Openness and Coordination

Hyeong-ki Kwon

Openness and Coordination

National Economies of the U.S., Japan, and Germany in a Globalized World

palgrave
macmillan

Hyeong-ki Kwon
Department of Political Science &
International Relations
Seoul National University
Seoul, Korea (Republic of)

ISBN 978-981-97-3351-4 ISBN 978-981-97-3352-1 (eBook)
https://doi.org/10.1007/978-981-97-3352-1

This Palgrave Macmillan imprint is published by the registered company Springer Nature Singapore Pte Ltd.
The registered company address is: 152 Beach Road, #21-01/04 Gateway East, Singapore 189721, Singapore

Preface

The concept of globalization came to me as a big shock before I left to study in the U.S. in 1995. As an undergraduate in the mid-1980s, the most eye-catching topic was democratization and the welfare state for my country, Korea, which replaced the existing goals of national modernization and economic growth that had dominated Korean society since the 1950s. When globalization first appeared in Korea, it seemed just political rhetoric to people focused on domestic power politics for welfare democracy. However, when the 1997 Asian financial crisis rippled through Korean society, globalization quickly emerged as a major concern for all.

Suffering a serious crisis that required urgent financial aid from the IMF, Koreans had to reconsider their social paradigms and value systems, whether voluntarily chosen or forcibly. They believed they had no option but to adopt liberalization and openness to the outside world. Koreans' thinking and lifestyles have changed fundamentally. Korea's existing statist developmentalism, long considered a model for economic growth and development for low-developed countries, was suddenly condemned as *Crony Capitalism* overnight, and the belief that democracy would solve every problem seemed to lose its place. No matter what one believed, national developmentalism or democracy, the existing beliefs fell into distrust, while globalization seemed irresistible and neoliberal free markets gained ascendancy as the only viable model.

In the 2000s and 2010s, when Korea moved beyond the crisis and grew rapidly through globalization, and flexibly adapted to rapidly changing technologies such as digitalization, globalization was no longer a buzzword or cause for concern. We acknowledged that we live in a globalized world, and still do, more open to a rapidly changing world. However, neoliberalism, regarded as the single viable alternative, reveals serious problems and limits in a globalized world. What alternative models are available? If the traditional one-nation-based model is no longer viable, how should a national economy be reconstructed in a globalized world?

By exploring three advanced capitalist countries—the U.S., Japan, and Germany, *Openness and Coordination* examines viable alternatives in response to the challenges of an open and rapidly changing world, and how such different patterns are newly constructed. In order to account for the various effects of globalization and modes of recomposing national economies, I have studied diverse models, including the U.S. as a liberal free market, Japan and Korea as statist coordination models, and Germany as a social coordination model. Concerning the evolution of Korea's statist coordination model, I draw it from my work *Changes by Competition: The Evolution of the South Korean Developmental State* (Oxford University Press, 2021). Now, *Openness and Coordination* focuses on these three types of advanced capitalism. This book highlights how each nation-state constructs industrial and innovative commons to improve national competitiveness in the process of national corporations' globalization and focuses on the politics of coordination: how actors coordinate with various interests to create industrial commons.

Over two decades have passed since I began research on globalization and diverse nation-states' responses, with a particular interest in the globalization of production. Over that span of time, I have come to owe much to many who have supported my work. I would like to express my sincere gratitude to all of them. First, I express deep gratitude to my teachers, especially to Professor Chey Myung and the late Professor Hwang Soo-Ik at Seoul National University, and to Professor Gary Herrigel at the University of Chicago. I also thank Professor Glenn Morgan at the University of Bristol for kind and insightful comments. In addition, I express my sincere gratitude to my colleagues, including Professors Chang Jae Baik, Joo Myung Song, Ha-lyong Jung, and Haeran Lim, who in 2008 formed a research team under the theme of "Globalization of Production." And I express sincere gratitude to many of my students, including Kyung Mi Kim, Eun-sik Yoo, Wonbin Choi, Yoo Lim, Seung-mi Kim, Ji-young Jeon, Hyun Lee, and Eun-young Cho, who researched data and created figures to illustrate the fruits of my research. This work was supported by the Ministry of Education of the Republic of Korea and the National Research Foundation of Korea (NRF-2020S1A3A2A01095861). I send my sincere gratitude for the Institute's support.

Finally, I would like to express my gratitude to my beloved brothers Oh-sung Kwon, Oh-soo Kwon, and my lovely sister Jung-hee Kwon. I also express many thanks to my mother-in-law Woojo Park, who consistently took care of my family during the whole research process. Above all, I would like to send my sincere gratitude to my wife Jung-hee Choi, who has always quietly helped and encouraged me. Without her assistance, I confess, this long-term project would not have been possible. Also, I express my sincere gratitude to Woo-hyuk Kwon, my lovely son who remains a bright light even in difficult times, and always invigorates me with joy and the vitality in his existence itself. Lastly, I want to express my immeasurable respect and gratitude to my parents, which cannot be fully expressed in words. I dedicate this book to my parents, Taekyong Kwon and Youngja Ko, who never let go of their faith in their son, even when I fumbled around pursuing somewhat vain and clumsy dreams, or when I edged toward precarious despair. I am deeply grateful that they have always believed in and felt proud of their son.

Seoul, Korea (Republic of) Hyeong-ki Kwon

Contents

List of Figures

List of Tables

CHAPTER 1

Introduction

What is the most viable model of national economy in a globalized world? How can we make it? *Openness and Coordination* examines how three nations representing diverse economic systems, including the free-market liberal U.S., the statist model of Japan, and the social coordination model of Germany, have redefined and reconstituted their national economies to face the dissolution of their existing national economic systems in a rapidly changing world.

Today, as technological development, including digitalization and nanotechnology, proceeds at a dizzying pace, and international competition accelerates day by day, companies can no longer stick to their existing production methods. They must innovate their entire value chains, by absorbing new ideas, adapting to new technologies and changing games. To meet these challenges, major corporations within national economies have been forced to reorganize themselves beyond their national boundaries in order to survive. Even top-tier and single-nation producers must enter the flow of rapid change in order to embrace new ideas and better inputs. Reorganization of entire value chains across national borders has become an irresistible trend.

For example, Apple's iPhone 14 Plus could not be produced in a decoupled and traditional one-nation-based system. The iPhone 14 Plus depends on worldwide resources, parts, and ideas of hardware chip designers and software engineers in Cupertino, the worldwide ecologic

H. Kwon, *Openness and Coordination*,
https://doi.org/10.1007/978-981-97-3352-1_1

applications developers, the remarkable productivity of the Shenzhen Pearl River Delta industrial complex, the excellent chip manufacturers in Taiwan, and semiconductor production machine designers and producers of ASML in the Netherlands and applied materials in San Jose (DeLong 2023). If we stick to the traditional single-nation production system or decouple the cross-border capabilities, we cannot produce such an extraordinary device at such a ridiculously low price. Due to the excellence and ascendancy of global production networks over the traditional single-nation model, global production networks over the last several decades have become inevitable and indispensable.

Events such as COVID-19 pandemic, wars in Ukraine and elsewhere, and the U.S. war for hegemony disrupt the existing system of global chains, drawing attention to the vulnerability of global value chains. Still, they have not brought an end to the trend of global production, nor reverted industrial nations back to traditional, single-nation models of production. Global production networks (GPNs) are still a trend because corporations cannot abandon GPNs' remarkable efficiency over traditional single-nation production. According to Oxford Economics' 2023 extensive analysis of bilateral cross-border trade of intermediate goods (IGs) that more accurately represent supply chain componentry than the final products in most analyses, global supply chains have continued to expand, despite talk of deglobalization and nearshoring (Nguyen-Quoc 2023; Kornprobst and Paul 2021; Felbermayr 2023). Even though decoupling has materialized for China's trade with the U.S. and Japan, China's inputs increased in trade with the Group of Seven (G7) developed economies. Despite de-risking, global value chains have not diminished but realigned. Intensified international competition has forced these companies to realign their methods of production at global levels, in order to mobilize labor, skills, parts, design, and R&D for competitive advantage beyond their national borders (Yeung 2022; Ponte 2019: 3–22; Herrigel 2010: 139–186; Dicken 2011: 13–74, 429–453). Now, a large number of corporations, representing their national economies, are reorganizing production competitively to survive in the international arena.

Yet serious tension arises between these national corporations' self-interests and survival and the overall interests of their national economies. Japanese enterprises such as Toyota captured enormous profits due to globalized production in 2008, while the Japanese national economy suffered from a production decrease of about US$420 billion and a loss of one million jobs (The Economist, 20 November 2010). And while American automobile and electronics firms have increased their production worldwide since the 1990s, domestic employment by these enterprises decreased to 66.5% in 2019, compared to employment in 1998 (OECD 2020; STAN Industrial Analysis 2020). The U.S. government attempted to limit imports from China to lower trade deficits and offset the loss of domestic employment. However, such a move contradicts business interests of American enterprises producing their products in China, as seen in the case where U.S. semiconductor industrialists opposed the U.S. government's tariff actions against China's Huawei (Bown 2020: 26–27).[1]

The perception of how national economies are constituted, alongside national corporations' globalization, is fundamentally changing. The past perception that "GM's interests are the interests of the U.S." (Holstein 2009: xi; Gereffi and Sturgeon 2004: 13)[2] made sense until the 1980s. But GM now produces and manufactures a larger number of vehicles overseas, in order to survive in international competition (Wall Street Journal 29 April 2005; US Newswire 13 November 2008). Toyota of Japan, in contrast, had been regarded as a main target of competitive vigilance as a foreign enterprise, but that, too, is no longer the case. Toyota is now perceived as a significant contributor to the U.S. economy because it produces a larger amount of value and employment in the U.S. compared with American-based companies (Berger 2005: 39; Wall Street Journal 29 April 2005). Robert Reich, the former Secretary of the Department of Labor in the Clinton administration, averred that "nationality not mattering" has become a universal trend which almost all nations will follow (Reich 1991: 172).

[1] The U.S. companies oppose the government's national protectionist and industrial policies against China. See Semiconductor Industry Association (June 15, 2018) "SIA Statement on Trump Administration Tariff Announcement," from https://www.semiconductors.org/sia-statement-on-trump-administration-tariff-announcement/; Semiconductor Manufacturing Industry Association (August 24, 2020) "SEMI Statement on New U.S. Export Control Regulations," *SEMI Press Release* from https://www.semi.org/en/news-media-press/semi-press-releases/semi-export-control.

[2] IN 1953, General Motors President Charles E. Wilson testified before Congress as follows: "For years, I thought what was good for our country was good for General Motors and vice versa. The differences did not exist. Our company is too big. It goes with the welfare of the country" (Holstein 2009: ix).

Openness and Coordination examines the tensions between the national economy and corporations' globalization and diverse ways of readjusting their nations' economies in the process of globalization. We focus on the major advanced economies, such as the U.S., Japan, and Germany, through the lens of these questions:

Does the globalization of national corporations' production necessarily conflict with their nations' economies? Despite the globalization of production, can national economies and corporate globalization be compatible? How can national economies reconstitute themselves in an era of corporate globalization? This book highlights that not only the impacts of corporate globalization upon national economies but also the ways nations adjust to these impacts vary across nations. What kinds of patterns could assist the reconstitution of national economies in the course of corporate globalization? What actions can lead to impactful solutions?

Global production networks, or global value chains, have been fortified by the optimistic views of neoliberalism. Refuting the pessimistic concern that national economies may experience deindustrialization as major corporations take production offshore, neoliberals argue that overseas production will strengthen national economic competitiveness. They hold that overseas outsourcing results in lower costs for parts, and creates a profit surplus, which increases investment in new technologies and creates more national wealth and more jobs for the nation's workers. Neoliberals suggest that the freer the flow of goods, humans, and capital across national borders, the more nations prosper (World Bank 2020; Friedman 2005; Farrell et al. 2003; Sirkin et al. 2011; Ramaswamy and Rowthorn 2000; Bhagwati 2010a, 2010b).

Considering the remarkable efficiency of global value chains over the traditional one-nation-based system, Global Value Chain (GVC) literature also emphasizes openness and flat-flow of inputs at the global level, accepting neoliberal theories, including comparative advantages, and neoliberal skepticism toward the state's active intervention (Singh 2023: 4–5; Werner 2016: 458–460). GVC literature suggests neoliberal policies, including liberalization of trade and investment and open links to global networks in order to develop the national economy (World Bank 2020; Aichele and Heiland 2018; Yeung 2022; Bair 2009; Gibbon et al. 2008).

Yet contrary to neoliberal and GVC optimism, not all states reap good results through national corporations' globalization. Some countries, such as Germany and South Korea, successfully strengthen their industrial competitiveness through globalization, while others like the U.S. do not. Then, why do certain countries succeed in upgrading their industrial competence in the globalization process of national corporations while others fail? How could the optimistic scenario of neoliberalism be realized? How can national economies increase their own industrial and innovative capabilities in the course of national corporations' globalization?

By comparing the different adjustments of the U.S., Japan, and Germany in the course of their national corporations' globalization, *Openness and Coordination* argues that in contrast to neoliberalism, globalization does not automatically result in the strengthening of national economic competitiveness. And in contrast to any nationalistic pessimism, we hold that national corporations' globalization does not necessarily cause the hollowing out of domestic production. The effects of corporations' globalization vary across national economies. While the U.S. and Japan have experienced a weakening of domestic industrial capabilities by losing much of their "industrial commons,"[3] Germany and South Korea have significantly improved industrial competitiveness and domestic production capabilities by establishing innovative industrial ecosystems at home while corporations go overseas.

In contrast to neoliberal globalism and recent GVC literature, openness to the free flow of inputs, including new technology, better parts, and innovative ideas, does not automatically lead to optimal outcomes. For example, as we shall see in the case of the U.S., individual companies' uncoordinated and free pursuit of individual rationality of maximizing profits in the course of globalization results in suboptimal outcomes and loss of industrial commons and innovation capabilities at the national economic level. Uncoordinated free globalization leads corporations to drift apart from their existing domestic industrial ecosystem, which can engender a dissipation of their industrial commons (Pisano and Shih 2012a, 2012b). Free relocation of national corporations to foreign countries can undermine the sustainability of the industrial commons at home

[3] "Industrial commons" refers to various complementary capabilities shared and commonly used by corporations, such as suppliers, customers, partners, skilled workers, universities, and research institutes and capital institutes. Firms do not rely entirely on their own materials and capital, but they need and utilize many complementary capabilities or industrial commons in order to improve their competitiveness in the market. Thus, the industrial commons are key sources of national economic competitiveness (Pisano and Shih 2012b; Berger 2013).

due to the hollowing out of specialized supplier networks, competitors, and qualified workforce, as well as experienced managers (Barzotto et al. 2018: 96).

Nevertheless, sustaining the given industrial commons without openness to a rapidly changing world can engender suboptimal outcomes. National protectionism or a nationally closed coordination system, as in the case of Japan, prohibits national firms from flexibly absorbing new ideas and better inputs, and from adapting to a rapidly changing world. Japanese firms based on closed circles of compensation might have better coordination capabilities than U.S. firms in the liberal open market, but they are relatively isolated from a changing world, showing so-called Galapagos syndrome (Calder 2017; Kushida 2011). Thus, even in their globalization, Japanese firms lagged behind innovation due to their nationally closed or Keiretsu-based networks on foreign soils.

Openness and Coordination highlights that industrial commons at home are a decisive factor in whether a national economy succeeds or fails in the course of national corporations' globalization. Industrial commons are the fundamental sources of innovation. As Janssen and Frenken (2019) argue, future innovation should aim at cross-specialization to reap the benefits of unrelated varieties. However, this collaboration of cross-specialization can be facilitated by interfaces based on common themes, and needs platforms or intermediaries—for example, the form in which to materialize. Industrial commons refer to the external economies which companies widely use in a district, such as R&D and manufacturing infrastructure, process-development skills, engineering capabilities embedded in firms, universities, and other organizations, that provide the foundation for growth and innovation (Pisano and Shih 2012b: 2). Industrial commons are rooted in firms, and also firmly geographically embedded (Götz 2019: 27; Pisano and Shih 2012b; Bailey and de Propis 2014; Buciuni and Pisano 2015).

The overseas production of multinational corporations can be beneficial not only for the companies themselves but also for the home economy. As international business literature shows, outward foreign direct investments are positively associated with sales increases for investing firms and their suppliers (Castellani and Pieri 2015: 2). In addition, domestic production can benefit from involvement in GVCs by learning from the strategies applied by global buyers (Barzotto et al. 2018: 99; Schmitz and Knorringa 2000). Openness to global networks can foster the development of links outside the home-based industrial district, and enrich the industrial commons at home, through reverse learning from overseas experiences and the introduction of new ideas and better inputs.

However, corporations' uncoordinated free mobility can also have negative effects to deteriorate the innovation capabilities at home by the loss of industrial commons. The fading of industrial commons can accompany the reduction of knowledge spillovers which need innovation in an economy (Capello and Lenzi 2015). The hollowing out of manufacturing activities due to corporations' overseas production has negative impacts on their home productivity growth and new job creation (Castellani and Pieri 2015; Bailey et al. 2010). Corporations' internationalization can have negative effects on the home production structure and reduce the reproducibility of the entrepreneurial factor or result in the erosion of the industrial commons, including loss of local suppliers and loss of the opportunity to learn and grow through a relationship with lead firms (De Marchi and Grandinett 2014; Elia et al. 2009; Berger 2013; Barzotto et al. 2018: 94).

Why do some countries succeed in improving innovation and production capabilities at home in corporations' globalization, while others do not? Again, this book highlights the industrial commons as the decisive factor for success. National economies which lose their industrial commons in the course of corporations' globalization will lose their economic competitiveness. By contrast, national economies which improve their industrial commons will achieve economic competitiveness despite any globalization of production.

The problem of how to improve the domestic industrial commons mainly relies on how to resolve the free-rider problems and coordinate collective action among various actors who are free to move their activities overseas. The use of industrial commons is difficult to exclude from potential beneficiaries, and thus it can easily fall into the situation of "tragedy of commons" and rapidly disappear (Barzotto et al. 2018; Götz 2019: 27).

Problem-solving collective action in corporate globalization varies across national economies, with diverse solutions coming mainly from key actors' strategies and interactions in historical and institutional contexts. For instance, the free market in the U.S. could foster high innovation for American enterprises. But, the free market could negatively affect the accumulation and improvement of domestic industrial commons. As we shall see, large U.S. corporations which pursue shareholder values in the absence of social coordination, easily undermine existing relationships with their local suppliers.

In contrast to the American free-market system, the statist coordination of Japan and the social coordination of Germany could more efficiently resolve the collective action problems and improve the industrial commons. Industrial commons are more likely to be built with key players' collaboration, resulting from societywide coordination. In the case of Germany, key actors, including labor organizations, suppliers, and trade associations, as well as lead firms and suppliers, collectively adjusted their processes of globalization. This form of social coordination improves the industrial commons at home even in the course of increasing overseas production.

However, trust and social coordination are needed among social actors for horizontal collaboration to build industrial commons; they cannot be built in a closed structure. Japan developed trustful relations to solve free-rider problems and build collaborative relations, based on the nationally closed circles of compensation and isolated from a changing world, even in the course of globalization. Japan's industrial commons became outdated and Japan suffered a long-term recession. Thus, *Openness and Coordination* emphasizes that in order to improve a national economy's innovation and production capabilities in the course of corporations' globalization, social coordination with openness to a rapidly changing world of technology and international markets is needed; social coordination within a closed structure or openness without social coordination is more likely to fail in building industrial commons at home and lose in international competitiveness.

To examine the various national adjustments in the course of corporate globalization, *Openness and Coordination* analyzes high-tech industries, such as electronics, automobiles, and ICT industries, which are major export drivers for the U.S., Japan, and Germany, and constitute core parts of their national economies. I focus on major high-tech industries because industries such as textiles and apparel have declined even apart from globalization. By contrast, high-tech industries are major export drivers as well as the key engine to national economic growth. These industries have seriously pursued the globalization of production, and serve as case studies on the impacts of corporate globalization upon national economies and their various outcomes in national adjustments.

Literature Review and Theoretical Alternative

We now briefly review prevailing views, including neoliberal optimism and pessimistic nationalism, regarding corporate globalization's impacts on national economies. Based on the critical review of existing theories, this section suggests a theoretical alternative.

Globalization of national corporations in advanced economies, including the U.S., Japan, and Germany, has generated significant concern about the hollowing out of domestic industries. In fact, corporations in these countries often threaten labor and government with their possible decisions to move production facilities overseas (Story 2012). Concern over the hollowing out of domestic industries leads pessimistic nationalists to suggest nationalist counter-measures, such as protectionism and an appeal to moral patriotism (Prestowitz 2010). A few states in the U.S. also passed laws that limit excessive outsourcing overseas in response to corporations' outsourcing practices. In the case of Japan, key players in the Japanese economy, including economic policy-makers and *Keidanren* (Japan Business Federation) emphasize Japanese patriotism, criticizing neoliberal groups such as *Keizai Doyukai* (Japan Association of Corporate Executives) which emphasize American-style shareholder capitalism and free market (Gotoh 2020: 135).

However, such nationalist policies based on a single-nation production model cannot effectively work in the new context of global competition based on the existing global production networks, which generate far more efficient and innovative achievements than a production system based in one nation. South Korean electronics companies in the early 1990s, for instance, could not avoid expanding production overseas, because they suffered from the disadvantages of single-nation-based production systems in competition with Japanese global production networks which combined Japanese high technologies and East Asian low-wage labor. As a result, South Korean companies expanded their production chains overseas to meet international competition. Clearly, nationalistic protection would have proved costly, while making it difficult for firms to catch up with high-speed technology innovation, as in the case of Japan, which suffered a long-lasting economic recession due to the so-called Galapagos syndrome, resulting from the nationally closed circles of compensation (Calder 2017; Kushida 2011).

In contrast to nationalist protectionism, neoliberal globalism emphasizes enhancing national competitiveness by optimally combining a variety of inputs, such as labor, skills, parts, and design, across national borders. Based on the theory of comparative advantage, neoliberals argue that globalization of companies is beneficial not only for the home economy but also for the host countries (Sirkin et al. 2011; Bhagwati 2010a, 2010b; Friedman 2005; Farrell et al. 2003; Ramaswamy and Rowthorn 2000). According to neoliberals, the outsourcing of advanced countries' corporations to developing countries like India could offer the developing countries opportunities to enhance human capital by increasing employment. As for the advanced home countries, the offshoring by their national corporations maximizes profits through cost reduction, which can result in more investment in new high-value-added industries, thereby creating opportunities for new employment. For neoliberals, the loss of domestic employment in the course of corporations' globalization is a kind of creative destruction by which they optimize the dynamic comparative advantages in the process of globalization. Neoliberals argue that the creative process of resource allocation should be done only through the operation of free markets; intervention of the state, or non-market social constraints, prevent the optimal solution of resource allocation (Pack and Saggi 2006: 276).

Reflecting upon the remarkable efficiency of global value chains over traditional single-nation system, GVC literature also emphasizes openness and flat-flow of inputs at global levels, confirming neoliberal globalism and convergence toward Washington Consensus for national economic development (Singh 2023: 4–5; Werner 2016: 458–460). Although GVC literature began over concern with asymmetrical power relations and uneven developments, they refocused their study on the mutual benefits reaped by global firms and local suppliers. Accepting neoliberal theories, including comparative advantages, and neoliberal skepticism toward the state's active interventionism, they argue for lowering tariff barriers and trade costs, investment liberalization, and little government intervention in markets, but fostering business-friendly environments to enable firms to make rapid and reliable connections with foreign partners (World Bank 2020; Aichele and Heiland 2018; Yeung 2022; Bair 2009; Gibbon et al. 2008).

However, unlike the GVC literature and neoliberals' argument for universal validation of free markets and openness to global value chains, upgrading from a low-value-added to a high-value-added economy does not automatically occur through free markets and uncoordinated open links to global value chains. Contrary to neoliberals' expectation, profit surplus created by American corporations' offshoring, for instance, may not be reinvested in upgrading domestic industries. As we will examine in Chapter 3, the U.S. trade deficit in high-tech industries since the 1990s has been severely aggravated with deficit amounts of US$178.1 billion in 2020—a dramatic drop from US$3.5 billion of surplus in 1990, while the U.S. goods trade deficit ballooned to a record $1.09 trillion in 2021 from $198 billion in 1996 (U.S. Census Bureau data). Economist Gregory Tassey points out that such trade deficit growth is due to the R&D expenditures of U.S. corporations which increased overseas while decreasing at home (Tassey 2010: 283–333). Also, as suggested by MIT and Harvard studies, the reduction of R&D within the U.S. is related to the loss of industrial commons, including the decline of parts suppliers and the loss of high-skilled labor in the course of American corporations' offshoring (Berger 2013: 20, 204–205; Porter and Rivkin 2012: 54–62).

By focusing on the quantitative aspect of value creation, neoliberals disregard the qualitative aspect of industrial linkages which have equally important effects in the sense of industrial and innovative capabilities. For example, neoliberals like Jagdish Bhagwati argue that if we earn the same profit, say $100, it does not matter whether we make potato chips or semiconductor chips (Bhagwati 2010a, 2010b). However, what neoliberal economists like Bhagwati overlook is the external effects of the industrial linkages, which an industry has on the innovation capabilities of other neighboring industries. Potato chips making $100 in profits may have the same value in the sense of value amount as semiconductor chips making a $100 profit. But their external effects in regard to innovative capabilities of other industries and an entire society are significantly different.

Neoliberalists overlook the fact that there is a marked difference in production capacity for computer chips and potato chips in terms of a country's collective technology and innovation capabilities. So-called "spillover effects" on other industries are drastically different between producing computer chips and potato chips. The former significantly increases overall productivity in society, while the latter does not. Cheap potato chips cannot produce Intel. Knowledge embedded in a relationship is not a simple product that can be bought and sold. Quantitative capital and intangible capabilities of a nation are not the same. Workers' talents and skills, organizational knowledge and institutional memory, and the industrial commons are not easily transferred to other regions, simply because experiential knowledge is embedded in organizational life. Moreover, the spillover effects, learning effects, and network effects of corporate activities are critical to the competitiveness of the entire national economy (Iversen and Soskice 2019: 1–4, 14–20; Atkinson and Ezell 2012: 94–95, 97). Innovation in one industry affects other industries. Therefore, potato chip production cannot keep up with the effect of computer chip production technology on front and rear industries. No matter how global a country is, if the industry that makes computer chips is lost abroad, it will result in the loss of entire industrial systems, including front and rear industries and various industrial commons simultaneously.

From the perspective of overall industrial capabilities based on industrial linkages, *Openness and Coordination* highlights the industrial commons as a decisive factor in whether a national economy can improve its innovation and production capabilities or not in the course of national corporations' globalization. As Janssen and Frenken (2019) argue, the collaboration of cross-specialization based on rich industrial commons is critically important for future innovation. Industrial commons refer to the common externalities for innovation, which can be necessary and utilized by more than one industry. Pisano and Shih (2009, 2012b) define industrial commons as critical components for innovation and competition, including encompassing knowledge, skills, institutions, and a broad R&D environment. Industrial commons, including technological know-how, operational capabilities, and specialized skills, are embedded in the workforce, competitors, suppliers, customers, cooperative R&D ventures, and universities, and often support multiple industrial sectors (Pisano and Shih 2009, 2012b; Barzotto et al. 2018: 96; Götz 2019: 27).

Individual companies need the industrial commons to compete in the market, since on their own they cannot make all of these goods. The industrial commons must be produced socially. They transcend financial value, and embed, animate, and support the industrial linkages produced through social interactions. Hence, we oppose the normative arguments that neoliberals such as Bhagwati pose, that potato chips and micro-semiconductor chips are the same if they produce the same value. We assume that even if they produce the same profits and wages, the potato chips and the microchips have significantly different external effects on the neighboring industries in terms of the effects of their productive capability in the industrial linkages.[4] For example, in the 2000s, the IT industry's

[4] In this work, I criticize the neoclassical economist conception of value theory and emphasize the productive capability and complementarity of the industrial commons. I

value should be considered not only for the value it created but also for its external effects that significantly increase the productivity and innovative capability of its neighboring industries.

From the perspective of industrial linkages and industrial commons, in contrast to the recent growth model literature which focuses on diverse models of demand management (Baccaro et al. 2022; Baccaro and Pontusson 2016), *Openness and Coordination* highlights the manufacturing and industrial capabilities for a nation's long-term growth (Carlin and Soskice 2015). Although demand management is important for economic growth, production, and innovation capabilities are critical for increasing productivity and long-term prosperity. If technology-based growth and innovation capabilities are not properly improved, household income structurally decreases, despite the economy's ups and downs. For example, from the 1950s to 1970s, the U.S. was able to dominate the global market and achieve economic growth based on superior technological competitive advantage. However, as commercialization of technology

rely on Friedrich List's conception of "the theory of productive forces" (Theorie der produktiven Kräfte) that criticizes Adam Smith's value theory (Die Theorie der Werte). So far, List's (2016 [1910]) *Das Nationale System der Politischen Oekonomie* has been understood as protectionism—a misunderstanding. List also suggests the opening of trade, rather than protectionism, if it improves the productive capability. List holds that the improvement of industrial capability matters regardless of opening or protection. He argues not protectionism but the theory of productive capability. According to List, Adam Smith did not develop further the conception of "productive forces" by focusing on the simple quantity of exchange value. Thereafter Smithian economists, including Jean Baptiste Say, who emphasize only the exchange value, disregard the different productive capabilities that resulted from various actors' complementary relations in the division of labor. According to List, the classical economists including Smith and Say emphasize the amount of exchange value in a national economy, and do not see how significantly different are the effects of manufacturing and agriculture on productive capabilities in the entire society. For example, agriculture currently produces the value of 3.3 billion dollars, 10 times more than manufacturing which produces 0.2 billion dollars. Thus, classical economists like Say may emphasize agriculture 10 times more than manufacturing. But List holds that classical economists do not see how agriculture's production currently relies on manufacturing's external effects on productive capabilities. List holds that the government's constructing of roads and bridges may not produce any exchange value in the market, but construction of infrastructure improves significantly the productive capabilities in the entire society. List also says that social institutions and laws may not produce any exchange value, but they significantly improve the productive capabilities of an entire society because they contribute to the combination of various labor. The industrial and innovative capabilities in a society rely on how to combine the various actors' labor and roles, rather than individual excellence. See Friedrich List's (2016 [1910]) *Das National System der Politischen Oekonomie*. 2nd version (Verlag von Gustav Fischer).

weakened, short-term economic activity and recession occurred over the past 20 years, but GDP growth rates decreased significantly compared to earlier (Tassey 2023: 1–2; Tassey 2014). Technology innovation brings long-term productivity, which in turn increases industrial competitiveness and market share, ensuring higher profits and incomes through long-term economic growth. Innovation requires industrial and technological commons such as new technologies, prototype labs, skilled labor, and technical infrastructure (Tassey 2023: 1–2).

To better understand how a nation's innovation capabilities rely on industrial linkages, we must look at the entire process of production, from concept development and prototype development to mass production and commercialization. In many cases, innovation and learning occur not only in the early stages of production but also in the process of moving to the prototype and commercialization stages. Innovation for production of high-value-added products is not determined solely by one or two brilliant ideas early on, but occurs through close interaction with researchers and designers, engineers, and high-skilled workers, in various stages of production and in every part-making process.

Notably, in contrast to neoliberal globalists' optimism and recent GVC literature, openness to global value chains and the rapidly changing world of technology does not automatically lead to national economic competitiveness. And in contrast to the nationalists' pessimism, national corporations' offshoring and overseas expansion do not necessarily hollow out the domestic industrial commons. Some countries succeed in improving their industrial competitiveness in the course of corporations' globalization, while others do not.

For example, in the process of overseas outsourcing, the U.S. has faced serious problems with loss of innovation capabilities because the uncoordinated globalization of individual corporations results in the loss of industrial commons and industrial linkages at home, including excellent parts suppliers, prototype makers, skilled laborers, and technology and training systems (Pisano and Shih 2012a, 2012b; Berger 2013; Porter and Rivkin 2012; Kochan 2012). By contrast, Germany and South Korea have upgraded domestic industrial capabilities in the course of globalization. Since the 2000s Germany and Korea have increased their trade surplus and employment in high-tech industries, despite a significant increase in overseas production.

Why do some countries succeed in improving production and innovation capabilities, while others do not? *Openness and Coordination* highlights not only openness to a rapidly changing world of technology and markets but more importantly, social coordination for building and improving industrial commons in the course of globalization. In order to build industrial commons, we emphasize, first, openness to a rapidly changing world of technology and markets. In the absence of openness, as in the case of Japan, too much coordination based on nationally closed circles of compensation can lead to stagnation or outdatedness of industrial commons, resulting in long-term economic recession. By contrast, simple openness without social coordination, as in the case of U.S., and individual companies' uncoordinated and free pursuit of individual rationality of maximizing profits in the course of globalization result in suboptimal outcomes and loss of industrial commons and innovation capabilities at the national economic level. Thus, *Openness and Coordination* highlights social coordination to build and improve industrial commons at home while national corporations go abroad.

In order to understand the multiple effects of national corporations' globalization on national economies, we focus on national coordination for creating industrial commons. Individual companies pay little attention to improvements and accumulation of industrial commons; their focus, instead, is on self-interests of profit maximization. Thus, an individual corporation's self-interest in the course of globalization can result in suboptimal outcomes in the national economy, such as the hollowing out of national industries, reduction in employment, and deterioration of productive and innovative capabilities across an entire national economy. The free and uncoordinated pursuit of individual business interests can create the so-called tragedy of industrial commons due to a free-rider perspective or resistance to collective action. Different outcomes rely on the *politics of coordination*—in other words, how to solve collective action problems in the course of national corporations' globalization.

Furthermore, *Openness and Coordination* emphasizes diversity of methods in societywide coordination to build the industrial commons. For example, Germany and Korea differ in their methods of improving innovation capabilities. Germany has achieved these improvements through a social coordination system, while South Korea has used active state intervention and coordination rather than a free-market system or social coordination. In the early 2020s, the U.S. and Japan also used state-led coordination methods to build the industrial commons in response to the decline of their industrial competitiveness.

Openness and Coordination highlights that the politics of coordination in creating industrial commons follow a variety of patterns, which are formed by key actors' proactive adaptations to new challenges against a backdrop of existing historical experiences and institutions. For instance, we will explore three distinct patterns of coordination politics, through the lens of Max Weber's ideal type.[5] These three patterns include the U.S. free-market system, the statist coordination model of Japan and South Korea, and the social coordination model of Germany.

Contrary to neoliberal arguments, social coordination or state intervention does not yield only negative effects. Still, not all interventionist states are always valid. For example, traditional and authoritarian developmental states, which previously existed in South Korea and Japan, may not produce a new innovative system. The traditional developmental states, with highly centralized authority, which focused on mobilizing massive amounts of capital and funneling it exclusively to a few corporations to realize an economy of scale, may not be valid for nurturing SME parts suppliers, nor building a flexible and decentralized innovation system in which various competent players can participate and collaborate for innovation. In Japan and South Korea, statist coordination must change existing developmentalism from the traditional and exclusive strategy to a more inclusive and decentralized form of developmentalism based on social cooperative networks.

While neoliberal and GVC theories disregard the effectiveness of state coordination, *Openness and Coordination* agrees with recent twenty-first Century Developmental State theories which emphasize the state's active role in coordination politics for building the industrial commons. Further, this book agrees that twenty-first century national economies depend not on inputs such as large infusions of capital, but on qualitative innovation capabilities of human capital and education (Williams 2014; Stiglitz et al. 2013; Evans 2010; Evans and Heller 2015). The twenty-first Century Developmental State theories emphasize that the method of economic growth should shift from large-scale capital accumulation to individual human capital-oriented innovation. According to this point of view, economic growth since the 1990s has been achieved not by the

[5] Weber's ideal type means not a reality, but what has been arrived at by the analytical accentuation of certain elements of reality in order to understand the reality. Only through ideal types does the individual case become explicit. See Weber (1949) "Objectivity in Social Science and Social Policy."

input of production factors such as capital and labor but through new ways of generating innovative ideas and information. Here, the personal capabilities of workers, and citizens in general, are the essential factors for economic growth. Therefore, societal support, education, and democratic institutions are emphasized to increase citizens' capabilities in today's developmental state theories.

However, we point out one limitation: twenty-first century developmental state theorists focus on improving individual human resources rather than on combining and organizing competent actors, that is, the systemic industrial linkages and commons. As twenty-first century developmental state theories argue, the driving force for economic growth has shifted from the accumulation of physical capital to the expansion of innovation capabilities and knowledge. However, we do not accept the simple causal relationship between economic growth and individual citizens' capabilities. For example, the decline in U.S. industrial competitiveness in the process of globalization is not due primarily to a setback in U.S. education or a reduction in new ideas from U.S. citizens. Rather, the decline is due to many holes in the industrial linkages, resulting from uncoordinated free globalization. Although U.S. universities generate world-class ideas, the commercialization of new ideas and innovation at the industrial level has grown feeble due to the loss of complementary goods as individual corporations freely move overseas in pursuit of short-term profits.

Contrary to the argument of new developmental theorists (Evans 2014: 37), large sums of money invested in education and social supports do not necessarily engender economic growth and industrial capabilities. France in the 2000s turned public expenditures from industrial policy to social policy while changing modes of developmentalism. However, as the expansion of social support expenditures soon reduced public support for R&D, the expansion of those expenditures made France a "social anesthesia state," pushing it into a long-term recession rather than strengthening the nation's innovation and production capabilities (Levy 2015: 402–403). By contrast, Northern European countries, such as Sweden and Denmark, were able to make a successful economic leap forward not by strengthening traditional social safety nets but by increasing their innovation capabilities through public investment (Huo and Stephens 2015: 410–425; Eliasson 2007: 214, 279). Support for social welfare and education matters in developing individual competencies which ultimately may contribute to the improvement of innovation and industrial capabilities in the entire society. More important in the process of corporations' globalization is how to reorganize and recombine various innovation factors at the societal level.

Finally, like the institutionalist varieties of capitalism, *Openness and Coordination* emphasizes the varieties of coordination patterns in the course of national corporations' globalization (Iversen and Soskice 2019; Hall and Soskice 2001; Whitley 1999, 2001, 2007; Amable 2003; Pierson 2004; Hancke et al. 2007). However, we do not agree with institutionalists' path dependency and self-reinforcement of patterns due to co-specificity embedded in national institutions. For example, institutionalists like Iversen and Soskice (2019) argue that despite corporations' mobility, national patterns of capitalism are self-reinforced due to co-specificity embedded in the nation:

> The skills of these workforces are tacit and cospecific both with each other and with company technologies. ... Quite generally it has pinned down advanced companies or their subsidiaries to the national environment where education and training take place; the high-value-added activities of an advanced company are thus generally embedded in the national or regional or local environment—advanced capitalism is geographically specific and not footloose. (Iversen and Soskice 2019: 7)

Institutionalists argue that even in the course of globalization, national patterns of capitalism persist or reinforce their original models, due to tacit knowledge and co-specific connectedness of skills, companies, and institutions, which are difficult to transfer due to their embeddedness in geographical clusters. They hold that even multinational corporations (MNCs) build subsidiaries in other advanced nations, and tend to not dissolve the existing national system, but reinforce the existing model because they utilize the comparative institutional advantages and complementary technologies on foreign soil, resulting from co-specific agglomerations embedded in multiple clusters or nations (Iversen and Soskice 2019: 7, 48; Hall and Soskice 2001: 38–40, 56–58).

However, contrary to institutionalist arguments, the existing national model of capitalism has undergone significant changes in the course of corporations' mobility across national borders. As seen in the the U.S., MNCs do not focus on utilization of existing complementary goods; rather, they freely move by comparing different regions' changing advantages, which result in devasting effects on the home economy. Again, against the decline of domestic innovation capabilities and employment, the U.S. does not reinforce its existing neoliberalism; rather, it changes its pattern of practices, from traditional taboo on industrial policy and state intervention toward more state-led coordination, to rebuilding industrial commons to revive its economy, as seen in recent industrial policies, including Manufacturing USA and the 2022 Chips and Science Act.

Meanwhile, institutionalists such as Richard Whitley emphasize "the country-of-origin effects" where national corporations transfer their original patterns of practices overseas. They identify the national differences of globalization as an "international projection of domestic institutions" (Whitley 2001, 2007; Harzing and Noorderhaven 2008; Lane and Probert 2009; Peng and Delios 2006; Yamakawa et al. 2008). In explaining the diverse patterns of global production networks, institutionalists like Whitely overlook the dynamic readjustments of actors in both home and international contexts. National corporations do not simply transfer their existing practices overseas, but readjust their practices on foreign soil. Sometimes they learn new strategies from overseas experiences and bring them back home.

Although we attempt to account for various patterns of globalization, we do not assume the unilateral projection of domestic institutions on the international context as institutionalists like Whitley assume. Reflecting upon the challenges in national and international contexts of competition, corporations make continuous strategic adjustments, readjusting their home institutions. For example, key actors in the U.S. in the 2010s attempted to establish a new coordination method, learning from the German coordination model. Reflecting upon the lost decades at home, Japan also tried to actively transform existing systems by taking inspiration from its competitor, the U.S.'s Silicon Valley model, to strengthen innovation capabilities at home. Germany and Northern European countries have significantly reorganized their traditionally inherited corporatist systems to improve collective learning and production capabilities. In other words, no country has persisted unconditionally with the existing institutional model. Rather, key actors in the advanced countries have struggled to change their existing systems, reflecting upon the contexts of domestic and international competition.

Diversity of national patterns is not the persistence of their traditional model based on unilateral constraints of institutions on actors or historical legacies. Rather, *Openness and Coordination* emphasizes the politics of active (re-)composition in the process of globalization. As seen in the case of Japan, the industrial commons based on traditional institutions can be outdated due to the absence of openness to and flexible adaptation in the rapidly changing world of technology and markets. Although we focus on the diversity of national patterns of building industrial commons in the course of globalization, these patterns are not reproduced by their traditional national institutions, including historical legacy, cultural delay, or institutional resistance. They are newly formed through the politics of proactive actors' new strategies and interactions in the context of domestic and international challenges.

In order to understand the different effects of corporations' globalization on national economies, we highlight the industrial commons in the course of corporations' globalization. Some countries succeed in enriching their industrial commons and improving their international competitiveness, while others do not. *Openness and Coordination* emphasizes that improving the industrial commons in the course of open globalization relies on solving free-rider and collective action problems in a more open way, flexibly adapting to the changing world. Decisive to building industrial commons is how key actors in a national economy, including lead firms, suppliers, skilled workers, trade associations, as well as national and local governments, coordinate collectively. Simple openness without social coordination, as seen in the U.S. free-market system, can deplete industrial commons; yet excellent coordination without openness to a world of changing markets and technology deteriorates industrial and innovation capabilities. *Openness and Coordination* emphasizes that there is no single best way to solve free-rider or collective action problems. Diverse ways include state-led coordination, as seen recently in the U.S. and Japan, and social coordination, as seen in Germany.

To better account for dynamic changes in patterns of building industrial commons, *Openness and Coordination* focuses on elite core groups as well as social alliances. The core group continuously generates new interpretation ideas to understand problems and suggest solutions, which facilitate the formation of social alliances for a particular regime of economic growth. More importantly, *Openness and Coordination* highlights the social alliances for the economic system's change. Following recent studies of growth regimes, we focus on elite politics as well as mass politics for social alliances at the level of noisy and quiet politics, to better account for the politics of regime changes (Baccaro et al. 2022: 30, 35–36; Bohle and Regan 2021: 78–79).

However, social alliances are not fixed but changing, as interest groups are not determined by their economic positions but through changing political discourses. As seen in the case of Germany, investment managers are persuaded to understand and accept the benefits of codetermination through collective deliberation. In order to better account for the changes of economic regimes, *Openness and Coordination* highlights discursive politics among elite groups as well as social blocs.

The book consists of nine chapters. Chapter 2 examines various effects of national corporations on national economies by offering an overview of globalization and comparing the various effects and patterns of the U.S., Japan, South Korea, and Germany. Coordination models include the uncoordinated and free market, statist coordination, and social coordination models, respectively.

The main body of empirical cases consists of three parts: part one for the U.S. (Chapters 3 and 4); part two for Japan (Chapters 5 and 6), and part three for Germany (Chapters 7 and 8), with each model examined in detail. Finally, Chapter 9 summarizes the main arguments based on the empirical findings, compares the three coordination models, and draws conclusions about the theoretical implications of different patterns and effects of national corporations' globalization.

CHAPTER 2

National Economies in Globalization

Globalizing production by national major corporations does not necessarily result in a "hollowing-out" of domestic production, as nationalist pessimists claim, nor in an upgrade of the national economy through creative destruction by free markets, as claimed by neoliberal optimists. While the U.S. has shown a tendency to hollow out domestic industries, this is not necessarily the case in Germany or South Korea. In Japan, too much coordination based on nationally closed circles eroded its international competitiveness by making the domestic commons outdated. Various aspects of reorganization of national economies through globalization of production are due to prominent domestic actors' reflective retrospection in the process of internationalizing production and the politics of reorganization based on it. Before examining specific methods of adaptation and adjustment of three ideal types of national economies, including the neoliberal U.S., the statist coordination model of Japan, and the social coordination model of Germany, this chapter examines the varied impacts of globalization on national economies in the process of production globalization. This chapter compares and analyzes how major advanced capitalist states variously reorganize their national economies in globalized production in major industries, including electronics and automobile industries.

H. Kwon, *Openness and Coordination*,
https://doi.org/10.1007/978-981-97-3352-1_2

Globalization and Denationalization

As international competition gets tougher and technology changes more rapidly, national major corporations cannot depend solely on their in-house capabilities and domestic inputs, but utilize better inputs beyond national borders. If they do not stay current with rapidly changing trends of markets and technology, even the best companies, like Sony in the 2000s, quickly lag behind the competition. National corporations were compelled to expand their production and development and build global value chains. Following this trend of corporations' globalization, neoliberals and the global value chain (GVC) literature based on neoclassical economics, as well as the Marxist-oriented global capitalism school, including Robinson (2004), commonly argue denationalization and convergence of national economies toward the free-market system. This section examines the different modes and effects of national corporations' globalization on national economies, in contrast to the denationalization view.

To better compare the effects of national major corporations' globalization, we focus on growth industries, especially in the U.S., Japan, and Germany, whose automobile, electronics, and ICT industries constitute the largest share of employment. In many cases, reduced employment in related industries may not be caused directly by globalization. In the case of sunset industries such as apparel, jobs can be reduced due to advances in science technology such as IT and improved productivity. In addition, automobile and electronics represent a national economy due to their size and industrial linkages. For example, automobiles, consisting of more than 20,000 parts, have been regarded by many scholars as a major industry, illustrating the developmental model of national economy. Therefore, the automobile industry provides a test case to measure changes in the national production model (Streeck 1996; Womack et al. 1990; Kwon 2004a, 2–4).

Notably, this section highlights first the point that globalization of production had recently established itself as an inevitable trend until the sudden COVID-19 pandemic and rising tension of U.S.–China hegemonic competition. In the 1990s, major national corporations expanded global production networks (GPNs) to organize their production chains. Development of information, communication, and logistics technologies has enabled companies to offshore their production bases to secure low-wage labor, new technologies, and competitive parts suppliers. In addition to the low costs of transportation due to improved technology, advances in computers and telecommunications have also encouraged international economic linkages, allowing businesses and customers to connect more easily across distances and borders and providing the data necessary to organize increasingly complex supply chains across borders (Grabow 2024).

Furthermore, as technology such as digitalization changes with accelerating speed, corporations have opened to global innovative ideas in technology, as well as information on changing markets (Yeung 2022). Competition itself at the global level has changed. Traditional national production methods (Porter 1990), mainly based on domestic science, skilled labor, and essential parts, are far less competitive than global production networks that combine best inputs, including design, skills, technology, and optimal market access, across global borders.

For example, in the U.S., General Motors (GM) faced market erosion caused by Japan's highly competitive automobiles in the 1980s. In response, GM reorganized its production method, as seen in New United Motor Manufacturing (NUMMI), a joint venture with Japan (Womack et al. 1990). Concurrently, GM organized a global production network to ensure a competitive market share. GM broke away from a vertically integrated organization system designed for in-house mass production toward a system based on a market relationship of outsourcing to external companies (Kwon 2004a, Chapter 2). Furthermore, disintegrated parts production was outsourced not only to domestic suppliers, but to foreign suppliers. Original equipment manufacturers (OEMs) like GM recombined the inputs across national borders to compete. For instance, by receiving designs from Italy, arranging design engineering in Germany, and assembling major parts in low-wage countries near the sales site, GM regained its competitiveness in the 1990s (Reich 1991: 123).

In response, Japanese companies also reorganized their production networks transnationally, shifting away from their existing one-country production method. South Korean companies, which are latecomers, did the same. As Japanese electronics companies expanded their production to Southeast Asia in the late 1980s and early 1990s, South Korean companies' competitiveness in exports into the U.S. market sharply declined. South Korean companies had relied on a domestic production system to compete with Japanese electronics companies that combined Japan's high technology and low Southeast Asian wages. As a result, South Korean companies were forced to turn production overseas for their own survival (Oh Moon-seok and Kim Hyung-joo 1996; Segye Ilbo 1992: 4, 7).

Due to companies' pursuit of the advantages of global value chains in the international competition, global production spread continuously even despite the recent COVID-19 pandemic. Considering the pandemic and U.S.–China hegemonic rivalry, some scholars expect the end of globalization, or deglobalization (Felbermayr 2023). However, many empirical studies reveal that globalization is far from over, but instead moves into a new stage in which not only free trade of products but also the flow of ideas and services become much more important (Levinson 2020). According to Oxford Economics' 2023 study of bilateral cross-border trade of intermediate goods (IGs) that more accurately represents supply chain componentry than the final products, global supply chains have continuously expanded, despite talks of deglobalization and nearshoring. For example, IG trade expanded to 126% in 2022 compared to 2018, although global value chains have undergone some changes: decoupling China's trade with the U.S. and Japan has materialized, while China has gained more importance as a source of inputs shipped to other G7 developed economies, including Germany and the U.K.; and, a few Asian economies, including Vietnam and Indonesia, are emerging as hotspots of IG trade growth (Nguyen-Quoc 2024).

Considering the superior efficiency of GVC over single-nation-based production systems, neoliberal globalists and GVC proponents, as well as many sociologists, such as Sassen (2006), and Marxist political economists (Cerny 2010; Harvey 2007; Robinson 2004) commonly hold the denationalization argument, despite their varied positions in the normative evaluation of globalization. They share the view that with globalization of major national corporations, diverse patterns of national economies will disappear and converge into the global free market.

Neoliberal globalists and GVC proponents (Singh 2023; World Bank 2020; Aichele and Heiland 2018; Yeung 2017; Bhagwati 2010a, 2010b; Gibbon et al. 2008; Friedman 2005; Edwards 2004; Ohmae 1990, 1995), based on neoclassical economics, hold that the free movement of capital, labor, and goods resulting from globalization guarantees the best efficiency; thus, almost all countries will competitively lift regulations and move toward the free market to attract capital and direct investment that moves freely across borders. Companies in nation-states that hold to more regulations, higher-cost welfare, or high-wage systems will transfer production to other countries to secure the advantages of lower wages and free economic activity. Therefore, neoliberals and GVC scholars argue that nation-states will abolish their patterns of economic development or nationalist elements and converge into the free market. Thus, neoliberals and the GVC literature hold that the decline of state interference, along with free markets across borders, will benefit not only home countries but also developing countries.

The view that globalization is denationalization is also shared by left-wing intellectuals who criticize neoliberalism (Cerny 2010; Harvey 2007; Robinson 2004; Jessop 1999; Giddens 1999). Left-wing intellectuals criticize globalization in that neoliberalism unilaterally strengthens the power of capital, reduces welfare, and expands social inequality, but they share the neoliberal view that globalization will eventually dissolve national economies into one global level economy, diminish the nation-state's decision-making role, and eliminate differences in national economic governance patterns.

For example, the global capitalism school, led by Robinson, a global networks analyst who builds on the Marxist tradition, argues that the emergence of a transnational production system will dismantle the existing national economy and accelerate convergence into a single global standard, as follows:

> But I want to emphasize here the qualitative differences between the world in the early twentieth century and the world in the early twenty-first century. The globalization of production has entailed the fragmentation and decentralization of complex production chains and the worldwide dispersal and functional integration of the different segments in these chains. Yet this world-wide decentralization and fragmentation of the production process has taken place together with the centralization of command and control of the global economy in transnational capital. In this way globalization is unifying the world into a single mode of production and a single global system and bringing about the integration of different countries and regions into a new global economy. (Robinson 2004: 15)

Philip Cerny (2010), a leading left-wing political economist, also stresses that, with globalization, countries can no longer play the traditional "strategic" or "developmental" role, and that economies are increasingly converging into marketization and "commodification," as neoliberal GVC proponents including Yeung (2017) argue.

Meanwhile, nationalists also share the denationalization view, worrying about the hollowing-out of domestic industries by national corporations' overseas expansion (Prestowitz 2010). In actuality, corporations in advanced economies, including the U.S., Japan, and Germany, often threaten labor and government with their possible decisions to move production facilities overseas (Story 2012). Many people in advanced countries have significant concern about the hollowing-out of domestic industries. Reflecting this concern, pessimistic nationalists suggest nationalist counter-measures, such as protectionism and an appeal to moral patriotism (Prestowitz 2010). A few states in the U.S. also passed laws to limit excessive outsourcing overseas in response to corporations' overseas practice. Japan's economic policymakers and *Keidanren* (Japan Business Federation) emphasize patriotism, criticizing neoliberal groups like *Keizai Doyukai* (Japan Association of Corporate Executives), which proposes American-style shareholder capitalism and a free-market system (Gotoh 2020: 135).

However, whether from a neoliberal GVC position or a left-wing position, arguments that globalization is denationalization may overlook the fact that patterns and outcomes of globalization vary across nation-states. Many empirical studies reveal that the ways of national corporations' overseas expansion differ by their nationality in the process of internationalization (Harzing and Noorderhaven 2008; Lane and Probert 2009; Lane 2001). As shall be examined later, contrary to the pessimistic nationalist expectation, national corporations' globalization does not necessarily result in the hollowing-out of national economies. And contrary to neoliberals' optimistic expectation, national corporations' uncoordinated globalization may not automatically upgrade domestic industrial capabilities. Rather, improvement of the industrial commons determines whether corporate globalization results in the hollowing-out of domestic industries or upgrades industrial and innovative capabilities at home.

Same Trend, Varied Outcomes

Against the background of rapidly changing technology and superior efficiency of global value chains, national corporations are impelled to recompose various inputs, including new ideas, skills, and parts, to secure their competitiveness. For example, Apple's iPod features innovative technology and design from the U.S.; parts such as memory chips produced in South Korea, display drives from Japan, and video processors from

Taiwan; and product assembly in low-wage China. This global production model vastly outstrips single-nation models of production, both in efficiency and in cost (Nanto 2010: 6–7). In order to meet the intensified global competition, companies are forced to build competitive edges all over the world. But, at a cost: Such national corporations' overseas expansion dissolves the existing national economic system.

The trend of globalized production of advanced countries' champions is causing a serious gap and tension between the interests of individual companies and the interests of national economies as a whole. The interests of nation-states, in general, lie in creating more economic activities, jobs, and added value at home, and avoiding trade deficits. Currently, however, national champions tend to worsen deficits by reducing domestic production, or increasing reverse imports from overseas production sites, while increasing their overseas production and establishing global networks for their own survival.

For instance, Apple, a national champion in the U.S. economy, produces its iPhone 14 Plus on Apple's global production networks, rather than with traditional one-nation-based production. The iPhone 14 Plus is made from worldwide resources, parts, and ideas, including hardware chip design and software engineering in Cupertino, and the excellent chip manufacturers in Taiwan and semiconductor production machine designers and producers of ASML in the Netherlands (DeLong 2023; Nanto 2010: 4–16). In this structure, Apple benefits from exporting its final product—the iPhone—from China to U.S. consumers; however, the U.S. economy suffers losses due to the current account deficit and decrease in domestic production activities.

This situation makes it unclear whether it is in the U.S. interest to limit imports to ensure jobs for U.S. citizens or to open imports for the benefit of U.S. companies. The question of which actors contribute more to the overall national economy between domestic enterprises increasing their overseas production and foreign companies creating more employment at home also becomes increasingly unclear.

However, not all national economies result in the same patterns and the same outcomes, although they undergo similar trends of their corporations' overseas expansion. Globalization of national corporations does not necessarily result in disadvantages for the entire national economy and denationalization. Unlike neoliberal globalism, national corporations' overseas expansion and growth do not automatically engender innovation capabilities at home. The relocation of national corporations to foreign countries may improve those corporations' competitive advantages, but can undermine the national economic ecosystem due to the hollowing-out of specialized supplier networks and qualified workforce. However, contrary to the pessimistic nationalists' worry about the hollowing-out of domestic industries, not all nation-states suffer from the loss of industrial commons in the course of national corporations' globalization.

As seen in Fig. 2.1, advanced economies including the U.S., Japan, and Germany, increased their outbound foreign direct investment (OFDI) in manufacturing, from 2006 to 2021: the U.S. increased to 214.7% in 2021; Germany to 178.2% in 2021; Japan to 299.4% in 2021, compared to the OFDI level of 2006.

However, the impacts of national corporations' globalization on domestic economies vary across nation-states. For example, as seen in Fig. 2.2, changes in manufacturing employment vary across advanced economies, including the U.S., Japan, Germany, and Korea, despite similar trends of national corporations' globalization. South Korea increased its employment to 126% in 2021, compared to the level of 2000, while its national corporations significantly increased overseas expansion to a significantly high level of 737.4% in 2021, compared to

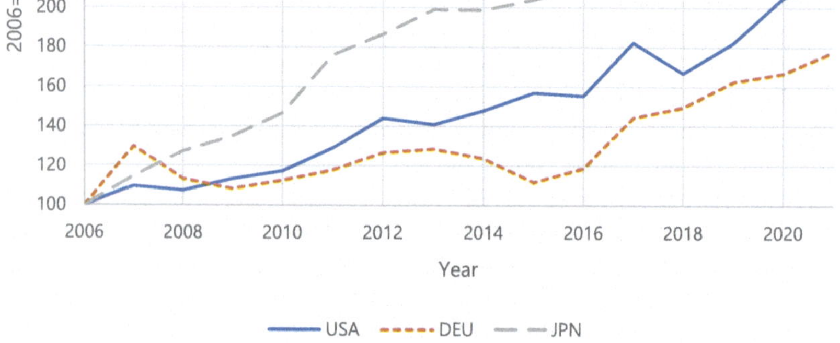

Fig. 2.1 Change in OFDI in manufacturing (*Source* OECD Database)

2006. Germany also successfully maintained its employment at 90–96% levels throughout the late 2000s and 2010s, compared to employment of 2000. By contrast, Japan and U.S. manufacturing employment at home significantly declined to 81% and 67% in 2021 respectively, compared to the 2000 employment.

In order to explore the impacts of national corporations' globalization on domestic economies, we focus on the automobile and electronics industries, which are the most globalized, and core industries of the U.S., Germany, and Japan. For example, automakers in these countries have rapidly increased overseas production since the 1990s, with their overseas production ratio reaching 65–72% as of 2016 (Table 2.1). In the case of South Korea, overseas production rapidly expanded, although delayed for a period compared to the U.S., Germany, and Japan. Almost all of South Korea's production was carried out domestically until early

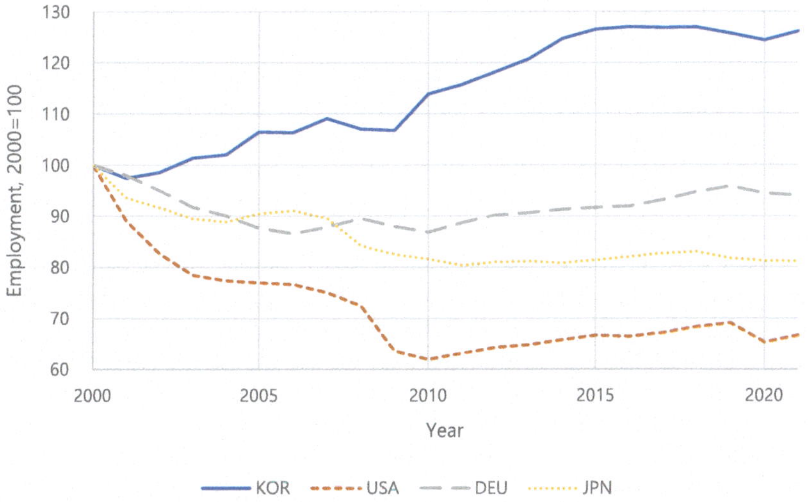

Fig. 2.2 Changes in manufacturing employment, 2000–2021 (*Source* The Japan Institute for Labour Policy and Training, https://www.jil.go.jp/kokunai/statistics/timeseries/html/g0204.html; ISTANS; U.S. Bureau of Economic Analysis (accessed Sunday, December 31, 2023); Statistisches Bundesamt, "Employees by industries" https://www.destatis.de/EN/Themes/Economy/Short-Term-Indicators/Long-Term-Series/Labour-Market/lrerw14a.html#fussnote-1-242422 [accessed December 31, 2023])

Table 2.1 Automobile corporations' overseas production in 2016

	U.S	*Germany*	*Japan*	*Korea*
Domestic production (cars)	4,853,403	4,480,655	6,597,736	3,237,000
Overseas production (cars)	9,369,148	9,754,716	12,506,924	4,653,000
Domestic production (%)	34.1	34.2	28.0	41.1
Overseas production (%)	65.9	65.8	72.0	58.9

Source OICA (Organisation International des Constructeurs d'Automobiles) Statistics
N.B.: U.S. automakers include GM, Ford; German automakers: Volkswagen, Daimler, BMW; Japanese automakers: Toyota, Nissan, Honda; Korean automakers: Hyundai, Kia

2000. In other words, it has maintained a one-country-based production system. However, South Korea rapidly increased overseas production in a short period of time. In 2012, Korean automobile corporations' overseas production began to surpass domestic production; as of 2016, overseas production accounted for 59% of total production, reaching a level comparable to the U.S., Germany, and Japan.

Despite similar trends of globalized production, and contrary to the denationalization views, the effects on national economies vary significantly. In Germany and South Korea, overseas production by corporations of electronics and automobiles representing their national economies did not result in denationalization, such as the hollowing-out of domestic industry and employment.

In the case of Korea, employment increased despite the fact that overseas production increased significantly over the past 20 years. Since the mid-1990s, South Korea's main industries—electronics and automobile—have increased Korea's outward foreign direct investment (OFDI) from $113 million in 1992 to $2.57 billion in 2008, about 22 times growth. Productivity also increased. However, domestic employment in the two industries increased from 6.53 million to 7.54 million during the same period (1991–2007).

As seen in Fig. 2.3, while national corporations in the electronics and automobile industries of the U.S., Japan, and Germany go abroad similarly, domestic employment changes vary across national economies. The U.S. and Japan suffered from declining domestic employment, to 66.4% and 77.9% in 2019 respectively, compared to the level of 1998, whereas employment in Germany's electronics and automobile industries increased to 110.3% in 2019, compared to the level of 1998.

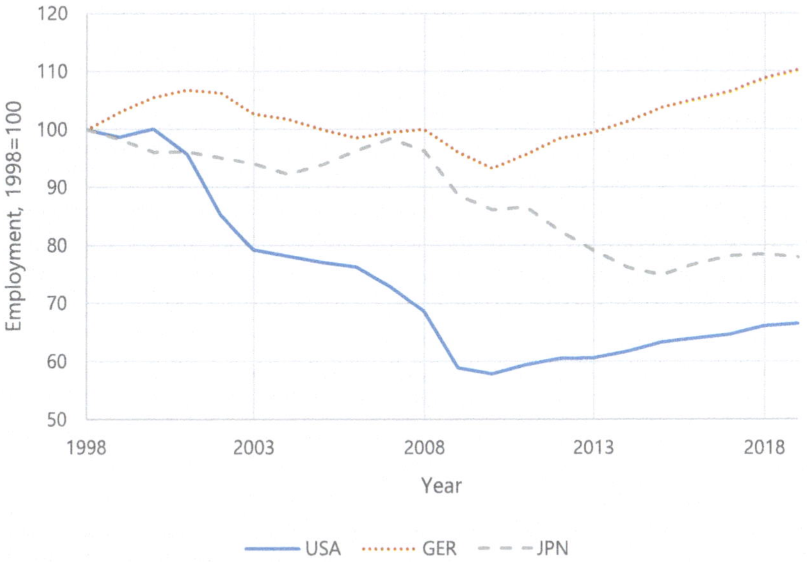

Fig. 2.3 Employment changes in automobile and electronics, 1998–2019 (*Source* OECD [2020], STAN Industrial Analysis 2020 ed. [Variable EMPN, Industries D26 and D29 added])

Moreover, the employment decline in the U.S. and Japan was due not to growth in productivity, but to the effects of national corporations' globalization, contrary to the neoliberal argument that job loss in domestic manufacturing is a natural phenomenon due to advances in technology and productivity, based on arguments by neoclassical economist Colin Clark (Clark 1940: 492). The neoliberal position takes reduction in U.S. manufacturing jobs as a given (Locke and Wellhausen 2014: 4). However, many empirical studies show that job reduction in the current U.S. manufacturing industry is difficult to be seen as a natural phenomenon resulting from increased productivity (Atkinson, et al. 2012; Houseman et al. 2011; Helper et al. 2012).

As seen in Fig. 2.4, labor productivity in the motor vehicle industry of Korea and the U.S. has similarly changed to 165% and 164% respectively in 2020, compared to 2000. However, in the similar trends of national automakers' globalization, U.S. employment declined to 77% in 2021, compared to 2000. By contrast, Korea's employment in the automobile industry increased to 159% in 2021, compared to 2000. This contradicts the neoliberal claim of reduced manufacturing employment due to productivity improvement.

Neoliberal globalists argue that expansion of overseas production is a "win–win" relationship between home country and overseas production sites, and that overseas production itself helps development of the home country's industry. In other words, overseas production, or offshoring, reduces costs compared to domestic production, and thus upgrades the domestic industry, by efficiently allocating resources to growth industries. In fact, transferring expensive sunset industries or low-value-added industries overseas may be inevitable. In this case, even if national corporations increase overseas production, as projected in neoliberal optimism, core innovation capabilities or high-value-added areas could be upgraded. However, evidence shows that companies' expansion of overseas production does not necessarily result in improved production competitiveness of domestic industries.

While major corporations in the U.S., Germany, Japan, and South Korea increased their overseas production between 2000 and 2022, their

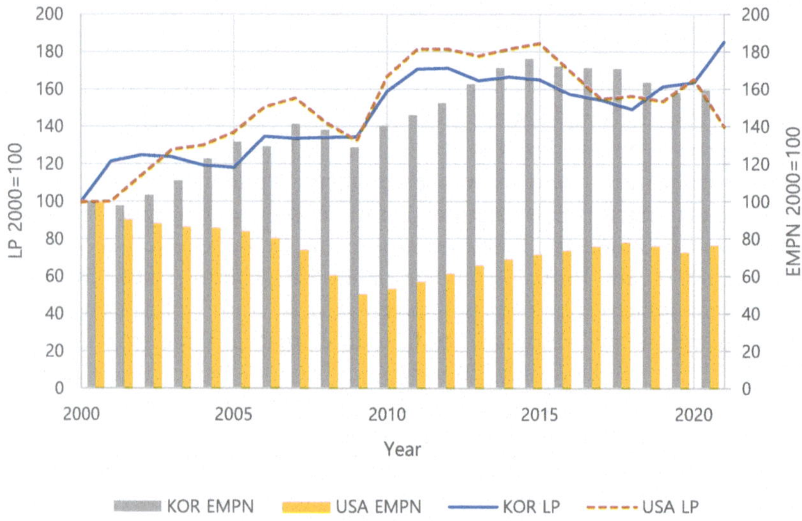

Fig. 2.4 Productivity and employment in automobile industry, Korea vs the U.S. 2000–2021 (*Source* ISTANS, US Bureau of Labor Statistics)

growth in the competitiveness of high-tech industries showed different patterns. As seen in Fig. 2.5, the trade balance of high-tech industries in the U.S. and Japan declined, while by contrast, those of South Korea and Germany increased. In particular, the U.S. trade balance of high-tech industries significantly declined from a $12 billion deficit in 2000 to a $350.7 billion deficit in 2022; Japan's high-tech trade balance also declined from a $54.98 billion surplus in 2000 to a $32.2 billion deficit in 2022. By contrast, Korea's high-tech trade balance increased from a $14.1 billion surplus in 2000 to a $52.9 billion surplus in 2022; and Germany's high-tech trade balance grew from a $2.29 billion deficit in 2000 to a $29.0 billion surplus in 2023.

Why does such a phenomenon occur? In the case of Germany and Korea, national corporations upgraded their domestic industries and innovation capabilities in the course of globalization, while the U.S. and Japan failed in doing so. These different effects result from different patterns of coordination politics to build industrial commons in the course of national corporations' globalization.

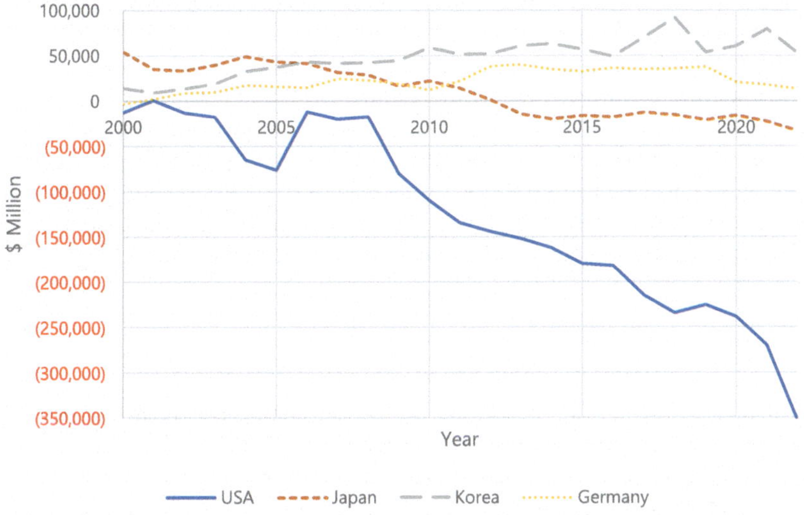

Fig. 2.5 Trade balance in high-technology sectors, 2000–2022 (*Source* UN Comtrade database 2016)

In the U.S. free-market system, individual firms expanded overseas production, freely pursuing the individualistic rationale of increasing shareholder value in the absence of social coordination, which resulted in the loss of industrial commons in the domestic industrial ecosystem. Japan lost its production and innovation capabilities due to too much coordination, based on closed circles of compensation. As seen in the so-called Galapagos syndrome (Calder 2017; Kushida 2011), Japan's coordination of closed circle stakeholders made its industrial commons outdated, losing competitiveness by isolating Japanese companies from rapidly changing technology and world markets.

In contrast to the U.S. and Japan, Germany and Korea improved their production and innovation capabilities at home through collective coordination, while their corporations expanded overseas production. In both cases, the domestic industrial ecosystems were newly upgraded through great struggles and collective coordination between labor organizations, industry associations, and governments in the process of globalizing corporate production. In particular, as shall be examined in Chapter 8, Germany improved its domestic innovation capabilities and industrial commons for commercialization through social coordination by labor organizations, industrial associations, and public research institutes.

In the end, contrary to neoliberal claims, the globalization process of companies does not necessarily result in upgrading their home industries, and unlike nationalist pessimists, production globalization does not necessarily lead to hollowing-out domestic industries. Whether industrial competitiveness will improve or result in industrial hollowing-out in the process of globalization depends on the extent to which industrial ecosystems can be rebuilt and industrial commons can be upgraded in the process.

Various Patterns of Coordination

Globalized production of national industrial champions is an irresistible and presumably inescapable trend in countries worldwide; however, the method and effects vary widely from country to country. In fact, globalized production of major U.S. corporations tends to have spurred denationalization, with export substitution, reverse imports, loss of domestic employment, and weakened domestic production bases. In Germany and South Korea, globalized production has spurred an upgrade of domestic production, an expansion of parts exports, and an increase in domestic employment, opposite the effects of denationalization and the hollowing-out of domestic industries. Such disparate outcomes result from differences in the "politics of coordination," in which a country's national corporations rebuild the domestic industrial ecosystem in the process of globalizing their production. Before we delve into each case of the U.S., Japan, and Germany in detail by examining how they have reorganized their national economy, this section briefly compares and summarizes the various politics of coordination.

Individual advanced countries employ various forms of politics of adaptation to coordinate changes in the national economy following corporate globalization. In order to flexibly adapt in a rapidly changing world of markets and technology, nation-states can open to the worldwide free flow of parts, skills, services, and ideas. But openness comes at a cost, including social and political instability and more difficulties in coordination. Even in the course of corporations' globalization to utilize best inputs, nation-states vary in their ways and degree of openness and coordination.

As seen in Table 2.2, the U.S. is more open to a rapidly changing world of technology and global markets due to its liberal free-market system, while at the same time it has a low level of coordination capabilities. By contrast, Japan shows a high degree of coordination but low openness to the outside world, based on its coordination through closed circles of compensation. Germany and Korea are more open to the outside world, compared with Japan, while possessing high coordination capabilities, compared with the U.S.

For example, Japan is relatively closed, compared to the U.S., Germany, and Korea, even in a globalized world. As seen in Fig. 2.6, Japan's position in terms of exports and imports, compared to its GDP, is one of the lowest among countries from 1990 to 2021, while Germany and Korea are the most open. As seen in Fig. 2.6a, in terms of exports

Table 2.2 Typology of openness and coordination

		Coordination	
		Low	*High*
Openness	High	U.S	Germany South Korea
	Low		Japan

compared to GDP, Germany and Korea show the highest levels around 40% to 50%, while Japan remains around 15% throughout the 2000s and 2010s. As seen in Fig. 2.6b, in terms of imports, the trend is similar: Japan ranks low, around 10 to 15%, with the U.S., whereas Korea and Germany rank high, around 40% throughout the 2000s and 2010. In terms of trade, Japan and the U.S. are oriented toward domestic markets, while Germany and Korea are oriented toward world markets. Although the U.S. has focused on domestic markets, unlike Japan, the U.S. is more open to the free flow of humans, ideas, and capital than Japan. U.S. universities attract high-quality students worldwide, while Japanese universities do not. As seen in Fig. 2.6c, in terms of openness to foreign direct investment, Japan ranks lowest among countries in attracting foreign investments, by 4.9% inward FDI compared to GDP in 2021, while Germany (25.8%), the U.S. (21.3%), and Korea (13.8%) are more open to FDI.

Even in the course of globalization, Japanese firms have focused on transferring their nationally-oriented networks nurtured at home onto foreign soil, rather than learning from experience on foreign soil and experimenting and flexibly adapting new ideas. As many empirical studies reveal (Shimada 2017; Calder 2017; Kazuhiko 2015; Kushida 2011), even while globalizing, Japanese companies have maintained a closed mentality and corporate governance. Japanese globalized firms use only Japanese managers and rarely recruit overseas talents. Japanese companies lack diverse nationalities in their executive boards and management circles. In contrast, European and U.S. companies actively recruit overseas talent and new operational capabilities through market relationships with overseas companies, thus outpacing Japanese management systems (Kazuhiko 2015: 59–60; Reisel 2017). Vassiliouk (2019) reports that Japan continues to maintain its insular outlook even in the course of globalization:

> Despite the Japanese government's efforts aimed at the globalization of the Japanese society since the 1990s, Japan is yet to reach an adequate level of openness and internationalization suitable for the world's third largest economy and a key global power. …Today, it can be observed that in comparison with the other OECD nations, Japan's society remains largely inward-looking and less competitive across various sectors, particularly in corporate culture, research, and education, English language proficiency, gender equality, and immigration policy. (Vassiliouk 2019)

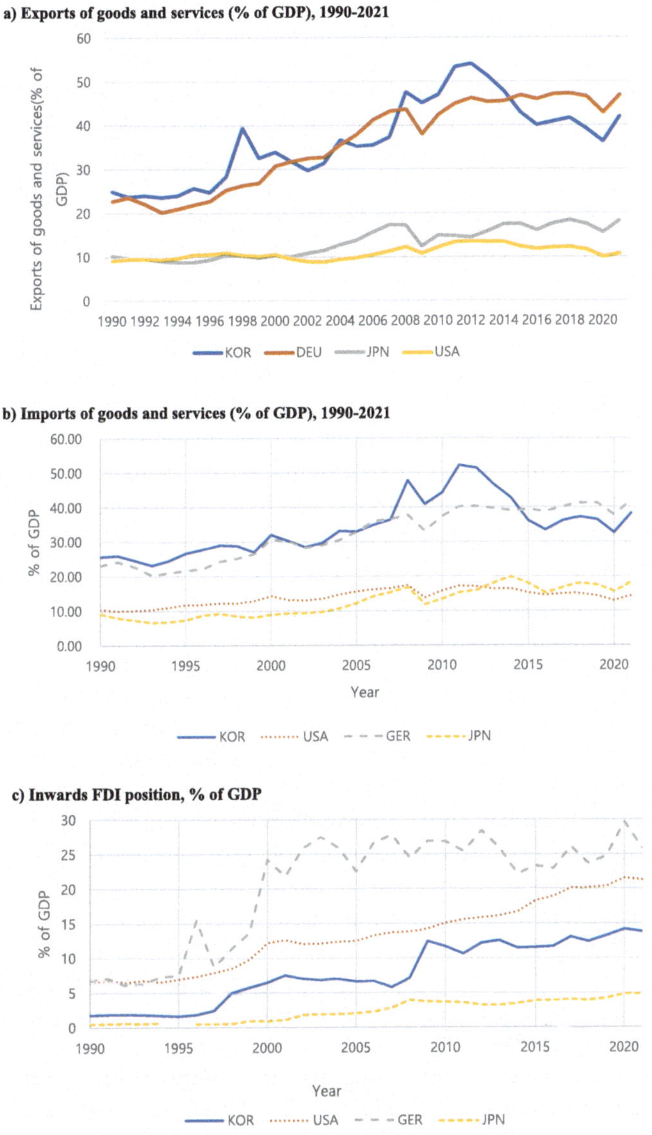

Fig. 2.6 Index of openness to global markets. **a** Exports of goods and services (% of GDP), 1990–2021. **b** Imports of goods and services (% of GDP), 1990–2021. **c** Inwards FDI position, % of GDP (*Source* OECD database; World Bank)

Japan's closed circles of compensation, including *Keiretsu*-based inter-firm relations, closed finance circles, and its so-called iron triangle of bureaucrats, large employers, and politicians, have insulated Japan from the outside world. Japan's strong social ties might facilitate domestic solidarity and inside coordination, but these ties are obstacles to change and flexible adaptation in the rapidly changing world of markets and technology (Calder 2017; Shimada 2017; Kushida 2011).

In addition to openness, types of coordination also vary across national economies. The U.S. tends to globalize by prioritizing financial capital through an uncoordinated free-market system. Germany and Northern European countries like Sweden upgrade their domestic industrial ecosystems through social coordination of social stakeholders including labor organizations, industry associations, and public institutions. Japan and South Korea employ a statist model of coordination to induce companies to create a new innovation system. Before delving into each case study, this section briefly outlines the typical coordination and adjustment methods along the line of these classifications.

Uncoordinated Free-Market System: The U.S.

The globalization process of U.S. companies is based on unilateral decisions by management focusing solely on increasing shareholder values. This free-market system rejects any social adjustment involving the state or labor organizations. Overseas production by major U.S. companies has increased dramatically since the 1990s, resulting in denationalization. U.S. companies' globalization could not induce advancement of domestic production bases because their driving concern was increasing short-term shareholder profits.

For example, U.S. innovations such as semiconductors, flat-panel displays, light-emitting diodes (LEDs), optical coating, high-tech batteries, precision bearings, photoelectricity, wind turbines, and ultra-large forgings were once created domestically, but are fast disappearing from U.S. production. Innovative ideas developed in the U.S. for production and commercialization have been quickly moved abroad, and complementary goods in the relationship between domestic industries are disappearing altogether (Pisano and Shih 2012b, 8–13; Atkinson and Ezell 2012; Berger 2013).

Due to the many holes in industrial linkages, even U.S. companies producing cutting-edge ideas have difficulty in commercializing them. Silicon Valley in California, Austin, Texas, and Cambridge, Massachusetts—the most innovative regions in the U.S.—are overflowing with innovative ideas. But young engineers with excellent ideas lack the ability to commercialize those ideas and scale up with products, due to lack of production technology, critical parts manufacturers, and long-term capital for commercialization (Berger 2013; Pisano and Shih 2012).

The U.S. method of globalization—simple openness without social coordination—has caused serious damage to the national economy because, unlike in Germany and Korea, social adjustment is not allowed. When companies began building global networks in earnest after the 1990s, the U.S. lacked capacity for collective social coordination. From World War II to the 1970s, the U.S. government's strategy and major companies' overseas expansion were somewhat coordinated because major U.S. companies' overseas production aligned with the government's policy to maintain U.S. hegemony. During that time, the U.S. government had coordinated companies' overseas production through carrots and sticks—generous subsidies and tax exemptions as carrots, and tariff cuts as representative sticks. However, the government's indirect industrial intervention retreated in the 1990s due to the dominance of neoliberalism to emphasize open and free flow of products, skills, capital, and ideas (Gilpin 1975: 139: Lynn 2005: 87–97). U.S. companies maintained formal market-facing relationships rather than developing close cooperative relationships with parts makers, while labor organizations and industry associations lacked a voice in determining corporate investment (Kwon 2004a: 92–105). These narrow-focused U.S. business relations and state-industrial relations worked aggressively against social coordination.

Financialization of the U.S. economy has accelerated since the 1990s, changing the focus of U.S. companies from supporting existing managers to supporting shareholder value (Davis 2011: 1121–1138; Orhangazi 2008). With financialization of the U.S. economy, improving the competitiveness of domestic industries in globalized production was not an important consideration. Professor Thomas Kochan explains financialization as prioritizing shareholder value, stock options, and frequent reshuffling of management by U.S. companies:

> The focus on maximizing shareholder value and an easy-come, easy-go attitude toward the workforce started during the 1980s. But there were larger forces at work: major innovations in capital markets, deregulation

> of financial institutions, and significant increases of debt deemed acceptable for the U.S. firms. Corporations were increasingly seen as bundles of tradable assets that could be reconfigured or restructured to maximize short-term financial returns. Power within corporations shifted from leaders responsible for production, human resources, and labor relations to finance executives, who served as agents of ever more demanding financial markets. CEO income rose rapidly as stock options and other incentives linked to share price became core elements of compensation packages ... These trends built stronger pressure for short-term returns, which in turn prompted firms to cut jobs as a preemptive act rather than a last resort. (Kochan 2012: 70)

In the past, U.S. companies maintained and developed various production factors within vertically integrated giants through cooperation and mutual coordination of various internal stakeholders, including capital, managers, and labor. More recently, social adjustment has proved more difficult as companies narrow their focus to shareholder value and exchangeable assets.

In this way, the U.S. stands in sharp contrast to other countries in terms of linkages between domestic and foreign production. Global production networks of Japanese, German, and Korean companies are closely integrated with the domestic production network, while U.S. companies' global production networks are severed from domestic production networks. As U.S. automakers' overseas production increased, U.S. parts makers' exports to countries where overseas production takes place, such as China, declined. Korean parts makers' exports have increased with the increase in overseas production, mainly because many Korean companies that produce overseas receive parts from Korea (Kwon and Kim 2020: 738–741).

Recently, in the late 2010s and early 2020s, the U.S. has revived its domestic innovation capabilities due to improved coordination capabilities, rather than simply pursuing openness and free flow of products, capital, and ideas. An emerging U.S. industrial revival could be possible, based not on a neoliberal free-market model but on newly established statist coordination built on strategic industrial policies. Chapters 3 and 4 will examine in detail the case of the U.S. in the course of globalization, including why the uncoordinated free-market model causes problems like loss of industrial commons, and how the U.S. improves its coordination capabilities by adopting the statist coordination model.

Statist Coordination: Japan and South Korea

In contrast to the U.S. uncoordinated free-market model, Japan and Korea developed statist coordination models in the course of globalization. Based on their similar models of industrialization of state-led developmentalism, both Japan and Korea pursued a similar path to globalization by building nationalistic production networks overseas. In contrast to the U.S., Japan and Korea developed close linkages between home and overseas production through a statist coordination model, which mobilized key actors to improve their domestic production bases in the course of globalization (Kwon and Kim 2020; Marukara 2006; Banenji and Sambharya 1996; Peng et al. 2001).

For example, as seen in Table 2.3, nationally diverse automakers operating in China have established a component procurement system, which reveals differences according to the nationality of the company. Compared to companies in the U.S., Germany, and France, Korean and Japanese companies have built overseas production networks in China with domestic parts makers that have joined them. In addition, Korea and Japan have forged a strong link between overseas and domestic production by establishing a nationalist network abroad (Kwon and Kim 2020; Yang et al. 2009: 152). Overseas production by South Korean and Japanese companies, coupled with domestic production, has boosted exports of related parts makers domestically as well.

However, both Japan and Korea as statist models are different in terms of timing and motives of globalization. Both countries pursued a state-led development method, yet they diverged in their globalization methods and effects on domestic economies. Despite similar statist coordination models, Korea successfully improved its domestic industrial ecosystem and increased innovation capabilities, while Japan failed to do so. The major reason for this difference lies in the degree of openness to a rapidly changing world of markets and technology.

When globalizing in the 1990s, Japan focused on transplanting its existing production system overseas, rather than absorbing new methods and innovation ideas, because it already had a world-class production system at home. Japanese companies entered together with domestic partners from the beginning and established a nationalistic overseas production network. Close cooperation between Japan's lead firms and parts makers has been a source of international competitiveness, to the extent that U.S. companies are learning from them. Japan focused on

Table 2.3 National differences in parts supplier networks on Chinese soil

		% of sharing stock with automaker (keiretsu) *(%)*	*Same nationality of automaker (%)*	*Chinese locals (%)*	*Others (%)*
U.S	Shanghai GM	–	16.6	42.1	41.3
	Beijing Jeep	–	15.0	57.1	27.9
Germany	Shanghai VW	–	13.4	53.9	32.7
	FAW-VW	–	13.3	54.2	32.5
France	Dongfeng Citroen	–	7.5	59.4	33.1
Japan	Tianjin Toyota	48.9	78.9	14.9	6.4
	Guangzhou Honda	15.1	54.8	24.7	20.5
	Zhengzhou Nissan	27.3	43.4	34.0	22.6
Korea	Dongfeng KIA	–	28.6	26.2	45.2
	Beijing Hyundai	–	81.3	6.3	12.4

Source Marukawa (2006)

transplanting its competitive advantage abroad. However, in the 2000s, Japanese companies wanted to switch to a more open innovation system in the aftermath of the long recession and the limited innovation capabilities of existing closed partnerships based on the *Keiretsu* system (Kwon and Kim 2020).

By contrast, as a latecomer, Korea lacked Japan's comparative advantage, so it changed its developmental strategy, from exclusively nurturing national champions to development of SMEs and collaborative industrial ecosystems in order to overcome difficulties abroad, rather than focusing on transferring domestic production overseas, as Japan did. For example, the Korean government supported and fostered the domestic parts and materials industry for ten years, based on the 2001 Special Act on Parts and Materials. As a result, Korea's parts industry, which suffered from chronic trade deficits with Japan and a lack of technology, grew rapidly (Industrial Research Institute 2012; Dong-A Ilbo February 3, 2015). In contrast to Japan, Korea was more open to new ideas and technology in order to improve its competitiveness (Kwon and Kim 2020).

Furthermore, the Japanese government's intervention sometimes hindered reform of the domestic industrial ecosystem, as reform and coordination weakened against the backdrop of unstable state power, as shown by the "lost decades" and frequent regime changes before Prime Minister Abe brought long-term and stable authority in the 2010s. In particular, Japan suffered from outdatedness of industrial commons, resulting from the so-called Galapagos syndrome (Calder 2017; Kushida 2011), due to coordination based on the nationally closed circles of compensation, as shall be examined in Chapter 5. However, since the late 2000s, Japan has enhanced its innovative capabilities, first by emulating the U.S.-style open and free-market system, and also by improving the state's coordination capability by centralizing state power with the Prime Minister and cabinet, as shall be examined in Chapter 6. Chapters 5 and 6 examine in detail why Japan suffered from long-term recession in the course of globalization, unlike the U.S. and Korea, and how Japan revived its economy in the late 2010s.

Social Coordination: Germany

Since the 1990s, major German corporations have increased overseas production, similar to the U.S. However, unlike the U.S. free-market model, Germany's expansion of overseas production has advanced production and innovation capabilities rather than reduced domestic production and employment. The great difference is that German companies' globalization is collectively adjusted by major actors inside and outside the corporation, to include labor organizations, industry associations, and local organizations.

Amid German national champions increasing overseas production, German production and employment grew or remained stable because of continuous upgrades and high-value-added domestic production along with globalization. Unlike the U.S., Germany's domestic job structure was upgraded qualitatively in the process of globalization. High-value-added and technology development-related jobs increased, while low-skilled jobs decreased (Nunnenkemp 2004: 8–26; Bernaciak 2010: 129; Jurgens and Meissner 2005: 227; Jurgens and Kraywdzinski 2010: 106; Kwon 2012: 587–588).

German companies were able to upgrade domestic production in the process of globalizing because major actors, including labor and trade associations, collectively discussed and coordinated the globalization process inside and outside the company. In contrast to U.S. finance-led, unilateral decisions in the free-market system, Germany improved its domestic production and innovation capabilities because of the linkage between overseas and domestic production resulting from collective coordination at home. Through *Mitbestimmung* (co-determination), German management and labor organizations have coordinated companies' globalization process to prevent expansion of overseas production from reducing or closing domestic factories. For example, when German automakers such as Volkswagen wanted to increase overseas production, labor organizations approved increased production in Hungary and the Czech Republic, while at the same time consulted with management to improve domestic production capabilities. Because of these joint efforts, Germany has maintained and strengthened domestic production capabilities amid the increasing overseas production (Kwon 2012: 590–592; Haipeter 2000: 353–355; Jürgen and Kraywdzinski 2010: 53–54; Klobes 2005: 177).

Notably, this method of globalization of production through collective bargaining at the firm level has spread to Germany's core industries. Company-level collective bargaining reorganizes the existing domestic corporatist system and centralized bargaining, contradicting the institutionalist argument that overseas production is a simple transplant of the domestic system. For Germany, overseas production is a comprehensive reorganization of the domestic production system based on experience and needs abroad. In other words, centralized labor–management negotiations were converted to decentralized company-level negotiations focused not only on wages and labor conditions but also on upgrading Germany's production methods. This social coordination model seeks to improve the innovation ability of Germany's domestic industry through cooperation with public and social research institutes such as the Industrial Association and the Fraunhofer Society (FHG). Chapters 7 and 8 will examine in detail how Germany improved its industrial commons in the course of corporations' globalization through social coordination, and how its institutions have changed to meet the challenges of globalization.

In summary, the globalization process of major industries does not simply mean denationalization or convergence to free-market relations, but takes various forms for each country. Outcomes depend on how domestic production is readjusted in the process of globalized production, and how the industrial commons are accumulated and improved.

The politics that reconstruct the industrial ecosystem follow various patterns by country. These patterns include liberal market principles, social coordination methods, and statist coordination adjustment. Adjustment methods are not determined by domestic institutions nor by a unilateral transplant of a domestic production method, as institutionalists argue, but by two-way processes that cause changes in the home country's production system based on the overseas experience. In the following chapters we will analyze how different politics take place in the process of globalization: in the U.S., representing the liberal market system; Japan, the statist coordination system; and Germany as a social coordination model.

PART I

Neoliberal Model: The Case of the U.S.

Against the backdrop of rapid development of information and communication technologies (ICT), globalization, and intensifying global competition, companies have built global value chains (GVCs) or global production networks (GPNs) that separate elements from existing value chains and freely reunite them at the global level. These chains and networks have shown superior efficiency over existing national production systems based on one-country national production factors, by optimally reorganizing production inputs, including technology, science, and parts, across national borders. Companies have tried to improve their competitiveness by dismantling existing domestic production systems and increasing overseas research and development (R&D) and production. As a 2024 Oxford Economics report reveals, despite talks of deglobalization and nearshoring, global value chains have continuously expanded (Nguyen-Quoc 2024).

Contrary to neoliberal arguments, companies' free pursuit of profits in an open world to utilize various inputs without national restrictions have not always produced beneficial results for their home countries or host countries. As seen in the case of the U.S., individual companies' strategic efforts in the absence of social coordination can result in suboptimal outcomes to national economies as a whole, such as loss of industrial commons and innovation capabilities. The more decentralized and open the world becomes, the more social coordination is needed. However, rigid coordination without openness to a rapidly changing world can also engender inferior outcomes, including outdated industrial commons, as seen in the case of Japan, which shall be examined later.

In part I, we show that the neoliberal argument—that companies' free globalization and openness to a changing world will result in improved production and innovation capabilities of the national economy—is not always correct, based on the case of the U.S. The U.S. trade deficit has expanded in the high-tech industries as those industries' capacity to commercialize innovative ideas weakens, despite great potential in the field of basic research. Unlike social coordination systems in Germany or state-led coordination systems in Korea, the U.S.'s free-market systems reveal weaknesses in the globalization of production. Contrary to neoliberal arguments, companies' simple openness to a rapidly changing world does not automatically produce beneficial outcomes to the national economy.

In the late 2010s and early 2020s, U.S. industries revived, following a long-term decline in the course of globalization. In 2018 alone, 264,000 manufacturing jobs were created. U.S. manufacturing employment increased from 11.22 million jobs in 2010 to 12.52 million jobs in 2022 (U.S. Bureau of Economic Analysis database). According to the Bureau of Economic Analysis, U.S. manufacturing output in 2017 was about $6 trillion, showing a record level of production (Ministry of Trade, Industry and Energy 2019: 34). This gradual U.S. revival does not confirm the effectiveness of a neoliberal free-market system. On the contrary, the revival of U.S. manufacturing competitiveness in the late 2010s was due to the U.S. government's active intervention based on the rationale of social coordination and state-led coordination models seen in Germany and Asian countries. As shall be examined later, following the 2012 report on manufacturing submitted to President Obama by the President's Council of Advisors on Science and Technology (PCAST, July 2012), along with the Manufacturing USA Program Act, the Trump administration's strategy for leadership in high-tech manufacturing industries, and the Biden administration's Chips and Science Act of 2022, the revival of U.S. manufacturing was due to the federal government's active intervention and support. The 2010s revival disproves the validity of the free-market model and shows that the state's active intervention may be still valid even in the era of an open and changing world.

Below, we first examine why the U.S. free-market system suffered from its companies' uncoordinated and free globalization; then we explore how the U.S. rejuvenated its economy and how its new methods for revival differ from traditional liberal methods. Finally, we examine how the recent revival policy has been established.

CHAPTER 3

Globalization and the U.S. National Economy

Contrary to the optimistic neoliberal outlook, the expansion of U.S. companies' free pursuit of best inputs and new ideas in a rapidly changing world has not always had positive effects on the domestic economy. Expansion of overseas production and investment by U.S. companies disrupted the domestic inter-industry linkage system and dismantled production. Sound industrial ecosystems for innovation suffered, as the expansion of uncoordinated free-market overseas production by individual companies led to the hollowing-out of domestic manufacturing. Before exploring how the U.S. has revived its economy with a new coordination model, and how it can change to a new system of state coordination (see Chapter 4), this chapter examines why the U.S. suffered from loss of production and innovation capabilities in the course of its companies' globalization.

Effects of U.S. Companies' Globalization on Domestic Economy

This section explores briefly what impacts U.S. companies' overseas expansion has had upon the home economy, and addresses why the U.S. economy suffered from its companies' globalization and how the U.S. began to rejuvenate its manufacturing in the late 2010s.

H. Kwon, *Openness and Coordination*,
https://doi.org/10.1007/978-981-97-3352-1_3

With globalization, core U.S. industries have experienced a sharp decline in jobs and production, and stagnation in productivity. For example, about 5.8 million jobs in U.S. manufacturing disappeared between 2000 and 2010. As seen in Fig. 3.1, U.S. manufacturing employment remained relatively stable until the year of 2000, at about 17 million jobs, decreasing sharply to about 11.22 million in 2010. Beginning with the first Obama administration, manufacturing increased eventually to 12.52 million jobs in 2022. Compared to 2010, 1.3 million new manufacturing jobs were created. Nevertheless, the industry has not yet recovered to its pre-2000 level (BLS Data from https://www.bls.gov/data/).

With corporations' overseas expansion, U.S. domestic production significantly declined. U.S. corporations' outflow of foreign direct investment (OFDI) increased from $1.18 trillion in 2000 to $4.26 trillion in 2021. Notably, the U.S.' outflow FDI has been bigger than its inflow FDI (IFDI) throughout the 2000s and 2010s. Particularly, from 2000 to 2010, the ratio of OFDI to IFDI significantly increased, from 104.9% to 145.5%, its highest peak, while after 2010, the ratio decreased to 111.6% in 2021 due to the government's reshoring and industrial policies (US

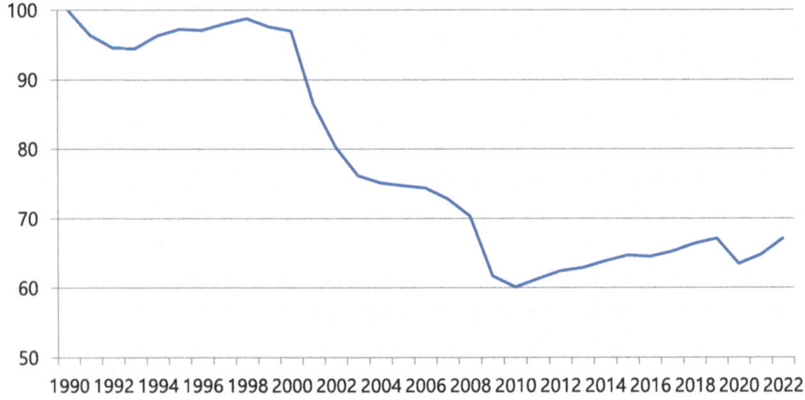

Fig. 3.1 Changes in employment in the U.S. manufacturing industry, 1990–2022 (**Source* U.S. Bureau of Economic Analysis, "Table 6.5C. Full-Time Equivalent Employees by Industry" [accessed Sunday, December 31, 2023], U.S. Bureau of Economic Analysis, "Table 6.5D. Full-Time Equivalent Employees by Industry" [accessed Sunday, December 31, 2023]. **Unit is a change relative to the jobs of 18.65 million jobs in 1990 [= 100])

Bureau of Economic Analysis database). Between 2001 and 2010, with increasing expansion of overseas production , U.S. production in the 13 manufacturing sectors accounting for 58% of its manufacturing employment decreased significantly, including production decline of electronic equipment and wood industries by 7%, fabricated metals by 10%, printing by 12%, apparel by 43%, and textiles and motor vehicles by 39% (Atkinson and Ezell 2012: 39, 57).

During the same period, U.S. manufacturing's global competitiveness weakened further. The U.S. accounted for about 25 to 30% of the world's manufacturing production from the 1970s to the 1990s. In the 2000s, the U.S. share of global manufacturing fell, to about 17% in 2012 (Kim Bo-min et al. 2014: 3). First to go was U.S. competitiveness in the machinery industry, the basis for all manufacturing technology development. In 2010, the U.S. portion of global machine tool production plummeted to 5%, while China's share increased significantly to 35%. Between 2005 and 2008, about 80% of the most sophisticated five-axis machines utilized in the U.S. were imported from Japan and Germany. And in the automobile industry, which shows the degree of intensity of a country's industrial linkage, the U.S. lost its edge. From 1999 to the 2008 crisis, the U.S. share of global passenger car production decreased from 14.5% in 1999 to 7.5%. In high-tech's printed circuit board production, the U.S. accounted for 29% of global production in 1998, decreasing to 8% in 2009. In global photovoltaic (solar panel) production, a next-generation technology, the U.S. share decreased from 40% in 1995 to 7% in 2011 (Atkinson and Ezell 2012: 44).

Decreased manufacturing production is by no means inevitable for advanced capitalist countries. In Germany, for example, production has shrunk in low-tech industries but increased significantly in high-value-added and high-tech industries, such as solar panels, high-tech machinery and automobiles (Atkinson and Ezell 2012: 43). In contrast to neoliberals' optimistic argument that the decline of domestic production in the course of globalization is a kind of "creative destruction" where high value-added production replaces the existing low-value-added production (Bhagwati 2010; Sirkin et al. 2011; Farrell et al. 2003), the U.S. high-tech industries continuously reduced production in the course of globalization.

As seen in Fig. 3.2, U.S. corporations increased outflow FDI from \$1.18 trillion in 2000 to \$4.26 trillion in 2021, while the U.S. trade balance with advanced technology products significantly declined from a

$32 billion surplus in 1997 to a $242.7 billion deficit in 2022. Companies' overseas production does not automatically result in a hollowing-out of domestic production. As seen in Chapter 2, Germany and Korea increased their production and innovation capabilities at home in the course of their corporations' overseas expansion. By contrast, U.S. production and innovation capabilities declined due to the hollowing-out of industrial commons at home.

Causes for the U.S. Manufacturing Decline

The U.S. suffered a decline in manufacturing production, jobs, and international competitiveness. The causes for decline are predominantly considered natural and inevitable phenomena, due first to productivity growth, and second to technology standardization. However, empirical evidence reveals that the U.S. decline in production was not natural and inevitable, but resulted from a lack of strategic coordination and market failure. This section explores two reasons why U.S. manufacturing has declined while manufacturing in Germany and Korea has improved in similar trends of globalization and digitalization.

First is productivity growth. Neoliberals hold that job loss in domestic manufacturing is a natural phenomenon due to advances in technology and productivity, according to arguments based on the work of neoclassical economist Colin Clark (Clark 1940: 492). The neoliberal position takes the reduction in U.S. manufacturing jobs as a given (Locke and Wellhausen 2014: 4). However, many empirical indicators show that job reduction in the current U.S. manufacturing industry is difficult to be seen as a natural phenomenon resulting from increased productivity.[1] In the 2000s, when U.S. manufacturing jobs decreased rapidly, as seen in Fig. 3.1, productivity decreased rather than increased. As seen in Table 3.1, labor productivity and total factor productivity (TFP) in U.S. manufacturing grew by 4.2% and 1.4% respectively between 1993 and 2002, higher than the 2.7% and 0.9% annual average productivity of 2003–2012 when U.S. manufacturing employment significantly declined. These data contradict the neoliberal claim of reduced manufacturing employment due to productivity improvement.

[1] See Atkinson et al. (2012), Houseman et al. (2011), Helper et al. (2012) for criticism of neoliberals' claim that reduction of jobs in the U.S. manufacturing industry is due to productivity improvement.

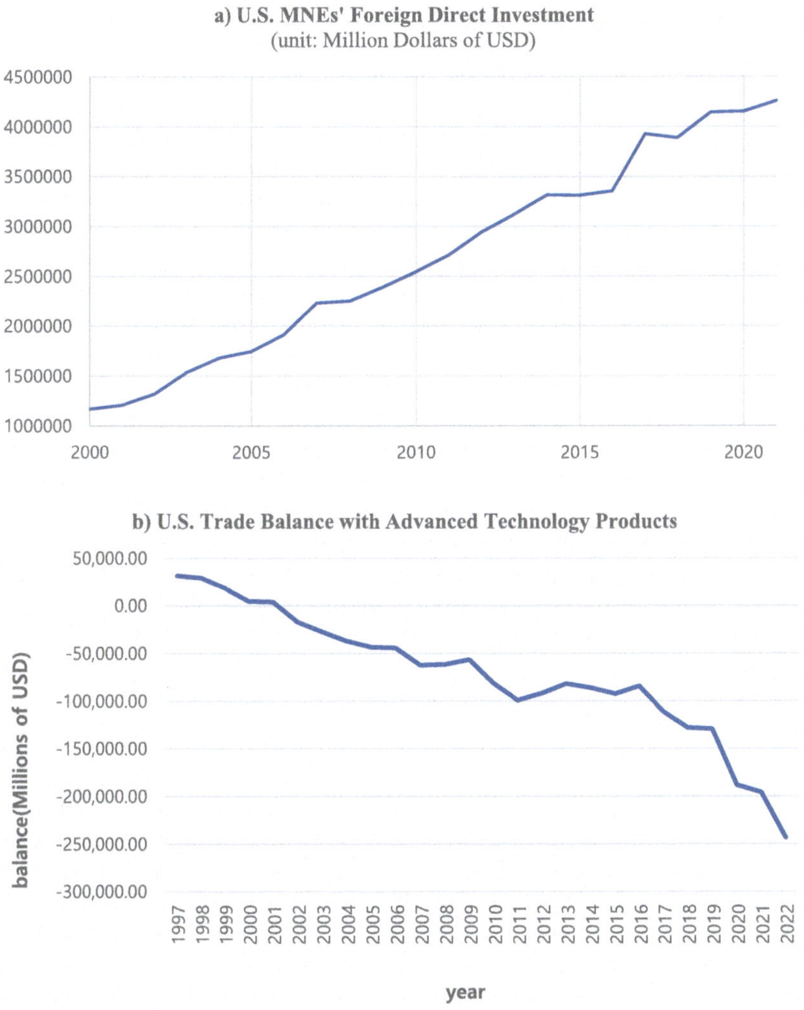

Fig. 3.2 U.S. OFDI and High-tech Trade Balance. **a** U.S. MNEs' Foreign Direct Investment [unit: Million Dollars of USD] (*Source* U.S. Bureau of Economic Analysis, "Data on activities of multinational enterprises" https://www.bea.gov/itable/direct-investment-multinational-enterprises [accessed Monday, February 12, 2024]). **b** U.S. Trade Balance with Advanced Technology Products (*Source* U.S. Census Bureau, Trade in Goods with Advanced Technology Products [2023])

Table 3.1 U.S. productivity growth in the manufacturing sector, 1993–2022

Time period	*Average annual labour productivity growth (%)*	*Average annual TFP growth (%)*
1993–2002	4.2	1.4
2003–2012	2.7	0.9
2013–2022	−0.4	−0.04

Source U.S. Bureau of Labor Statistics

The second position on the cause of manufacturing's decline is based on production cycles. This theory proposes that when an industry becomes old and standardized, it offshores to a low-wage country. Old and standardized low-tech industries are difficult to maintain in developed countries, so the logical move is to transfer them to low-wage countries. This argument is supported by the recent offshoring of simple labor. The neoliberal argument is that the relocation of companies' production abroad will not lead to hollowing-out of domestic industries, but rather bring positive outcomes to both home and host countries (Friedman 2013: 37, 298–299; Bhagwati 2010a, 2010b; Ramaswamy and Rowthorn 2000; Sirkin et al. 2011). The neoliberal argument holds that the current reduction in manufacturing due to overseas production facilitates new technologies and opportunities to upgrade to the next level. Neoliberals envision the loss of U.S. manufacturing jobs to be supplemented by higher-tech industries.

However, the current problem in the U.S. is not just the transfer of low-tech standardized industries, but the overseas relocation of cutting-edge industries as well (Pisano and Shih 2012a, 2012b). In low- and medium-tech manufacturing industries such as rubber, plastics, and metals, the U.S. maintains its edge. From 1995 to 2010, the U.S. global market share in low- and medium-technology industries fell by only 1%. In terms of absolute quality, American high-tech products are still the best in the world. Nevertheless, as seen in Fig. 3.2, the U.S. share of the high-tech industry and its relative competitiveness are rapidly decreasing, causing the rapid growth of trade deficits in the 2000s and 2010s, from a $4.45 billion surplus in 2001 to a $218.9 billion deficit in 2023 (US Census Bureau database).

Why has the U.S. not replaced old industries with high-tech industries even with its world-leading innovation and advanced research, contrary to the neoliberal expectation? Even though the U.S. invented many high-tech products available in global markets, production and commercialization occur abroad, due to individual U.S. corporations' rational pursuit of profits. The decline of U.S. manufacturing is not a natural phenomenon, but a market failure in which individual firms' rational action in the absence of collective coordination results in suboptimal outcomes.

As shown in Table 3.2, many high-tech products have disappeared in the U.S. as of the 2010s, although they were researched and developed in the U.S. Compact disc players, high-definition TVs (HDTVs), and dynamic random access memory chips (DRAM) were originally researched, designed, and developed in U.S. academic and corporate laboratories. Since then, Asian countries have received these technologies, made them available for commercialization and mass production, and now export these high-tech products back to the U.S. More recently, state-of-the-art high-tech products such as lithium-ion batteries, compact fluorescent lightbulbs, and solar panels have also been researched and developed in the U.S., but commercialized and mass-produced by Korean, Chinese, and Japanese companies (Atkinson and Ezell 2012: 112–113).

As these state-of-the-art products were "designed at home, produced overseas," the U.S.'s innovation capacity dropped sharply in the 2000s and 2010s, since innovation occurs not only in the laboratory but in every area of the value chain, through continuous feedback and interaction, from basic research and R&D to testing prototypes and mass production. As a result, the U.S. share of domestic innovation has seriously lagged, ranking 43rd out of 44 countries in the rate of progress between 2000 and 2011 (Atkinson and Ezell 2012: 2). In 2017, the San Francisco Bay Area, where Silicon Valley is located, gave up first and second place to Beijing and Berlin as the most innovative ecosystem for the high-tech industry (Hynes 2017; Primabase Team 2018).

As Berger's (2013) *Making in America* and many other scholars' empirical studies have shown, U.S. high-tech production and innovation capabilities have declined because industrial ecosystems, or industrial commons for domestic production and innovation were lost in the process of production globalization.[2] According to Berger's MIT research

[2] See Berger (2013), Locke and Wellhausen (2014), Helper et al. (2012), Houseman et al. (2010), Fuchs and Kirchain (2010), Wesner and Wolf (2012) and Pisano and Shih

Table 3.2 Types of U.S. industries that have disappeared or are at risk

Types of industrial capabilities that have disappeared or are at risk	*Current situation*
Ultra-heavy forgings	Pressurized forging is a method of making a large high-strength structure such as a nuclear reactor or steam generator. The external container of the reactor can weigh more than 500 tons and is generally composed of seven very large containers. The third generation of innovative Areva Power Generation Unit uses four steam generators, each weighing 500 tons. This means that each steel mill must produce an ingot weighing 500 ~ 600 tons. As the production of such large-scale metal ingots has been stopped, the US gave up its large forging industry 40 years ago. Currently, only Japan, Korea, China, France, and Russia are performing large forging
Machine tool: metal cutting	From 1990 to 2009, total metal processing machine shipments were reduced by 43%, metal cutting by 40%, grinding and polishing machines by 62%, lathes by 43%, station type machines by 77% and metal molding machines including punching and shearing systems, bending and moldering systems, compressor, forger and other metal molder by 51%
Permanent magnet electric motor and generator (electric drive)	Neodymium-iron-boron magnets used in permanent magnet generators and small, high-performance traction motors are currently driving innovation. Of these 10–12 permanent magnet suppliers, 8–10 are in China and none in the United States

(continued)

Table 3.2 (continued)

Types of industrial capabilities that have disappeared or are at risk	*Current situation*
Rare earth elements: purification of rare earth element, and fabrication of devices using rare earth	The refining of rare earths was no longer carried out in the US after Molykov closed Mountain Pass mine and moved to China. The chain impact of this is a perfect example of the destruction of (industrial) commons. This is the same as the previous permanent magnets case, but the range of influence is greater
Rechargeable battery	This market is mainly occupied by Korean, Japanese, and Chinese manufacturers. This is because these companies have excellent expertise in customer solutions to lithium-ion batteries The Asia–Pacific region is a manufacturing hub for all electronic components and has all the support infrastructure needed for large-scale production of batteries for hybrid electric vehicles and plug-in hybrid electric vehicles North America and the European Union are facing fierce competition with manufacturers in the Asia–Pacific region, which produce lithium-ion phosphate batteries using cheap manganese compounds instead of expensive nickel and cobalt. These manufacturers are strengthening their expertise in lithium-ion batteries by investing in high-tech materials such as nanofiber electrodes
LED manufacturing: energy-efficient display and lighting	In the first quarter of 2010, only one of the US LED producers was included in the world's top 10 LED producers, ranking fifth with a global market share of 6.7%. Meanwhile, growth in China, Taiwan, and Korea accelerated. Chinese companies such as LDK Solar are expanding to produce sapphire substrates, the standard material for blue and white gallium nitride LEDs

(continued)

Table 3.2 (continued)

Types of industrial capabilities that have disappeared or are at risk	*Current situation*
Semiconductor manufacturing (foundry service)	70% of the world's semiconductor foundry plant production capacity is in Taiwan
LCD display	All flat-panel display factories in the world are located in Korea, Taiwan, Japan, and China
Precise glass	Precision glass manufacturing is rapidly developing in China, while Japan is leading the industry. Some competencies are still held by Germany
Optical fiber components including gallium arsenic GaAs laser diode	As a key component of the electronic device supply chain for communication devices, most of these major components were manufactured locally in China

Source Pisano and Shih (2012b, pp. 11–12, Table 1.1)

team, each country's own innovation capabilities are important for high-value-added production upgrades and economic development, especially given the progress of globalization. However, acquiring these innovation capabilities requires close interaction among various organizations and technology stages. These stages include equipping R&D capabilities, technology and manufacturing readiness to create and materialize innovative ideas; testing suitability, stability, and reliability for basic research, prototype building and mass production; and coordinating and testing the production processes. In other words, innovation in R&D needs to be supported by relationships of close feedback from production and manufacturing operations (Tassey 2023, 2014). Industrial innovation ecosystems, or industrial commons such as vocational training, cooperation between companies and universities, various parts manufacturers, industrial consortiums, and technology research centers, remain important, especially in the rapidly changing world of technology and globalization. These industrial ecosystems and industrial commons are

(2012a or 2012b) for further readings on the globalization of American companies and declining American manufacturing industries.

crucial to improving collective innovation capabilities by providing individual companies with various complementary goods that they cannot produce on their own. Therefore, in a country's innovation ecosystem, manufacturing has positive externalities that cannot be measured simply by the contribution to value production or quantitative value.

Loss of Industrial Commons

The U.S. finds itself in the collapse of its innovation ecosystem and industrial commons due to its uncoordinated and free globalization of production. Berger (2013) observes that as overseas production increased, the phenomenon of "invent it here, make it there" became common in the U.S. Her team concludes, based on extensive empirical research: "The US production ecosystem has been hollowed out over the past decade" (Berger 2013: xii). How does this happen?

According to Berger (2013), innovative U.S. startups are established in innovative regions such as Silicon Valley and Boston, but commercialization of new technologies is carried out mainly overseas. Numerous U.S. parts manufacturers have disappeared as large corporations outsource parts and unilaterally relocate without coordinating with manufacturers. (In Germany and Japan, many social actors and stakeholders coordinate their globalization, as shall be examined later.) In the U.S. in the 2010s, small and medium-sized enterprises (SMEs) could not find complementary capabilities in the surrounding industrial ecosystem, so they had to rely mainly on insufficient internal resources. U.S. SMEs struggle as traditional local banks disappear due to buyouts and financialization,[3] and the consequent lack of external funds for those companies. In addition, SMEs lack connection with local community colleges, resulting in weak R&D capabilities, loss amid global competition, and a weakened U.S. industrial ecosystem. This unsustainable loop incites companies to accelerate their overseas production bases, which intensifies the weakening of the industrial ecosystem (Berger 2013: 5, 13, 204–205).

[3] Although financialization is variously defined by scholars, it generally refers to the development of capitalism for financial advantage which occurred from the 1980s to the present. It refers to a situation in which profits are advantageously generated through capital channels rather than through product production or trade. More specifically, it refers to the ascendancy of shareholder values and capital market advantage as a form of corporate governance (Epstein 2005: 3–16). See Orhangazi (2008) for financialization in the U.S.

In high innovation areas such as Silicon Valley and Boston, new inventions constantly emerge from laboratories supported by venture capital and outstanding universities. The U.S. remains far superior in generating innovative ideas and developing them to the experimental stages. The amount of U.S. venture capital has increased considerably. In the 1970s, only a small amount of venture capital existed, but in 2000, about 6420 companies held $100 billion total, and this increased to $248 billion in 2022 (dealroom.co database). Venture capital usually invests for five years, applying pressure for rapid scale-up for ample return on investment. Therefore, it is not a suitable funding source for long-term commercialization. In particular, venture capital does not work well for manufacturing companies that require intense capital for commercialization. Therefore, most of Silicon Valley's innovative startups (about 98%) decide to exit through mergers and acquisitions (M&As) rather than raise capital through Initial Public Offerings (IPOs). This process has caused a huge loss of U.S. capacity for innovation capabilities (Locke and Wellhausen 2014: 10; Berger 2013: 67, 82, 87; Pisano and Shih 2009, 2012a, 2012b; Delgado et al. 2012; Moretti 2012).

For example, innovative American companies such as QD Vision excel at creating new products within high-innovation laboratories. As these ideas progress to the prototype production stage, they can be helped, though insufficiently, by nearby parts manufacturers. Proceeding to large-scale production, U.S. innovators sign contracts with foreign parts giants, because mass production requires complex research and intellectual ownership. So, U.S. innovative companies move abroad to scale up production, weakening U.S. innovation capabilities and international competitiveness (Reynolds et al. 2014: 82–84; Tassey 2010, 2023).

Collapse of Traditional Commons Not Replaced by New Ones

U.S. manufacturing innovation encountered a problem with the globalization of production due to individual companies' rationale for profits, without coordination by society or the state in the process of globalization and financialization of production. As a result, the traditional American innovation system has collapsed, based on the single-minded mission of vertically integrated giant corporations. No new innovation ecosystem and industrial commons have emerged to replace it.

Until the 1980s, the U.S. economic system had been governed by vertically integrated industrial giants. Created in the early twentieth century, these vertically integrated giants ensured a stable flow of parts and materials for mass production and performed R&D, design, manufacturing, sales, and service functions within the company. These companies were able to build innovative systems that required close cooperation in various stages and fields by integrating R&D and manufacturing capabilities internally, and by forming various technologies and accumulating skilled labor (Locke and Wellhausen 2014: 3). For example, giants such as AT&T operated Bell Labs, Xerox PARC, and Alcoa Research Laboratory, hiring numerous scientists and engineers to support their long-term massive-scale projects (Gertner 2012). These centralized internal research institutes were the driving force of American innovation (Reynolds, Samel, and Lawrence 2014: 81).

Moreover, various research projects, vocational training, and new technologies accumulated by these industrial giants have provided a "spillover" effect of abundant public goods to local communities and numerous nearby companies. Other regional companies were able to easily benefit, even though they did not directly contribute to the formation of industrial commons which these corporate giants provided. Indirectly, these industrial leaders have also played a major role in building and improving the American industrial ecosystem by pressuring the federal government to build infrastructure such as railroads, highways, and road networks to benefit industry. However, with the 1990s financialization and globalization decoupled from social coordination, many of the complementary and shared public goods these industrial giants had previously provided began to dry up, replaced by a focus on amassing short-term financial profit and slashing costs through outsourcing (Berger 2013; Porter and Rivkin 2012).

Since the 1980s, American innovation has emerged from smaller, more agile creative firms within the innovation ecosystem. Industrial giants now rely on external innovators, technicians, and producers for research, experimental testing, and production. These small but innovative companies make new developments through cooperative interaction with each other, an important benefit of shared industrial commons.

But in the 1990s, in-house innovation systems were dismantled before new, robust external innovation ecosystems could replace them, due to the rush toward offshoring. U.S. companies have relatively lagged in domestic R&D investment. In terms of absolute R&D investment, the U.S. remains the world's strongest, but in terms of ratio to national income as a whole, U.S. R&D efforts fall sharply compared with other countries. Comparing R&D to gross domestic product (GDP), the U.S. investment ratio was ranked 8th in 2011 among 27 OECD (Organisation for Economic Co-operation and Development) countries worldwide. The U.S. R&D expenditure to GDP is 2.8%. Israel, on the other hand, is 4.3%; Finland 4.0%; Sweden 3.6%; Korea 3.4%; Japan 3.3%; Denmark 3.0%; and Switzerland 3.0%. While these competitors have since continued to increase investment in R&D, the U.S. maintained its status quo of around 2.6% to 2.7% throughout the 2000s and 2010s. By contrast, Korea increased its R&D investment relative to GDP from 2.12% in 2000 to 4.93% in 2021, while Japan invested around 3.2% to 3.47% throughout the 2010s despite its economic recession (OECD Database; Ministry of Science, ICT, and Future Planning 2014: 17–18).

As U.S. companies increase overseas production and related overseas R&D investment, these R&D investments have waned. Between 1999 and 2008, U.S. companies' R&D share of GDP increased by only 3%, while investment by Chinese companies increased 187%, along with 58% in Korea, 28% in Finland, 27% in Japan, and 11% in Germany (Atkinson and Ezell 2012: 64). Coupled with U.S. disinvestment, companies have also reduced work force development. Between 1999 and 2007, U.S . companies' investment in worker training decreased by 45% (Atkinson and Ezell 2012: 65; Atkinson 2009).

Individual U.S. companies that pursue short-term financialized returns are less likely to invest in technology infrastructure which takes longer to realize. According to National Institute of Standards and Technology (NIST) Senior Economist Gregory Tassey (2023), U.S. companies' underinvestment in the four technology assets—technology, capital formation, skilled labor, and infratechnologies—which are needed for sustained growth of corporate profits and worker incomes, have resulted in loss of innovation capabilities and declining U.S. labor productivity, which were 4.1% annual growth on average from 1949 to 1978, but from 2013 to 2022, shrank to a −0.4% average annual growth rate (Tassey 2023: 4; US Bureau of Labor Statistics database).

The result of a weakened U.S. innovation ecosystem is a loss of U.S. international competitiveness in many high-tech industries, ranging from desktop and laptop PCs to liquid crystal displays (LCDs), high-tech batteries, and compact fluorescent lightbulbs (CFLs). Moreover, American leadership has lagged in industries such as high-performance computing, artificial intelligence, biotechnology, nanotechnology, robotics, energy storage, and clean energy production, and future innovative growth engines are not guaranteed.

Politics in Neoliberalism

In an era of globalization, individual companies abandon existing domestic production relationships to pursue global production networks for their own benefit at the risk of dismantling the national economy. Representative companies' interests no longer reflect and reinforce the interests of the entire national economy. In the U.S., the rational choice of free companies has resulted in the loss of industrial commons and a weakened innovation ecosystem at the national level.

A remedy will not be easy. The U.S. lacks a cooperative coordination method between labor organizations and capital, as in Germany and Northern Europe. Organized labor remains weak, and attempts toward traditional social coordination gain no traction. Industry innovation experts in the U.S. have emphasized strategic reproduction of industrial commons through active state intervention, including public policy to nurture industrial commons and regional innovation clusters (Tassey 2014, 2023; Bonvillian and Singer 2017; Atkinson and Ezell 2012; Locke and Wellhausen 2014; Berger 2013)—an intervention strategy not well received by U.S. industry giants. The U.S., a traditionally liberalist nation, has a strong tendency to leave things to free-market relations rather than state-led strategic intervention, as in Korea and Japan. Despite recent intervention and coordination by the U.S. government, as shown in its Manufacturing Revival Policy and Chips and Science Act of 2022, this intervention has never been complete or smooth. Private capital's fundamental distrust of the state, and neoliberal theories and ideologies, have blocked efforts toward state intervention. Before examining the transformation of politics in the next chapter, this section explores how U.S. liberal politics affects the absence of effective coordination and loss of industrial commons.

Lack of Strategic Coordination by the State

Destruction of the U.S. industrial ecosystem and job reduction due to globalization have been noted since the 2000s. The issue of industrial hollowing-out due to globalization arose during the 2004 U.S. presidential campaign. Democratic presidential candidate John Kerry criticized President George Bush for giving tax cuts to companies moving overseas. Regarding the destruction of the domestic industrial ecosystem and reduction of jobs due to the expansion of overseas outsourcing, people easily agreed on the seriousness of the problem, regardless of political affiliation.[4] Many involved in the industry, many innovation experts, and policy-makers pointed out that it is difficult to recover the industrial ecosystem by relying on individual companies, concerned though they may be about the destructive effects of globalization. The government offered little strategic intervention, unlike Korea and Japan. In the 2000s, even mentioning the industrial policies of Korea or Japan was considered "not allowed" among Americans. Professors Locke and Wellhausen (2014) describe the situations in which U.S. industrial policy is needed for an economy based on innovation:

> In the current political atmosphere, "industrial policy" has become a taboo in the United States. However, targeted investments with strategic intention to foster the foundation that supports the industrial ecosystem—financial or energy, or education and R&D-related infrastructure—is crucial to maintaining the US innovation economy. (Locke and Wellhausen 2014: 10)

Many industrial experts in the U.S., including Atkinson and Ezell (2012: 12–13) and Tassey (2014, 2023), also emphasize the need to create an industrial ecosystem and the importance of government's active intervention to do so. They argue that in order for the U.S. to effectively compete, it needs an entrepreneurial and capable business community that is willing to invest in innovative projects, even if it cannot make profits within a quarter or a year, and that such investment requires innovative government policies. Many researchers and industry experts, including Berger's MIT research team, have expressed the need for active government intervention to restore industrial and innovative ecosystems.

[4] Financial News (October 18, 2004), "US companies are likely to increase outsourcing after the presidential election: overseas relocation will be accelerated to reduce costs.".

However, the U.S. government has not easily drafted nor implemented industrial and strategic innovation policies. Why the resistance?

Within the liberalist tradition, the U.S. rarely uses the types of industrial policies seen in Japan, Korea, and France (Kwon 2021: 19–31; Vogel 1978). An Anglo-American liberalist state does not imply the absence of national expansion or intervention. In the U.S., the role of the liberal states has changed in various ways. Following World War II, it was never considered a minimalist or laissez-faire country. We distinguish Anglo-American liberal states from interventionist France and Japan in their way of intervention, not the degree of state expansion itself. After World War II, the U.S. actively intervened in the market through fiscal expansion, welfare expansion, and Keynesian-based currency control centered on fiscal and monetary trade, a macro approach neutral to private market actors. Even with interventions affecting industries, the liberalist U.S. used a horizontal industrial policy neutral to private market actors. Horizontal intervention allowed all private actors to benefit from common initiatives, such as the construction of a national highway system in 1956, military technology for defense during the Cold War, and pure academic-oriented basic research support (Blyth 2002: 49–95; Eisner 2014: 85–109; Di Tommaso and Schweitzer 2013).

Even under the neoliberal system introduced in the 1980s Reagan administration, U.S. state intervention remained in effect, expanding market principles in terms of direction and method, though with decreasing influence compared to the postwar Keynesian state (Prasad 2006). Reagan in the U.S. and Thatcher in the U.K. weakened organized labor; and in the U.K., state-owned enterprises were privatized. Public services such as aviation and electronic communication were de-regulated, and market principles were introduced. The market contract principle was introduced into many public service areas, as well as in public education.

Still, to understand the U.S. government's consistent lack of industrial policy, we need to focus more on the mindset of economic policy elites, who set economic policy within the U.S. Department of the Treasury. Other departments become secondary players. Along with the Department of the Treasury, the Office of Management and Budget and the President's Council of Economic Advisers are other major policy-makers. Rather than nurturing domestic production and innovation capabilities, U.S. economic policy is mainly monetary and fiscal policy, focusing on quantitative control of the macroeconomy including interest rates, inflation, savings, exchange rates, and international balance. Issues at the center of discussions on economic policy have focused on the degree of marginal tax rates for individuals, whether to join free trade provisions, whether to reduce budgets or reduce corporate taxes. These issues are only peripherally linked to the issue of industrial revival (Atkinson and Ezell 2012: 81).

The reason for neoliberalism's continuance is due not only to the social bloc of dominant growth strategy based on finance, insurance, and real estate (FIRE) sectors but also to the continuous dominance of neoliberal elites in economic policy-making. For example, according to van Apeldoorn and de Graaff's (2017) study, the Obama administration continued a finance-led, neoliberal strategy because finance-led elite group networks led its economic policy. This finance-led elite group continued its neoliberal policy across the Clinton and Bush administrations. Despite the 2008 finance-led crisis, the Obama administration did not make a radical break with the neoliberal policies of its predecessors. Although Obama was elected on a platform of change, his economic policy showed continuity (Hirsh 2010; Susskind 2011; Panitch 2012), due to the continuous dominance of American liberal corporate networks, dominated by financial interests. While U.S. state executives may act more independently, their agencies are a part of a powerful corporate elite, dominated by finance. U.S. government agencies are closely affiliated with or directly recruited from liberal corporate elite networks. According to the van Apeldoorn and de Graaff (2017) analysis, top economic policy-makers are largely affiliated with corporate positions. Of the 19 selected top economic policy-makers in the Obama administration, 14 occupied a total of 48 top-level corporate positions before serving in the Obama administration. Of these affiliations, finance, including insurance and real estate, was the biggest sector representing with 38% of all the linked companies. The second largest, at 29%, is law and consultancy (van Apeldoorn and de Graaff 2017: 357–359). For example, in the Obama administration, Geithner and Summer who had direct ties with Wall Street continued its economic policy of global liberalization of financial markets initiated by the Clinton administration and further deepened by the Bush administration (van Apeldoorn and de Graaff 2017: 363).

In addition, policy planning bodies, including the Brookings Institution, the Trilateral Commission (TC), the Bilderberg Conference, the World Economic Forum, the Bretton Woods Committee, and the Committee for Economic Development, were mostly associated with promoting neoliberal economic policies. These policy planning bodies and think tanks, including most notably the Council on Foreign Relations and Brookings Institution, are bipartisan but slightly Democrat-leaning. These bodies within the corporate elite networks focus on finance-led growth with neoliberal globalism (Blyth 2002: 152–201; van Apeldoorn and de Graaff 2017: 363–365).

Discursive Politics Among Social Actors

U.S. economic policy-makers tend to pay little attention to actual industrial composition or ecosystems. In a neoliberal environment, they tend to pay more attention to helping the finance sectors, represented by Wall Street, than to helping Industrial Street, and by extension, Main Street. When industries lose their share in the international market and show trade deficits, the foreign exchange market underestimates the exchange rate of these deficit countries so that companies can regain export competitiveness. However, the U.S. government tends to focus on defending monetary value because it is financial capital-friendly rather than industry-friendly. For example, although U.S. industries continue to suffer from trade losses due to a lack of international competitiveness, Timothy Geithner, the Obama administration's Secretary of Treasury, confirmed, "We will never weaken our currency." Such a stance turns a blind eye to the fact that strong-dollar policy acts contrary to promoting U.S. exports.[5]

On the other hand, economic policy discourses surrounding Congress and lobbying likewise lack focus on industrial policy. Such discourses consist of a confrontation between Wall Street, focused on finance, and "mom-and-pop" businesses owned by everyday Americans. Although groups promoting the government's role in fostering innovative industries in Massachusetts, New York, New Jersey, Colorado, and Florida are not absent, they have been overwhelmed by conflicts between dominant neoliberal groups such as Wall Street and "mon-and-pop" businesses (Pereira and Plonski 2009: 456–457; Amsden 2013: 5–6). So-called "Industrial Street" and "Office Complex Street" tech-oriented companies, competing in the international market, including software, Internet, information and communication, and global engineering companies

[5] "Geithner: US Won't Seek to Weaken Dollar to Spur Growth," *CNBC.com* (November 11, 2010); Takashi Nakamichi, "Geithner Affirms Strong Dollar Policy," *Wall Street Journal* (2009, November 11).

(Atkinson and Ezell 2012: 271–275) are underrepresented, compared to the muscular "Wall Street" finance companies and "Main Street" SMEs oriented toward domestic markets, represented by the right-leaning National Federation of Independent Businesses (NFIB). The association, composed of independent small businesses, is enthusiastic about reducing top individual tax rates, rather than corporate tax rates which would favor Industrial Street and Office Complex Street. While tax cuts for high-income individuals are advantageous to NFIB members, they do not help to improve innovative industrial competitiveness. The NFIB argues that federal workforce expenditure for labor training should be reduced rather than increased (Atkinson and Ezell 2012: 276–277). In the 2000s, the contentious discourse between Wall Street and those focusing on SMEs and tax justice derailed efforts to support and reorganize innovative companies and export-oriented high-tech industries.

Meanwhile, conflicts in the "noisy" politics, mainly between right-leaning Main Street organizations such as NFIB, and left-leaning citizen groups such as Citizen for Tax Justice (CTJ), deter serious deliberation about industrial policies in national politics. "Liberal redistributionists" groups such as CTJ which emphasize redistribution of wealth to low-wage Americans and workers through tax increases on high-income earners, such as the right-leaning NIFB, do not focus on improving competitiveness based on U.S. industry and innovation. Rather, they similarly oppose policies designed to improve productivity or competitiveness, which run counter to the interests of Industrial Street and Office Complex Street groups (Atkinson and Ezell 2012: 277–278). From reducing high-income tax rates to relief for the unemployed, this protracted confrontation shows the chasm between support for innovative companies and the immediate social needs of society.

Growth Strategy and Dominant Social Bloc

Even liberal states like the U.S. and the U.K. use growth policies. However, Anglo-American neoliberal countries have mostly focused on boosting consumption for growth, rather than industrial policies to nurture production and innovation capabilities. Hence, expansion policies relied on the liberalization of financial markets and the revitalization of domestic consumption. Until the 1960s, economic growth in the U.S. relied on productivity improvement, but after the mid-1990s, money available to households had expanded, especially due to financial deregulation. With changes in dominant social actors, from industrial giants to finance-led sectors, the U.S. increasingly depends on consumption-led economic growth through finance-led demand stimulation, which results in short-term and modest spurts in growth up to the limits that inflation allows, rather than improving the structural growth based on industrial and innovation capability. This section examines the U.S. growth strategy and its social bloc.

The U.S. is a finance- and consumption-led growth regime, while Germany is an export-led growth regime (Baccaro and Pontusson 2016; Baccaro et al. 2022). For economic growth, the U.S. expands domestic demand, credit expansion, and consumption, whereas Germany relies on wage restraint, savings, and repressed consumption to secure export competitiveness. For example, in 2019, private consumption was 68% of U.S. GDP, while exports were only 12%. By contrast, Germany's exports constitute 47% of its GDP, while private consumption was 52% (OECD Stat; Reisenbichler 2022: 8–9).

The U.S. finance- and consumption-led growth model operates through two distinct but related channels. One is the housing channel, while the other is the income-maintenance channel. The housing channel operates through real estate markets, in which rising house prices increase homeowners' wealth, thus boosting household borrowing and consumption. The income-maintenance channel works through credit markets that allow households to maintain their rising expenditures given weak public welfare (Reisenbichler and Wiedemann 2022: 215; Baccaro et al. 2022: 17; Baccaro and Pontusson 2016: 185–186; Reisenbichler and Wiedemann 2022: 215–23231; Hall 2015: 431–435).

Such consumption-led growth strategy increasingly relies on lower interest rates to indirectly drive economic growth through demand stimulation, causing a continuous decline of treasury yield, from more than 10% in the early 1980s to about 3% in the late 2010s (Tassey 2023: 6). U.S. economic elites with liberal ideas increasingly depend on consumption-led growth strategies resulting in short-term and modest spurts in growth, while disregarding industrial policy of improving structural technology and innovation capabilities.

Even in response to the economic crisis of 2008, which resulted from a finance-led growth strategy, the U.S. government used a further finance-led consumption strategy to recover economic growth. For example, facing the 2008 crisis, the U.S. increased generous mortgage subsidies to resuscitate economic growth, in contrast to Germany's economic policy which reduced housing subsidies and focused on export-led growth by improving its industrial competitiveness. Facing the financial crisis of 2008, the Bush administration and the Democratic Congress adopted the Housing and Economic Recovery Act of 2008. Even free-market conservatives and Republicans supported massive public spending to revive the housing financing system. The U.S. government took over two crisis-ridden government-sponsored enterprises, Fannie Mae and Freddie Mac. In 2020, ten years after the crisis, the U.S. government still owns $5.5 trillion in mortgage debt or almost 50% of the residential mortgage market (Reisenbichler 2022: 2, 5).

In contrast to the U.S. consumption-led growth strategy, Germany' policy-makers had begun to reduce mortgage subsidies even before the 2008 crisis, and facing the crisis, reduced the subsidies further (Reisenbichler 2022: 5, 17; Tooze 2018: 173). Germany's subsidies for homeownership today are lower than those of any other country. According to the mortgage credit index, developed by Johnston et al. (2020), which measures the degree to which national mortgage regimes encourage or discourage mortgage credit through subsidies and other regulatory actions (the higher values indicate restrictiveness on a 0–10 scale), the U.S. (0) encourages mortgage credit the most, followed by the Netherlands (1), Ireland (2), the U.K. (2), and Spain. By contrast, Germany (9) is the most restrictive country, followed by Austria (8), Italy (8), and France (7) in 2007 (Reisenbichler 2022: 6).

The reason for the differences between the U.S. and Germany in response to the crisis is Germany's national growth strategy and its dominant social alliances. Housing markets are embedded in this national macroeconomic growth regime. For the U.S. where the finance sector dominates social alliances, housing is a major growth engine of the consumption-led regime, where high housing prices stimulate consumption and spur economic growth. In Germany, where policy-makers and dominant social blocs prioritize export-led growth, high housing prices and easy credit run counter to its macroeconomic priority to restrain domestic prices, credit, and wages, in order to secure cost competitiveness (Reisenbichler 2022). Facing minus growth in 2002 and 2003,

Germany's SPD-Green coalition government enacted a law for financial support of innovation through the reduction of housing subsidies,[6] considering that housing subsidies are a hindrance to growth and shift public funds from the unproductive housing sector to support for innovation capabilities (Reisenbichler 2022: 24–25).

The U.S. consumption-led growth, focused on domestic expansion of credit and disregard for industrial policy to improve industrial competitiveness, is based on a political coalition for its strategy. Political coalitions based on the finance-led and credit-driven U.S. growth model, which share a common interest in facilitating easy access to credit and debt-fueled consumption, include producer groups in the financial services industry, asset-owning voters, and mainstream left and right political parties (Reisenbichler and Wiedemann 2022: 214, 221).

The dominant group in the U.S. growth social bloc, the so-called FIRE (finance, insurance, and real estate) sector, includes banks, insurance companies, credit card companies, hedge funds, mortgage brokers, home-builders, and realtors. They do not agree on all policies, but share a common interest in gaining from the expansion of consumer credit, property markets, and household consumption. This FIRE group has a significant influence on policy-making for growth strategy, while U.S. trade unions play no significant role in deciding economic policy (Bergholt et al. 2022; Iversen and Soskice 2019; Thelen 2019).

In regard to election politics, the coalition includes current and aspiring homeowners who are interested in accessible and expanding credit markets to increase home values. Even poorer voters have interests in easy access to credit to smooth income losses and finance their expenditures. Both center-left and center-right political parties also favor policies of generating consumption and domestic demand, particularly in moments of economic crisis (Reisenbichler 2022; McCarthy et al. 2013).

For example, after the 2008 crisis, the U.S. government, including both the Democratic and Republican parties, has continuously supported measures to boost housing and mortgage markets. Bipartisan consensus is a rare phenomenon in U.S. politics, except on housing policies, because both parties benefit from the FIRE sectors' lobby and homeowning voters, and because policies that stimulate mortgage debt, housing

[6] Bundesregierung, "Entwurf eines Gesetzes zur finanziellen Unterstützung der Innovationsoffensive durch Abschaffung der Eingenheimzulage," Berlin, September 27, 2004.

activity, and prices contribute to growth (Acharya et al. 2011: 171–172). By contrast, during Germany's mid-2000s economic crisis, policy-makers reduced housing subsidies to secure export competitiveness, despite opposition from housing interest groups—building societies, construction industries, and mortgage banks, because the housing sector plays a minor role in Germany's economy, while export sectors lead (Thelen 2019; Baccaro and Pontusson 2016; Carlin and Soskice 2008).

Despite the 2008 financial crisis, the U.S. reinforced its existing finance- and credit-led growth with support from the U.S. finance-led and housing-based political coalition. Housing-related interest groups include the National Association of Realtors (NAR), whose 1.5 million members are active in every electoral district nationwide, the Mortgage Bankers Association (MBA), the National Association of Home Builders (NAHM), and other financial institutions. These well-organized interest groups lobby hard in favor of expanding government support for housing. NAR is one of the most powerful lobbies, spending $133 million in 2020, fourth in size following the pharmaceuticals, electronics, and insurance industries (Reisenbichler and Wiedemann 2022: 226–227). Following the lead of this dominant social bloc, both the Democratic and Republican parties have continuously supported measures that favor the housing and mortgage markets.

Financialization and Industrial Commons

Changes in the U.S. growth model and its dominant social alliances are based on the financialization of the U.S. economy and its shift from managerial capitalism to shareholder capitalism since the 1980s (Fligstein 1990, 2021; Mazzucato 2020: Chapters 5, 6; Kruse and Zelizer 2019). With financialization, the U.S. growth model increasingly depends on the finance and consumption-led growth model, which further limits the improvement of structural growth capabilities based on technology and innovation. In the absence of social coordination, the industrial commons rapidly dissolve by the unilateral decision for the singular rationale of profits.

With this shift in the U.S. economy from managerial capitalism to shareholder capitalism, capital markets, and compensation systems under shareholder activism are driven by rapid processing and quarterly numerical values. Traditional managers who performed sustained, local-specific investments for long-term productivity improvement become business vagabonds who shift their business activities to areas that offer the best deals of the day, with no attachment to any specific region. Investment needed to improve productivity and innovation capabilities, such as skilled labor, R&D, advanced manufacturing capabilities, parts manufacturing networks, and local educational institutions, continues to decline (Porter and Rivkin 2012: 59).

As managers of U.S. companies continue to pursue short-term profits, investments in large companies that once provided public goods for industrial ecosystems are further decreasing (Pisano and Shih 2012b: xiv; Krehmeyer et al. 2006). According to Clayton Christensen of Harvard Business School, many U.S. companies focus on Return on Net Assets (RONA) as so-called performance indicators of companies (Denning 2011)—the reason why U.S . companies are concerned about reducing fixed assets, which are the denominators of performance measurements. A recent statistical analysis on approximately 1500 U.S. large firms from 1990 to 2018, with about 51% of U.S. R&D expenditures in 2018, confirms the effects of U.S. managers' short-termism on micro and macro level outcomes (Terry 2023). For micro-level firms, short-termism boosts firm value by about 1%. But at the aggregate level, short-termism reduces economic growth by 5 basis points yearly and lowers social welfare by about 1%, because U.S. managers facing short-term profit pressure reduce long-term investments like R&D, which have higher social returns than the private return due to standard channels including knowledge spillovers.

U.S. business leaders who focus on maximizing short-term shareholder value through financialization have shown an easy-come, easy-go preference for wherever they can make the best profits, regardless of where. They tend to easily relocate overseas disregarding domestic labor training, robust R&D, and fostering domestic parts makers. For U.S. managers, companies are gradually considered as chunks of exchangeable assets that can easily be restructured to maximize short-term financial returns (Kochan 2012: 70).

In the case of short-term profits, reducing costs through the dismissal of skilled labor was not the final measure but a preemptive and easy one. Overseas relocation was decided in a similar way. And since U.S. companies have already invested in low-cost production facilities overseas, they tend to choose low-cost overseas production for short-term profits, rather than improve domestic capabilities as Germany does, which takes a longer time to foster (Bonvillian and Singer 2017: 4–5). As U.S. conglomerates changed their parts procuring lines and decided to relocate overseas independently, many remaining SME domestic parts manufacturers struggled to endure the global competition alone, with no choice but to perish. This disappearance of various parts manufacturers soon caused serious gaps in the U.S. industrial ecosystem (Berger 2013: 20).

In summary, even with the world's best innovative ideas, yet the loss of industrial ecosystems in the process of globalization, the U.S.'s industrial gap has deepened as weaknesses in organizing actual commercial production come into clear view. The U.S. suffers a lack of social coordination to establish an innovation system to meet the demands of a globalized process. Prior to globalization, the innovation system was based on interactions between universities and government in the basic research stage, and interactions between large corporations' R&D and manufacturing companies in the commercialization stage. U.S. innovation also was based on the external effects of those combined interactive relationships, achieving the production and spread of industrial commons within local communities. More recently, against the backdrop of financialization and globalization, these industrial giants have transformed into light asset organizations and moved overseas through outsourcing and offshoring, creating a gap in the industrial commons. Many SMEs have had to choose whether to stay in U.S. domestic markets, lose their consumers, and eventually perish, or go abroad as well, in search of cheap production costs. Weakened innovation capacity and loss of national competitiveness reflect the chilling consequences inherent in the neoliberal model: industrial and social fallout due to the absence of a coherent policy and process of political coordination. Since the late 2010, the U.S. has shown signs, albeit weakly, of reviving its manufacturing industry and innovation ecosystem. To what extent does the recent U.S. revival policy differ from its traditional neoliberal free-market model? How can the U.S. transform its economic policy? These questions will be examined in the next chapter.

CHAPTER 4

Recent Transformation of the U.S. Economy

Recently U.S. manufacturing has shown some recovery from its trend since the mid-2010s. Manufacturing employment turned around after a decade-long sharp decline, increasing from 11.22 million jobs in 2010 to 12.52 million jobs in 2022. Even amid the COVID-19 pandemic 3,541,000 manufacturing jobs were created within two years, from 2020 to 2022 (U.S. Bureau of Economic Analysis database). Notably, this manufacturing revival does not confirm the effectiveness of the neoliberal free-market system. The revival was mainly due to the U.S. government's strategic intervention. Following the President's Council of Advisors on Science and Technology (PCAST) 2012 report, the Obama administration produced the Manufacturing USA Program Act and established 13 manufacturing research institutes across the U.S. The Trump administration continued this industrial policy, and the Biden administration added the 2021 Endless Frontier Act, the Inflation Reduction Act, and the Chips and Science Act of 2022, to rebuild the industrial ecosystem for high-tech manufacturing industries.

Unlike the 1950s and 1960s Keynesian state intervention, recent manufacturing revival policies focus on factors necessary for front and rear industries in terms of supply and not demand. These revival policies break from the former path; While it's too early for these new policies to become the dominant discourse, they have shown some remarkable results that even the government officials of the Korean developmental

H. Kwon, *Openness and Coordination*,
https://doi.org/10.1007/978-981-97-3352-1_4

state, recognize and attempt to emulate.[1] As of 2022, the signs of revival in the U.S. manufacturing industry are the effectiveness of state-led industrial policy and readjustment, even in an open and rapidly changing world. This chapter examines to what extent the recent U.S. revival policy differs from its traditional neoliberal free-market model, and how and why the U.S. can transform its economic policy.

Changes in Growth Strategy

The tradition of deep-rooted distrust toward the state's active intervention is never immutable. The space for change is always open, through crisis or new ways of practice. In the face of a weakened industry and innovation ecosystem following globalization during the 2000s and 2010s, the U.S. tried a new form of interventionism distinct from the existing liberalist neutral state model. New solutions and new discourses raised by various forces provided a possibility of change in traditional practices. Starting with the Obama administration in the wake of the 2008 economic crisis, the U.S. government actively sought new solutions to revive U.S. manufacturing that were distinct from existing neoliberal policies. This new position emphasizes strengthening the competitiveness of high-tech manufacturing industries. This section examines to what extent the recent U.S. revival differs from traditional neoliberalism.

While industrial policy was taboo outside the defense sector in the liberalist tradition, the recent U.S. government has legislated the United States Innovation and Competition Act of 2021 (USICA), formerly known as the Endless Frontier Act, the 2022 Inflation Reduction Act, and the 2022 Chips and Science Act. All three serve to build regional innovation hubs and manufacturing research institutes across the U.S.

Most important in the U.S. revival policy is its massive R&D investment to improve the production of high-tech industries and build industrial ecosystems. For example, the 2021 Competition Act (USICA) authorized $110 billion for basic and advanced technology research over a five-year period (S. 1260 from Congress website). The Chips and Science Act of 2022 provided $280 billion for semiconductor R&D and manufacturing to boost the U.S. domestic economy. The 2022 Inflation

[1] See the report of the Ministry of Trade, Industry and Energy (2019), Park Yoo-mi (2019) from KIET, and Kim Bo-min et al. (2014) for a recent introduction of the U.S. state-led manufacturing revival policy into Korea.

Reduction Act also provided $30 billion in tax credits to increase domestic production of solar panels, wind turbines, batteries, and critical minerals processing. The Act also provided $10 billion in tax credits to incentivize domestic investments in clean technology manufacturing facilities (Quinn 2022; Tassey 2023: 10; O'Donnell 2022).

Figure 4.1 shows how the U.S. has rapidly increased its R&D investment since the mid-2010s. Traditionally, compared to the size of GDP, the U.S. spent relatively less R&D investment (around 2.7%) than other advanced countries, including Japan and Germany, throughout the 2000s. However, by increasing R&D for high-tech industries from 2.73% of GDP in 2010 to 3.46% in 2021, the U.S. surpassed Japan and Germany. Between 2010 and 2020, U.S. R&D growth accelerated by 127.75%, outpacing Germany's 114.63% and Japan's 105.28%.

Along with the rapid growth of R&D investment since the mid-2010s, U.S. capital expenditure by companies as a key source of productivity

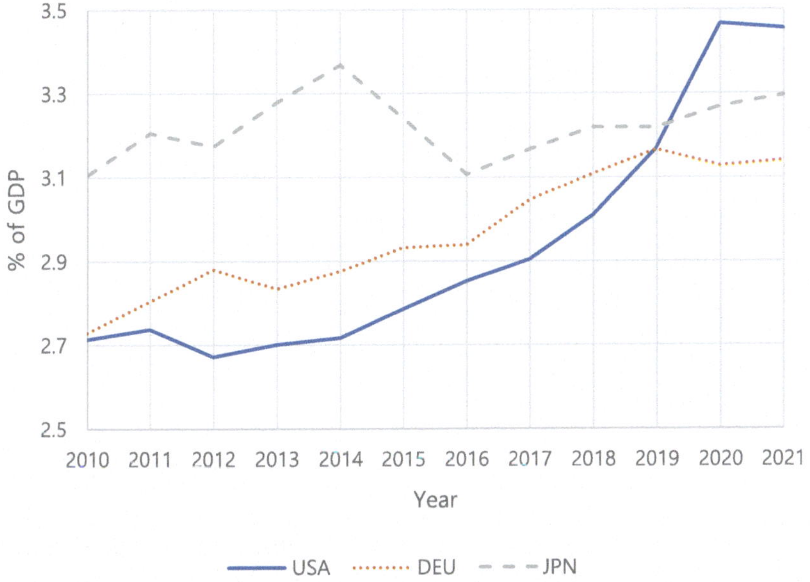

Fig. 4.1 R&D expenditure, 2010–2021 (unit: % of GDP) (*Source* UNESCO Institute for Statistics [UIS]. UIS.Stat Bulk Data Download Service [Accessed November 27, 2023]. apiportal.uis.unesco.org/bdds)

and production growth also began to turn around. As seen in Fig. 4.2, banks have shifted capital from existing housing and consumer loans to industrial loans. When analyzing the assets of U.S. commercial banks, the ratio of industrial and commercial loans to real estate and consumer loans fell rapidly, from more than 80% in the early 1980s to 38.76% in 2000 (Atkinson and Ezell 2012: 21), and further to 22.97% in 2004, as the U.S. economy shifted into a finance- and consumption-led growth regime. However, the ratio of industrial and commercial loans to real estate and consumer loans reversed, increasing from 24.26% in 2010 to 40.41% in 2020, although it did not recover the level of the early 1980s.

In a personal email with the author, National Institute of Standards and Technology (NIST) Senior Economist Gregory Tassey evaluates the recent U.S. industrial policy as a serious transition of the U.S. growth strategy, from demand management to a high-tech based, productivity-focused growth model:

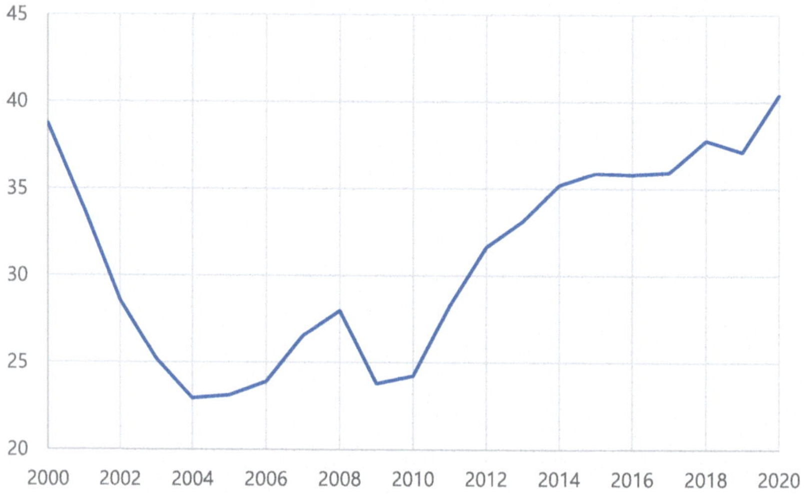

Fig. 4.2 Ratio of U.S. banks' industrial and commercial loans to real estate and consumer loans, 2000–2020 (*Source* FDIC [2023], "Loan Performance" https://www.fdic.gov/analysis/quarterly-banking-profile/ [accessed February 12, 2024])

> The U.S. economy is finally in a serious transition away from "demand management" (really "business-cycle" management) to an increasing emphasis on investment in productivity, which clearly means an "investment-oriented growth strategy." In the past three years, the three major pieces of legislation that have been passed are all targeted at investment in more high-productivity assets. You note the last two (the first one targets a long overdue upgrading of existing, more conventional, infrastructure). Together, they mark the beginning of what will become an increasingly "productivity-focused" growth strategy. (Author's personal email of October 14, 2023)

More noteworthy are the changes in R&D investment and the state's role in managing the economy. While neoliberal policy focuses on market-neutral basic science while leaving commercialization to private companies, recent U.S. industrial policy uses strategic targeting for commercialization of high-tech industries, emulating Germany's Fraunhofer model.

Changes in U.S. Industrial Policy

Traditionally, the U.S. liberalist pattern of the government's role in economic development was market neutral, focusing on regulation and investment for general purposes such as national defense and highway construction. The U.S. government intervened in the regulation and distribution of public funds, but strategic intervention in production and manufacturing was negligible, compared to other countries. However, recent revival policies focus more on production and commercialization of high-tech industries than on basic science. The revival policy also is more strategic and selective. This section briefly explores how the U.S. revival policy differs from the traditional U.S. neoliberalist state role.

Since the early twentieth century, the U.S. government has focused on macroeconomic stability through fiscal and monetary policy, but has not pursued strategic intervention and selective industrial policy at the production level (Vogel 1978). This policy was essentially based on the liberal understanding that state intervention should be fair and neutral for every private market actor, setting rules that apply equally to all private actors. These liberalist market-neutral policies are clearly distinct from strategic industrial policies which foster specific industrial groups and provide selective benefits through specific strategic choices.

Traditionally, the U.S. government's R&D policies focused on basic science serving broad missions such as national defense and health care, while production and commercialization were left to private market actors (Di Tommaso and Schweitzer 2013: 146–148, 168–172; Ruttan 2006). Following World War II, Department of Defense (DoD) research institutes, among others, led R&D worldwide in the aviation, space, nuclear power, electronics, computing, semiconductors, and the Internet,[2] while neglecting commercialization of production and innovation.

For example, in 2011, 51.2% of the U.S. federal R&D budget went to defense-oriented R&D, while defense-oriented R&D averaged 3.9% in most OECD countries. U.S. spending on economic growth in its R&D budget accounts for only 5% of the total R&D budget, while the OECD average is three times larger. In particular, 40% and 44% are budgeted in Finland and Korea, respectively (Atkinson and Ezell 2012: 76–77; OECD Main Science and Technology Indicators Database). As the innovative basic studies of the U.S. DoD show, research institutes under the U.S. government have led state-of-the-art research, but have lacked commercialization or manufacturing processes (Di Tommaso and Schweitzer 2013: 146–148, 168–172).

However, in special cases, the U.S. government attempted strategic industrial policy. As the postwar U.S. economic golden age disappeared, and Japan's and Germany's industrial competitiveness strengthened in the late 1970s and 1980s, the U.S. sought new economic policy quite distinct from the past. The Democratic Party introduced an active industrial policy as an alternative to neoliberal policy and the existing Keynesian demand-control approach (Blyth 2002: 190–192). With Japan's developmentalist industrial policy in mind, Democrats emphasized relief for collapsing companies and industries and maintaining the labor force. However, a remarkable U.S. industrial policy was implemented during the Republican Reagan administration (1981–1989), which instituted many pseudo-industrial policies in actual actions, even while insisting on adhering to the liberalist tradition. The Reagan administration institutionalized comprehensive legislation to strengthen U.S. competitiveness in response to the U.S. economic crisis from the early to mid-1980s, due

[2] In the United States, the DoD's role has been important, as Vernon Ruttan emphasizes. See Ruttan (2006) for the role of the DoD in innovative research in the U.S.

to Japan's rapid advancement. This period saw many institutional reforms to support the American innovation ecosystem.

In addition to the 1980 Bayh–Dole bill, the U.S. generated various bills and organizations to revive the manufacturing industry. The legislation included the Stevenson-Wydler Technology Innovation Act, the Manufacturing Extension Partnership (MEP), the Small Business Innovation Research (SBIR) program, the Advanced Technology Program (ATP), along with the Malcom Baldrige National Quality Award, and the Semiconductor Manufacturing Consortium (Sematech) (Bonvillian and Singer 2017: 42; Atkinson and Ezell 2012: 102; Di Tommaso and Schweitzer 2013: 73–76).

In particular, Sematech has been mentioned as a representative example of U.S. industrial policy. Sematech, a cooperative partnership organization created in 1987 by the U.S. Department of Defense (DoD) and 14 private companies, has served to strengthen the competitiveness of the semiconductor industry, a key U.S. industry (Atkinson and Ezell 2012: 102–103; Browning and Shetler 2000; Bonvillian and Singer 2017: 41; Di Tommaso and Schweitzer 2013: 77).[3] Sematech's public–private partnership to restore the innovation ecosystem and revive the manufacturing industry was a state-led new alternative to the traditional liberal model. Clearly, new paths to industrial innovation were possible, even in liberalist America.

However, these attempts in the 1980s, including Sematech, had limitations in their temporality and strategic methods. First, considering the overall economy, the scale of state support was both limited and temporary. Most public support disappeared with the collapse of communism and the 1990s decline of the Japanese economy. Although Sematech, a public–private consortium, is a representative example frequently quoted during discussions on the American innovation system, this model was not widely adopted until recently. Sematech was legitimized based on the

[3] The partnership was established by the crisis-conscious U.S. government to restore its industrial competitiveness when the Japanese semiconductor industry overtook the U.S. in the mid-1980s. Sematech began operations in 1988, and received about $500 million in public funds from the DoD and the Defense Advanced Research Projects Agency (DARPA) for about five years. Sematech focused first on production of semiconductor chips, and later played a crucial role in constructing semiconductor supply chains. Although President Reagan was a strong advocate for free trade, he established and supported the National Center for Manufacturing Sciences to improve U.S. industrial competitiveness, while externally restricting machinery imports from Japan and Taiwan.

logic of national defense which worried over the U.S.'s relative decline in military power, rather than on economic and industrial capabilities. As military threats disappeared, the legitimacy of the state's industrial policy intervention also weakened. Without these external threats, the legitimacy of state support has disappeared (Bonvillian and Singer 2017: 28–30, 43–44; Atkinson and Ezell 2012: 104–107).

Furthermore, most of the U.S. government's support focused on breakthrough research, with little attention to commercial production.[4] Publicly funded R&D policy focused on breakthroughs based on basic science toward broad missions including national defense, strictly separating from commercialization and production areas (Tassey 2014, 2023).

However, recent U.S. revival policies, including the Chips and Science Act of 2022, the Inflation Reduction Act of 2022, and the Manufacturing USA Program Act of 2013, strategically target selected industries interested in commercialization and production.

For example, in contrast to the traditional liberalist focus on market-neutral basic science, the Chips Act strategically targets U.S. high-tech industries, such as the commercialization of semiconductors. The Act provides $52 billion in public funding directly to domestic semiconductor device production, giving a 25% tax credit to private companies in semiconductor manufacturing, and supports the critical high-tech workforce and expansion of American-made 5-G technology (Tassey 2023: O'Donnell 2022).

The 2022 Inflation Reduction Act provides $30 billion in tax credits to increase domestic production of solar panels, wind turbines, batteries, and critical minerals processing. This Act also provides $10 billion in additional tax credits to support domestic investments in clean technology manufacturing facilities, such as those that make electronic vehicles and solar panels. In addition, the Act aims at significantly increasing jobs in R&D and manufacturing through workforce development grants (Quinn 2022: Tassey 2023).

In addition, the 2013 Manufacturing USA Program and the 2022 Chips and Science Act focus on building industrial ecosystems and manufacturing for high-tech industries, to boost commercialization and production. For example, in 2012 the U.S. government established its network of manufacturing innovation institutes called Manufacturing

[4] See Hughes (2005, pp. 45–49, 50–51, 74–77, 85, 153–168, 170–198) for further explanation of the U.S. response to Japan's production and quality control innovation.

USA, supported by the DoD and DoE (Department of Energy) through its NIST. As seen in the appendix, each institute was organized around specific high-tech industries, including 3D printing, photonics, digital production, and robotics. Based on this network of manufacturing innovation institutes, the U.S. has created public–private partnerships consisting of industry, academia, government, and nonprofits that boost scientific and technology innovation and support the prospect of major long-term economic growth. These public–private partnerships have further developed into innovation hubs under the Chips and Science Act of 2022 (Bonvillian 2022: 18; Tassey 2023: 9).

The Advanced Manufacturing Partnership (AMP), established in the Obama administration, embodied a more detailed practical organization to improve U.S. manufacturing's competitiveness. AMP modeled innovation in advanced manufacturing industries in America, pivoting from existing policies focused on taxes and trade barriers. AMP drew a roadmap for key technologies such as advanced sensing, process control, informatics, advanced material design, and visualization, and aimed to establish manufacturing innovation institutes (MMIs) to link SMEs with large companies. Manufacturing innovation organizations aim to enhance processes for federal research institutes to commercialize technology and systems development, as well as provide shared facilities and organize worker training (Park Yoo-mi 2019: 63–66; Bonvillian and Singer 2017: 113–114).

Politics of Transformation

With the government's recent industrial and economic intervention, the U.S. now strategically coordinates its industries and improves its innovation capabilities, fostering technology-driven growth over consumption-oriented growth. Why, and how, has the U.S. changed from neoliberal policies to create an alternative path of national developmentalism?

Notably, neoliberalism lost its relative influence in the U.S. through recent events, including the 2008 financial crisis, the COVID-19 pandemic, wars in Ukraine and elsewhere, and U.S.–China rivalry. These events may facilitate the state's active interventionism, but they do not necessarily result in statist developmentalism or strategic industrial developmentalism. The post-World War II rivalry with the Soviet Union and competition with Japan in the 1980s did not lead to Asian-style developmentalism but resulted in a neoliberal consumption-led growth regime.

The degree of economic crisis does not set the direction for a solution, as seen in the postwar U.S. of 1980s where the serious economic crisis led to a shift in U.S. capitalism. Professional managerialism gave way to a neoliberal finance- and consumption-led growth regime, rather than state-led industrial developmentalism. The recent dominance of U.S. industrial policy occurs in competition between political and discursive interpretations concerning national crises. To examine why the U.S. could develop a new state-led developmentalism, this section focusing on discursive politics analyzes first why neoliberalism declined, and then, why state-led developmentalism has prevailed over alternatives, including New Progressivism, Conservative Populism, and Hamiltonism.

Neoliberalism's Decline, and Industrialism

Against the background of the 2008 crisis and national rivalry with China, neoliberalism lost its public influence, as Americans searched for new alternatives, including new progressivism and national developmentalism. However external threats, such as the war in Ukraine and hegemonic war with China, unemployment due to offshoring, and the 2008 financial crisis, may not be sufficient to explain why the U.S. government has actively pursued industrial policies. Even under Soviet threats and U.S. economic decline in competition with Japan, the U.S. did not adopt today's industrial policy. The question is how to see a crisis or threat, and from what perspective and paradigm to understand normal economic and industrial management. This section explores why neoliberalism based on neoclassical economics lost its influence among the American public.

First, we will explore the logic of neoliberalism's opposition to the industrial policy and its critics' arguments concerning economic management, which shape the interpretation framework of economic crisis. Neoliberal financial-oriented thinking, among liberalist traditions, was the dominant paradigm in the U.S. before the rise of the U.S. revival policy. Based on neoliberal thought and the neoclassical economic paradigm, U.S. policy elites have criticized the state's active intervention as unnecessary and inefficient. For example, as of 2011, the U.S. showed very low R&D support measures compared to GDP, and ranked only 26th worldwide. Yet regarding efforts to expand R&D tax support, many U.S. policy elites preferred instead to stabilize the budget, arguing from a neoliberal perspective that a sound budget is more important, and chose instead to sacrifice R&D support. Neoliberal conservatives and neoclassical economists opposed President Obama's proposal to support facility investment in the 2010s (Bonvillian and Singer 2017: 6; Atkinson 2010; Atkinson and Ezell 2012: 63, 75).

Mainstream American economists and economic policy-makers focus on financial returns, and show little interest in collective innovation and production capabilities based on manufacturing and industrial links. In the early 2010s' "Potato chips vs semiconductor chips" debate, neoclassical economists argued that if semiconductor chips and potato chips are of the same value (e.g., $100 worth of production), it would be best to invest in a profitable way, whether semiconductors or chips.[5] These discussions of false equivalence were argued in the 1990s by Michael Boskin, the head of the Presidential Economic Advisory Committee of President George W. Bush: "What is the difference between potato chips and computer chips? The former is $100 and the latter is $100, and the two are still the same at $100" (Prestowitz 1992: 67–87). Mainstream American economists and neoliberal policy-makers argue that as long as profits are generated, whether through semiconductor chips or potato chips, there is no need to consider ripple effects in terms of technological innovation and productivity in certain industries. Jagdish Bhagwati, a professor at Columbia Law School and a key adviser to the WTO and UN, criticized the position that potato chips and semiconductor chips are different:

> I have argued that you can produce semiconductor chips, exchange them for potato chips, watch TV while chewing the chips, and become a fool. On the other hand, you can produce potato chips, exchange them for semiconductors, mount them on PCs, and become computer geniuses. In short, the question of what kind of person you will be and how it will affect your economy and society depends not on what you "produce" but on what you "consume". (Bhagwati 2010b)

U.S. economic policy-makers argue that strategic state intervention to foster specific industries or manufacturing is inappropriate. Kenneth Green of the American Enterprise Institute, a conservative neoliberal

[5] See Bhagwati (2010a, 2010b), Ramaswamy and Rowthorn (2000), Sirkin et al. (2011) for a detailed explanation on the neoliberal arguments.

economic research institute, denies the need to maintain the U.S. manufacturing base: "As long as China sells the products we need, the location of manufacturing is not so important to our economy" (Green 2010). Christina Romer, head of President Obama's Council of Economic Advisors, criticized the president's manufacturing policy, arguing that there is no need for "special treatment" for the manufacturing industry. There is no particular reason to treat the manufacturing industry differently from the service industry such as haircuts, and it is only sentimental to do so (Romer 2012). David Yoffie, professor of business administration at Harvard University, also argues that the decline in U.S. high-tech industries such as computer software, telecommunications, and electronics can be compensated for by the growth of the service industry (Yoffie 2009).

According to these American mainstream economists and neoliberalists, what is most important is to make a lot of quantitative profits regardless of whether it is a high-tech or simple service industry. Therefore, if the state intervenes to foster a certain industry, whether that industry is high-tech or simple service, it will only lead to inefficiency and waste (Pack and Saggi 2006: 289). The position that bureaucratic intervention is absurd was a dominant idea among mainstream American economists and policy-makers.

However, neoliberal arguments, which focused only on individuals' free choices, overlooked the real possibility that individual rational choices can lead to unreasonable results at the collective level. In actuality, as U.S. firms' free globalization in pursuit of profits engendered loss of production and innovation capabilities and massive trade deficits in the 2000s, neoliberalism has slowly lost its grip on America's public mind (Atkinson 2023: 2). Many industrial experts criticized that neoliberalists overlooked the marked difference in production capacity for computer chips and potato chips in terms of a country's collective technology and innovation capabilities, mentioning the "spillover effects" of computer chips to other industries, which are critical to the competitiveness of the entire national economy (Tassey 2012; Atkinson and Ezell 2012: 94–95, 97).

Concerns about the decline of U.S. manufacturing due to globalization and the search for alternatives began to be publicized in the early 2000s. In the 2004 U.S. presidential debates, Democratic candidate John Kerry criticized President George W. Bush's policy of tax cuts for companies moving abroad, publicizing corporate relocation and the decline of domestic industries.[6] According to a poll in the early 2000s, about 51% of Americans believed that jobs are unstable due to globalization (Berger 2005: 3, endnote 1). In the early 2000s, numerous U.S. newspapers and experts predicted that jobs in America would disappear due to the globalization of companies. For example, according to one consulting firm's 2003 survey, 1.4 million U.S. jobs would be offshored within the coming 12 years, and 80% of the total population expected real wages to fall (Janco Associates 2003; Berger 2005: 3–5).

However, the decline in U.S. industry and innovation capabilities began to draw the most attention during the 2008 U.S. economic crisis, which seemed to manifest pessimism toward globalization rather than neoliberal optimism. At that time, the unemployment rate exceeded 10% and long-term unemployment reached its highest peak since the 1930s Great Depression. Despite the seriousness of the 2008 crisis, in the early stage of crisis management neoliberalism still prevailed over state-led structural reform. The crisis was so serious that the government had no choice but to use short-term economic stimulus measures to stabilize the economy rather than set long-term policies. Prescriptions for the crisis were suggested mainly by still-dominant neoclassical economists, and most of them focused on price signals that revive investment to show positive growth rather than fundamental structural reform. These short-term macroeconomy stabilization policies had only a limited effect in improving the structure to address the problem of underinvestment in economic assets or to strengthen innovation capabilities for long-term growth (Bonvillian and Singer 2017: 101–102).

Despite the dominance of neoliberalism, the position that emphasized technological innovation and active national structural improvement for innovation slowly began to gain strength by raising questions about the existing neoclassical economists' prescriptions. For example, Gregory Tassey, former chair of NIST, criticized the makeshift neoclassical macroeconomic response, and offered new alternatives:

> The US trade deficit for 35 years in industrial products cannot be explained simply by business cycles, monetary shifts, trade barriers, or inefficient use of currency and short-term fiscal policy. High productivity growth is the solution. High growth in productivity can only be achieved through

[6] Financial News (October 18, 2004) "US companies are likely to increase outsourcing after the presidential election: overseas relocation will be accelerated to reduce costs."

> long-term and continuous investments in intellectual, material, human, organizational and technical infrastructure and capital. To carry out this urgent mission, a "public-private asset growth model" is needed that emphasizes investment in technology. (Tassey 2012: 2)

Groups emphasizing the revival of the U.S. high-tech industry criticized neoclassical economists' measures against the backdrop of the crisis, arguing that those measures cannot reverse the trend of declining competitiveness and low growth, and suggested policies to create an innovative ecosystem through a public–private cooperation model.[7] The groups emphasizing the revival of the U.S. manufacturing industry began to gain strength as the Obama administration, which took power against the backdrop of the crisis, struggled with the existing neoliberal position.

Formation of Core Groups for Industrial Revival Policy

Despite neoliberal policy elites' opposition, the Obama administration came to visualize and materialize the U.S. manufacturing revival policy. This did not come about naturally but resulted from serious political struggles. In order to gain strength to continuously interpret the crisis and suggest an alternative to neoliberalism, a core group for industrial revival policy was needed. Embedded in the new theoretical alternative for the revival of U.S. manufacturing is the formation of the main force that promoted the policy: discussion of new alternatives centered on MIT and the White House Department of Science and Technology, and the formation of consultative bodies led by them. However, their arguments raised much opposition, requiring persuasion in the struggle against the neoliberal position. This political process is our focus in this section.

MIT and the White House Office of Science and Technology Policy are noteworthy as the visionary forces emphasizing the revival policy. Each remained a respected, independent force, focused on studying issues in U.S. manufacturing and suggesting new alternatives. Based on their research and search for alternatives, the U.S. government has applied

[7] The Obama administration's initial response focused on short-term intervention and stabilization of finance due to the urgency of the crisis. See Di Tommaso and Schweitzer (2013: 96–111) for further explanation on the Obama administration's initial response to the crisis.

efforts for revival of the U.S. manufacturing industry. Many policy-makers and politicians made efforts to link those organizations.

Among them, Ron Bloom notably began working for the Obama administration as senior advisor on the President's Task Force on the Automotive Industry in 2009. He later played a pivotal role in the government's acquisition and restructuring of U.S. automakers GM and Chrysler, contributing greatly to preventing the collapse of the U.S. manufacturing industry. After that, Bloom led a White House science and technology team and organized the Advanced Manufacturing Partnership (AMP) on January 24, 2011, leading the revival of U.S. manufacturing industry as the co-chair of AMP, with Dow Chemical CEO Andrew Liveris and MIT President Susan Hockfield (Bonvillian and Singer 2017: 102, 107).

Hockfield convened a roundtable of 11 MIT faculty on March 1, 2009, to devise an innovative plan for the U.S. to escape the recession.[8] They then decided to focus on "advanced technologies for manufacturing" in a follow-up roundtable meeting on March 29, 2010. Since then, the MIT research team, led by Suzanne Berger, a professor of Politics at MIT, has addressed problems and alternatives in U.S. manufacturing through extensive research.[9] The MIT team formed a Production in the Innovation Economy (PIE) team and started its research in 2013 following a 2012 study by AMP. The PIE team diagnosed that the U.S. innovation ecosystem had weakened, as U.S. conglomerates became obsessed with short-term financial returns and turned to outsourcing and offshoring (Locke and Wellhausen 2014).

Simultaneous with the MIT research team's efforts, the White House Office of Science and Technology Policy (OSTP) actively produced research and reports as part of its efforts to revive U.S. manufacturing. According to an OSTP study, studies by government defense research institutes and universities had focused on basic science that is somewhat isolated to commercial research, while private research institutes

[8] "Summary of MIT Roundtable on Developing National Innovation Policies" March 1, 2010 from https://dc.mit.edu/sites/default/files/pdf/MIT%20Innovation%20Roundtable.pdf.

[9] See MIT Washington Office (from http://dc.mit.edu/resources-links) for MIT's briefing activities for advice and linkage to the Washington administration in various high-tech fields.

focused more on technology and production processes than on fundamental technology development. OSTP revealed that this separation of basic research and manufacturing led to the absence of manufacturing-led innovation, causing the decline of the U.S. manufacturing industry in the 2000s. Therefore, OSTP suggested innovation through close links between research and industry as an alternative, with the idea of Germany's Fraunhofer model in mind (Bonvillian and Singer 2017: 104–105, 133).

Most notable in the development of the U.S. manufacturing revival policy is the combination of third-party forces that emphasize fostering high-tech manufacturing as a way to overcome the crisis, and that differs from Keynesianism which advocates distributive justice, and from neoliberalism which emphasizes free markets. A typical example is the AMP.

The AMP consisted of key personnel from industry, academia, and government who agreed on the revival of U.S. manufacturing and appointed three co-chairs—Ron Bloom from government, MIT President Susan Hockfield, and Dow Chemical CEO Andrew Liveris. Major industry conglomerates, including Dow in chemicals, Northrup Grumman and United Technologies in aviation, Proctor and Gamble in consumer goods, Ford in automobiles, and Intel in semiconductors, participated, along with presidents from six research and academic institutions—MIT, *Carnegie Mellon, UC Berkeley, Stanford, Michigan, and Georgia Institute of Technology*—and the chair of the National Economic Council Gene Spurling, Secretary of Commerce Rebecca Blank, Jason Miller from the White House Economic Committee, and David Hart and Charles Thorpe from OSTP. In addition, key personnel contributed from major research-related government agencies, including NSIT, National Science Foundation (NSF), DoE, DOD, and the President's Council of Advisors on Science and Technology (Ministry of Trade, Industry and Energy 2019: 15–16; Bonvillian and Singer 2017: 107–109). AMP's goal was to convert the previous American "invent here and manufacture there" model to "invent here and manufacture here." AMP attempted to establish a public–private partnership to design continuous innovation for the manufacturing industry.

Although the U.S. high-tech manufacturing revival policy was formed by actors and projects inside and outside the Obama administration, this initiative was not easily achieved. This process materialized through extreme opposition and struggle both inside and outside the government.

Manufacturing revival groups faced serious opposition, especially from groups holding dominant neoliberal positions.

For example, the White House OSTP experienced difficulty in even publishing its report on the revival of the manufacturing industry due to questions raised by Richard Levin, president of Yale University and chair of the President's Council of Advisors on Science and Technology (PCAST). Levin worked closely with Lawrence Summers, director of the White House Economic Committee and former president of Harvard University, to write a report expressing opposition to OSTP's manufacturing revival project (Bonvillian and Singer 2017: 105). Christina Romer, chair of the Presidential Economic Advisory Committee (2009–2010) in the Obama administration, also opposed the administration's support measures for the revival. In a New York Times article, Romer raised a question: "Do manufacturers need special treatment?" (Romer 2012). This process became a confrontation between neoclassical economists and new groups with an engineering perspective.

Despite opposition from neoclassical economists and neoliberalists, President Obama actively supported the U.S. high-tech manufacturing policy and ruled in favor of a group claiming revival in manufacturing. President Obama actively supported the revival of U.S. manufacturing in his State of the Union Address in February 2012.[10] And in March, 15 manufacturing research institutes called for the revival's creation. In his State of the Union address in February 2013, President Obama once again supported the creation of manufacturing research institutes.[11] Along with the AMP team, President Obama wanted to include the establishment of manufacturing research institutes in the FY2013 budget. However, due to serious conflict in Congress, he chose a detour to create manufacturing research institutes under the U.S. Federal Administration Department rather than directly. So-called "Man-Tech" (manufacturing technology) crews at the administration's DoE and DoD, who emphasized the revival of U.S. manufacturing, agreed to support manufacturing research institutes and to have research institutes under the DoD lead and support the processes. The Obama administration and AMP worked to

[10] *Wall Street Journal* (February 12, 2012) "President's State of the Union Address."

[11] White House (February 12, 2013) "Remarks by the President in the State of the Union Address," from https://obamawhitehouse.archives.gov/the-press-office/2013/02/12/remarks-president-state-union-address.

create Advanced Manufacturing Institutions based on Germany's Fraunhofer model. Advanced Manufacturing Institutions are organizations that realize ideas for high-tech development evaluated by AMP groups, like Fraunhofer organizations, through cooperative partnerships between SMEs, giant conglomerates, and engineers at academic research institutes (Bonvillian and Singer 2017: 111).

Three Main Alternatives to Neoliberalism

The decline of neoliberalism did not automatically result in the current U.S. industrial policy, which reflects various alternatives to neoliberalism. Notably, despite the differences in their definitions of industrial policy and policy priority, diverse alternatives to neoliberalism share state-led industrial development. As an alternative to neoliberalism, three main currents are proposed: New Progressivism to focus on green equity and anti-globalism, National Developmentalism or Hamiltonism to emphasize technology-based national development and Conservative Populism. They have different priorities, but share common goals to revive U.S. manufacturing as an alternative to neoliberal finance- and consumption-led growth, as seen in the Chips and Science Act of 2022. This section examines which of these competing alternatives to neoliberalism commonly support the manufacturing revival policy.

New Progressivism is the most dominant alternative to neoliberalism. New Progressives, mainly based in small and local firms, propose that the U.S. withdraw from the global economy and that expenditures should be expanded, focused on redistribution (e.g., college debt forgiveness, free daycare, and other social needs). However, their policy priority is green equity, arguing that the U.S. should reengineer away from fossil fuels (e.g., public transit instead of cars, rail instead of planes, urban instead of suburban, vegan instead of meat, decentralized energy instead of centralized) (Nicholas 2024; Atkinson 2023: 2).

Social alliances for New Progressivism include small and local firms, so-called political "progressives" and many moderates on the political spectrum. For example, former Clinton administration officials Gene Sperling and Brad DeLong embraced New Progressivism, putting redistribution first and growth a distant second, at best. In terms of voters, Progressives include college graduates, women, and growing minorities, rather than white male workers (Tucker 2019; Atkinson 2023: 2; Teixeira 2009).

Conservative Populism as a second alternative to neoliberalism is supported by a small but growing number of Republicans.[12] Emphasizing America first, they support a fair deal for U.S. workers through such measures as limiting low-skill immigrants (especially prohibiting illegal immigrants), reducing financialization of the economy, and crafting policies to ensure U.S. advanced industry ascendancy. However, this stream often shows an excessive anti-corporate and anti-globalization sentiment, along with unaffordable spending and tax incentives to address social issues (see American Compass website). The main social group of Conservative Populism includes less productive employers and workers, particularly in suburban areas rather than metropolitan areas, where economic decline has been underway throughout neoliberal globalization (Broz, Frieden, and Weymouth 2021).

The third alternative to neoliberalism is National Developmentalism or Hamiltonism.[13] National Developmentalism emphasizes "competitiveness-focused industrial policy" in a global context of national competition, criticizing the structural and systemic failures of free-market neoliberalism. Instead of short-term profit-taking and the enrichment of financial elites, they focus on real value creation by a technology-based growth strategy. Unlike the Progressives and Populists, they embrace large corporations as engines of progress and prosperity. They hold that corporations' value creation should meet goals that align with state goals, especially greater competitiveness (Atkinson 2022, 2023; Bonvillian and Singer 2018; Bonvillian 2022). Proponents of Hamiltonism include an array of political tendencies, including pragmatists and moderates from all political stripes of Right, Center, and Left. They commonly focus on strengthening U.S. economic and technological power, especially in rivalry against China (Atkinson 2023: 3).

In light of the rise of recent U.S. industrial revival policy against neoliberalism, all the three alternative streams—including New Progressives, Conservative Populists, and Hamiltonians—support industrial policy as an

[12] American Compass is an example of this new conservative populism https://americancompass.org.

[13] Alexander Hamilton the first Treasury Secretary was the first political leader to propose the federal government's active role in industrial policy in his report on manufacturing to Congress. Hamilton's main policies are the U.S. manufacturing by tariff-based trade policies. His plans were opposed by agriculture-oriented southerners led by Jefferson and Madison (Bonvillian and Singer 2018; Bonvillian 2022: 5).

alternative to neoliberals' finance-led growth strategy, even though they differ in the policy priority.

For example, Hamiltonians support large corporations in developing technology-driven growth because they consider large corporations as vital to their goal of national competitiveness. By contrast, New Progressives propose support for small firms and small businesses.[14] Criticizing the Hamiltonian industrial policy to emphasize large corporations, New Progressives hold that the Hamiltonians disregard income equity and the social justice of redistribution (Baker 2022). Hamiltonians use industrial policy to ensure that the U.S. stays the strongest nation on earth economically, technologically, and militarily (Atkinson 2023: 6), whereas New Progressives want to use industrial policy to achieve social missions including reduction of economic inequality and green equity (Mazzocato et al. 2020; Mazzucato 2020). Hamiltonians such as Suzanne Berger (2021) emphasize that the goal of industrial policy is technology goals, not broad societal goals, while New Progressives such as the Roosevelt institute put the priority of industrial policy on equality, justice, and opportunity, stating that government policy should benefit workers, child care, elder care, and housing. In contrast to Hamiltonians who emphasize technology-driven development, New Progressives, including neo-Brandeisians such as Barry Lynn, Matt Stoller, and Federal Trade Commission (FTC) Chair Lina Khan, rail against large corporations, criticizing Hamiltonians' patriarchy, supporting Trump's forces including white working-class males, and instead proposing policies that emphasize race, gender, and sexual orientation (Tucker 2019: 35–36; Atkinson 2023: 8–9).

However, despite their differences in industrial policy, these three main alternatives to neoliberalism commonly support state-led industrial policy over finance-led growth. Reflecting the negative impacts of neoliberal globalization on domestic manufacturing and local community (particularly in suburban areas), Conservative Populists support the recent U.S. state-led revival policy. For example, according to a 2023 survey by the American Compass, when asked to rank the most important challenges

[14] Chris Stein, "How Bernie Sanders and conservatives united against US semiconductor bill." The Guardian, July 31, 2022; Bethany Blankley, "Opponents of CHIPS Act say it could subsidize construction of semiconductors in China, not America." The Center Square, July 26, 2022.

facing America, 50% of Republican voters answered "American manufacturing has been gutted by globalization and trade with China" as one of the top issues, far ahead of issues including taxes and regulation. And a great majority of Republican voters (78%) support industrial policies like the Chips and Science Act.[15]

Bipartisan and Societywide Support

Despite the strong and long-held dominance of liberalist thinking, the U.S. shifted from neoliberal finance-led growth strategy to state-led industrial developmentalism. This was possible not only due to the formation of a core group for industrial developmentalism but also due to societywide supports. Despite the growing conflicts within both the Republican and Democratic parties, state-sponsored industrial developmentalism gained bipartisan support, a rare phenomenon in the U.S. How is this possible?

Notably, industrial groups' efforts against the backdrop of the 2008 economic crisis, the COVID-19 pandemic, wars in Ukraine and elsewhere, and national rivalry with China facilitated the U.S. shift from neoliberalism to new industrial policy. In particular, the pandemic collapsed the consumer market and destabilized global supply chains. Trump's Republican government, which traditionally had supported fiscal conservativism, abandoned that policy path. Supplementing the Federal Reserve's unprecedented steps of supporting direct credit to large employers by buying debt or loans from corporations and supporting the public debt markets for state and local governments, the Trump administration signed a $2.3 trillion COVID-19 relief package in 2020, and the Biden administration backed $1.9 trillion in 2021.[16] With the COVID crisis consciousness, even a fiscally conservative Republican government abandoned its longstanding position, and mobilized the government spending methods, including major tax cuts, without spending reduction offsets. Facing the economic emergency and the pandemic, fiscal restraints were lifted.

[15] American Compass (November 8, 2023) "Issues 2024: Industrial Policy" from https://americancompass.org/issues-2024-industrial-policy.

[16] The Hill (December 27, 2020) "Trump signs $2.3T relief, spending package"; CNBC (March 11, 2021) "Biden signs $1.9 trillion COVID relief bill, clearing way for stimulus checks, vaccine aid."

Furthermore, with the rise of national rivalry with China, active industrial policies are considered essential to competition, rather than relying on simple Keynesian demand policy. China's massive spending on industrial policy efforts served as a spur for U.S. revival policy (Broz et al. 2021: 2). Americans began to recognize the rapid growth of China based on nationalistic industrial policy as dangerous to the U.S. economy. For example, in 2019, China's manufacturing (28.7% of the world's manufacturing output) surpassed the U.S.'s 16.8%, a reversed position compared to 15 years ago. More serious is that in the international competition for advanced technology products, the U.S. held a $195 billion deficit in 2021, whereas China has rapidly advanced (Bonvillian 2022: 21–23). Many Americans believe that China's substantial surplus in trade with the U.S. has been unfairly distributed; the U.S. receives too small a portion, whereas China holds too large a share of the liberal trade. Many Americans believe the surplus needs to be redivided (DeLong 2023).

With the rise of national rivalry, industrial policy has gained bipartisan support and societywide consensus, as seen in Table 4.1. As crisis consciousness against the rise of China's manufacturing and advanced technology has grown, both Republicans and Democrats in the Senate and House of Representatives have proposed nationalist developmental laws, including FIRRMA of 2018, ECRA, Chips & Science Act, and USICA across the Trump and Biden administrations. As the populist backlash grew societywide against the negative effects of neoliberal globalization, particularly against U.S. manufacturing's decline with the rise of China, both Republicans and Democrats in the Senate and House of Representatives have supported nationalist industrial policies because they are concerned with national security as well as with voters' jobs in their districts (Broz et al. 2021).

Due to declines in employment, both Republicans and Democrats have transcended their political factions and supported for manufacturing revival policy. In particular, industrial states such as Michigan and Ohio, which were severely damaged by manufacturing's decline, supported the policy. Both capital and labor turned from opposition to support of state intervention, giving support to Congress to pass the legislation. For example, Ohio Democratic Senator Sherrod Brown, in collaboration with

Table 4.1 Legislation proposed in the context of U.S.–China Rivalry

Laws		*Primary sponsor*	*Time to propose*
Foreign Investment Risk Review Modernization Act (FIRRMA)		[Senate] John Cornyn (R-TX)	November 8, 2017
		[Senate] Dianne Feinstein (D-CA)	
		[House] Robert Pittenger (R-NC)	May 16, 2018
		[House] Denny Heck (D-WA)	
Export Control Reform Act (ECRA)		[House] Ed Royce (R-CA)	February 15, 2018
CHIPS and Science Act		[Senate] Chuck Schumer (D-NY)	July 1, 2021
USICA	a. CHIPS for America Act	[Senate] John Cornyn (R-TX)	June 11, 2020
		[House] Mark Warner (D-VA)	
		[House] McCaul, Michael (R-TX)	
		[House] Doris Matsui (D-CA)	
	b. Endless Frontier Act	[Senate] Chuck Schumer (D-NY)	April 21, 2021
		[House] Todd Young (R-IN)	
		[Senate] Ro Khanna (D-CA)	
		[House] Mike Gallagher (R-WI)	

Missouri Republican Senator Roy Blunt, introduced the Revitalize American Manufacturing and Innovation (RAMI) Act on August 1, 2013.[17] The bill approves the creation of 15 manufacturing institutes under the guidance of NIST. Other members of both parties expressed support for the bill. Senate legislation was supported as well by major manufacturing associations and labor organizations. Following the Senate's legislative initiative on August 2, 2013, RAMI was introduced in the House of

[17] House of Representatives 2296, Revitalize American Manufacturing and Innovation Act, 113th Congress 2nd Sess., Congress.gov, bill actions, from https://www.congress.gov/bill/113th-congress/house-bill/2996/actions.

Representatives, with bipartisan support (Bonvillian and Singer 2017: 126–127).

In addition to concerns for jobs in their districts, significant efforts by core groups of industrial development in the federal government contributed to bipartisan support for legislation of more recent industrial policies. For example, Deputy Secretary of State Keith Cragg under the Trump administration contacted both Republican and Democratic lawmakers and emphasized the importance of legislation and congressional support in securing manufacturing capabilities in the U.S. Thus, legislation in Congress related to semiconductor support began to accelerate in 2021. The Semiconductor Support Act and the Foundry Act were passed and included in the National Defense Authorization Act in January 2021. In June of the same year, the American Innovation and Competition Act, which effectively combined the Semiconductor Support Act and the Frontier Act, was passed in the Senate (Global Tech Security 2023).

Many Americans have begun to recognize that a strong industrial base is vital to workers and their communities, to the rate of technological and economic progress, and to national security. However due to rapid offshoring, U.S. manufacturing output and productivity are declining; only public industrial policy will restore the American leadership. According to Deloitte-MI Report (2011), public opinion in the U.S. supports manufacturing revival. Approximately 80% of respondents saw manufacturing as important to ensuring U.S. living standards and economic prosperity. Two-thirds support the government's policy to invest in manufacturing and to take a strategic approach towards it (Bailey and Propis 2014: 384).

As seen in Table 4.2, another 2021 survey by the Chicago Council,[18] shows that an absolute majority of Americans support strategic industrial policies, such as the Inflation Reduction Act (IRA), the Chips and Science Act, and the Infrastructure Investment and Jobs Act (IIJA). Regarding the question of whether to support or oppose government assistance to promote semiconductor chips, 65% of Americans support it, while only 13% oppose it. In addition, regarding the question "which of the industrial policy measures, if any, do you think the U.S. government should take to promote investment in strategically important industries?" overall

[18] The Chicago Council on Global Affairs (January 25, 2023) "Free Trade with Exceptions: Public Opinion and Industrial Policy," from https://globalaffairs.org/commentary-and-analysis/blogs/free-trade-exceptions-public-opinion-and-industrial-policy.

79% support the policy that the U.S. government should fund R&D of emerging technologies to give U.S. companies an edge over foreign businesses in these new industries; and overall 72% express that the U.S. government should financially support U.S. companies in key industries competing against foreign business that receive support from their own government.

In addition to core policy elites' leadership, a wide-ranging social bloc of Americans, including Conservative Populists comprised of suburban communities and white male workers, New Progressives comprised mainly of SMEs and female workers, and Hamiltonians based in high-tech and large corporations, supported U.S. strategic industrial policy to promote national industries. With the policy elites' persuasion and the pressure of popular supports, U.S. industrialists, who initially opposed government interventionism, changed their attitude toward supporting the industrial policies in 2020.

Table 4.2 Public opinion on industrial policy Acts, 2021 (unit: %)

		Support	*Don't know*	*Oppose*
Q1. Support for Chips Act	Overall	65	22	13
Do you support or oppose	Democrats	68	25	8
government assistance to	Republicans	63	23	14
promote semiconductor chips?	Independents	62	20	18
Q2. Support for Industrial Policy Measures		% of should take action		
a. The US government should fund R&D of emerging technologies to give US companies an edge over foreign businesses in these new industries		Overall	79	
		Democrats	83	
		Republicans	74	
		Independents	79	
b. The US government should financially support US companies in key industries competing against foreign business that receive support form their own governments		Overall	72	
		Democrats	73	
		Republicans	72	
		Independents	72	

Source Chicago Council Survey, July 7–26, 2021; $n = 2086$

Actually, U.S. industrialists opposed the U.S. government's intervention policy until 2018, including tariff actions against China's Huawei, because the target corporations of U.S. export control, such as China's Huawei, are those U.S. corporations' customers (SIA June 15, 2018). In the summer of 2020, the toolmakers' industry association (SEMI) opposed the U.S. government's second export control, complaining that the May 2020 export controls alone caused $17 million in lost sales of U.S.-origin items to firms related to Huawei (Bown 2020: 26–27; Semiconductor Manufacturing Industry Association August 24, 2020).

However, industry associations, including the Semiconductor Industry Association (SIA), changed their attitude toward support for the government industrial policy. In the Biden administration, they became the government's partners to provide a rationale for industrial policy. For example, the SIA's 2021 report "Strengthening the Global Semiconductor Supply Chain in an Uncertain Era"[19] emphasizes the need for the government industrial policy to boost domestic chip production in the situations where supply chains are uncertain due to geographic specialization. This SIA 2021 report was cited in the U.S. supply chain evaluation report pursuant to Presidential Executive Order (No. 14017). The SIA report highlights supply chain vulnerabilities as semiconductor production is concentrated in East Asia. According to the report's analysis, if Taiwan's semiconductor industry encounters a problem, Taiwan will lose about $42 billion per year, but the entire electronics production market will lose $490 billion per year. As a solution to address these vulnerabilities in the semiconductor supply chain, the SIA report argues that the resilience of the supply chain must be established by building domestic manufacturing capabilities in the U.S.

In another 2021 SIA report, "The Positive Impact of the Semiconductor Industry on the American Workforce and How Federal Industry Incentives Will Increase Domestic Jobs" (SIA May 2021), the SIA justifies the Chips Act, emphasizing its positive effects on employment. The report holds that more than $50 billion in funds to be invested through CHIPS will have a positive impact not only on the semiconductor industry but

[19] Boston Consulting Group (BGC) and Semiconductor Industry Association (SIA) (April 2021) "Strengthening the Global Semiconductor Supply Chain in an Uncertain Era" Policy Report, SIA from https://www.semiconductors.org/wp-content/uploads/2021/05/BCG-x-SIA-Strengthening-the-Global-Semiconductor-Value-Chain-April-2021_1.pdf.

also on surrounding industries, creating not only 42,000 direct jobs in semiconductors but also 347,000 indirect jobs in manufacturing, design, and professional occupations and approximately 185,000 temporary jobs per year from 2021 to 2026. U.S. industries have changed their attitude of opposition to state intervention toward support or partnership with the government's developmental policies, although some companies, including Intel and Qualcomm, still oppose the U.S. government's nationalist developmental policies.[20]

To sum up, against the background of the decline of U.S. industries in the course of uncoordinated finance-led offshoring, the U.S. has shifted from traditional neoliberalism to state-led industrial development. Against the backdrop of the 2008 financial crisis, wars in Ukraine and elsewhere, and national rivalry with China, neoliberalism is losing its grip on the U.S. public mind. Three main alternatives to neoliberalism, including New Progressivism, Conservative Populism, and National Developmentalism, share common interests in the state's active developmental role to revive U.S. industries, despite differences in their policy priorities. They have continuously provided interpretations of socio-economic problems and suggested solutions, reflecting their social bases. Due to their efforts, societywide support for industrial policy has spread. And reflecting upon constituents' concerns for jobs in their districts, both Democrats and Republicans provide bipartisan support for U.S. revival policies. Industrialists who initially opposed the state's intervention have undergone a change of attitude toward support for the revival policies, due to policy groups' persuasion and social pressures.

Appendix 1

The following table summarizes 13 manufacturing research institutes.

Manufacturing Research Institutes in Manufacturing USA

[20] Wei Sheng, "Briefing: Qualcomm, Intel lobby against Huawei ban," *Technode*, Jun 18, 2019 from https://technode.com/2019/06/18/briefing-qualcomm-intel-lobby-against-huawei-ban/.

Name of institutions	*Description*
DMDII-Digital Manufacturing and Design Innovation Institute	DMDII was established in Chicago in 2014. Digital manufacturing uses an integrated computer-based system along with simulations, three-dimensional visualization, analytics, and collaboration tools for simultaneous production and definitions of the manufacturing process. Design innovation refers to the ability to apply these technologies, tools, and products to reinterpret the entire manufacturing process from end to end The DMDII is attended by 201 members from a wide range of areas, including major companies, many small companies, and 11 leading universities. The institute operates on a \$70 million budget from an Army Mantech fund of the Ministry of Defense, and \$2.48 billion from an industrial and state response fund. Its task is digital manufacturing that fosters close connections between suppliers to lower production design costs, reduces capital requirements through better connections from end to end of the product life cycle, and saves production costs. Furthermore, it aims to shorten the time to the market through faster iteration, develop and apply innovations in digital design, digital processes, and digital supply chain, develop new products, and innovate existing legacy products
LIFT-Lightweight Innovations for Tomorrow (lightweight and advanced metals)	LIFT was established in 2014 with a hub in Detroit, Michigan, and has geographically expanded to Michigan, Ohio, Indiana, Tennessee, and Kentucky via I-75 roads. Lightweight and advanced metals provide improvement in key performances and greater energy efficiency that can enhance the performance of various systems in defense, energy, transportation, and general engineering production. Lightweight metals are applied to wind turbines, medical technology, pressure vessels, and alternative energy resources

(continued)

(continued)

Name of institutions	*Description*
	LIFT has 78 members, including 17 universities and companies from various fields, including metal, aerospace, and automobile suppliers. The institute is receiving $70 million in funding through naval research by the Navy Headquarters and its Mantech program. The lab's mission is to innovate the production of lightweight, high-performance metals and expand such new technologies with industrial-based applications. The institute is working on projects on melting, thermo-mechanical treatment processes, powder processes, agile low-cost tooling, plating, and joining, which are widely applicable to automobiles, aerospace, shipbuilding, railroads, manufacturing, and other various areas. As will be discussed in Chapter 8, this institution plays a leading role in human resource education
Power America-Next Generation Power Electronics	Power America was launched in 2015 to develop wide-bandgap semiconductor technology. This technology has improved the energy efficiency and reliability of power electronics through smaller, faster, and more efficient semiconductor materials than silicon-based technology. These semiconductor materials were able to operate at higher temperatures, prevent higher voltages, and enable faster switching at less power loss, as well as be more reliable with significant advantages at the system level. These capabilities could reduce weight, volume, and life cycle costs in various fields of power application. Such technologies will be applicable to various fields, including industrial motor systems, home appliances, data centers, and conversion to renewable energy such as solar and wind power. If extensive introduction of the technology in a limited area is achieved, significant electronic power savings, including industrial production, can be achieved annually. The high cost of broadband technology is expected to decrease along with achieving higher production levels Power America receives $70 million from the Energy Efficiency and Renewable Energy High-tech Manufacturing Division of the Department of Energy with another $70 million from the matching fund. The institute is located in Raleigh, North Carolina, with the participation of 17 industrial partners, 5 universities, and 3 laboratories

(continued)

(continued)

Name of institutions	*Description*
IACMI-Advanced Composites Manufacturing Innovation	IACMI was established in 2015 and aimed to develop and demonstrate advanced fiber-reinforced polymer composites within decades that are 50% cheaper, 75% less energy, and more than 95% reusable and recyclable Lightweight, high-strength, and high-stiffness synthetic materials are recognized as key technologies that enable energy-saving transportation, efficient power generation, and the promotion of renewable power generation across multiple areas. The scope of application of these lightweight and high-strength composites varies from automobiles to aviation and wind power wings Constraints in achieving this include high cost, low production rate, high manufacturing energy density of synthetic materials, non-recyclability, as well as the need to improve design modeling and inspection tools, and the suitability to regulatory conditions. Technology acceleration and manufacturing research need to meet production costs and performance goals criteria during the process, from component material production to final composite structure production IACMI is located in Knoxville, Tennessee, and receives \$70 million from the Energy Efficiency and Renewable Energy High-tech Manufacturing Division of the Department of Energy along with a \$180 million matching fund. The institute involves 57 companies, 15 universities and laboratories, and 14 other organizations
AIM Photonics-American Institute for Manufacturing Integrated Photonics	AIM Photonics was established in 2015 in Albany and Rochester, New York. The institute's goal is to develop a device that enables telecommunications, new high-performance computing, and a high-speed signal transmission that enables sensors and imaging that will bring progress in the health industry

(continued)

(continued)

Name of institutions	*Description*
	For integrated photonics, various photons and electronic devices (e.g., laser, detector, wave-guides, passive structure, modulator, electronic controls, optical interconnects, etc.) needed to be integrated into a single nano-sized substrate. The advantage of this integration was considerable. This simplifies system design, improves system performance, reduces configuration space and power consumption, and improves performance and reliability, enabling the realization of important new capabilities and functions at low costs. The current photonic manufacturing area is interrelated, but it still is only a fairly independent set of businesses, organizations and activities. This area has the developmental potential quite independent businesses, organizations, and activities. It has the developmental potential to construct an ecosystem. However, it still lacks the organization and integrated market power necessary to efficiently innovate manufacturing technology for cost-effective design, manufacturing, testing, assembly, and packaging of integrated optical equipment
	AIM Photonics' focus is on creating a photonics ecosystem that encompasses domestic foundry, integrated design tools, automated packaging, assembly, inspection, and human resource development. The institute receives more than $2 million in matching funds from state and industries along with federal government support
NextFlex-Flexible Hybrid Electronics	NextFlex was founded in 2015 with Silicon Valley, San Jose, California as its hub. The institute aims to develop a highly applicable device that forms a flexible and expandable gas that combines thin CMOS elements with new elements added in the printing sequence. This means flexible and mixed elements for circuits, communication, sensing, and power sources which are inappropriate in current silicon processing machines

(continued)

(continued)

Name of institutions	*Description*
	Flexible Hybrid Electronics (FHE) also enables the full operation of traditional electronic circuits in new flexible structures and formats, such as bending, stretching, or folding. These highly functional devices can be part of a bent, irregular, and stretched material. These technologies enable traditional electronic packaging to expand into a new form that will enable new stages of commercial and military technology. Examples of these include medical devices and sensors, sensors for monitor-structural or method-performance, interoperability sensors over the Internet, sensors that detect physical locations, wearable performance or information devices, robotics, human-robotic interface devices, and lightweight portable electronic systems. This includes applications such as wearable technologies, new information devices and sensors, medical prostheses and sensors, and portable sensors
	For this institute, DoD Mantech bears $75 million, and industries, state and local government bears $96 million. 22 corporate members, from semiconductor companies, and their suppliers to aerospace and life science companies, 17 universities, and state and local institutions are participating in this institute
AFFOA-Advanced Functional Fabrics of America	AFFOA was announced in April 2016 and began its operation in 2017 with 80 members, including large and small companies, universities, and local colleges. The institute's headquarters is located in Cambridge, Massachusetts, and is planning to create several regional hubs
	Advances in science have allowed textiles and fabrics to have special properties, including strength, salt resistance, and electronic conductivity, which can be used in electronic devices, sensors, and telecommunication elements. This new range of fibers and fabrics includes various forms of special fibers, industrial fibers, electronic fabrics, and advanced fabrics. These enable communication, lighting, cooling, health monitoring, battery storage, and other new functions that have not previously been connected to the fabric. These technical fabrics are based on a mixture of synthetic and natural fibers and multi-material fibers, which can be applied in various commercial and military fields beyond traditional wearable fibers

(continued)

(continued)

Name of institutions	*Description*
	AFFOA has received $75 million from Mantech funds of DoD, along with $240 million from industrial and state-level matching funds. The institute's goal is to serve as public–private partnership in an innovative ecosystem for revolutionary textile and textile manufacturing from end to end, and also serve as a leverage for domestic manufacturing facilities that develop manufacturing processes and increase scales. The institute plans to ensure rapid production realization opportunities based on design and simulation tools, pilot production facilities, cooperative infrastructure with suppliers, and opportunities for manpower development. The institute seeks to revolutionize textiles and fabrics while combining IT technologies and knowledge devices
Smart Manufacturing Innovation Institute	The winner of the new Smart Manufacturing Innovation Research Institute was announced by President Barack Obama in June 2016, and is now at the startup level, recruiting its members. The institute's headquarters is in Los Angeles Smart manufacturing is characterized by the convergence of knowledge and communication technologies in the manufacturing process to enable a new level of actual time control between factories and companies in terms of energy, productivity, and costs. This is regarded as a high-priority manufacturing technology area that requires federal support in the AMP2.0 report. Combined with advanced sensors, controls, information technology processes and platforms, and advanced energy and production management systems, smart manufacturing has the potential to improve energy efficiency and manufacturing capabilities in various industrial areas

(continued)

(continued)

Name of institutions	*Description*
	Of the institute's $140 million budget, federal funds from the Department of Energy's high-tech manufacturing division have already been set at $70 million for more than five years and the rest are allocated to matching funds. The institute will focus on combining information technology with the manufacturing process through equipment such as smart sensors that reduce energy consumption. For example, the institute will collaborate with the Department of Energy's "Institute for Advanced Composites Manufacturing Innovation" to test advanced sensors in carbon fiber production. The institute expects to sign partnerships with more than 200 companies, universities, national laboratories, and non-profit organizations. Microsoft Corp., Alcoa Inc., Corning Inc., ExxonMobil, Google, the National Renewable Energy Laboratory, and numerous small companies are their partners. The institute plans to launch five centers. Those are planned to be established and operated in collaboration with universities and laboratories in each region, such as in California (UCLA), Texas (Texas A&M), North Carolina (North Carolina State University), New York (Renselaer Polytechnic Institute), and Washington (Pacific Northwest National Laboratory), focusing on technology development and transfer, and on human resource education
RAPID-Rapid Advancement in Process Intensification Deployment Institute	On December 9, 2016, the Department of Energy's Office of Energy and Renewable Energy (EERE) announced that a consortium led by the American Institute of Chemical Engineers would be the fourth research institute sponsored by the Department of Energy, which would be a key step in its efforts to double US energy productivity in 2030. RAPID, which has received $70 million in federal funding along with private cost sharing more than 130 partners, focuses on making a technological breakthrough that improves domestic energy productivity and energy efficiency by more than 20% within five years in the manufacturing process of industries such as oil, gas, pulp, paper making, and various domestic chemical manufacturers

(continued)

(continued)

Name of institutions	*Description*
	Traditional chemical manufacturing relied on large-scale energy-intensive processes. The new agency will raise the leverage of the modular chemical process strengthening method by combining various complex processes, such as integrating mixing, reaction, and separation into a single step, with goals of improving energy productivity and efficiency, reducing work costs, and reducing waste. The rapid development of the process can drastically reduce the space of facilities in factory workplaces and reduce waste while efficiently using raw materials. For example, by simplifying and reducing the process, this approach enables direct natural gas purification from the source, preventing half the energy loss that occurs during the current ethanol cracking process. Even considering the chemical industry alone, these technologies can save more than $9 billion in process costs in the United States
NIIMBL-National Institute for Innovation in Manufacturing Biopharmaceuticals	On December 16, 2016, the Secretary of Commerce announced that he would award $70 million to the new NIIMBL Research Institute. The institution is the first research institute to deal with the areas proposed by the industry and the first research institute funded by the Department of Commerce. The agency pursued an open topic approach, which allowed this new institute to deal with any areas that are not currently targeted by other existing institutes. NIST held the Industry-proposed Institutes Competition to provide a bottom-up topic selection process that enables industry-led consortiums to propose key technical areas of local manufacturing. The result was NIIMBL

(continued)

(continued)

Name of institutions	*Description*
	NIIMBL aims to transform the production process for biopharmaceutical products. Overall, the institute aims to further develop the U.S. leading position in the bio-farm industry, improve medical treatment, and produce qualified personnel to match specific technologies of bio-farm through the development of new educational programs. The announcement was made at the University of Delaware, which will be a partner with NIST of the Department of Commerce. In addition to federal funding, the new institute received an initial investment of $129 million from a consortium of 150 companies, educational institutions, research organizations, coordination organizations, non-profit organizations, and manufacturing expansion partnerships
ARMI-Advanced Regenerative Manufacturing Institute	On December 21, 2016, the Department of Defense announced that it would establish ARMI, at a White House event to commemorate the progress achieved by the National Network for Manufacturing Innovation, which has become the Manufacturing USA today. It will be the seventh laboratory led by the DoD

(continued)

(continued)

Name of institutions	*Description*
	New Hampshire's senator and governor simultaneously participated in the announcement of $80 million in support to establish a bio-manufacturing consortium headquartered in Manchester Millyard in a bipartisan manner. Led by a coalition including DEKAR R&D Corporation, the University of New Hampshire, and the Dartmouth-Hitchcock healthcare system, the institute aims to develop and biomanufacture transplantable tissues and organs for patients. DEKA founder Dean Kamen will lead the institute. The institute plans to pioneer next-generation manufacturing technologies to fix and replace cells and tissues. If this is successful, such technology will enable the ability to manufacture life-extension organs for numerous Americans waiting for a new skin or organ transplant turn. The institute will focus on solving the challenges of cross-cutting manufacturing in the way it produces new synthetic tissues and organs, such as improving manufacturing materials and technologies, the effectiveness of processes, reproducibility, accessibility, and standardization. Cooperation is expected with various fields ranging from 3D bioprinting, cell science, and process design to automated pharmaceutical screening methods to supplier chain experts for the rapid production and transport of these lifesaving materials
REMADE-Reducing Embodied Energy and Decreasing Emissions in Materials Manufacturing	REMADE was selected by the Department of Energy in January 2017 and will be operated by the "Sustainable Manufacturing Innovation Alliance" with its base in Rochester, New York. The institute will operate at $70 million from federal funds and $70 million from more than 100 private partners. The agency aims to reduce costs of technologies for reusing, recycling, and reproducing materials such as metals and textiles, polymers, and electronic waste, and to improve 50% of total energy efficiency by 2027. According to the DoE, these efficient ways can save billions of dollars in energy costs and improve the economic competitiveness of the United States through innovative new manufacturing technology

(continued)

(continued)

Name of institutions	*Description*
	The institute aims to reduce the overall life cycle energy use of materials manufactured through reuse and recycling. The institute performs this through the development of a new "cot-to-cot technology" for reuse, recycling, and reproduction of human-made materials. Manufacturing consumes one-third of the country's total energy use, most of which is implemented in physical products made during the manufacturing process. New technologies that recycle these materials in a better way can save 160 trillion BTU of energy each year for US manufacturing and the country, equivalent to 280 million barrels of crude oil or monthly crude oil imports across the country
ARM-Advanced Robotics Manufacturing Institute	The Department of Defense proposed the new manufacturing lab to focus on establishing the leadership of the United States in smart cooperative robotics. Cooperative robotics, along with humans, deals with advanced robots that carry heavy objects or handle complex or dangerous tasks that require precision on the process line smoothly, safely, and intuitively. They argue that as people collaborate with robots that assist them and efficiently produce high-quality and customized products with trust, they have the potential to change the wide path of the manufacturing area from national defense and space to automobiles and health
	The ARM, announced as the 14th 'Manufacturing USA' lab, was designated by the Department of Defense on January 13, 2017. The headquarters will be located in Pittsburgh, and the proposal group was convened by Carnegie Mellon University. The institute consists of a fairly large team, including 84 industrial partners, 35 universities, and 40 other groups from 31 states. Industry, state and the federal government share costs of $250 million total, of which the federal government bears $80 million. Clemson University's Center for Workplace Development will be in charge of the institute's manpower training program
	In a statement, the DoD explained the lab's needs as follows:

(continued)

(continued)

Name of institutions	*Description*
	"The use of robotics already exists in a manufacturing environment, but today's robots are typically expensive, performing only a single purpose, difficult to reprogram, and require isolation from humans for safety. The need for robotics gradually increases to achieve the precision required for the need for defense and other industrial manuals. However, the complexity of capital cost and use makes it difficult for small and medium-sized manufacturers to use these technologies. Therefore, ARM's mission is to create and deploy robotics by integrating industrial practice and institutional knowledge from various fields, such as sensor technology, end-effector development, software and artificial intelligence, material science, human and mechanical behavior modeling, quality assurance, etc., to materialize the promise of active manufacturing innovation ecosystem. Technologies that have matured considerably within ARM include cooperative robotics, robotics control (learning, control, repurposability), skillful manipulation, operation with navigation devices, perception and sensing, and testing, inspection, and verification" Referring to the need for more advanced organizations and cooperation in order for the U.S. to take a better position in international competition in this field, the DoD evaluated that domestic manufacturing robotics technology capabilities are currently fragmented

PART II

Statist Coordination Capitalism: The Case of Japan

Despite the challenges of globalization, not all economies have suffered from deindustrialization as did the U.S. Some coordination market economies, including Korea and Germany, have succeeded in improving their domestic production and innovation capabilities through strategic coordination. Through active state intervention, Korea succeeded in changing to a knowledge-intensive innovation economy (Kwon 2021). Coordination economies do not necessarily perform better than uncoordinated market economies. Japan's coordination economy failed to improve its international competitiveness due to stasis resulting from too much coordination and too little outside stimulus and openness to new ideas.

In the late 1980s, Japan was one of the most enviable economies in the world. Most countries tried to emulate Japanese companies' practices like just-in-time and trustful subcontracting. Japanese companies in the automobile and electronics industries, including Toyota, Sony, Panasonic, and Hitachi, grew into high-value-added manufacturers for exports under the statist industrial policy and dominated global consumer markets, challenging many U.S. industries and triggering a trade war with the U.S. (Schaede 2020: 1, 7).

However, since its bubble burst in 1990, the Japanese economy fell into a long and deep economic abyss, called "the lost two decades." Japan's average annual GDP growth rate was 0.8% in the 1990s and 1.4% in 2000 to 2007, in contrast to 9.7% in the high growth period of 1955 to 1970 and 4.4% in the 1980s (Calder 2017: 5). In late December 1989, the Tokyo Stock Exchange's Nikkei 225 index average reached almost 39,000, whereas 25 years later, the Nikkei index still stood at less than half of its 1989 level, despite massive stimulus efforts and a host of structural reform attempts. In the 2000s, Japanese electronics companies lost their market to Apple in the U.S. and Samsung in Korea. On Fortune's Global 500 List, Japanese companies fell from 141 in 1995 to 71 in 2010. The size of the Japanese economy globally shrank from 15% in 1999 to 8% in 2012 (Calder 2017: 7; Kazuhiko 2015: 56, 58).

Why did Japan's statist coordination market economy lose its way and undergo a long-term stagnation after the 1990s, in contrast to its growth until the 1980s? How can we understand such success and failure under the same institutions of the statist coordination model? Why do the statist coordination economies of Japan and Korea yield markedly different outcomes, while each facing challenges of globalization and digitalization? Why has Japan experienced more severe stagnation than Korea despite similar statist coordination systems?

In the late 2010s, Japan slowly revived its economy. According to a 2018 Morgan Stanley report, Japan presents "the most interesting and underrecognized turnaround story in global equity markets" (Morgan Stanley Research 2018). As of 2020, Japanese companies have become key players in cutting-edge technologies for the digital transformation, occupying dominant market shares in hundreds of critical input products. For example, Japanese companies provide more than half of the semiconductor industry's most critical materials and one-third of the world's semiconductor manufacturing equipment. Japanese companies command over 80% of the global market for specialty chemicals, and 100% at the top end, like ultrapure fluoride etching gas, and approximately 90% of the photoresist's world market, both highly valuable and critical for the production of current chips as well as development of next-generation 5-G semiconductors by Korea's Samsung and SK Hynix. Japanese companies anchor global supply chains with cutting-edged materials and intermediate inputs (Schaede 2020: 1-2, 69-70).

The revival of Japanese economy is due to recent reform measures, particularly industrial policy by the Abe administration (2012–2020), which successfully changed Japan's traditional innovation system to a new "open innovation" system (Jung 2020; Fukuda 2020, 2015; OECD 2021). How has Japan rejuvenated its economy since the 2010s after long-term inertia? What is Japan's new innovation system?

This part of our study of statist coordination capitalism focuses on the case of Japan to understand how a statist coordination economy can fail in adapting to the challenges of globalization and digitalization, challenges which are distinct from free-market economy and social coordination capitalism. The Korean case will be briefly mentioned in terms of comparison with Japan.[1] Notably, Japan was a fast starter in industrialization and globalization compared to Korea, with an advanced economy similar to the U.S. and Germany. Japan has been comparatively analyzed in political economic literature as an ideal type of statist coordinated capitalism. The pre-1980s heyday of Japanese statist capitalism, the subsequent long-term recession, and enhancement of new innovation capabilities with recent reforms illustrate the strengths and weaknesses of statist coordinated capitalism compared to other models.

To examine successes and failures under the same statist institutions, we focus on insiders' close collaboration in bureaucracy, business, and politics, termed "bureau-pluralism" by Aoki (1988), communitarian "Kaisha model" by Kazuhiko (2015), and "circles of compensation" by Calder (2017). The Japanese insider clientelist circles might work effectively for stable and incremental innovation in competition with rigid mass producers in the 1980s. But in the highly turbulent world economy and rapidly changing technology environment, closed collaboration among insiders blocked flexible innovation, and Japanese innovation outmoded and unable to compete. Circles of compensation brought investment-driven growth to Japanese economy until the late 1980s. But in an increasingly globalized and volatile world, Japan's insider circles resisted adaptation to the rapidly changing world market. Japan's circles of compensation enhanced internal stability, but intensified parochialism, as the so-called "Galapagos syndrome" of Japanese companies shows (Kushida 2011; Dujarric and Takenaka 2019; Calder 2017: 30–34).

In Chapter 5, we examine why the traditional Japanese statist coordination model encountered obstacles to globalization and digitalization following its enviable economic performance, and why Japan failed in reforms and adjustments, leading to long term stagnation. In Chapter 6, we explore the politics of transformation, and how Japan revived its

[1] For detailed accounts on the adaptation process of the Korean economy in globalization, see Kwon (2021), and my articles co-authored by Dr. Kim Kyung Mi in *Politics and Society* (2017) and *Journal of International Relations and Development* (2020).

economy in the mid-2010s through a statist coordination model. We will track the politics of change by focusing on how Japanese capitalism changed in the 2010s, and why Japan developed a new statist system rather than an American-style free-market system.

CHAPTER 5

Japanese Model of Capitalism and Globalization

Japan's surprising growth and development surged until the 1980s. The Japanese model of capitalism, including statist industrial policy, collaborative interfirm relations, lifetime employment, and trustful labor relations, had attracted worldwide attention. However, the situation changed notably. With the 1990s, Japan entered a serious, long-term recession called "lost decades" (Schaede 2020: 1–3). This chapter examines first what the traditional Japanese model of capitalism is, and how it achieved such surprising economic success. And then we explore why Japan failed to make a turnaround and suffered from such long-term recession.

Traditional Characteristics of the Japanese Capitalist Model

In much of comparative political economic literature, the traditional characteristics of the Japanese capitalist system stand apart from both the U.S. and British liberalist models, and the social coordination capitalist model of Germany and Northern Europe. In government-business relations as well as interfirm and employment relations, Japanese practices, including the developmental state's industrial policy and bureau pluralism, collaborative subcontracting and *keiretsu* system, and company union and collaborative employment relations, significantly differ from the liberal

H. Kwon, *Openness and Coordination*,
https://doi.org/10.1007/978-981-97-3352-1_5

free market system. Unlike the social coordination model and liberal regulatory states, the Japanese "developmental state" (Johnson 1982) played an active role in economic development. Japan's powerful Ministry of International Trade and Industry (MITI), established in 1949, evolving later into the Ministry of Economy, Trade and Industry (METI), played an aggressive coordinating role in choosing priority sectors for economic development and nurturing certain forms of collaboration between firms (Johnson 1982; Nakano 2011: 2–3; Schaede 2000: 2).

This Japanese capitalist model developed a flexible "lean production" system that overcame the weaknesses of rigidity and lack of innovation found in America's mass production system based on Fordism or Taylorism, and enabled continuous innovation in the production process. The Japanese model showed remarkable competitiveness during the 1970s and 1980s (Womack et al. 1990). The advantage of the Japanese model of fostering strategic industries and incremental innovation by the state through closed but trust-based cooperation led Japan to rise to world-class in industries including precision machinery, electronics, automobiles, materials, and heavy machinery (Johnstone 1999). Notably, Japanese electronics companies surpassed IBM in the computer industry in the early 1980s. In the mid-1980s, the market share of Japanese companies also grew significantly in the memory semiconductor market (Macher et al. 1998: 107–136; Cole and Whittaker 2006: 9). Among core elements of Japanese capitalism model, many political economists cite capital organizations, cooperative labor–management relations, and business relations that enable long-term investment along with the government's strategic industrial policy (Aoki 1988; Fujimoto 2004; Johnson 1982).

This chapter examines first what the classical Japanese model of capitalism was, and why it performed better in international competition. Then we examine why the Japanese model of capitalism turned problematic amid challenges of globalization and digitalization since the 1990s. We focus first on state-business relations, interfirm relations, and employment relations.

State-Industry Relationships

The Japanese capitalist model is most commonly referred to as the developmental state. Japan's state played an active role in choosing and nurturing strategic industries, through MITI's industrial policy. Japan's developmental state differs from an Anglo-American liberal state in that it strategically intervenes in the private economy. And unlike Europe's welfare state system, the state directly and strategically intervenes in supply, not demand.

Japan's MITI-led industrial policy selected and intensively fostered core strategic industries based on three main criteria: Industries expected to have high productivity growth rate (productivity growth), industries expected to increase income due to a significant increase in demand within the global economy (income elasticity), and industries expected to cause ripple effects to increase employment in other industries (employment relevance). Based on these criteria, MITI selected major industries including machinery, automobiles, and electronics, and intensively supported and fostered them through domestic market protection, tax benefits, and subsidies. MITI also limited domestic competition in order to maintain competitiveness in the global market. To this end, private investment was artificially adjusted to induce specialization, and company mergers were promoted to realize economies of scale (Okuno-Fujiwara 1991; Okimoto 1989).

Another characteristic of the Japanese developmentalist state was its "small government." Despite active government intervention in the economy, the state had no large bureaucracy or public sector, as in advanced countries. For example, in the mid-1990s, the Japanese workforce employed in central and local governments accounted for only 6.5% of the total Japanese workforce. In contrast, the U.S. had 14.2%, Germany 14.1%, and U.K. 11.9%. In terms of government spending relative to GDP, Japan was relatively small (Hatch 2010: 48, footnote 16; Amyx 2002).

Despite a small government, the Japanese state was able to coordinate relations with industrial elites using a distinctive method based on cooperative relationship, or *Gyoseishido* (administrative guidance). METI and the Ministry of Finance exercised great discretionary power. Industry also preferred informal forms of regulation, which allowed for the possibility of continuous negotiation with the government. Government officials were able to exercise their discretion based on the exclusive nature of informal cooperation and trust that prevents information leakage. The alternative method was often called *Amakudari* (or "hostage" system) in which retired bureaucrats were hired by private companies to ensure good relations with the government (Calder 1989; Okimoto 1989; Hatch 2010: 48–50).[1]

However, it is particularly noteworthy that Japan's developmental state is not dirigisme based on the state's unilateral plan and command system. Rather, it is characterized by circles of public–private insiders, called "bureau pluralism" (Aoki 1988, 1998), where representatives of specific industries take part in collective deliberation within the government (Lechevalier 2016: 76). In contrast to the dirigisme of Korea and France, where the powerful state initiates and executes developmental policies unilaterally, the Japanese statist coordination system works in a form of public–private collaboration. In this sense, the Japanese state is a "catalytic state," intimately bound up in networks of coordination and allowing them to work effectively without commanding them (Tiberghien 2016: 31; Amyx 2002; Okimoto 1989). Japan's bureau pluralism as a circle of public–private stakeholders also differs from the U.S . liberal state in which lobby groups of private industries, separate from the state, influence congressional committees (Calomiris and Himmelberg 1995).

In the process of strategic allocation of finance for economic development, for instance, the Japanese state did not unilaterally command. Instead, private bank and industry representatives collaborated with state bureaucrats for credit allocation. After 1958, the secretary general of *Zenginkyo* (Japanese Bankers Association) served on the Industrial Capital Subcommittee of MITI's Industrial Structure Rationalization Council, evolving after 1964 into the Industrial Structure Deliberation Council (*Sangyo Kozo Shingikai*). This private–public partnership committee within the administration remained the most authoritative voice on Japan's sectoral credit-allocation issues. *Zenginkyo* succeeded in defeating MITI's attempts to centralize government control over credit allocation in its own hand in 1962 to 1964, while bank and industry associations normally did not challenge government preeminence in the credit-allocation process (Calder 2017: 47–59).

In the insider circles of bureau pluralism, private interests primarily aggregated into a trade association and then approached its bureaucratic counterpart, called the "original bureau" (*genkyoku*), which is in charge of the industry. Within the government, the original bureau collectively

[1] Okimoto (1989) defines *Amakudari* as a bureaucratic system, while Calder (1989) sees it as an industry-led system.

deliberates and bargains with industry representatives under its jurisdiction. This system is pluralistic: private and public interests participate in policy-making. Bureau pluralism in the Japanese political economy is reflected in the deliberative council, most notably the Industrial Structure Council of MITI established in 1964. The Industrial Structure Council had 19 branches, consisting of 505 members, of which 108 (21.3%) were representatives of industrial associations (Okazaki 2001: 323–325).

This bureau pluralism of Japanese political economy had significant advantages. First, local information scattered throughout the industries could be incorporated quickly into government policy (Aoki 1988: 284–85). Also, trustful relations of insiders within the circles facilitated solutions to bottleneck coordination problems among industries. For example, Japan in the 1950s pursued development of its machinery industry, because its textile industry could not sustain Japan's international competitiveness. However, developing machinery industry required interindustry coordination. But the price of the iron and steel had to come down, requiring lower costs for freight, which depended on high-cost shipping. Individual industries alone could not solve this interindustry coordination problem (Lechevalier 2016: 76–77; Aoki 1998).

Japan's bureau pluralism worked well in the heyday of Japan's developmental state. The circle of insiders in the private–public partnership facilitated an appropriate and simultaneous investment supported by government policies, creating a path out of a coordination failure. Simultaneous investment depended on policy finance, which was coordinated through a "deliberative council system," a circle of stakeholders in a forum of public–private partnership. Under MITI's First Iron and Steel Rationalization Plan, the total investment in the mining, steel, and machinery industries rose sharply in the 1950s (Okazaki 2001: 331–334). The problem of interindustry coordination was easily resolved by bureau pluralism, in which associations of private industries, MITI, and Ministry of Transportation took part. Together they secured the necessary supply of steel (Okazaki 2001). MITI also worked with other related ministries, such as Ministry of Transport, to build necessary infrastructure and to resolve issues between industrial associations of the steel and shipping industries. Through the coordination of public–private stakeholders within the state, Japanese industries could be competitive. For instance, through bureau pluralistic coordination, the price of iron and steel declined enough to compete with the U.S. (Shimada 2017: 171).

Japan's statist coordination capitalist model, referred to as Japan Inc., saw rapid growth from 1960 to 1973, the heyday of Japanese industrial policy. Between 1960 and 1970, Japan's average annual real economic growth rate was 11.6%, a rapid growth due to a surge in exports in the heavy machinery and chemical industries. During the rapid growth, the Japanese government actively utilized industrial policies to strengthen the international competitiveness of domestic companies while pursuing trade liberalization and exports.

However, as noted above, Japan's statist developmentalism, different from Korea's authoritative developmental state during the 1970s, featured close negotiations and cooperation based on mutual agreement in a tight-woven network of government officials and business elites. In Korea's authoritative developmental state model, the state created and unilaterally guided a "master plan" independent of private actors, while in Japan, the state served as an industrial midwife through collective negotiations, not authoritative leadership (Evans 1995: 13–16). In Japan, relations between government and industry were informal, mainly characterized by repetitive negotiations or an "unusual amount of mutual consultation" between government officials, representatives of related industrial associations, and corporate representatives (Schaede 1995; Okuno-Fujiwara 1991: 278–279). Outsiders were restricted from participating, although the scope of key participants has expanded recently due to the participation of experts from academia (Hatch 2010: 50). Collective negotiations tended to take place behind closed doors rather than open to the general public. Between April 1986 and July 1998, the Japanese government introduced, revised, or abolished about 10,000 regulations. However, only 100 of them were publicly noticed prior to actual implementation, and only 16 went through a public comment process (Yomiuri Sinbun, Oct. 15, 1988; Kishii 1999, 56; Hatch 2010: 48–49).

The exclusive circles of stakeholders in Japanese developmentalism, like bureau pluralism or circles of compensation, worked effectively for rapid growth until the 1980s, through large and long investment by risk-diffusion, as well as through resolving bottleneck problems and interindustry coordination problems by public–private partnership. However, as international competition has changed through globalization and digitalization since the 1990s, the exclusive circles of insiders have become problematic with flexible and rapid adaptation due to the vested interests of existing industries and bureaucracy, as shall be examined later.

The circles of insiders were effective in developing trustful coordination, but deterred radical decision and reform.

Interfirm Networks

In much of political economic literature, Japan's long-term cooperative interfirm relations, including *keiretsu* and subcontracting relations, have been considered the source of innovation within industry. *Keiretsu* consists of horizontal networks of financial institutions, trading companies, and manufacturing companies, while vertical networks of subcontracting consist of manufacturing prime contractors (original equipment manufacturers, or OEMs) and their subcontractors. The *Keiretsu* system is a kind of network capitalism that enables secure collaboration and long-term investment through risk-diffusion among stakeholders in the network. Japanese subcontracting enables companies within the networks to achieve better incremental innovation than the vertically integrated U.S. mass producers (Lechevalier 2016: 74–75; Nishiguchi 1994; Lincoln and Gerlach 2004).

Japan's interfirm network is distinct from the American corporate network. First, Japanese companies developed subcontracting relations, while American corporations developed vertically integrated in-house production for stable mass production. For example, in the 1980s, approximately 50% of the total value added of vehicles produced by General Motors (GM) came from its in-house production, whereas Toyoda sourced about 70% of total value added from its subcontractors (Clark and Fujimoto 1991). In addition, subcontracting relationships in Japan were more trustful and collaborative, while similar relationships of the U.S. were held at arms' length.

The Silicon Valley model, an example of American innovation and entrepreneurship, is also a network-based model (Saxenian 1994). However, it is much less durable, with relationships between individuals who "have lunch together." By contrast, Japan's interfirm networks are based on cross-shareholdings, director transfers, and preferential trade and lending flows at the macroscopic level, and on typical customer–supplier relationships of trust, reciprocity, and relationship stability at the microscopic level. Japan's interfirm networks facilitate the mutual exchange of relation-specific information and cooperation (Williamson 1996; Lincoln and Gerlach 2004).

Japan's long-term interfirm relations do not rule out competition. However, competition might not occur at the market price level, nor at the level of individual companies. Competition between companies has often occurred at the level of quality and service, and at the level of affiliated blocs of companies. In Japan, excess competition has been perceived to yield harmful outcomes, affecting the overall national interests. For example, the government has often intervened to prevent excessive competition in winning construction contracts (Hatch 2010: 51–52).

In the Japanese model, vertical cooperative subcontracting relationships enable international competitiveness and continuous innovation, unlike the U.S. model. In U.S. market relations, no synergy results from cooperative relations because OEMS refuse to access the expertise of parts manufacturers (Helper 1991). Conversely, Japanese OEMs and subcontractors facilitate the flow of relationship specific information through cooperative relations based on relationship stability, allowing OEMs to use the expertise and creative ideas of parts suppliers from the early stages of product development. Cooperative learning and innovation flourish, as one company accesses the practical knowledge of another company as a source of innovation and commercialization of Japanese technology (Imai et al. 1985; Teece 1998).

Traditionally, Japan's R&D was mainly done by large corporations which in turn helped neighboring small and medium-size (SME) parts manufacturers to commercialize their parts in the production process. In Japan's *keiretsu* relationship between companies, the lead company helps to innovate and commercialize the entire network by leading major learning and innovation rather than controlling the entire process. And lead companies focus on their expertise with the help of parts makers working as satellites. This arrangement is possible because *keiretsu* was formed by companies that participated with available capital in the process of innovation and commercialization (Aoki 1987).

Cooperative Employer-Employee Relations

Another characteristic of traditional Japanese capitalism is that Japanese companies pursue continuous innovation (*Kaizen*) in the production process based on long-term collaborative employment relations, including lifetime employment, seniority-based pay, and enterprise unions. Unlike adversarial U.S. labor–management relations driven by free market principles, Japan's cooperative employment relations are based on principles of mutual reciprocity and one family or one village thinking. Long-term collaborative employment relations enabled Japanese firms to accumulate technological and business expertise, and to incrementally innovate in the production process as well as continuously modify products, making Japanese firms competitive with the rigid U.S. mass manufacturers.

Japan's long-term employment relationship is an implicit social agreement based on the loyalty of skilled laborers in exchange for job security and seniority-based pay from companies. Cooperation within Japanese companies based on these agreements became possible after labor abandoned its ideological struggle (Hatch 2010: 59). Management's interests lie in the company's long-term development rather than maximizing short-term profits or shareholder value. Japanese corporate managers act as arbiters between capital and labor. Japan's corporate governance model could be called an "insider" model or a "communitarian *kaisha* (company) model," while corporate governance in the U.S. and U.K. could be called an "open" model (Hatch 2010: 58; Kazuhiko 2015: 65).

For example, according to Booz & Company's (2013) thirteenth annual examination of CEO succession trends, approximately 97% of Japanese corporate CEOs are internally promoted, a much higher percentage than in North America and Western Europe. Additionally, 75% of Japanese CEOs have worked at only one company, while the figure in Western countries lies between 7 and 20%. In the communitarian *kaisha* model of insiders, where nearly 90% of directors and executives of Japanese companies have risen to their current position after long-term promotions at their current company or affiliates (Kazuhiko 2015: 65; Suehiro and Wailerdsak 2004), managers and employees of Japanese companies tend to identify themselves with the company, becoming socialized through a sense of unity and internal culture (Dore 2005).

Until the 1980s, the communitarian circles of insiders in Japan, including bureau pluralism or circles of compensation in state-business, *keiretsu* and subcontracting in the interfirm relations, as well as the *kaisha* model in employment relations, enabled Japanese companies to be internationally competitive through close collaboration and incremental innovation, compared with rigid Western mass producers. However, such Japanese practices became outdated because they could no longer handle new challenges rapidly, resulting from new international competition and environments, fundamentally changed by globalization and the digital revolution. The next section examines why the Japanese capitalist model suddenly dropped in competitiveness.

The Crisis of Japanese Models in the 1990s

The Japanese capitalist model, which had been in the spotlight until the 1980s, faced problems in the 1990s. When the bubble economy exploded in the early 1990s, a crisis rippled through the financial sector, and in the late 1990s problems emerged in the previously competitive manufacturing sector. Japanese manufacturing companies' profits declined, and large electronics companies suffered from a serious deficit. Global competitiveness in the semiconductor and electronics industry, which had been at its highest level until then, began to collapse. Japan's electronics companies, world-class until the early 1990s, have since lagged in global competition (Cole and Whittaker 2006: 4; Schaede 2020: 7–9; Kazuhiko 2015: 56–58).[2] The main response of Japanese companies was to establish new global networks by relocating production to Southeast Asia and other countries. As such global production networks were established through numerous negotiations and coordination between the Japanese government and corporate representatives, so also cooperative links were established between home and overseas production bases. Nevertheless, Japan experienced the adverse effect of delayed problem-solving as it transplanted the problems faced by domestic production to overseas. Why did the Japanese capitalist model, in the spotlight until the 1980s, suddenly fall into crisis in the 1990s?

First, international competition changed during the 1990s, as U.S. and European competitors learned and creatively adapted to the excellence of Japanese production models. U.S. and European companies, which lagged in competition, adopted new flexible production methods and proceeded with reforms emulating the Japanese model. As a result, Japan's competitiveness began to erode as rival companies sharpened their competitive edge (Kwon 2005; Cole and Whittaker 2006: 4–5). For example, in the 1990s, European and American companies made strides in information and communication technology (ICT) industry, while Japanese companies' growth weakened. As shown in Table 5.1, Japan's

[2] Recently, with the advent of automated driving cars pioneered by U.S. companies such as Google, Tesla, and Uber, even Japan's strong automobile industry is threatened (Kushida 2018a: 13–14).

annual average growth rate in exports of computer devices, communication devices, and electronic parts from 1995 to 2000 was -1.4%, 3.3%, and 3.1%, respectively, compared to growth rates of 9.7%, 13.6%, and 20.4% in the U.S., and 7.2%, 21.2%, and 9.0% in Europe.

European and U.S. companies began to regain competitiveness by imitating Japan's method and applying it creatively to their circumstances. U.S. and German companies reorganized their workplaces, based on the Japanese flexible model, into cross-functional teams to bridge the gap between concept and execution inherent in mass production systems (Womack et al. 1990; Kwon 2004b: 330–335; Kwon 2002: 51–65). Outsourcing and cooperative systems emerged between companies that utilize the expertise of various parts makers in key areas.

New methods of production have emerged. U.S. electronics companies which focused only on design have formed partnerships with the Taiwan's foundry model, creating organizations with much faster innovation capabilities than Japan, based on domestic circles of insider suppliers (Sturgeon 2002; Cole and Whittaker 2006: 5). In semiconductors, for instance, in the 1990s U.S. companies regained market share by moving away from vertically integrated production systems in favor of outsourcing and developing networks with external professional companies. U.S. companies have linked international production with Taiwanese module producers through global networks—the so-called foundry model, creating international networks using close links with those companies (Macher et al. 1998: 119–120; Chesbrough 2006; Sturgeon 2002). Competitors' "open

Table 5.1 Amount of ICT exports (Units: million US$; Growth rate: %)

Exports		*1990*	*1995*	*2000*	*Average annual growth rate 2000/95*
Computer devices	US	23,005	34,476	54,685	9.7
	Japan	18,584	29,521	27,558	−1.4
	Europe	40,119	66,460	94,131	7.2
Communication devices	US	4,063	10,933	20,680	13.6
	Japan	5,614	6,904	8,106	3.3
	Europe	9,541	26,440	69,179	21.2
Electronic parts	US	13,826	27,668	70,001	20.4
	Japan	14,678	43,270	50,348	3.1
	Europe	16,330	36,393	55,972	9.0

Sources OECD, ITS Database; Cole and Whittaker (2006: p. 4)

innovation system," based on digital technology and global production networks, showed significantly higher innovation capabilities and economic efficiency than Japan's "one-nation closed structure-based cooperation system" (Inagami and Whittaker 2005: 141–142).

Latecomers such as Korea and Taiwan also made strides by developing new adaptation models, while Japanese companies hesitated. For example, Korea's Samsung Electronics grew rapidly in the global market in the mid-1990s with the aggressive introduction of global standards in the cell phone business. Meanwhile, Japan's global market competitiveness weakened as it mainly focused on the domestic market, despite its global technological abilities. For example, Japanese companies' share in the LCD market decreased, from 62% in 1999 to 24% in 2002. In 2004, the average profit rate of Japanese LCD companies (Sharp, Toshiba, Hitachi) was only 5.4%, while the average profit rate of Samsung and LG in Korea was 34.2%, and the average profit rate of Taiwanese companies such as AUO, CMO, CPT (TFT), GDI, and Hannstar was 25.9% (Cole and Whitaker 2006: 7). Japanese companies have entered a vicious cycle of relative loss of competitiveness, resulting in reduced profits, and reduced reinvestment.

Until the 1980s, Japan achieved continuous and incremental innovation of products and production process based on the trustful *kaisha* model and collaborative interfirm relations within closed circles of stakeholders. This model enabled more flexible and continuous innovation, compared to short-term U.S. free market relations and vertically integrated corporate mass production (Baldwin and Clark 2000; Sturgeon 2002; Fujimoto et al. 2001; Fujimoto 2002: 23).

However, in the changed contexts of international competition, the Japanese model based on communitarian circles of insiders became inefficient and outdated, closed to new ideas, and slow to adapt to rapidly changing technology and international competition. Although Japanese *kaisha* was effective for incremental innovation in a stable world, it was ineffective for speedy decision-making and adopting radical and sweeping changes in a globalized world (Kazuhiko 2015: 65). Lifetime employment and accumulation of firm-specific know-how fettered employees from experiencing new ideas, thus isolating Japanese companies from a rapidly changing world (Dujarric and Takenaka 2019: 278). Japan's "circles of compensation" enhanced collaboration in a stable world, but intensified parochialism in the turbulent world Calder 2017: 34).

The so-called "Galapagos syndrome" exemplifies Japanese parochialism in a globalized world (Kushida 2011; Kazuhiko 2015; Dujarric and Takenaka 2019). Galapagos syndrome originally referred to the failure of Japanese 3G mobile phones that dominated Japanese markets but were ill-prepared for overseas markets, despite their advanced technology. In the 2000s Japanese companies developed a great number of products fitted for domestic markets but unable to be used outside Japan (Kazuhiko 2015: 64).

Japan led the world technologically in deploying a specialized high-speed communication networks by Integrated Services Digital Network (ISDN). But in the late 1990s the costly ISDN infrastructure was suddenly rendered obsolete by current broadband Internet access technologies, notably Digital Subscriber Line (DSL). Japanese firms also developed sophisticated mobile phones, but Apple's iPhone spearheaded a worldwide shift toward high-performance smartphones. Japan also pioneered a dynamic, multi-billion-dollar mobile Internet content ecosystem, confined to Japan, while the iPhone and Android platforms quickly became the dominant global mobile Internet platforms (Kushida 2011).

The Galapagos syndrome in the ICT sector, due to the parochially closed circles of compensation among insiders, affected the Ministry of Posts and Telecommunications (MPT), Nippon Telegraph and Telephone (NTT), NTT family companies (NEC, Oki Electric, Hitachi, and Fujitsu), as well as politicians (Calder 2017: 145–146; Kushida 2011: 281–282). The Japanese ICT sector's circle of compensation enabled a highly advanced information society based on optical-fiber and local area networks, due to the NTT family system's high profitability and high investment in the 1980s. Yet it retarded the development of the Internet as well as innovative telecommunications services, at high cost to the entire society. The circle of ICT insiders in Japan encouraged Japanese firms to create "their own parochial communication universe" in terms of protocols, standards, and performance levels. Japanese distinctive technical standards and services, congenial to the circle of insiders but unacceptable to foreign preferences, kept Japanese firms from competing in the world market, with higher costs compared to Korea, and the U.S. (Calder 2017: 146–150).

The bureau pluralism of bureaucracy, business, and politicians, praised for high growth until the 1980s, became problematic in the 1990s, deterring flexible adaptation to globalization and digitalization due to vested interests in a politically captured system (Shimada 2017; Calder 2017; Okazaki 2001). Until the 1980s, the financial circle of compensation consisted of bureaucrats, banks, industries, and politicians to achieve economic success by investment-driven growth through a risk-diffusion system. Japanese development banks, based on bureau pluralism, solved the failure of the free-market where new sectors and new technology tend to be underfunded (Vittas and Cho 1996; World Bank 1993). Due to their ability to promote strategic long-term and massive investment and defuse intragroup conflicts, the bureau pluralism of the financial circle contributed to Japan's high economic growth.

However, in a volatile and increasingly globalized world, circles of compensation often reduced the incentives of their insider members to respond rapidly and creatively to external challenges (Calder 2017: 30). The bank-centered nexus tended to prohibit new entrepreneurial entrants and venture capital from emerging in the market. Circles of finance, including the Ministry of Finance's convoy system, slowed the response of Japanese banks and insurance companies to dynamic globalization and rapidly changing technology (Calder 2017: 19, 166).

For example, public funds in the Fiscal Investment and Loan Program (FILP) contributed to high growth in the stage of catch-up industrialization, but deteriorated particular spending based on vested interests. The FILP, considered Japan's "second budget," is funded by postal savings and public pension monies. FILP is almost one-third of the size of the general account (GA) budget. As the financial bubble burst in 2000 and deposits surged back into the post office, the FILP peaked at over 40% of the size of the GA budget. In the 1960s and 1970s, public funds were by and large invested in programmatic spending for national development. However, in the 1980s and 1990s, FILP deteriorated as interest-induced politics grew more particularistic and less dedicated to industrial development, telecommunications, and science (Curtis 1988: 236; Noble 2010: 244). For example, the R&D share of Japan's public spending in 2001 was noticeably lower than in most other Organisation for Economic Cooperation and Development (OECD) countries. In contrast to Korea's significant increase in R&D, Japan's government-funded R&D spending as a share of GDP declined during the bubble economy (MEXT 2008: 9). Instead, a larger portion of FILP went to the Japan Housing and Urban Development Corporation because Liberal Democratic Party (LDP) politicians were interested in homeowners' votes (Noble 2010: 245–246).

Since the late 1980s, public banks and development banks have revealed rent-seeking, corruption, particularly the problem of political capture. Development bank programs, which contributed to high economic growth through investing long-term funds to new sectors and new technologies frequently underfunded by the market, were now used for non-performing loans due to interest-induced politics (Shimada 2017: 157). Bureau pluralism had advantages in the catch-up period with easy collection of scattered local information and coordination among industries and sectors. However, in a fast changing world, the vested interests of existing industries and bureaucrats made flexible decision-making and adaptation much harder.

For example, as a new industry such as IT emerged, the vested interests of bureaucrats and industries were difficult to coordinate. In Japan, telecommunications and broadcasting were under the jurisdiction of the Ministry of Postal Service (MPS), while the computer industry was under the jurisdiction of MITI. But, as the information and telecommunications industries began to develop, the two ministries struggled severely over jurisdiction. Development of Japan's IT industry slowed because drafts developed by MITI and MPS respectively were not realized (Kawakita 1985: 123–126).

As seen in the case of NTT privatization, the vested interests in the circle of compensation retarded Internet reform and development, which in turn increased communication costs and negative externalities to other industries. Telecommunication equipment producers like NEC focused on areas of special interest to NTT within Japan, rather than on broader global markets because they relied on the circle of communications dominated by NTT and were driven by lucrative price parameters provided by the NTT family (Okazaki 2001: 339; Calder 2017: 150).

To sum up, Japan's political economy, described as a "developmental state" (Johnson 1982), or an "bureau pluralism" (Aoki 1988, 1998) or "circles of compensation" (Calder 2017), had achieved economic success through effective allocation of resources and collaborative coordination in a closed and stable circle of stakeholders. However, the arrangement turned problematic in a changed context of globalization and technology. Japan's circles of compensation created strong vested interests as well as entry barriers for competitors in politics or business (Schaede 2012: 168). They revealed the inability to quickly adapt amid rapidly changing technology and competition. Circles of interests in bureau pluralism, bank-nexus, and industries such as communications and agriculture have directly worked to insulate Japan from external stimuli of a volatile world, and thus prohibited or delayed any flexible response to globalization and rapidly changing technology. The parochialism of the circles made industrial and innovative commons obsolete.

Delay of Reform in Japanese Globalization

Over decades of economic recession, Japan's government and business elites debated and pursued alternative policies to revitalize the economy. Many measures were implemented to rejuvenate the economy, including financial deregulation, dissolving the existing *keiretsu*, and expanding subcontracting to global value chains. However, Japan fell short of intended outcomes. With the onset of the lost decades, Japan lost its way. Reform measures to revitalize Japan's economy were delayed due to the tardy response, thus postponing any significant economic turnaround (von Staden 2012; Kazuhiho 2015; Warner 2011; Tiberghien 2007). By contrast, Korea, a developmental state similar to Japan, illustrates the speed with which it made deep structural reforms in the wake of the Asian financial crisis of 1997, with immediate economic growth from 1999 to 2003, following the deep recession of 1998 (Gourevitch and Shinn 2005: 123–131; Tiberghien 2007: 156–179). Why did Japan fail while Korea succeeded in structural reforms with rapid speed and depth? This section contrasts Japan's nationwide economic crisis with Korea's radical reform.

Vested Interests and Confidence in a Traditional Model

Even in such deep and long-term economic recession, Japan was slow to reform, and revealed inertia during the two lost decades. Upon a thorough study of Japan's reform measures, Lincoln holds that "the surface image of change is misleading" (Lincoln 2001: 5). Despite reforms including financial deregulation and abandoning the old-style developmental state, Japan's government continued to intervene in the economy. General mistrust in the market remained, and social considerations tempered the drive for economic efficiency (Lincoln 2001: 5; Kalinowski 2015). Corporate governance tended toward rigid conservatism, while pervasive reliance on indirect finance based on stakeholder dominance prevailed, although some marginal changes have been discernible since the mid-2000s (Calder 2017: 165). Fundamental reform of the economic system has been impeded, perpetuating economic stagnation. Japanese elites in both state and business seemed unwilling to embrace reform. Why the delay?

First, the ironclad business networks of *keiretsu* and closed subcontracting fettered any radical reform (Schaede 2012: 168). They insulated Japan from global competition, and directly resisted fundamental reform by emphasizing domestic collaboration, suggesting "virtuous capitalism" and rejecting neoliberalism.

Although neoliberal ideas spread societywide, particularly in academia and mass media, the anti-liberal forces supporting the traditional Japanese model prevailed in management and social affairs, as well as in bureaucracy. Vested interests remained strong across the circles of compensation. Conservatives of the dominant LDP were involved in almost all clientelist circles of interests. Most big businesses were also involved in the circles, while individualistic entrepreneurs' support for neoliberal reform was weak. Groups of high officials and conservative politicians with close links to specific interest groups managed to hold neoliberalism in check (Tiberghien 2016: 32–33; Calder 2017: 161–162).

For example, the bank-centered circles of finance in Japan, whose key members include Japanese Bankers Association (*Zenginkyo*), the Ministry of Finance (MOF), the Bank of Japan (BOJ), commercial banks, and long-term credit banks, and insurance firms, contributed to the high investment-driven growth through the system of risk-diffusion, particularly through the expansionary policy of "invest, then save" by the finance-land nexus until the 1980s. However, since the 1990s, the bank-land nexus favoring banks, politics, and real estate, inhibited not only the emergence of innovative technology-driven capitalism, delayed financial reform based on global financial standards, and impeded economic recovery through toxic loans. Bank-centered circles of compensation resisted adapting to global standards, and delayed reform by maintaining the economically outmoded but politically influential land-finance nexus. Even with the disappearance of long-term credit banks, the circles of finance failed to build a new alternative system. The circles' vested interests have impeded economic reconstruction, perpetuated stagnation, and made it difficult for the Japanese economy to adapt to global competition (Calder 2017: 27–29, 36, 43–44, 165).

Secondly, these elites could resist reform because their justification of the traditional Japanese model was widely shared. Bare interests and power cannot sustain policy effectiveness without shared belief and confidence. Resistance to neoliberal reform in Japan occurred not just at the macro level of national politics, but societywide at the micro level. Almost all reform-oriented CEOs in Japanese corporations faced strong internal resistance at the micro level (Kazuhiko 2015: 65–66; Schaede 2020: 85–93, 176–180).

Japanese state and business elites were confident in the old system and resisted reform (Schaede 2012; von Staden 2012). Despite the long-term recession and severe debates among state and business elites, Japan illustrates inertia concerning reform because they responded to new challenges with confidence in the old system. Japanese elites accepted the need for change, but they "framed it within a vision of a political economy inspired by the past" (von Staden 2012: 188). For example, a survey of 480 Diet members in 2005 revealed that Japanese Diet members did not want radical reform, although attitudinal differences existed between generations (Boyd and Samuels 2008: 48). After examining Japan's reform initiatives in detail, Lincoln accounts for Japan's delay of reform with "belief in the value of the existing system" (Lincoln 2001: 8). With confidence in the old system and vested interests in the existing system, Japanese elites cautiously observed that old ways "should not be carelessly abandoned in the hopes of a better performance" (Lincoln 2001: 8, 221). After analyzing the reform debates of *shingikai* (Council of Deliberation) for key policy-making, where elites in ministries, business, and academia prepared a wide spectrum of reform bills after a decade of recession, von Staden concludes: "The debates of key policy makers in 1999, after a decade of economic turmoil, show that they continue hold on to values and beliefs of a political economy that resembled that of the high growth period" (von Staden 2012: 199). Japanese state and business elites pursued a "virtuous capitalism" with a sense of joint responsibility, unity and sacrifice for the nation, rejecting neoliberalism and higher competition in the liberal market.

Japan's Globalization and Reform Delay

Japanese companies remained passive to changes, based on their confidence in the excellence of the existing model. However, beliefs alone cannot delay the implementation of fundamental reform without confirming and justifying in the practical context. Ironically Japan's globalization worked to delay domestic reform, rather than achieving reform as Korea did. To adapt to its competitors' global networks, Japan has also built a global production network in earnest, but domestic reforms were delayed until the first half of the 2010s. This section examines why Japan's globalization served to delay domestic reform, in contrast to Korea.

Japan's early production globalization consisted of establishing a nationalist global production network overseas by transplanting the home country production model. Reducing costs became the main purpose. This method resulted in a quantitative growth of Japanese companies, but home country production and innovation capabilities failed to improve Japan's international competitiveness, since it still relied on an outdated model. Relocation of the production base overseas contributed to a delay in reforming domestic production.

Japan turned to overseas investment in the 1960s amid a huge trade surplus. Since the 1985 Plaza Accord, Japanese companies further expanded overseas, with foreign direct investment (FDI) aimed mainly at North America, an export region, with the main purpose of avoiding export barriers. However, until the early 1990s, Japanese companies were still reluctant to increase overseas production, and lacked the vision to establish a full-fledged global production system. As of 1994, overseas production accounted for only 8.6% of the gross product of Japanese manufacturers. However, since the mid-1990s, Japan has continuously increased its overseas production, and as a result, overseas production in Japan's core automobile and electronics has exceeded domestic production (METI yearly surveys).

In particular, Japan's 1990s overseas investment aimed at full-fledged cross-border production based on an international division of labor in the Asian region. Asia's share of Japanese manufacturers' total FDI increased consistently in the 1990s, exceeding 40% of the total in 1995. A large number of Japanese SME parts makers entered Asia in the first half of the 1990s. For example, 74% of computer components, 59% of audiovisual components, and 84% of electrical and electronic parts were distributed in Asia in the mid-1990s. Since then, China has emerged as a new investment area as it has replaced ASEAN-4 countries (Hatch 2010: 74–79).

Establishing an Asian-based international production system was Japan's response to liberalization pressure from the U.S. and other Western countries (Schoppa 1997). It also was a response to Japan's late 1980s economic crisis. Japanese elites' two options were to dismantle the existing statist coordination and closed cooperation system and introduce unfettered markets, or to expand existing production networks overseas. Japanese companies' response to domestic problems in the 1990s was to expand in Asia because manufacturing companies investing in Asia were achieving tremendous success. When government officials actively encouraged entry into Southeast Asia, Japanese scholars applauded this direction. Faced with a crisis, Japanese elites sought overseas expansion of the existing system rather than overall system reform. This choice further delayed the reform of the Japanese domestic system. Next, we examine the uniqueness of Japanese globalization to analyze how Japanese companies' globalization process has hindered the reform of the innovation system at home, compared with Korea's globalization.

Uniqueness of Japan's Globalization

Globalization of Japanese companies was a coordinated process, unlike the free-market overseas expansion of American companies. Japan's globalization also differs from Western European companies' coordination methods in the sense that Japanese globalization was based on nationalism (Doremus et al. 1998: 3; Pauly and Reich 1997). Three characteristics of the Japanese globalization method include: (a) home country centralism based on hierarchical and close relations between the home country and its overseas branches; (b) transplanting from home to abroad the closed cooperative relationship model between companies; and (c) active state coordination. Let's take a closer look at these characteristics.

Regarding home country centralism based on hierarchical and close relations between the Japan-based parent company and overseas branches, production and intrafirm trade between overseas subsidiaries and other parts companies in Asia was based on Asia's international division of labor. Accordingly, overseas and home country production and exports are closely related (Kwon and Kim 2020; Hatch 2010: 83–84).

Many empirical studies on Japan's initial production globalization process show that in cross-border corporate expansion and construction of production networks, Japanese home-based parent companies control almost everything. Hiroyuki Itami argues that Japanese companies' overseas branches and headquarters are closely connected (Itami 1998: 21). Jochen Legewie holds in an empirical study of Japanese and American companies in Southeast Asia that Japanese overseas branches have much lower autonomy than U.S. overseas branches (Legewie 1999, 18). Similar studies by Mitchell Sedgwick and Takamasa Nakashima also point out that overseas branches of Japanese companies rarely modify the management principles and policies delivered from their headquarters (Sedgwick 1996:

29–30; Nakashima 1998: 14). Other studies, such as Singh et al. (1998: 155–79), Chen and Wang (1997: 96), Tu (1997: 73), Ali (1994: 121), and Takahashi (1996: 58) show that the relationship between Japanese headquarters and overseas branches is carried out through well-defined hierarchical divisions of labor. According to these researchers, Japanese companies that have expanded to Asia typically operate overseas branches in a top-down or bureaucratic way, complying faithfully with demands and instructions from headquarters in Japan (Ernst 2006).

Japanese companies sensed a need to maintain their home country's production methods when they entered overseas markets, and accordingly, transferred the existing Japanese production techniques, including on-the-job training and seniority-based systems, to overseas branches. Overseas local production has tended to rely on Japanese managers rather than appoint local staff. According to Mingsarn (1994: 84), Thai managers working for Japanese subsidiaries in Thailand are rarely promoted to top positions. In comparison, about 55% of non-Americans are in top management positions at overseas branches of U.S. companies, while only 23% of non-Japanese are in key positions at overseas branches of Japanese companies (Ali 1994: 119; Sedgwick 1996: 20; Stewart 1985; 2010: 14).

Another uniqueness of the globalization process of Japanese companies is that they have transferred existing subcontracting relations of their home country to overseas. Japanese companies' overseas local parts procurement system and interfirm relations reveal a tendency to transfer Japan's established vertical labor division system to overseas. Most Japanese subcontractors have begun overseas local production in the form of follow-the-leader investment (*zuihan shinshustu*). In fact, 56% of Japan's FDI in 1995 was made by Japanese subcontractors, most of which were follow-the-leader investment (JETRO 1997: 190; Mukoyama 1996: 7). According to an empirical survey of *Kikai Shinko Kyokai* (1995: 94), a Japanese mechanical industry association, Japanese subcontractors in the metal working industry followed their Japanese customers and relocated their production sites to northeast China. And in the automobile industry, when Toyota built a factory in Tianjin in 2000, major parts companies also built a series of factories in the same region.

This phenomenon happened similarly in China, Thailand, and Southeast Asia. According to Anuroj (1995: 113), Japanese companies in Thailand relied more on subcontractors from their home country than did Western companies. In the process of Japanese companies establishing an overseas parts procurement system based on subcontracting relations formed in their home country, existing local parts manufacturers have been pushed out, and Japanese subcontractors have replaced them (Suehiro 1998: 31). Based on this practice, in the 1990s Japanese companies mainly used parts made by Japanese subsidiaries or affiliated parts makers scattered around Asia. This trend was particularly prominent in electronics and automobiles, identified as Japan's core industries. According to Japan's MITI survey (MITI 1998: 213, 220), about 60% of exports to Asia by Japanese electronics companies consisted of intrafirm channels, and about 46% of imports from Asia also consisted of corporate internal transactions.

Lastly, establishment of a nationalistic overseas production network by Japanese companies is characterized by active state intervention and coordination, unlike the globalization of U.S. and Western European companies. In the process of building overseas production bases, Japanese companies worked closely with Japanese government officials, and the Japanese government actively coordinated and supported companies to establish stable production systems overseas (Mingsarn 1993: 24; Panglaykim 1983: 17). This cooperation was based on a shared perception that Japanese companies could increase their competitiveness by building an international "flying geese" division of labor led by Japanese companies in Asia (Hatch 2010). MITI actively intervened in the formation of these international divisions at the regional level. Japanese bureaucrats' intervention was mainly through development aid plans where the Japanese government identified and supported specific projects that individual countries would develop.

For example, in 1989, the Japanese government created the Overseas Economic Cooperation Fund (OECF) through the Japan International Development Cooperation (JAIDO) to support Japanese companies' entry into Asia. JAIDO formed a team with the Japan Business Federation (*Keidanren*) to provide low-interest loans to developing countries, which formed the link between production in developing countries and in Japan. The team provided low-interest loans to developing countries on the condition of purchasing Japanese materials and machines or hiring Japanese engineers. For example, the Miyazawa Initiative, an Official Development Assistance (ODA) package worth about $30 billion, provided to Asian developing countries, was mainly a loan that supports the construction of infrastructure for production, such as dams, bridges, electrical facilities, and telephone services. Through this assistance, the Japanese government has helped Japanese companies to easily build production systems overseas, and linked developing countries to purchase most of the equipment, materials, and parts needed for the infrastructure construction process from Japanese companies (Hatch 2010: 80–81, 95).

The Japanese government's overseas development aid process was ultimately carried out in accordance with the strategies of individual Japanese companies or corporate networks (Hatch 2010: 82, 86). For example, Japan has required Asian countries to accept very detailed conditions when importing technology from Japan, so that the introduction of technology from Japan becomes linked to the purchase of certain Japanese products or transactions with certain companies. It also placed restrictions on exporting products with Japanese technology to specific markets (Hatch and Yamamura 1996, 108).

The Asian production network, established in the 1990s with the overseas expansion of Japanese companies, was based on ODAs through cooperation between the Japanese government and companies, policy advice from bureaucrats, FDI, production technology guidance, and adjustment of export payments. In fact, Japan was the largest aid country of bilateral ODAs in Asia and the largest investor in FDI in Asian manufacturing. In addition, the Japan International Cooperation Agency (JICA) has deeply intervened in establishing industrial and macroeconomic policies in developing countries. For example, Japanese economic bureaucrats provided policy advice for Thailand's five-year economic development plan in the 1980s and 1990s. Japan's MITI intervened to establish and coordinate development plans for Asian countries through significant organizational capabilities in Asia (Inomatsu 1998, 57; Kano 1996, 81). Through these interventions, Japanese government officials and industrial managers promoted a common strategic goal of building a regional international division of labor structure based on various levels of technological development in Asian countries in the 1990s.

Effects of Japan's Globalization on Domestic Reform

Japan's statist coordination system, characterized by the construction of a nationalist production network abroad and close links between overseas production and home country, did not lead to a hollowing out of domestic production, as seen in the U.S. Rather, increased overseas production promoted exports of parts and materials. However, Japan's overseas production strategy relatively weakened the innovation capabilities of Japanese companies as a whole by avoiding and delaying efforts to reform in the face of international competition . Here, we will look at how Japan's globalization affected domestic production and innovation capabilities.

Unlike U.S. companies, Japanese companies had a fairly low rate of reverse imports from overseas. A closed structure based on Japan's selective relationalism and an overseas-home linkage structure prevented domestic companies and subcontractors from being damaged by reverse imports. According to an empirical study by Kimura (1996: 12), Japanese companies ensure that overseas production strengthens their home country's production system. Japanese parent companies effectively prevent reverse imports from reducing domestic production and employment, and maintain strong relationships with home-based supplies to counteract rapid overseas expansion without coordination. MITI's study of 900 Japanese manufacturers entering Asia in 1994 (MITI 1996: 73–74) illustrates this trend well. According to the study, even foreign companies doing business in Japan that have worked in Asia for 15 years or more continue to import and use a large portion of the intermediate goods from parts manufacturers of Japanese parent companies. This study examined the volume of intermediate goods the Japanese overseas branches imported from mainland Japan. The results of the study were contrary to MITI's expectation that imports from home countries would decrease over time and become increasingly localized. Another analysis by MITI (1998b: 260–261) showed that Japanese companies' overseas production in Asia did not reduce home country exports but rather contributed greatly to the home country's trade surplus.

Japanese companies' overseas expansion increased their home country's production due to an international division of labor based on the coordination system of the state and companies, as discussed earlier. As Japanese companies expanded to Asia, Japanese companies exported capital goods, intermediate goods, and high-value-added parts to Asia; in turn, Asian countries assembled the intermediate goods and core parts and exported products to the U.S. and Europe (Kawai and Urata 1996; Ernst 2006: 172).

For example, Japanese companies in the electronics industry have established a chain of subcontracting transactions that are actively vertically affiliated throughout Asia. In this structure, technology-intensive production was located in Japan, capital-intensive production in emerging

Asian industrial countries, and labor-intensive production in China and ASEAN-4 countries (Asian-4). For example, Sony in Malaysia runs a VCR assembly line in Bangi, Malaysia, imports integrated circuits or high-tech parts from Japan, and imports rather simple printed circuit boards from Singapore. Tape decks and other simple standardized parts are procured from Malaysian local parts makers or Malaysian-based Japanese companies. The Japanese automobile industry shows a similar structure of international division of labor. Toyota produced transmissions at its subsidiary in the Philippines, gasoline engines in Indonesia, electric parts in Malaysia, and diesel engine parts in Thailand (Hatch 2010: 82–83). According to a study by Tamura (1996: 22), Japanese multinational corporations mainly produce prototypes that require high technology in Japan, while standardized parts are mainly produced in Asia.

While Japan's coordinated production globalization, centered on overseas relocation of domestic production relations, had a relatively weak effect on the hollowing out of domestic industries, it delayed the reform of the domestic production system. Japanese companies were already experiencing weakening competitiveness before expanding overseas production, due to limitations in innovation capabilities from the parochialism of Japan's *kaisha* model, as seen in the Galapagos syndrome. Japan focused instead on quantitative expansion through global networks rather than addressing the problems of its nationally insulated and closed structure.

Many Japanese political economic researchers, including Schoppa (2006), Pempel (1998), Tiberghien (2007), and Hatch (2010), address Japan's delay in domestic reform along with the expansion of overseas production in the 1990s and 2000s. According to these researchers, pressure on domestic reform weakened as large companies, or key insiders who could demand domestic reform, chose to exit to Southeast Asia or overseas rather than raise the call for reform. In the 1990s, overseas production was a way Japanese companies could avoid high domestic cost structures, while overseas branches generated huge profits. For example, even when Matsushita, an electronics company, lost a total of \$211.8 billion in North American, European, and Japanese markets in 2001, it posted a surplus of 45 billion yen in Asia. Asaka Toshimasa, director of Matsushita Global Strategic Plan, confessed: "Without that profit, I wonder if we could have kept going the way we did for so long at home" (Hatch 2010: 144). Japanese elites did not abandon the traditional *kaisha* model by relocating production overseas; rather, by relocating the

Japanese problem abroad, they maintained the Japanese domestic system just as it was.

Continuing the rigid closed structure in the context of changed international competition was costly to Japan. Japan's closed relationalism based on the circles of compensation reduced transaction costs and enabled relatively flexible adaptation compared to the U.S.'s rigid mass production system and free market relations, until the 1980s, through strong insider ties. However, Japan's production system became expensive compared to the U.S. and Germany, which introduced an innovative and flexible system in the 1990s. With Japan's closed network limited to fixed insider trading, Japanese companies struggled to capture new information and opportunities, while outsiders with new information and opportunities had difficulty accessing existing network resources. These costs increased income imbalance, and lowered entrepreneurial and innovation capacity.

Weakened innovation capability was the most serious problem.[3] In particular, Japan's traditional closed system had difficulties in accepting new information and innovation from high-tech industries (Rtischev and Cole 2003: 3; Steffensen 1998: 519; Okimoto and Nishi 1996: 203). In the 1990s and 2000s, Japan's innovation capacity significantly declined. For example, in terms of citations received for its patents, Japan performed poorly by a significant reduction of non-U.S. citations of Japanese patents, contrast to the superior performance of Japanese patents in the pre-crisis period (Yamashita 2021). Using the patent data from the Institute of Intellectual Property (IIP) Patent Database, Ito et al. (2023) reveal that from 1995 to 2011, Japanese firms' patents declined. Many former superstar Japanese innovators have disappeared from the list of top assignees at the U.S. Patent and Trademark Office. Notably, Ito, et al.'s study (2023) holds that the trend of slowing innovation intensity is closely related with declining centrality in global production networks (Ito et al. 2023: 2, 8). According to the Global Entrepreneurship Monitor, Japan ranked near the bottom in innovative startup capabilities among 21 advanced capitalist countries in 2000 (Hatch 2010: 188). Japan's startup rate is only 3%, far lower than 14% in the U.S. Most of Japan's startups are

[3] Several theories and explanations analyze Japan's decline. For example, Fingleton (2000) and Posen (1998) focus on the mixing of incorrect policies. And Katz (1998) criticizes Japan's excessive protection and regulation from a neoliberalist standpoint. Some scholars argue that Japan's traditional culture delayed innovation.

related to large companies. Even compared with Korea, Japan's venture capital investment is low. Korea's ratio of venture capital investment to GDP in 2015 was nearly twice as high as that of Japan (OECD 2015: 103). Japanese venture startups independent of large companies struggle to find new consumers, parts makers, skilled workers, and capital outside the existing network (Hatch 2010: 188–191).

As Japanese political economy expert Yamamura (2003) points out, in the twenty-first-century era of innovation competition, the Japanese model based on cooperative insiders is bound to be less competitive. The closed structure of the circles of compensation weakens opportunities for innovation. Despite the efforts of Japanese overseas companies to survive the international competition of the 2000s, including opening subcontracting and using more local suppliers (Hatch 2010: 214–219), Japan seemed unable to actively respond to the crisis of the existing model. Domestic reform was still delayed. Japan, based on a statist coordination system, had difficulty undergoing a fundamental transformation, let alone consistent structural reforms, due to the lack of political will for reform based on elites' confidence in the traditional model combined with political instability until the Abe administration was established in 2012.

Korean Globalization, Compared with Japan[4]

Japan's failure in the process of globalization and digitalization does not mean that statist coordination necessarily weakens domestic production and innovation. Korea's experience of production globalization of major industrial companies since the late 1990s, a little later than Japan, shows different results. Similar to Japan, Korea developed a method of connection between overseas networks and home production, while establishing overseas supply networks using domestic parts makers. But unlike Japan, Korea's domestic innovation and production capabilities have been further enhanced through globalization. In what ways were the statist coordination systems of Korea and Japan different? What marks the differences between the two statist coordination economies in globalization?

[4] The Korean globalization experience, compared with Japan, relies on my articles, including Kwon (2021), Kwon and Kim (2020), and Kim and Kwon (2017).

The first answer may be the curse of the past for Japan. Japanese elites in both state and business had strong confidence in their traditional model based on high growth, as examined earlier, which made them reluctant to embrace reform at home (von Staden 2012). Thus, they transferred unilaterally their existing practices overseas rather than reversely learning from experiences on foreign soil. By contrast, the initial failure of Korean companies on foreign soil caused significant reform at home through learning from experiences in globalization. In the initial stage of globalization, most Korean lead firms pursued an independent overseas expansion rather than collectively going abroad with domestic partners, and they failed due to serious problems in establishing a parts procurement network in overseas production. For Korean companies on foreign soil, global parts suppliers like Bosch and Delphi were already doing business with competitors, which undermined small Korean latecomer companies' competitiveness. Local firms were cheap but hardly reliable in quality (Kwon and Kim 2020).

In order to overcome the latecomer disadvantages, large Korean companies tried to use their home partners. However, in order to use domestic parts suppliers, Korea needed to reform its domestic production system and foster domestic SME parts makers, because unlike Japanese SME parts suppliers, Korean SMEs were underdeveloped and less competitive due to Korea's traditional developmental strategy to exclusively support large conglomerates. In the process of globalization, large Korean conglomerates reformed their existing domestic practices like the exploitative and adversarial interfirm relations, reflecting upon their experience on foreign soil. Thanks to the Korean government's efforts to expand SME companies' innovation capabilities and develop the industrial ecosystem, Korean lead firms were able to successfully build global production networks.

The role of the Korean and Japanese governments differs in their statist coordination systems. In Japanese companies' globalization, the government actively cooperated with and supported them to establish a vertical international division centered on Japan in the Asian region. Yet the Japanese government delayed reform by not addressing problems in the existing production system. The Korean government focused on innovating domestic production models rather than directly intervening in the globalization of companies. The government recognized the globalization of major industrial companies as a crisis of domestic production, and focused on innovating the domestic production system.

Since the late 1990s, the Korean government has shifted its industrial policy from fostering national champions in the finished product assembly industry to parallel development of the innovation-led parts and materials industry. The focus moved from mobilizing physical resources to strengthening support for R&D. According to the OECD Main Science and Technology Indicators, Korea's R&D expenditure relative to GDP was only 1.7% until 1991, but increased to 4.3% in 2014, the highest level among OECD countries. Meanwhile, other major developed countries did not significantly change their percentage of R&D expenditures during the same period. The U.S. remained almost unchanged from 2.6% in 1991 to 2.7% in 2014, and Germany's R&D expenditure increased only slightly from 2.4% to 2.9% during the same period. Korea's growth in the scale of R&D expenditure reflects the government's policy direction to establish an innovation-led industrial system (Kwon 2021).

The Korean government's support in constructing a cooperative innovation ecosystem and strong industrial linkages enabled its new industrial policy to play an important role in domestic subcontracting relations in the production globalization of companies. For example, the Korean government strengthened its R&D consortium to create an innovative ecosystem. In this R&D consortium, in which government-funded research institutes, finished product conglomerates, parts companies, and university research institutes jointly participate, the government and government-funded research institutes serve as coordinators, and companies become the actual subject of R&D.

The government first conducts a needs survey in technology development, targeting researchers from industries, academia, and public and private research institutes to identify technologies that should be developed first. In this process, the government seeks help from various industrial associations. When a technology development project is selected, government-funded institutes such as the Korea Institute of Production and Technology act as practical government policy enforcement agencies. They conduct project competitions for companies, and public and private research institutes select participating companies, and conduct monitoring and evaluation throughout the project (author's interviews with Korea Automotive Technology Institute, May 31, 2010; Electronic and Telecommunication Research Institute interview, April 18, 2013; Korea Institute of Advanced Technology interview, June 24, 2015; interview with a camera lens manufacturer, November 12, 2015).

Korea's official innovation network and informal network between private companies and research institutes have provided mutual synergy to the collective innovation ecosystem and industrial commons. Information shared through formal and informal networks enables rapid innovation and increases the likelihood of potential innovation. Formal and informal innovation networks outside of companies play an important role in continuing technology development, despite the limited capabilities and conditions of SME parts companies that lack their own technology development capabilities (author interview of a semiconductor equipment manufacturer, November 19, 2015).

Korea's innovation capabilities of domestic production were strengthened and continuously reproduced rather than lost in the process of globalization, thanks to the state's intentional efforts to strengthen industrial capabilities, and private actors' adaptation of those state actions. Although Japan had greater competitive production and innovation capabilities, globalization delayed reform of the existing system and threw it into crisis. Resolving the crisis required a new vision and implementation of national development through political reform. Japan's domestic reform politics were sluggish until the Abe administration took office in 2012, bringing stable power and consistent policy enforcement.

CHAPTER 6

Transformation of Japanese Political Economy

The Japanese economy began to revitalize under Prime Minister Shinzo Abe in 2012. Through silent but significant reforms, Japan's manufacturers occupied key inputs components and materials, including LCD panels, semiconductors, batteries, and medical devices, in the global value chains (Schaede 2020: 68–69). Anchoring Asian supply chains with advanced materials and components, Japanese companies became key players in cutting-edge technologies for the digital transformation and occupied dominant market shares in hundreds of critical global input products. For example, Japanese companies command more than 80% of the total global market for advanced chemicals, including fluorinated polyimide, hydrogen fluoride, and photoresist, and 100% at the top end of the market (Schaede 2020: 1–2, 70). With Japanese companies' profitability, they accumulated large amount of cash to enable strategic global acquisitions and investments in Southeast Asia, the U.S., and Europe (Ando 2019). A 2018 Morgan Stanley research reports that Japan offers "the most interesting and underrecognized turnaround story in global equity markets" (Morgan Stanley Research 2018). As seen in Fig. 6.1, the stock price index of Japan's Nikkei peaked at 38,712.88 in 1990, and after the bubble burst, it stagnated for two decades, until 2012 with Abe's return to power, and the price index rose to 29,301.79 in 2022.

How has the Japanese economy revived? Throughout the two lost decades, Japan made reform attempts but delayed fundamental changes

H. Kwon, *Openness and Coordination*,
https://doi.org/10.1007/978-981-97-3352-1_6

Fig. 6.1 Changes in Nikkei index stock prices, 1981–2022 (*Source* Nikkei 225 Official Site; https://indexes.nikkei.co.jp/en/nkave)

due to the resistance of vested interests, including the iron triangle of bureaucrats, business leaders, and politicians. However, the second Abe administration initiated and implemented fundamental changes based on long-term development plans, with stable power centralized in the Prime Minister's office. The revival of the Japanese economy, so-called Abenomics, relied on expansionary monetary policy as well as fundamental policy and institutional changes. The Abe administration transformed the Japanese economic model of closed circles of insiders into an "open innovation" system. Despite efforts to imitate the Silicon Valley model, Japan has adopted a new hybrid system different from the American neoliberal capitalist system (Schaede 2020). What changed with the reform, and how much reform has been achieved? The next section examines the extent to which Japan has changed, and what has made the reform possible.

Transition from Closed to Open Innovation Systems

Before examining the politics of the transformation process, this section first explores the recent changes in Japanese political economy. From around 2013, the Japanese government, businesses, universities, and public research institutes pursued the Japanese version of the "open innovation model."[1] Japan's 2010s Open Innovation Strategy aims to create a new innovation ecosystem in which large companies, SME venture companies, universities and public research institutes, venture capital, and the government participate as major innovators (Jung 2020: 17–19).

Japan's traditional innovation system among large corporations was a closed system in which large firms established a network of innovation with some core business partners, coordinated at a central research institute within the organization. Until the 2000s, the internal research institutes of Japan's large corporations conducted applied research to drive innovation in products or processes. Japanese companies maintained a cooperative closed-structure relationship between large companies and a few trading companies. Large companies pursued exclusive protection strategies for technologies and intellectual property rights developed internally. Under this system, universities and public research institutes conducted basic research separate from market demand. Any cooperative studies between companies and university-based researchers were small and irregular, rather than full-scale comprehensive cooperation between organizations (Jung 2020a: 1; 2020b 17–18).

Although Japan's closed innovation system produced successful results until the 1980s, the innovation system revealed its limitations after the mid-1990s, not only because competitors like Korea and Taiwan were in rapid chase, narrowing the technological gap, but also because technology development was too rapid for Japan's stable but closed system to adapt. However, despite the long-term loss of international competitiveness, Japan's innovation system had not changed fundamentally until 2010 due to state and business elites' confidence in their existing model (Jung 2020a: 1–2). Since the 2010s, through gradual changes and reforms, Japan established a more open Silicon Valley-style startup ecosystem, as studies by Kushida (2017, 2018a, 2018b) show. Table 6.1 tracks how Japan developed open innovation system in which innovative companies

[1] The concept of "open innovation" was first proposed in 2003 by Professor Henry Chesbrough of Harvard University, and was noted as a new paradigm for innovation that intentionally distributes and utilizes ideas and technologies not only inside but also outside the company (Chesbrough 2003 "Open Innovation: The New Impact for Creative and Profiting Technology").

can grow, strengthen flexibility in the labor market, and establish an innovative ecosystem through industry-academic cooperation and openness of large companies.

Japan's first focus has been the change in traditional relations between companies. Many empirical studies in the 2000s argue that Japanese interfirm networks of the past acted adversely to rapid changes in technology and global networks. As a result, the closed interfirm relations, including horizontal *keiretsu* and vertical subcontracting relationships, are gradually pivoting to a new relationship between companies since the 1990s. Today, the boundary of the *Keiretsu* is hard to define. *Keiretsu* members are no longer stable, and their relationships are not reciprocal but sensitive to various tradeoffs (Lincoln 2006: 217; Schaede 2006; Lechevalier 2016: 77). Japan's subcontracting relations have also become more open and fluid compared to those of the past (Isogai et al. 2000). Today, Japan's subcontracting has become less stable and more sensitive to short-term gains.

For example, Nissan announced a revolutionary plan, in which it would reduce the number of subcontractors from 1145 to 600 and adopt open competition for purchasing, in contrast to traditional closed but collaborative relations (Lechevalier 2016: 78). The subcontracting relationship of Toyota, a representative model of Japan's close cooperative relationship, also changed in the 2000s (Nishiguchi and Beaudet 1999; Dyer and Nobeoka 2000). With the traditional closed-structure *keiretsu* relationship yielding to a more open form, Toyota's subcontracting yielded to more open relations with parts makers with new technologies in order to expand production to new product lines such as trucks (Hino) and minicars (Daihatsu) in a short period of time. Toyota moved production of electrical-related parts inside the company to meet increasing demand, which resulted in a reduction of the volume of orders previously placed with Denso (Ahmadjian and Lincoln 2001; Lincoln 2006: 224–228).

Although Japan's interfirm relations based on traditional *keiretsu* and subcontracting systems have the advantages of trust, familiarity, and easy organizational maintenance among internal companies, closed intragroup alliances are unable to take advantage of multiple combinations of production, such as materials, technology, and culture. Particularly in R&D, according to a Japanese study by Ritschev and Cole (2003), "R&D aimed at the inside of *Keiretsu* hinders the benefits of the alliance across *keiretsu*." Traditionally, Japanese interfirm cooperation has placed a taboo on trading across *keiretsu* groups. However, an empirical study focusing

Table 6.1 Japan's Innovation Ecosystem: comparison of the mid-1990s and 2016s

	Mid-1990s	*Change after 2016*
Finance The degree of venture capital	Bank-centered financial system: Most innovative companies raise funds through traditional bank loans	Growth of the venture industry and new finance; growth of independent venture capital; financing through the small and medium-sized capital market
Labor market Diversity and liquidity of skilled manpower	Long-term employment based on seniority; low labor market liquidity; Elite workforce guarantees lifelong employment centered on large corporations	Increased labor market liquidity; especially in IT and foreign companies; opportunities to work in large corporations and their prestige are lowered
Industry–University-Government Cooperation Industry–University-Government Linkage	Cooperation is difficult due to numerous official regulations	Active efforts of universities, venture companies, and governments to foster startups with innovative technologies of the universities
Large corporations and Small- and Mid-sized companies Synergy between large corporations and innovative SMEs	A closed innovation system based on research and development within a large company; large companies are not interested in transactions with startups	Large companies are more interested in open innovation systems; participate in venture funds; and form collaborative transactions with startups
Innovative Entrepreneurship (Entrepreneurship): A social system to foster innovative entrepreneurs	Innovative companies have a low reputation for large corporations and governments	Becoming an innovative company gains high social confidence in large corporations; the number of successful startups increases
Professional services Specialist services for entrepreneurs	The professional service environment is poor	Law firms and accounting firms increase in services focused on startups; foster startups and benefit from them

Source Kushida (2018b: 94)

on interfirm relationships among 128 Japanese electronics companies, conducted by Japanese interfirm relations experts Lincoln and Gerlach, reveals that changes in interfirm relations began to appear in the 1990s (Lincoln and Gerlach 2004). In other words, between 1986 and 1991, Japanese companies mainly formed alliances with other companies within the same group, while between 1992 and 1997 this form of traditional alliances gradually decreased. The meaning of traditional vertical *keiretsu* had almost disappeared in R&D. Lincoln and Gerlach (2004) report the changes in the Japanese *keiretsu* companies as follows:

> Japan's business linkage has symbolized the [Japanese model] over the past 50 years through stable macro-structural cooperation represented by *Keiretsu*. ... [However] Post-bubble networks are different: ... it has become less quantal and less *Keiretsu*. Japanese capitalism is still network capitalism. ... However, it is fundamentally changing. In a different way than in the past, companies are using interfirm relations to strengthen their business agenda. Rather than being bound by *Keiretsu*, they are pursuing partnerships that can benefit the competitiveness of a company (Lincoln and Gerlach 2004: 103, 354)

Traditional Japanese interfirm relations, based on a closed relationship, became a disadvantage for innovative startup companies striving to emerge. By contrast, in a new environment, startups find it easier to get established and to cooperate with existing conglomerates. Recently, horizontal cooperation between large companies or between large companies and venture companies is increasing in Japan. For example, 10 Japanese companies, including Honda, Konica Minolta, and Onkyo, jointly established three companies for robotics-related businesses. The creation of such a coalition company is unusual in Japan (Kushida 2018a: 25). Changes in relations between companies, along with changes in the finance model, contribute greatly to the emergence and growth of innovative companies.

Changes in Finance and Growth of Venture Companies

Japan's increase in innovative venture companies relies heavily on the institutional reform of the finance model, along with changes in interfirm relations. Following World War II, Japan's financial system was bank-centered. Banks were basic capital mediation organizations that loaned to industries and households, based on domestic savings. In Japan's main bank system, large banks monitored companies that received their loans. This system was not designed for venture capital investing in high-risk innovative companies with new technologies. In the 1990s, when venture businesses became popular, entrepreneurs who wanted to establish startups had to provide personal assets as collateral to secure loans from banks. It was personally too risky to pursue innovative entrepreneurial projects because failure, under this finance model, could soon result in personal bankruptcy (Imai, ed. 1998). This bank-centered system lasted into the 2000s. Since then, many venture investment companies emerged, but mostly as subsidiaries of traditional financial companies.[2] Employees of these venture companies were evaluated for individual performance by a point subtraction system, which forced them to opt for risk-averse behavior (Kushida 2018a: 17).

However, as shown in Table 6.2, Japan's innovation ecosystem began to change significantly in the 2010s. Compared to the earlier absence of venture capital in Japan, recently it has grown significantly. Venture capital's domestic investment in 2018 (excluding the investment of CVC Japan, a corporate venture capital firm) was 164 billion yen, showing an increase for the sixth consecutive year. Venture firms built by existing large corporations (CVC), not by venture capital, also increased significantly. The investment amount in 2018 was about 350 billion yen, an eight-fold increase from 2013. In addition, Japanese startup investment also steadily increased year by year, reaching an all-time high of about 446.2 billion yen in 2019, from 70.5 billion yen in 2010. The number of Japanese startup companies also increased significantly, from 968 in 2010 to 2055 in 2018, just before the COVID-19 pandemic (Cha 2020; Jung 2020: 103).

The increase in venture capital also affected the policy of fostering ventures in universities. As of 2020, many university-based venture companies are growing in Japan, including Cyberdyne from Tsukuba University, which makes robot suits that help humans move, Spiber from Keio University, which makes spider synthetic silk, and Nuprotein, which

[2] Reform of Japan's finance system does not lead to Anglo-Saxon-style free-market, in contrast to many neoliberals' expectation. Credit financing, particularly for SMEs, continues (Aoki, Jackson, and Miyajima 2007). Most companies rely on self-financing, rather than on stock market. There also is some revival of cross-shareholding (Nitta 2009; Lechevalier 2016: 79).

Table 6.2 Comparison on the amount of venture capital investment (Unit: billion dollars)

Country | Years	*2010*	*2015*
Japan	1.29	1.11
Germany	0.97	0.87
France	0.80	0.84
United Kingdoms	0.79	0.62
Israel	0.41	0.65
Korea	0.96	1.78
USA (total)	23.52	59.70
Silicon Valley	9.39	27.76

Source Kushida (2018b: 89, Table 4.3)

was established by professors in Nagoya University. In addition, new innovative startups are being created in government-affiliated research institutes, including Agri Info Design that develops GPS apps for farmers to help them drive tractors more easily (Kushida 2017: 12–15).[3]

Japan's recent "open innovation ecosystem" means that Japanese capitalism has become a system based on the synergy between innovative startups and established large companies, which remain at the center. In Japan, large companies traditionally have been reluctant to trade and collaborate with startups. However, since the 2010s, the cooperative symbiosis between innovative startups and existing large companies has played an important role in the tremendous growth of the startup ecosystem in Japan.

For example, Preferred Networks, a startup founded in 2014 by computer scientists at the University of Tokyo, is developing AI-based machine learning, algorithms, and tools, and is working with Toyota, a Japanese auto industry giant, and Fanuc, a factory robot producer, to develop new factory robotics. And Komatsu, the world leader in the heavy equipment industry, is increasing its competitiveness by actively utilizing AI innovation. Komatsu purchased sensor technology and artificial intelligence systems for automated dump trucks from outside sources and integrated them internally. Komatsu also is partnering with drone companies through open innovation (Kushida 2017: 17, 27–28).

Recently, large companies have begun to actively collaborate with innovative startups and sometimes actively engage in mergers and acquisitions

[3] For list of specific venture startup companies, see Kushida (2017: 21–22, Fig. 3).

to benefit from their innovative technologies. Implicit market protection is now difficult to find in Japan. Large conglomerates expanded their collaboration with external innovators to create new core businesses and find new sources of innovation. These open innovation strategies are strengthening large companies' connection with domestic innovation startups as well as with Silicon Valley innovation companies in the U.S. (Kushida 2017: 2, 28–37).

Establishing Industry-Academic Cooperative Relations

Japan is shifting its industry-academic cooperation system to a more open innovation model away from closed and self-centrist, dedicated to commercial R&D within large companies. These efforts began in earnest in the 2010s, and show clear signs of change as of 2020. We identify four markers in particular.

First, research funds earned by universities through joint research, entrusted research, and intellectual property with industries increased by 4.3% year-on-year to about 343.2 billion yen in 2018. The amount of research funds imported from pure private companies, excluding public funds, was 107.5 billion yen, a 12.0% increase from the previous year. In terms of content, about two thirds of funds from joint studies of private companies and universities. Income from joint research increased from only 1.5 billion yen in 2003 to 68.3 billion yen in 2018. The number of industry-academic joint studies also increased by about 2.5 times from 11,054 in 2005 to 27,383 in 2018 (MEXT 2018; Jung 2020: 41–42). Although small-scale studies (with fund of less than 10 million yen) account for 95.5%, and large-scale studies (with more than 10 million yen) account for only 4.5%, the increase is significant compared to the first half of the 2000s.

Second, as of 2018, the number of patent applications was 9529, showing a continuous increase over the previous five years. The number of patents held by Japanese universities increased significantly from 2755 in 2005 to 46,038 in 2018. The intellectual property activities of Japanese universities clearly have increased. Japanese universities' revenue from intellectual property rights in 2005 was less than 1 billion yen, increasing to 6 billion yen in 2018. These universities' intellectual property production activities show a marked increase, especially after the Abe administration's university reform in 2012 (MEXT yearly database; Jung 2020: 45–47).

Third, universities' industry-academic cooperation includes venture company activities. Universities in Japan are experiencing a venture boom, and related activities are rapidly increasing. According to a survey by the Ministry of Economy, Industry and Energy, the number of venture companies at universities increased from only 97 in 1994 to 2278 in 2018 (METI 2019). Sales from these venture companies' outputs have continued to increase since the global financial crisis, more than doubling from 105.3 billion yen in 2007 to 232.7 billion yen in 2016 (Jung 2020: 53–56).

Fourth, expansion of staff for university research administrators allows administrators to plan and manage research activities with researchers, and provide support activities to researchers to increase their results. The research administrator needs a broad understanding of the entire process to guide it from the discovery of technical "seeds" to commercialization. In Japan, 169 institutions assigned university research administrators in 2018, an increase of 23 institutions from 146 in 2017. The number of university research administrators also increased, from 696 in 2013 to 1,459 in 2018. In addition, 42% of research administrators are from private companies, 40% from universities, and 10% from public research institutes. They are mainly in their 50s and 60s with extensive work experience in companies (MEXT 2018; Jung 2020: 49–50).

Innovation Success Story: Biotech Industry

Japan's changed innovation system strengthened innovation capabilities in its high-tech industries. Here, as a representative example, we will briefly look at the growth process of Japan's biotech industry. In the 1980s and 1990s this industry lagged behind major European countries and the U.S. in terms of technology development and commercialization (Okamoto 2007: 2–7). Until the 1990s, biotech industry's innovation structure showed the characteristics of Japan's typical innovation structure of the past, when commercialization efforts led by large companies dominated the patent process in the pharmaceutical sector, accounting for 86% of total biotechnology patents. In contrast, most U.S. biotech patents occurred at universities, research institutes, and venture companies (Lehrer and Asakawa 2004: 927). Unlike the U.S., cooperation and joint research between Japanese universities and companies was not robust.

Since the 2000s, Japan's biotech industry has grown rapidly. In the early 1990s, Japan's biomedical sector accounted for only 12.6% of global sales, but in 2005, it accounted for about 22% (Okamoto 2007: 5). In the 1990s only 100 biotech ventures existed, but in 2017 about 659 biotech ventures existed at universities alone, forming the core of Japanese university-based ventures, along with 614 IT-related ventures. In 2017, the number of biotech-related startups increased by about 13%, compared to the previous year, with 86 startups growing (Rodergas 2018: 30–31; Kim Si-yoon 2012: 698–699).

Looking specifically at the bioplastics industry, as the existing petrochemical-based plastics industry declined due to environmental and climate concerns, bioplastics emerged as a new, alternative technology industry that could cope with international environmental regulations. According to the 2013 Kyoto Protocol, the competitiveness of the petroleum-based polymer industry that generates carbon dioxide had weakened due to the introduction of carbon taxes and production of eco-friendly polymer materials based on new biotechnology. In this high-tech innovation industry, Japan is growing rapidly through an open innovation system. For example, from the early 2000s to 2012, in terms of bioplastic patent applications by nation, Japan leads with 55%, followed by the U.S. with 13% and Europe with 5% (Jung et al. 2014: 498). This increase in Japan's patent applications is due to an open cooperation system. Of Japan's top 10 applicants, Toyota applied for 56 patents, Toray for 24 patents, Teijin for 20 patents, and Musashino Chemical Laboratory for 14 patents. Japan's open innovation system is mainly characterized by the cooperative relationship of three or more entities from industry and university (Jung et al. 2014: 500; Jung 2020: 59–99).

Open innovation in the Japanese bioplastics industry shows the developmental and strategic nature of Japanese government intervention. Japan has focused on the use of biomass since the early 2000s, and in the 2010s, the government actively intervened to develop and utilize technologies for bioplastics. In 2002, related government departments enacted a comprehensive Biotechnology Strategy Overview, and in 2007, a Biotechnology Strategy Roadmap was announced to introduce measures to promote the utilization of biomass. In addition, the 2010 Basic Plan for the Utilization of Biomass focused on strategies to accelerate the commercialization of next-generation biomass such as cellulose and algae, and technology development for the utilization of biomass by linking industry, university, and government research institutes (Jung et al. 2014: 504).

Changes in State's Role: New Developmentalism Under the Abe administration

Although Japan was influenced by the U.S.-style free-market open system, it opted instead for a statist coordination model of open networks through state's active role for developmentalism. Reforms in Japanese capitalism, including more open interfirm relations, venture-friendly changes in finance, and new collaborative industry-academic relations, resulted from private companies' strategic reflection upon the competitive nature of rapid technology changes and the rise of neighboring competitors including Korea, Taiwan, and China. Reform also resulted from changed incentives introduced by the government's new developmentalism (Lechevalier 2016: 80). Japanese firms' motives to engage in open innovation mainly emerged from the government's industrial policy. Similarly, new industry-academic cooperation and the rise of venture companies in the 2010s were based on the government's reform of universities and new industrial policy to nurture venture companies. As the will and efforts of the state materialized, innovation efforts to redirect major private actors, especially companies and universities, began to take hold. In this section we examine to what extent new developmentalism, particularly under the Abe administration, differs from the U.S. free-market system, as well as from its traditional developmental state.

Japan's traditional industrial policy of coordination had been eroded since the 1990s, due to the influence of neoliberalism and much academic criticism of the developmental state. Traditional bureau pluralism broke down (Toya et al. 2003; Lechevalier 2016: 78–79). However, Japan's developmentalism did not disappear completely regaining ascendancy in a new form under the Abe administration. Starting in 2012, the Abe administration reformed industrial policy through a new Industrial Competitiveness Council and a new Deregulation Council. "Abenomics," promoted during this period, featured three main aspects: aggressive policy for monetary expansion, fiscal stimulus for economic revitalization, and economic structural reform. Abe's new industrial policy implemented a package of structural reforms to pursue open innovation systems, along with liberal policies including deregulation, special economic zones, and efforts to join the Trans-Pacific Partnership (TPP) (Tiberghien 2016: 51–54; Fukuda 2015, 2020; OECD 2021).

The Abe administration's new industrial policy differs from both Anglo-Saxon-style neoliberalism and European social coordination model, in the sense that the state leads developmental initiatives through strategic industrial policies (Watanabe 2020; Kalinowski 2015). Important differences exist also between the Japanese and U.S. models of state intervention. Following basic defense research at the U.S. Department of Defense (DoD), the state pursues innovative commercialization through spin-offs, and plays a major role in economic innovation by strengthening its research capabilities. However, the DoD tends to focus on basic research, such as general infrastructure construction, that is neutral to market actors and available to everyone, based on liberal principles. In Japan, a developmental state, most research support corresponds to a strategic industrial policy, which selectively fosters economic and industrial aspects of major industries. For example, Japan recently strategically fostered its biotech industry for economic growth, along with industries such as robotics for health management and advanced sensor (Rodergas 2018: 32; Kushida 2018a: 23–24).

The Abe's strategic developmentalism also differs from Japan's existing industrial policies, with a focus on R&D support rather than direct subsidies, as well as on nurturing an industrial innovation ecosystem rather than supporting individual industries. In the 1980s and 1990s, Japan's industrial policies mainly focused on market-correcting policies, but from the late 1990s, they shifted back to strategic selective fostering of industries. While earlier industrial policies mainly focused on supporting large companies, recent industrial policies focus on nurturing innovation capabilities of large companies, SME venture companies, universities, and on creating open innovation networks that bring them together. The core of Japan's new industrial policy is to link universities' technologies, knowledge, and inventions so that they can be commercialized quickly through strong links with companies (Kim Si-yoon 2012: 14).

While the Japanese government's industrial innovation efforts began in the 1990s, only with the Abe administration did these efforts lead to a full-scale state-led reform. Throughout the 2000s and the prior Abe administration, the Japan's industrial policies were small-scale, dispersed, and inconsistent. While in the 1990s Japan's traditional industrial policies were criticized as engendering dysfunctional effects and causing economic recession through the closed nature of interfirm relations (Tilton 1994; Beason and Weinstein 1996; Rodrik 1996), the Japanese developmental state's role receded and its industrial policies reduced to bare survival (Hoshi 2017). From 1996 to 2006, Japan experienced some neoliberal reforms, particularly under the Koizumi administration. However, as most experts of Japanese political economy point out, Japan during this period featured "decentralization with serious inertias in the system of political economy" (Tiberghien 2016: 27; Amyx 2004; Katz 2003; Schoppa 2001; Lincoln 2001; Tiberghien 2007). After Koizumi left in 2006, Japan underwent inertia with pause and reversal of reform until 2009, followed by social backlash to neoliberal reforms from 2009 to 2011 (Tiberghien 2016: 29–30).

However, with Abe in 2012, Japan turned around with new state-led reform. Abe's developmentalism may be similar to Koizumi's neoliberalism in the sense that it pursued further liberalization to dissolve the traditional closed circles of vested interests. But Abe's developmentalism differs from Koizumi's neoliberalism in the sense of its return to state-led initiative. In short, Abe's developmentalism is open but state-led coordination (Tiberghien 2016: 30).

Abe's developmentalism also differs from traditional industrial policies in the sense that it developed a comprehensive and full-scale policy to link industries and industry-social policies, rather than the traditional policy of protecting and promoting individual industries (Lee 2023: 144; OECD 2021). Unlike Kozizumi's neoliberalism which focused on regulation reform with stable fiscal balance, Abe pursued a comprehensive developmentalism which closely linked expansionary fiscal and monetary policies with structural reform and growth strategy (Lee 2018b: 98–99). Rather than focusing on simple redistribution of financial resources, Abe's new industrial and innovation policies encompassed traditionally separated policy areas such as education, industry, and science and technology. In particular, unlike the Democratic government (2009–2011) which pursued sound fiscal and social policy, Abe's developmentalism linked social policy with industrial developmentalism, as seen in Japan's "Society 5.0" (Holroyd 2022; Fukuyama 2018; OECD 2021).

The Abe government's developmental policies are well illustrated in the *Japan Revitalization Strategy* which had been revised and expanded since 2013, as seen in Table 6.3. According to the roadmap, the government first needed to boldly support capital investment so that private companies can exert their maximum capabilities and create new businesses at an unprecedented rate. Second, as an economic reconstruction project, the roadmap emphasized regulatory reform and worker training, especially for women and youth who had not had training. Third, it created new markets through the development of new products, services, and systems. These measures were designed to transform Japan into a

Table 6.3 Abe's state-led developmental strategies

Year	*Title*	*#Key Performance Indicators (#new)*
2013	Japan Revitalization Strategy: Japan Is Back	24
2014	Japan Revitalization Strategy 2014 Revision: Challenge Towards the Future	48 (25)
2015	Japan Revitalization Strategy 2015 Revision: Investment into the Future, Productivity Revolution	51 (9)
2016	Japan Revitalization Strategy 2016: Towards the Fourth Industrial Revolution	60 (14)
2017	Future Investment Strategy 2017: Reforms Towards Society 5.0	60 (13)
2018	Future Investment Strategy 2018: Transformation Towards "Society 5.0," "Data-Driven Society"	70 (19)
2019	Growth Strategy (2019)	63 (5)

Source Prime Minister's Office, Kushida (2021: 397), Lee (2023)

technology-driven nation by mobilizing government, universities, and private companies in strategic areas, with the support of the Council for Science and Technology Policy (Kushida 2018a: 7–11; 2021; Lee 2023).

Above all, Abe's developmental strategies emphasized building an open innovation system with university reform, fostering venture companies, and cooperation policies between universities and SMEs, as well as strategically selecting and promoting 23 cutting-edge technology development programs (Lee 2022: 85). The government's specific goal was to double the number of large-scale joint studies between companies and universities by 2020, triple corporate investment in universities and national research institutes by 2025, and support universities with strategic reform initiatives by providing subsidies for university operating costs (Kushida 2018a: 22; Nagata 2018). The Innovation Network Corporation of Japan (INCJ), established in 2009 as a system jointly operated by the government and private companies, led investment for a startup innovation ecosystem, the core of the open innovation system. INCJ collected 14 billion yen from 26 major Japanese companies, including Toyota and Canon, and started with a total of 300 billion yen in funds. The government provided an additional 180 billion yen as a loan guarantee, allowing INCJ to invest a total of 200 million yen (Kushida 2017: 19).

These measures played an important role in significantly increasing Japanese venture capital, compared to other developed G7 countries, and contributed greatly to the increase in independent venture capital apart from traditional banks and financial firms. According to 2014 and 2015 indicators, independent funds accounted for the largest portion of capital invested in new funds. In 2014, independent venture capital accounted for 42%, and corporate venture capital for 43%; in 2015, independent funds accounted for 35%, corporate venture capital (CVC) 28%, and financial institution ventures 18% (Kushida 2018: 18).

The Abe government also introduced many open innovation measures: "open innovation promotion tax system" in which, if a large company invests more than 100 million yen in an unlisted company less than 10 years after its establishment, 25% of the investment will be deducted (Cha 2020; Jung 2020: 103); lawyers and supportive companies can enable venture entrepreneurs to work more easily (Kushida 2018a: 28); and a high-quality workforce can support a flexible labor market, especially to foster venture companies.[4]

Above all, the Abe government called for active reform of universities based on large selective subsidies to promote open innovation strategies. Since 2013, the Japanese government has implemented the Research University Reinforcement Promotion Project to select universities with world-class research activities and provide 200 to 400 million yen in annual subsidies for 10 years. In 2016, the National University Corporation Act was revised to establish a designated national university corporation system, enabling universities to increase their autonomy and receive and distribute various incentives, including government subsidies such as grants for operating expenses (Nagata 2018; Jung 2020: 32).

The Abe government's policy of industry-academic partnership was in line with the creation of regional clusters. Originally, regional clusters were designed to attract large companies to specific regions, but more recently Japanese policy has aimed to advance new projects through cooperation between local companies and universities, to help local industries

[4] The Abe administration strengthened labor market flexibility, allowing workers to change jobs seamlessly, with a focus on training in IT-related technologies, including cybersecurity (Kushida 2018a: 21). With many foreign companies able to enter Japan due to regulatory reform, paths have opened for elite university graduates to demonstrate their entrepreneurship, creating an environment in which new innovative venture companies can be activated. As of 2015, the majority of innovative startups were established by graduates of elite Japanese universities (Kushida 2017, 2018a: 21).

gain global competitiveness. Regional clusters are a response to regional hollowing out of industries following the globalization of production. For example, the Industry-Academic-Government Cooperative Program supports 200 large-scale programs using technologies developed in each region since 2021, and promotes 1000 projects over the next five years, specifically to enhance the competitiveness of SMEs (Kushida 2018a: 23).

Japan was able to shift from its closed system based on the circles of vested interests to a new open innovation system which included new venture companies and universities, thanks to the Japanese government's reform policies of the 2010s. This transition would have been impossible without the active cooperation and innovation efforts of large companies and universities. Next, we will look at changes in the perception of large corporations and the reform of universities that enabled transformation.

Politics of Transformation

Japan, which had been sluggish even after decades of economic turmoil due to delays in industrial reform, has succeeded in switching to a state-led open innovation model since the 2010s. The 1990s saw various attempts and experiments, but political instability and lack of consistent national policy delayed reforms. The traditional Japanese political economy, based on closed circles of compensation, delayed fundamental reforms, insulating Japan from foreign stimuli and prohibiting the entrance of new ideas and entrepreneurial attempts. In order to shift toward a more open innovation and economic system, Japan needed to break or change the existing circles of vested interests at various levels, including the so-called iron triangle of bureaucrats, business elites, and LDP politicians at the national level, as well as bank-centered *keiretsu* and closed subcontracting relationships at micro levels.

How was Japan able to switch to a new open cooperation system, despite its past and the global milieu? Reform initiatives come mainly from national politics and governments, as seen in the Koizumi and Abe administrations. In particular, the second Abe administration, starting in 2012, brought the longest period of political stability since the postwar period, and centralized the power of decision-making with the prime minister and cabinet, which enabled the dissolution of clientelist circles, structural economic reforms, and a consistent national policy based on innovation. Before examining why and how Abe could successfully build a new statist coordination system, in contrast to Koizumi's failure in structural reform, we first explore the direction of reform—why Japan did not converge toward Anglo-Saxon-style neoliberalism—by exploring the discursive politics, with an overview of the political process of reform throughout the lost decades.

Overview of Discursive Politics in Transformation

In the 1990s, Japan has established an industrial production network abroad based on Japanese closed circles of insiders, while domestically it has turned to pursue American-style shareholder capitalism to reform the Japanese capitalist model based on existing networks. But Japan did not undergo a wholesale change to American shareholder capitalism. As can be seen from Japan's corporate governance structure reform, it only introduced a formal outside director system; in a practical sense, the large framework of the existing stakeholder capitalism has not changed. Why has Japan's reform neither led to a full-scale transition to an American-style free-market nor adhered to the existing Japanese model? By focusing on the discursive politics among key actors, this section examines why and how Japan's new alternative system like the state-led open innovation system has been created and empowered since the 2000s, while not converting to an American-style free-market.

Vogel (2019), an expert on Japanese political economy, broadly considers the reform process of Japanese capitalism and divides it into two rounds. The first round was between 1995 and 2005, when American-style neoliberal alternatives prevailed.[5] During this period, with the collapse of the Japanese economy as the U.S. economy revived, various government and industry discussion panels argued that they needed to learn the secret of success in the U.S. neoliberal shareholder capitalist model. Neoliberal groups established the Japan Association of Corporate Executives, or *Keizai Doyukai*, a new capitalist association, and actively advocated the American-style free-market model, with neoclassical economists as an alternative. In particular, key neoliberal elites entered the cabinet during Prime Minister Koizumi's term and further strengthened their influence.

The second round of reform followed the decline of neoliberalism beginning in 2006. With the retirement of Prime Minister Koizumi

[5] Ulrike Schaede stipulates that 1998 to 2006 was the time when Japan's policy and corporate-level reform became a "strategic inflection point" (Schaede 2008: 1–2).

in 2006, neoliberalism weakened, while traditional groups emphasizing Japanese coordinative capitalism regained their power. In particular, since the start of the second Abe administration in 2012, the Japanese government has led the reform by presenting new growth strategies different from the American free-market system through new industrial policies and coordination. In the second round, the shift in the direction of reform showed a new mix of neoliberal-style openness and changes in the existing network capitalism not only in the political sphere but also at the level of private business (Gotoh 2020; Vogel 2019: 122).

Since the 1990s, Japan's capitalism reform method has been an adaptation process through continuous consultation and coordination between stakeholders, rather than an American model of winner-take-all based on the power of groups such as financial capital. Japan's politics of overcoming the capitalism crisis was a slow process through network-based mutual consultation and coordination (Schaede 2020: 10–16). To borrow Hirschman's terminology, Voice (consultation and negotiation) was more important for Japan than Exit (relationship break). Companies did not break ties with traditional stakeholders, workers, and key parts makers, but continued to consult and coordinate with them for new adaptations, thus avoiding a unilateral switch to new anonymous market relationships. Rather than dismissing workers in a recession, Japanese companies restrained the wages of key workers and negotiated the movement of labor within the entire business group. Instead of giving up core parts makers, they sought ways to improve quality or lower prices by applying pressure on parts makers (Schaede 2020: 43–67). These mutual consultations in Japan's reform took time. We look next at the discursive politics surrounding Japan's reform in two rounds after the mid-1990s.

Round 1: Dominance of Neoliberal Discourses (1995–2006)

Since the mid-1990s, Japan's neoliberal elite groups advocating an American-style free-market reform of Japanese capitalism have become aggressive. In particular, neoliberalism gained ascendancy in Japan after Prime Minister Hashimoto (1996–1998) began the neoliberal reform, and next, Prime Ministers Obuschi (1998–2000) and Koizumi (2001–2006) attempted many neoliberal reform measures. The media and academia also supported neoliberal reform, criticizing the traditional Japanese model of capitalism. Several waves of structural reforms included the Hashimoto government's financial reform and the Obuchi government's central bank independence and establishment of the Financial Supervision Authority. However, each wave of reform was followed by a lull and a loss of budgetary rigor; thus, the actual reforms of neoliberalism are limited (Tiberghien 2016: 40–42). For example, the Obuchi administration established the Industrial Competitiveness Council (ICC) and, through eight meetings which involved the Prime Minister, ministers, and private companies (Toyota and Sony), the ICC produced a dozen new laws for neoliberal reform, including the Law on Industrial Revitalization of August 1999, the Bankruptcy Law, and the Law on Temporary and Dispatch Workers of December 1999. But they failed to achieve the intended outcomes (Tiberghien 2016: 42–43).

Why is that so? Japan's neoliberal forces lacked sufficient authority to overcome the resistance of vested interests. But anti-liberal conservative elites also failed to persist with Japan's traditional network capitalism model. Before examining why neoliberals, like elites of the Koizumi administration, failed with radical reform, this section explores the discursive politics between neoliberal and traditional conservative elites.

In the course of Japan's reform, neoliberal groups have been mainly reformist bureaucrats, politicians, neoclassical economists, *Keizai Doyukai* (the Japan Association of Corporate Executives), non-Japanese companies, and U.S. credit rating agencies. Foreign (primarily American) shareholder groups have become more influential in the debate over the reform of Japanese corporate governance as their stock ownership increases. As of 2005, foreign stockholders owned about 25% of Tokyo stock-listed companies. The American Chamber of Commerce in Japan (ACCJ) pressured the government to appoint at least one outside director, and to adopt America's free-market shareholder capitalism (Gotoh 2020: 126, 130; Vogel 2019: 122). Countering this movement were anti-liberal conservative camps, including interventionist bureaucrats, conservative politicians, *Keidanren* (Japan Business Federation), Japanese law elites, bankers, and Japanese credit rating agencies. They resisted American neoliberal reform and advocated a Japanese network, or stakeholder capitalism (Gotoh 2020: 126, 130).

In particular, the business association *Doyukai* and the conservative *Keidanren* were key organizations in creating specific, distinct ideologies and programs on behalf of neoliberal shareholder capitalists and stakeholder capitalists, respectively. *Doyukai* originally had a Marxist influence, but accepted the idea of the post-WWII New Deal, and since the 1980s it has advocated neoliberal reform influenced by American ideology (Okazaki et al. 1996). *Keidanren* is a successor to the Important Industry Control Council, which helped the government by controlling and delivering war supplies to major industries in wartime Japan. Naturally, *Keidanren* embraced anti-free-market ideologies and institutions. As Japan's largest industrial association, *Keidanren* encompasses the widest range of large-scale manufacturers.[6] Its key affiliates are manufacturers of mechanical chemistry and steel, Japan's major industries, and traditionally influenced by the Japanese government's economic policies and credit institutions through bureau pluralism (Calder 2017: 30–34; Aoki 1988; Matsutani 2009: 111–113; Teranishi 2003: 202–208).

In the ideological conflict that lasted from the mid-1990s to the mid-2000s concerning alternatives to Japan's capitalism, the two camps competed toward different outcomes. *Doyukai*'s shareholder capitalism pressed for individualism, entrepreneurship, market liberalism, commerce morals, and refusal of a supportive system. *Keidanren*'s stakeholder capitalism argued a collectivist perspective, coordination by administrators, anti-free market coordination, a moral standard, and consent to a supportive system. The so-called "Imai-Miyauchi controversy" in February 1994 illustrates the two opposing positions. Imai was a member of *Doyukai*, but also a key member of *Keidanren* as chairman of Nippon Steel (Kawakita 2011: 227–229; Asahi Shimbun 2009: 2–3).

> Miyauchi argued, "The most important thing for the company is the extent to which it can compensate shareholders. The company manager needs not to consider employment and its condition." Then Imai replied, "If you really think so, you are a traitor to our country. We haven't run our companies for that purpose," Yoshikaju Hanawa, vice chairman of Nissan Motor, while supporting Imai, said: "If lifelong employment ends, the CEO will have to take responsibility and step down first." On the other hand, Ushio said as follows, advocating Miyouchi: "Lifelong employment and seniority wage systems will no longer be sustainable under the conditions of our reversed population pyramid and aging society". (*Asahi Shimbun* 2009: 2-3; requoted in Gotoh 2020: 135)

[6] *Keidanren* is a comprehensive economic organization with a membership comprised of 1,512 representative companies of Japan, 107 nationwide industrial associations and the regional economic organizations for all 47 prefectures.

Unlike *Doyukai* entrepreneurs, *Keidanren*'s Imai and Hanawa were internally promoted administrators in large corporations, and at the center of a traditional elite network that connected bureaucrats, large corporations, and the LDP. *Doyukai*'s neoliberals such as Ushio, Miyauchi, and Shiina were either CEOs of U.S. subsidiaries or founders of their own corporations. The two elite groups had vastly different career backgrounds. Against this backdrop, *Doyukai* argued that capitalists and entrepreneurs should not be restricted by social links, and that vested interests in Japan represent the inefficiency of stakeholder capitalism. *Keidanren* CEOs believed that uncontrolled capitalism would not only threaten the lifelong employment of regular workers and subordinate allies, but jeopardize the independence of their company's management from the influence of capital markets. Therefore, lifelong employment and the independence of internally promoted managers should be protected through systematic support (Gotoh 2020: 135–136).

However, the neoliberal group gained strength first in the 1990s and early 2000s. In the 1990s, Japan's traditional stakeholder capitalism faced crisis. The Liberal Democratic Party lost the general election in July 1993 due to corruption scandals concerning Japanese officials, including Treasury officials,[7] and money for politics scandals by LDP lawmakers. Claiming conservative Japanese-style capitalism became the subject of criticism and reform.

Along with this, the number of market liberals in the parliament, bureaucracy, and private industries increased, and market liberals prevailed within *Doyukai*, bringing about a change in its ideology (Okazaki et al. 1996). Masaru Hayami, chairman of the *Doyukai* Association from 1991 to 1995, emphasized that the existing Japanese model, which relied on a sense of social unity during the period of rapid growth, no longer worked and should be changed. Hayami insisted on deregulation and free-market transition in retail markets, real estate, healthcare, groceries, finance, transportation, and IT industries.

Jiro Ushio, who succeeded Hayami and served as chairman of *Doyukai* from 1995 to 1999, further strengthened *Doyukai*'s neoliberal tendency. Ushio graduated from the University of California, Berkeley, in 1957, and

[7] Treasury officials provided selective benefits and treatment to financial institutions, while receiving drinks and dinner entertainment in return. As this scandal made headlines, five senior Treasury officials were arrested, and the Minister of Finance resigned, which weakened the power of the Ministry of Treasury.

founded Ushio Electric, a lamp manufacturer, in 1964. Because Ushio Electronics was small, it lacked influence in the existing *Keidanren* Association. Ushio had long served as a neoliberal business leader emphasizing reform of the existing Japanese capitalist system. He was deeply involved in the privatization of Japan National Railways, Nippon Telegraph and Telephone, and Japan Tobacco, and later was actively involved in the deregulation of the information and communication industry.

After the bubble economy ended, the *Doyukai* appointed four market liberals as vice presidents of the association: Yotaro Kobayashi (Chairman of Fuji Xerox), Yoshihiko Miyauchi (CEO of Orix), Takeo Shiina (Chairman of IBM Japan), and Yuzaburo Mogi (Chairman of Kikkoman). All were educated at American universities and ideologically close to Hayami and Ushio. Their appointments were coupled with the political event of the LDP's dismissal and launch of the Hosogawa administration (1993–1994). The Hosogawa administration consisted of a coalition of eight political parties other than the LDP, criticizing the LDP's failure and emphasizing reforms for deregulation and prevention of political corruption (Rosenbluth and Thies 2010: 99–101; Tiberghien 2007: 109). Yotaro Kobayashi and his three *Doyukai* colleagues tried to introduce an American-style free-market model as an alternative to overcome the Japanese capitalist crisis. They gained strength, especially in the Hashimoto administration (1996–1998) and the Koizumi government (2001–2006) (Gotoh 2020: 127).

Hashimoto Ryotaro (Prime Minister, 1996–1998) was a conservative politician, but when he took power, the LDP was criticized for political scandals and faced a serious debt problem in the financial sector. The LDP had to counter the New Frontier Party, which insisted on neoliberal reform, and Sakigake, a new party, insisted on reform of the existing bureaucratic system. The Hashimoto administration established an Administrative Reform Council in the Cabinet and sought reform in six areas: administration, fiscal structure, financial system, social safety, economic structure, and education (Toya 2006: 174–175).

In 1996, the Deregulation Committee was newly established as part of the Hashimoto administration's reform. Miyauchi Yoshihiko, vice chairman of *Doyukai*, became chairman of the committee, on the recommendation of *Doyukai*. Miyauchi believed that bureaucratic authority, control, and regulation were obstacles to business and economic development (Kawakita 2011: 151–153). Miyauchi's view of capitalism was quite different from that of existing Japanese company executives who were promoted internally. The Deregulation Committee gradually expanded, and in 2001, the Koizumi administration renamed it the Council for Regulatory Reform. Thanks to his close friendship with Prime Minister Koizumi, Miyauchi served as chairman of the council once again (Kawakita 2011: 151–152). During this period, the Regulatory Reform Council attracted key *Doyukai* executives and scholars close to the association, focusing on reform in areas such as temporary jobs and financial services.

Doyukai's political influence was at its highest in 2001 to 2006 when Ushio, then chairman of *Doyukai*, participated in the Koizumi administration's Council on Economic and Fiscal Policy, the most important policy-making body in the administration, with the Prime Minister as its chairman, plus 10 members. Council members included the Minister of Economy and Finance (Heijo Takenaka), the president of the central bank, and four private sector members, plus Ushio, Toyota Chairman Okuda, and two neoliberal economists Masaki Homa and Hiroshima Yoshikawa. Minister Takenaka was a key figure in the Koizumi administration's reform program, and his perspectives were similar to those of Ushio and Homa. *Doyukai* executives' neoliberal policy proposals included fiscal soundness, suspension of bad loans, deregulation, tax reform, and privatization (Gotoh 2020: 133–134).

As an alternative to the existing Japanese model of capitalism, the Koizumi government carried out neoliberal reforms in a wide range of areas—deregulation of finance, telecommunications, and retail markets; reduction of public works; and privatization of the postal savings system and highway construction agency (Kamikawa 2010: 1–10; Gotoh 2020: 133–134). However, this reform did not bring Japan to pure American shareholder capitalism.

The Koizumi administration's neoliberal reform weakened with the Prime Minister's resignation. A representative example of the failure was the failure of free-market financial reform. The Japanese government pursued deregulation of the financial sector during the 1990s. However, no fundamental transition resulted from the existing bank structure. Japanese corporate bonds had decreased slightly, from 62 trillion yen in 2000 to 60 trillion yen in 2016, representing 11% of GDP, in contrast to American-style stock capitalism, where U.S. financial market corporate bonds account for 45% of GDP. Bank loans still account for most of the capital raised within Japanese companies, with about 400 trillion yen in 2016. In addition, Japan has considerably less inward FDI than other developed countries. The inward FDI to GDP in 2016 was only 3.8%, far less than 35.2% in the U.S. and 55.7% in the U.K., and quite small compared to China's 24.5% and Korea's 12.4%, other nearby coordinated capitalist countries (Gotoh 2020: 127).

The attempts of Japanese institutional investors, who spoke up in the 2000s claiming neoliberal reform, were unsuccessful as well. Some institutional investors suggested active investment strategies to monitor corporate performance in more detail and increase profits. Japan's hedge funds at home and abroad earned some profits due to their active strategies in the early 2000s. However, these efforts were eventually restrained and failed to change the business strategies of major Japanese companies (Buchanan et al. 2012: 153–239; Vogel 2019: 127–128). Japan's neoliberal reform failed to establish a fundamental shift to the U.S.-style neoliberalism because the resistance of traditional elites was formidable, even during the period of neoliberalism superiority.

The power of anti-liberal conservative groups, such as *Keidanren*, had weakened since the 1990s, but they never lost their social voices. Even during the peak of the Koizumi administration's neoliberal reforms, *Keidanren* was defensive compared to the dominant *Doyukai*, but still contributed to maintaining the basic framework of the Japanese-style stakeholder capitalist model. *Doyukai* argued that Japan's difficult economic conditions posed limits to pursuing fundamental structural reforms, and the Koizumi government could not ignore the systemic support claimed by stakeholder capitalist elites such as *Keidanren* to relieve the pain of ordinary citizens. Introduction of measures such as Resona Bank's public relief, establishment of corporate restructuring funds based on government support, and quantitative expansion of currencies to alleviate economic difficulties caused by structural reforms were the result of *Keidanren*'s influence (Gotoh 2020: 139–140).

Furthermore, anti-liberal conservatives could defend their rationale of communitarian stakeholder capitalism by seeking new alternatives amid changes in the international political and economic order, rather than sticking to their traditional practices. Their reform efforts differed from the arguments of neoliberals, while presenting the possibility of a new direction different from the traditional model. Amid Japan's "lost decade" crisis, supporters of the existing Japanese network capitalism were forced to adapt to the new environment. Now, lifelong employment had to cover the cost of wages with the strong yen. *Keidanren* agreed to deregulate the temporary service industry, although *Keidanren*'s goal differed from that of *Doyukai*. *Keidanren*'s deregulation purpose was to protect the existing lifelong employment system by hiring low-wage non-regular workers, while *Doyukai* sought deregulation of both regular and non-regular workers (Gotoh 2020: 136–137; Yun 2016: 485; Vogel 2006: 56). Unlike *Doyukai*, *Keidanren* regained their influence among citizens by demanding more realistic options of systematic government supports during the recession, including taxes and support policies to boost the economy rather than relying on the laissez-faire free-market system (Schoppa 2006: 147).

Round 2: Resistance and Change of the Anti-liberal Group

With the 2006 resignation of Koizumi, neoliberal reform turned toward Japanese-style relational capitalism. Prime Minister Koizumi, lacking LDP-insider power, relied on popularity among voters. However, critical public opinion concerning neoliberal reform of the Koizumi cabinet gained strength, especially since the government's neoliberal structural reform further deepened income inequality (Kamikawa 2010: 311). Amid these criticisms, the Koizumi government could not continue its reform, and the pendulum began swing toward anti-liberal criticism. This criticism did not result in the revival of traditional statist coordination, because those tools, including credit control and support mechanisms for coordinating institutions, had been abolished throughout the neoliberal reform of 1996–2006 (Tiberghien 2016: 29). Japan's government lacked capabilities to rebuild a new statist coordination before the Abe administration regained them. Before examining how Abe could successfully establish organizational capabilities for a new statist coordination system, this section explores how anti-liberal critics regained influence by building a new alternative to their own traditional model, as well as to neoliberalism.

The anti-neoliberal coalition's criticism of neoliberal reform has increased, as fears of neoliberal financial capitalists' power have risen among traditional Japanese model supporters such as regular workers and SME subcontractors. The Japanese government carried out quantitative expansion of currencies to ease the pain of neoliberal structural reform, which encouraged speculative money games by aggressive investment funds and entrepreneurs in the Japanese financial market. Anti-free market elites, full-time workers, and SME capitalists took a critical view of these speculative funds and so-called entrepreneurs reaping great profits.

Keidanren did not give them membership until the end of 2002, even if major consumer credit companies had grown significantly (Mainichi Shimbun, 12 November 2002).

In addition, the 2006 Livedoor and Murakami Fund incidents spread antipathy toward neoliberals throughout society. In January 2006 the Japanese Prosecutors' Office arrested Takafumi Horie, CEO of Japan-based internet company Livedoor, which grew rapidly in the IT and finance sectors, for violating securities laws, and indicted him on charges of fraud. Livedoor rapidly increased capital through stock splits and a series of mergers. As a young and ambitious CEO, Horie received social attention by criticizing existing Japanese capitalism and strongly advocating new shareholder capitalism. Five months after the arrest, the Tokyo Stock Exchange withdrew the company's listing on the grounds that the annual stock report submitted by Livedoor was false. The Japanese Prosecutors' Office also arrested Yoshiaki Murakami, a reformist official and founder of the active shareholder Murakami Fund, for internal transactions of Livedoor stocks (New York Times July 19, 2007; Japan Times June 6, 2006). Horie and Murakami were socially notable neoliberal elites and close to each other. Though their accounting fraud was small compared to the accounting fraud of existing giants such as Olympus and Toshiba, Horie and Murakami were criticized in mass media and public opinion as "immoral money worshipers" and "greedy neoliberals." These criticisms soon spread to criticism of neoliberal shareholder capitalism which they advocated. Japan's legal elites, like other conservative elites, shared anti-free-market norms, and took a critical view of such extreme profit-seeking forces. Strict punishment for Horie and Murakami was a clear warning to other financial capitalists and similar entrepreneurs.[8]

The Livedoor and Murakami incidents weakened the power of market liberals, especially *Doyukai,* because of Murakami's close relationships with key members of *Doyukai* and with key reformist figures in the cabinet. In the wake of these incidents, criticism of the structural reform promoted by the Koizumi administration intensified. Critics argued that the volume of low-wage non-regular workers increased and income inequality intensified due to Koizumi's neoliberal reform. The global

[8] New York Times (July 19, 2007) "Murakami gets two years in jail in Livedoor scandal"; Japan Times (June 6, 2006) "Murakami arrested over insider trading"; The Wall Street Journal (October 29, 2010) "Japan Insider Trading Flashback: Murakami and Livdoor."

financial crisis, which began in the summer of 2007, further fueled criticism of neoliberal financialization and shareholder capitalism, and the anti-neoliberal trend received strong support in Japan (Gotoh 2020: 141–142).

In the wake of the global financial crisis, groups that emphasized the existing Japanese-style relational capitalist model gained strength by criticizing American-style shareholder capitalism and suggesting new alternatives. Stakeholder model advocates such as *Keidanren* had suggested alternatives to neoliberalism since 2006. Shortly before the Koizumi administration resigned in June 2006, *Keidanren* published a policy proposal titled *A Suitable Corporate Governance System for Japan* (*Keidanren* 2006). The arguments in this report are as follows: First, companies have a social responsibility to create social values in consideration of various stakeholders such as employees and local communities. Second, corporate management should be based on various cultures, traditions, and social norms and customs of individual societies. Third, when introducing a new, foreign corporate governance method, it should be indigenous to Japan and not unconditionally accepted.

Arguments of stakeholder model advocates such as *Keidanren* never meant to return to the model of the past. They admitted that Japan could no longer rely on the past model, but nevertheless argued that it cannot accept American neoliberal market capitalism as it is. They gained support by acknowledging the need for new adaptations in the changed situation and suggesting new alternatives. Their most important question was: How will Japanese manufacturers increase overseas production, preventing industrial hollowing out from occurring in Japan, and restore international competitiveness?

Japanese companies began to relocate domestic production to other Asian countries in the mid-1980s, as their international competitiveness weakened due to the growth of Asian developing countries along with the strong yen. And jobs and wages for domestic workers were cut. Japan's FDI to GDP increased sharply from 5.3% in 1996 to 30.7% in 2007, high compared to China's 12.3% (Schoppa 2006; Hatch 2010: 199). However, while companies moved production overseas, Japan failed to foster new entrepreneurial companies, and failed to attract global capital and talented personnel. In the end, Japan's overall industrial competitiveness had weakened since the 1990s, and Japan's average household income decreased. Efforts to protect existing jobs and regular workers led to an increase in non-regular jobs. In this economic situation, the main concern of relational model advocates such as *Keidanren* was how to foster new innovation capabilities apart from neoliberalism, while accepting the changed situation of globalization and openness of companies.

Moreover, the METI officials advocating the stakeholder model regained the rationale of active industrial policy by suggesting new policies, rather than adhering to traditional industrial policy. METI officials suggested new industrial policies, including upgrading innovation capabilities based on basic science and linking social agenda and industrial policy, in the changed contexts of intensified competition for innovation and platform, and Japan's delay in digital transformation (Lee, S.J. 2023: 148).

Bureaucrats in the past paid little attention to companies' low return on equity, contrary to neoliberals who advocated for the shareholder capitalist model. Officials thought that even if companies' return on equity was low, investors would invest on their own if the industry's infrastructure and the economy as a whole were strong. However, economic and industrial officials began to consider the neoliberal arguments and the importance of financial profitability. They said, "If the return on equity is low, companies may leave Japan. It is difficult to sustain the economy simply with the natural virtuous cycle that R&D and investment in infrastructure can bring; so, a new virtuous cycle structure, or financial path, should be considered" (Vogel 2019: 126). Therefore, the METI organized a research group led by Kunio Ito, a respected financial professor at Hitotsubashi University, to investigate how to increase the profit rate of Japanese companies. METI also organized working groups to promote dialogue between investors and companies as a way to increase corporate value (Vogel 2019: 126).

As the neoliberal groups faced limits to pursuing reform as they intended, the atmosphere reversed beginning in 2006 and turned to a relational capitalist model. *Keidanren* and economic industry officials were not wedded to the past model, but gained strength by finding new alternatives to address neoliberals' concerns. In the midst of these struggles and confrontations, Japan's reform neither converged into American neoliberalism nor continued the traditional stakeholder model.

Changes in Power Alignments and Coordination Capabilities

The Koizumi administration (2001–2006) attempted comprehensive reforms in problematic areas, including privatization of postal services, banking reform, tax, medical and pension systems, and restructuring of 163 public corporations (Pempel 2004: 241). However, in contrast to the Abe administration (2012–2020), Koizumi's reforms failed, remaining "superficial, incomplete, and unconsolidated" (Mulgan 2002: 238). By contrast, Abe's reforms achieved significant success, as seen above. What makes the difference? This section explains why and how the Abe administration succeeded in reform, while the former government did not.

To understand Abe's success, we first look at political stability. Japan's prime ministerships were too short and unstable to coordinate conflicts of vested interests and to make fundamental reforms. In the past, bureaucrats could rule in policy-making because they could address key agenda over a longer period than prime ministers and politicians. In the past, when politicians they disliked became prime ministers or cabinet members, bureaucrats sat back and hoped that the next leaders would come with a new set of priorities they could appear to implement while pursuing their own policy preferences (Winter 2016: 2). Japan's prime ministerships were too short, except in the cases of Koizumi and Abe. Even after Koizumi stepped down, between 2006 and 2012, Japan had five prime ministers. By contrast, Abe's prime ministership was one of the longest, and Yoshihide Suga, during the Abe administration, was the longest serving Chief Secretary. This long-term stability served to overcome conflicts among various ministers and to coordinate different circles of invested interests.

However, considering that Koizumi also enjoyed a relatively long-term prime ministership (2001–2006), but failed in reform, the institutionalization of strong political leadership, like centralization of power at the Prime Minister's Office *Kantei*,[9] and realignments of power alliances in the Abe administration should be noted. Although the Koizumi administration had good conditions for reform, including a political honeymoon, strong and visionary leadership, social consensus, use of the media, and a fragmented and demoralized opposition, it failed in achieving its intended

[9] This is equivalent to the Blue House in Korea or the White House in the U.S.

reform, due to the lack of political leadership and coordination capabilities (Mulgan 2002). By contrast, Abe centralized the power at the Prime Minister's Office and Cabinet, creating new power alignments by changing the existing iron triangle of bureaucrats, LDP politicians, and business elites (Lee 2022: 74–75; Mikuriya 2015).

In former governments, including the Koizumi administration, most of Japan's prime ministers lacked strong political leadership and sufficient institutional coordination capabilities to implement reforms, although Japan was traditionally a strong developmental state. In particular, in the 2000s, when multiple industrial sectors, both globalized and domestic, were now less complimentary to each other and more difficult to coordinate, government policy became less coherent and interdependent compared to the 1980s. Japan's reforms in the 2000s did not achieve expected outcomes due to the lack of central government's coordination capabilities in response to the conflicting circles of vested interests (Tiberghien 2016; Lee 2022: 82–83).

Although Japan adopted the Westminster parliamentary system, its actual operation is not the true Westminster system in which the ruling party and bureaucrats are subordinate to the Prime Minister's cabinet. But in Japan, the ruling party and bureaucracy had their own political structure that unofficially prevented reform from being carried out. In the absence of strong executive authority, all executive directives in Japan confronted powerful parallel channels of policy-making within both the ruling LDP and the fragmented and often uncoordinated ministries of bureaucracy (Mulgan 2002: 146).

By contrast, Abe could reduce policy uncertainty and increase political authority by the long-term seizure and centralization of power at the Prime Minister's Office (*Kantei*) and cabinet. Indeed, Koizumi also tried to centralize power at the Prime Minister's Office, while reforming the existing clientelist iron triangle system, but Koizumi failed in the institutionalization of policy-making reforms, relying instead on his personal popularity outside the LDP (Krauss and Nyblade 2005; Lee 2018: 100–101; Kabashima and Steel 2007: 79–83). The major confrontation in Japanese politics during the Koizumi administration was not between the ruling LDP and opposition parties, but between the Prime Minister and pro-reform ministers in the cabinet on one side, and dominant factions within LDP outside the cabinet and bureaucrats with vested interests on the other (Mogaki 2019: 6–7; Kabashima and Steel 2007: 79–83).

However, in the Abe administration, the power balance in Japanese policy-making radically changed, although Abe's centralization of policy-making authority at the Prime Minister's office (*Kantei*) does not make the system presidential and collective decision-making remains the norm. After examining the changes in Abe's policy-making process, George Mulgan (2019) rightly points out that the LDP *zoku* (policy tribe) politicians "no longer exercise blocking power over policy initiatives coming from the ministerial executive" (2019: 68). The iron triangle of business elites, bureaucrats, and LDP politicians dissolved. Mulgan notes that "A key aspect of the Abe prime ministership is thus the way he has managed to build and sustain centralized control over both the bureaucracy and the party. The structural change also altered the direction of policy from bottom-up to top-down" (2019: 71).

How could Abe increase its institutionalized power? To achieve this, Abe first shifted the center of policy-making from bureaucracy to the Prime Minister and Cabinet Office by increasing the number of councils and their policy-making expertise under the offices. For example, Abe concentrated policy-making expertise in the Prime Minister's Office by installing no less than five councils advising him on his growth strategy alone, plus a number of individual advisers for various agendas. The Cabinet Office also increased councils by 211 in January 2022 to improve their policy-making and coordination capabilities. The Cabinet Office, based on its special councils, directly managed giant projects such as the Strategic Innovation Program (SIP), Innovative Research and Development Promotion Program (ImPACT), and Regional Revitalization, which individual departments could not control (Cabinet Office homepage; Lee 2023: 150). For example, the Council for Science, Technology and Innovation (CSTI) in the Cabinet Office, under the leadership of the Prime Minister and the Minister in charge of Science and Technology Policy, is institutionalized with 1 regular meeting per month, and serves as a control tower, responsible for planning and coordinating comprehensive "basic science, technology and innovation policies from a position higher than each ministry" (Cabinet Office homepage). This council also oversees and manages the implementation of programs of individual departments (Lee 2023: 154; Larrue 2021). The Abe administration not only increased the number of councils under the *Kantei* and Cabinet Office, but also improved their policy coordination power.

This movement of building councils under the Prime Minister's Office and Cabinet Office shifted much of the core competence and expertise of policy formulation, from ministerial deliberative councils, where laws used to be drafted, almost exclusively to the Prime Minister's Office, *Kantei*. In other words, power shifted in policy-making from the traditional Iron Triangle of LDP diet politicians and big business to a new triangle of *Kantei*, business, and handpicked advisers (Winter 2016).

Abe also strengthened the institutional basis of power over bureaucracy by increasing the Prime Minister's involvement in bureaucrats' appointments. Abe established the Cabinet Bureau of Personal Affairs in 2014, which granted the prime minister control over more than 600 bureaucratic appointments, tripling the previous number. The Cabinet Bureau of Personal Affairs ensured the supervision of the cabinet on administrative reform and the appointment of high-ranking government officials. In addition, Abe increased political appointments in the upper echelons. For example, in the past, political appointments in the Ministry of Agriculture, Forestry and Fisheries (MAFF) were only the minister and his deputy. More recently they have included five to seven political appointees. In the Abe administration, the powers of *Kantei*, the authority of Chief Cabinet Secretary, and the authority of other Cabinet Ministers were strengthened, whereas each ministry's status as a key strategist weakened in the Abe administration (Mogaki 2019: 8–9). The clear influence of government ministries referred to by Chalmers Johnson (1982) has been limited since 2012.

In the Abe administration, the power bloc of policy alliances also changed. In the past, government councils such as the Industry Competition Council under the METI were largely composed of bureaucrats and representatives of large conglomerates. However, after the 2000s, new entrepreneurial companies including Rakuten and Pasona increased their presence in such government industry councils. Abe strengthened this trend. For example, of the twenty members of the Industrial Structure Deliberation Council under the METI in 2021, only three are traditional private partners representing large conglomerates, including Hitachi, Mitsubishi, and Japan General Research Institute. By contrast, representatives of new enterprises established in the 1990s, including Netyear Group, Saki, Nonstress, and K2Marketing established in 2013, took part in the Council. The increase of newly established enterprise participation in government councils indicates the changes in the policy alliances (Lee 2023: 155).

Electoral reform, prior to the Abe era, also amplified prime ministerial leadership, as elections focused more on party leaders and led to the weakening of factions within the LDP. Due to the electoral system change from a traditional medium-sized constituency to single member districts in 1994, LDP politicians became more concerned with party-versus-party competition, rather than the traditional intraparty competition and reliance on delivery of pork barrel spending as a way for candidates to differentiate themselves. The role of factions declined, while party leaders gained more effective control over nominations. In particular, weakening its rule enforced LDP to change its policy positions, from a traditional particularistic approach toward a more centralized and reform-oriented approach to pursue its comprehensive reform policies targeting the median voter (Rosenbluth and Thies 2010; Noble 2010; Hiwatari and Miura 2002).

More importantly, Abe made a full strategic use of changed institutions to bring the ministries to toe the line and to reform the clientelist circles of vested interests (Winter 2016). The Ministry of Agriculture, Forestry and Fisheries (MAFF), for example, used to be a typical case of iron triangle or clientelist circle of vested interests. Despite MAFF's opposition to the loss of power, Abe first appointed Hisao Harihara (an internationalist and proponent of agricultural reform) as vice minister by the Prime Minister's personal appointment. Abe also appointed Ken Saito (a former pro-reform METI official) as head of the LDP's powerful agricultural policy groups (*norin bukai*) in order to weaken MAFF's and farmers' opposition to the Trans-Pacific Partnership (TPP).

However, Abe's strategy to reform the closed circles of iron triangle was not to destroy, but to strategically utilize the traditional organizations. For example, in the reform process of the clientelist circle of agriculture, Abe first shifted the LDP policy center from the existing LDP *joku* (policy tribe) members to the official Regulatory Reform Promotion Council, which enforced the agriculture *joku* members to agree with the need for agriculture reform, a stance shared broadly by LDP members. Based on weakened factions and centralization within the LDP, Abe transformed LDP *joku* politicians to move from traditional roles to represent agriculture interests in LDP and bureaucracy, now to a new role to promote and persuade the necessity and effectiveness of agricultural liberalization. Then, the Abe administration changed the preferences of the private partner JA (National Agricultural Cooperative Federation) by using the LDP agriculture *joku* politicians as promoters of reform and by making tradeoffs between not dissolving JA and implementing agricultural reforms (Lee, Junghwan 2018; Lee, Sungjoo 2022: 91–92; Honma and Mulgan 2018).

Abe succeeded in reform by strategically utilizing previously changed institutions, strengthening centralized power of the Prime Minister's Office, and by transforming existing relationships with vested interests. Not only in agriculture, but in many other areas including medical and energy, the Abe administration introduced the practical use of regenerative medicine earlier than expected, and liberalization in the energy sector, untouched by previous governments (Sasada 2015; Incerti and Lipsey 2018). Despite the opposition of traditional vested interests, the Abe administration successfully pursued growth and innovation policies based on support from a wide range of voters and centralized power of the Prime Minister.

To sum up, in the late 2010s, Japan began to revive its economy in a rapidly changing world, not by American-style free-market model, but by a new statist coordination model. Through recent industrial policies, the Abe administration successfully changed Japan's traditional innovation system to a new "open innovation" system. By centralizing power at the Prime Minister and cabinet and reforming the existing bureau pluralism of vested interests, the Abe administration succeeded in reforming the traditional Japanese statist coordination model which encountered obstacles to globalization and digitalization.

PART III

Social Coordination Model: The Case of Germany

National corporations' globalization does not always have a negative effect on a nation's domestic economy. Germany strengthened the competitiveness of its domestic industry in the process of globalization of production. Germany has maintained its employment levels in manufacturing, while converting that employment to high-value-added professional jobs. Germany's automobile and machine tool industries have strengthened their international competitiveness by enhancing domestic innovation capabilities. And Germany's high-tech industry leads to an increased trade surplus.

How was Germany's remarkable competitive growth possible? How could Germany strengthen its domestic production and innovation capabilities despite globalization and game-changing technologies? Germany neither resisted liberalization and openness to world markets through closed coordination, as Japan did, nor did it practice openness without coordination, as in the U.S. Germany embraced world markets through its export-oriented growth strategy. Germany has strengthened its domestic industry and innovation ecosystem in the process of globalization and liberalization, through openness and social coordination. Through struggle and social consultation, Germany mobilized coordination among various social actors, including labor and trade associations, small- and medium-sized parts markers (SMEs), prime contractors, and original equipment manufacturers (OEMs). It upgraded its domestic industrial ecosystem through collective coordination and taming the priority of shareholder value.

In Part III, we will first look at German company's globalization impacts on the national economy. We briefly compare Germany's development path with the U.S. and Japan during the process of globalization. Then we will analyze why Germany has taken a different path, despite the similar globalization of production. To distinguish Germany's process, we will first analyze how and why German companies have linked overseas and domestic production in the process of globalization. The political process will be analyzed in terms of macro- and micro-level politics, including interfirm relations between prime contractors and SMEs and labor–management relations surrounding corporate governance.

CHAPTER 7

German National Economy in Globalization

German companies, similar to American and Japanese companies, have greatly expanded overseas production since the 1990s. In particular, Germany's main industries—automobile, chemical, and machine tools—were forced to utilize new global networks to adapt to global competition. However, Germany, unlike the U.S., did not engage in the hollowing-out of domestic production. And unlike Japan, Germany's domestic production did not result in outdatedness and inertia. Before looking at the politics of transformation through which Germany adapted to globalization, this chapter examines how Germany improved domestic production and innovation capabilities, and actually sustained its economic development, despite liberalizing and globalizing trends.

Effects of German Companies' Globalization on National Economy

The greatest impacts of globalization on a nation's economy occur in high-tech electronics and automobile industries, where overseas relocation immediately results in the hollowing-out of domestic production. Such actions change the way the national economy develops. Focusing on major industries such as automobile and electronics, this section briefly examines the effects of German companies' globalization on the domestic

H. Kwon, *Openness and Coordination*,
https://doi.org/10.1007/978-981-97-3352-1_7

economy, before we explore how Germany has upgraded its innovation and production capabilities at home.

Since the 1990s, German companies have seriously expanded their production overseas to meet international competition. For example, in 1995, German auto companies' overseas production accounted for 33.2% of Germany's total passenger car production. However, 15 years later, in 2010, the ratio increased to 52.3%, surpassing domestic production, and reached 68.7% in 2018.[1] As automobile OEMs moved overseas, German SMEs followed and expanded their overseas production. According to a study of German parts makers, by 2006 approximately 47% of German parts makers already had expanded their production to Eastern and Central Europe (Ernst and Young 2006; Kwon 2012: 585).

Germany's overseas relocation of major industries was by no means smaller than in the U.S. Foreign investment by U.S. and German companies in the automobile and machinery industries increased steadily between 1995 and 2009, when the trend in production globalization accelerated. In particular, overseas investment in Germany's flagship automobile and machinery industries increased from $20.5 billion in 1995 to approximately $71 billion in 2009, an increase of 345%. The U.S. also increased overseas investment from $46.6 billion in 1995 to $117.8 billion in 2009, an increase of approximately 238% (OECD statistics database). The amount of overseas investment similarly increased in other major industries such as electronics. As shown in Fig. 7.1, German and the U.S. foreign direct investment (FDI) between 2005 and 2021 in the automobile and machinery industries shows a similar trend: Germany grew to 240% in 2021, compared to 2005, while the U.S. 257% in 2021, compared to 2005.

Despite similar patterns of overseas production expansion, the impact on the domestic economy varies greatly from country to country. In the U.S., domestic production and jobs have been reduced due to overseas production, as discussed in Chapter 3. However, in Germany, overseas production in major industries did not result in industrial hollowing-out, as Fig. 2.2 in Chapter 2 shows the change in the total number of jobs in manufacturing in the U.S., Japan, Korea, and Germany from 2000 to 2021. In the U.S., the number of jobs decreased by about 6 million: from

[1] For automobile production indicators in Germany, see the official indicators from *Verband der Automobile Industrie* (VDA). VDA figures from https://www.vda.de/en/services/facts-and-figures/annual-figures/automobile-production.html.

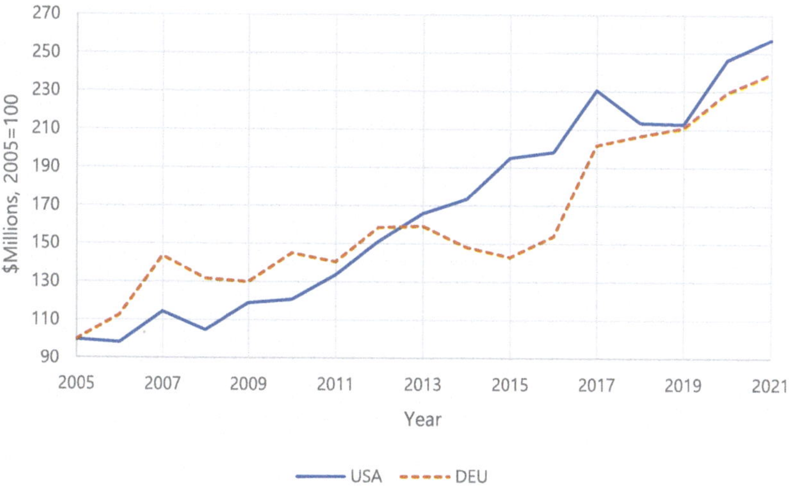

Fig. 7.1 Changes in outward FDI in Germany and the U.S. in the automobile and machinery industries, 2005–2021 (*Source* OECD International direct investment database [added 2900, 3400 and 3500 from FDI Statistics according to BMD3], OECD FDI by counterpart area and by economic activity, BMD4 [accessed on 22 March 2024])

18.09 million in 2000 to 12.09 million in 2021. In 2021, employment in U.S. manufacturing decreased to 67% compared to 2000. In contrast, Germany remained relatively stable: from 10.64 million jobs in 2000 to 10.01 million in 2021, decreasing slightly to 94% compared to 2000.

Despite Germany's expansion of overseas production, the maintenance or expansion of domestic production is more pronounced in major German industries such as automobiles, electronics, and machinery. The automobile and electronics industries are the most globalized, as well as the core of U.S. and German industries. However, between 1998 and 2019, the period when the percentage of overseas production was continuously increasing, domestic employment changes in Germany and the U.S. differed greatly. In the automobile and electronics industries, as seen in Fig. 7.2, the U.S. employed about 3.0 million people in 1998, but employment dropped significantly to approximately 2.0 million in 2019, a 66.5% compared with 1998. In Germany, capacity increased from 1.18 million in 1998 to 1.30 million in 2019, a gain of 110.4% compared to 1998.

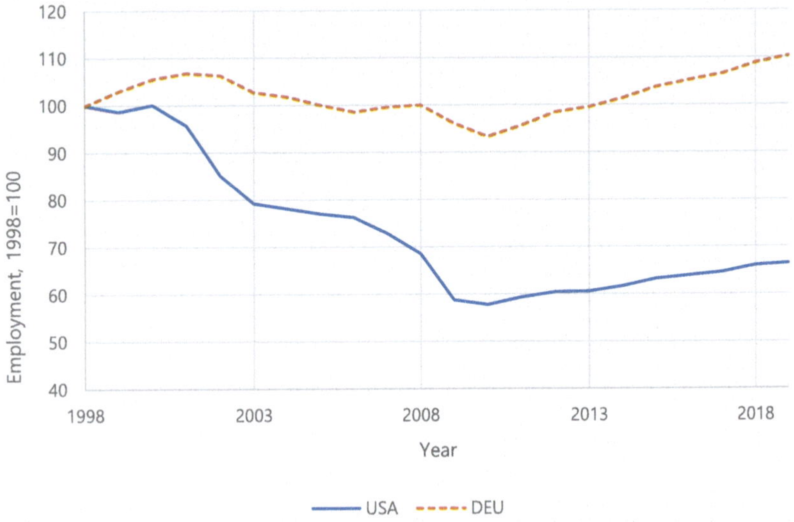

Fig. 7.2 Employment changes in Germany and the U.S. in the automobile and electronics industries, 1998–2019 (*Source* OECD [2020], STAN Industrial Analysis 2020 ed. [Variable EMPN, Industries D26 and D29 added])

However, more important than the maintenance or creation of jobs is whether international competitiveness is strengthened by enhancing high-value-added production and innovation capabilities. In the U.S., as noted in Chapter 3, domestic production and innovation capabilities were weakened due to the production relocation of major companies and the overseas transfer of R&D. However, in Germany, companies' overseas investment and reorganization of global production networks took place along with adjustment to domestic production methods and strengthening of innovation capabilities. Therefore, even in the process of expanding overseas production, international competitiveness in high-tech industries in Germany and the U.S. shows significant differences. Between 2000 and 2015, the U.S. high-tech trade balance decreased significantly from a deficit of approximately $28 billion in 2000 to a deficit of $180 billion in 2015. Germany's high-tech industry, the trade balance increased significantly by about 272%, from a surplus of $150 million in 2000 to a surplus of $40 billion in 2015. In the process of globalizing production, German companies further strengthened their domestic production and innovation capabilities. Beyond relocation and upgrade of human resources, Germany reorganized its production style and development model. We explore this in more detail in the next section.

Improvement of Domestic Innovation and Production Capabilities

Facing rapidly changing global competition and gaming-changing technologies, Germany sustained its economic growth through exports, rather than expanding domestic consumption. How did German companies increase exports despite the expansion of overseas production? This section explores how Germany improved its international competitiveness in the course of globalization.

Export growth was a method of Germany's overall economic growth. Even with expanded overseas production, German companies increased exports from 20.3% of total GDP in 1993 to 52.8% of GDP in 2022, while U.S.' remained around 10 to 11% from 1995 to 2021, and Japan's exports slightly grew from 10.0% in 1990 to 18.2% of GDP in 2021 (OECD 2024, *Trade in goods and services*). Germany's exports survived the 2008 global financial crisis, at first contracting, but rapidly rebounded, leading to economic growth and creating new jobs (Reisenbichler and Morgan 2012: 553; Rattner 2011). Growth of manufacturers' domestic exports also created new demand for services. Rattner (2011) explains how Germany gained a virtuous cycle of export growth: "More exports have generated more profits and created more jobs, and these in turn have fueled domestic demand for consumer products" (Rattner 2011: 8).

How did Germany improve its export competitiveness? Much comparative political economy (CPE) literature highlights Germany's capacity for wage coordination and wage restraints, which has delivered strong cost competitiveness to Germany's export-oriented manufacturers (Baccaro and Benassi 2017; Di Carlo 2018; Hall 2018; Hassel 2014; OECD 2012). Focusing on relative unit labor costs, Stockhammer (2011) argues that "German gains in competitiveness (since the introduction of the Euro) have not been founded on superior technological performance, but more effective wage suppression." Lapavitsas et al. (2011: 2) claim a similar story: "Germany has gained [cost] competitiveness within the Eurozone for the sole reason that it has been able to squeeze its workers harder."

Although German wage moderation may to some extent contribute to Germany's export competitiveness, the cost competitiveness alone cannot account for German export growth. Many other statistics reveal the weakness of the wage restraint thesis. For example, many econometric analyses, including Schröder (2011), Gaulier and Vicard (2012), and Gabrisch and Staehr (2014) reveal that changes in relative unit labor costs do not affect changes in the account balance for Germany and EU countries in any statistically or economically significant manner. In actuality, the wage gap between Germany and 16 other Eurozone countries increased from 24.3% (on average) in the 1990s to 28.2% in the 2000s, while the gap of the hourly productivity of workers between Germany and the rest of the Eurozone countries increased from 0.4% in the 1990s to 9.3% (on average) in the 2000s. The key driver of this productivity gap is Germany's core export manufacturing industries. The productivity level of German export manufacturers was 8% higher than that of the Eurozone in the 1990s, but the gap increased to 11% in the 2000s (Storm and Naastepad 2015: 15).

Much other CPE literature rightly points out non-price competitiveness, including improved quality and innovation capabilities, for the growth of German exports (Storm and Naastepad 2015; Braun and Deeg 2019). Unit labor cost development accounts for only a small fraction of German export growth, while non-price competitiveness, such as quality, accounts by and large for the growth of German exports. For example, according to the analysis of Storm and Naastepad (2015), the unit labor cost advantage was not transferred to the lower product price in German export companies. In other words, the price of German export products has not reduced as much as the decline of domestic wages.

How did Germany's manufacturing export sectors improve their non-price competitiveness, despite overseas expansion? Notably, Germany improved its export growth, not by creating new industries but by improving international competitiveness of its existing industries. German flagship industries, including automobile and machinery industries, were the main drivers of export and economic growth, with a strikingly similar set of products for the past four decades (Thelen 2021). Germany's top exports in 2017 were automobiles and auto parts, which accounted for approximately 17% of all goods exports. Germany also maintained its global preeminence in the export of industrial goods, including machinery and equipment (Diessner et al. 2022: 125–126).[2]

On the surface, the picture of German export sectors shows a continuity. But, this image of continuity obscures the fundamental changes that took place in the manufacturing industry during Germany's transition to the knowledge economy. For example, German carmakers sharply increased internal expenditure on R&D, from €15.77 billion in 2011 to €45.7 billion in 2021 (Statista 2023, Car industry in Germany). According to the U.S. National Science Foundation's R&D intensity data, the degree of R&D in the U.S. automobile industry accounted for only about 2.5% of total sales, while the intensity of R&D in the overall manufacturing industry was about 2.3% on average. In contrast, the German automobile industry invested 7% to 8% of its annual sales in product development and innovation (Jürgens and Meissner 2005: 22; Jürgens and Krzywdzinski 2010: 107; Kwon 2012: 587–588). This story applies to German manufacturing firms in general, which substantially increased R&D expenditure by 33 percent between 2007 and 2017 (Diessner et al. 2022: 126).

German manufacturers have also increased skilled labor, especially in R&D jobs, while increasing overseas production, as many empirical studies show (Nunnenkamp 2004; Bernaciak 2009). According to empirical studies on employment changes in the German automobile industry (Jürgens and Krzywdzinski 2010: 106; Jürgens and Meissner 2005: 227), unskilled white-collar workers (*Ungelernte Angestellte*), less involved in production innovation, decreased by about 55% between 1996 and 2001, while the number of skilled workers (*Facharbeiter*) increased by about 16% for the same period. In particular, while German lead firms cooperated with parts makers to build a flexible innovative production system in the process of globalization of production, SMEs increased the number of skilled workers by 64%. In addition, German automakers increased their qualified, professional employees (*Qualifizierte Angestellte*) in management and R&D by 94%. From 1995 to 2002, the number of R&D-related personnel in the German automobile industry

[2] The fact that Germany's export relies on the same manufacturing industries, including automobiles and machinery industries, differentiates Germany from Sweden and the Netherlands which increased exports by building new industries, including IT and financial services (Thelen 2021).

increased by about 50%, to 77,000. By contrast, in the U.S. the proportion of skilled workers changed little during the production globalization process. For example, between 1980 and 2004, the proportion of production blue-collar workers in the U.S. automobile industry remained fairly constant, at around 80% (Kwon 2012: 587–589).

Originally, Germany had a high proportion of skilled workers, and in the process of globalizing production that proportion increased to amplify development and innovation capabilities. By 2008, skilled labor increased to about 78.6% of all employment, while unskilled labor was reduced to 16.6%. While U.S. companies moved production overseas to reduce costs, in Germany, investments were increased to strengthen domestic R&D for high-quality German production at the global level.

Contrary to the prevailing claim that Germany improved its international competitiveness through wage cuts (Baccaro and Benassi 2017; Di Carlo 2018; Stockhammer 2011), Germany's average wages increased. Rather, it gained competitiveness through quality of products based on skilled labor. As seen in Table 7.1, university graduates employed in the German manufacturing sector increased by 401,974 jobs between 2002 and 2017, while jobs of low-qualified workers decreased by 403,393. During globalization of production, low-skilled, low-wage jobs decreased in Germany, while high-value-added R&D-related jobs increased significantly (Bernaciak 2010: 129).

Table 7.1 Changes in the employment and compensation by skill group in the German manufacturing sector, 2002–2017

Education levels		*2002*	*2017*	*Change 2002–17*
No formal qualifications	Compensation share	12.5%	6.9%	−5.6%
	employment	1,425,955	1,022,561	−403,393
Intermediate	Compensation share	56.7%	57.9%	+1.2%
	Employment	4,733,746	4,669,165	−64,580
University graduates*	Compensation share	30.8%	35.2%	+4.4
	employment	1,527,300	1,929,273	+401,974

Source Calculation based on Diessner et al. (2022: 133, Table 3)

**Note* University graduates refer to those with educational attainment at ISCED levels 5 and 6

German manufacturing companies also upgraded their international competitiveness by improving domestic innovation capabilities. In 2020, Germany remained at the top of the Bloomberg Innovation Index, owing to top-five scores in value-added manufacturing, high-technology, and patent activity (Jamrisko and Lu 2020). German exports were heavily concentrated in advanced, high-tech goods, with 52% of exports in high-tech products, and 31% in medium–high-tech products in 2015 (OECD 2018). Germany also was a leading producer of IT manufactured goods, including computers, electronics, and optical products. According to an OECD (2017) study, Germany was rated as Europe's most "central" IT manufacturing hub, highlighting its influence in global and domestic production networks for IT manufacturing goods. Contrary to the expectation of Varieties of Capitalism (VoC) literature (Hall and Soskice 2001), considering the importance of Information & Communications Technology (ICT) to advanced manufacturing in the knowledge economy, German manufacturing companies shifted away from traditional forms of innovation toward more radical forms. For example, since the mid-2010s, German automakers have registered as many patents that pertain to radically innovative technologies (in the areas of digitalization, electric mobility, and electronics) as those that pertain to conventional power trains (Koppel et al. 2018: 22–23; Diessner et al. 2022: 126).

The continuity of Germany's export profile and its sustained competitiveness does not mean no changes occurred. German export industries have undergone significant and deep structural changes in the course of transition to a digital economy and globalization, which involved severe conflicts and coordination among key actors, including government, trade associations, unions, and works councils. Next, we will explore how German companies expanded overseas before examining the domestic adjustment efforts.

German Pattern of Globalization

In this section, we examine the kinds of challenges German companies faced in globalization, and how they managed their overseas expansion, which required new coordination both at home and overseas to establish a global production network. To systematically manage global production and enhance innovation capabilities, Germany reenvisioned its role as the home country and center of management and innovation. Therefore, with overseas relocation of production, the home country's R&D

and innovation capabilities were further strengthened. The globalization process of production demanded dissolution of the old and reorganization of a new production model based on the existing national system. In other words, along with reorganization of the international division of labor, the home country's production system was reorganized through social coordination.

How did Germany achieve this transition? Before looking at the political process that caused German companies to pursue a domestic production path different from the U.S. and Japan, this section examines how German companies organized international divisions of labor in the course of globalization, and how domestic production methods were reorganized.

How German Companies Globalized

This section examines how German companies uniquely managed their overseas expansion and why Germany improved its domestic innovation capabilities even while expanding overseas production.

Notably, German companies globalize in ways different from the U.S. German companies systematically coordinated home and overseas production through division of labor, giving priority to the German home sites. By contrast, U.S. companies' link between overseas and domestic production was weak on systematic organization of production, instead freely selecting production sites based on domestic cost reduction and high returns. However, U.S. multinational corporations (MNCs) are more likely to centrally coordinate subsidiaries on foreign soil through formal, codified, and standardized global policies than German MNCs (Ferner et al. 2004, 2013). German companies were less likely than U.S. firms to develop transferable and codified rules for controlling their subsidiaries on foreign soil. Instead, they organized a global production network focused on production management rather than prioritizing financial value. German firms pursued close links between overseas and domestic production bases, and strengthened domestic management and innovation capabilities to organize global production.

Germany's reorganization in the course of globalization also differed from Japan's path. Japan focused on transferring its existing model of production system overseas, confident in its traditional practices rather than reverse learning from overseas production. With its globalization based on nationally closed circles of stakeholders, Japan delayed its reform of domestic production, as seen in Chapter 5, and Japanese production and innovation systems became outdated in the course of globalization. By contrast, Germany improved its domestic production and innovation system through opening to new challenges and reverse learning from overseas production. In contrast to Japan's unilateral transfer of its production model overseas, German firms made various experiments on foreign soil, and learned in the process (Baccaro et al. 2018: 627–629; Herrigel 2015).

Before examining Germany's dismantling of the old and introduction of the new adaptations of production methods, let's look first at how German companies globalized and established overseas parts procurement systems. In Germany's globalization process, the most notable feature has been the strengthening of home country production bases, including research and innovation. German companies invested in strengthening domestic production and innovation capabilities, while in the U.S., increasing overseas investment meant reducing domestic investment in a zero-sum relationship. While U.S. manufacturers increased their overseas investment from 33% in 2000 to 77% in 2009, domestic spending of U.S. companies decreased by 50%. The same trend can be found in R&D investment. Between 1998 and 2007, U.S. overseas R&D investments increased 2.5 times more than domestic investments. Most of that investment in the high-tech industry has flowed to Asia. Between 2009 and 2013, Asian countries such as China, Japan, and South Korea became the center of investment, absorbing $509 billion, compared to only $172 billion invested in the U.S. (Atkinson and Ezell 2012: 23–24, 45, 65).

By contrast, Germany's overseas relocation of R&D facilities increased, but the role of R&D in overseas bases was limited, and investment in domestic R&D as a global center to coordinate engineering and development was expanded. German companies' R&D transfer increased from 1.4% in 2006 to 2.6% in 2012 (Zanker and Hovat 2015). Overseas R&D facilities were limited to providing technical support for local facilities to produce specialty products for local markets. In other words, core R&D took place in Germany (Krzywdzinski 2014; Herrigel et al. 2017).

German companies' overseas expansion shows a more coordinated pattern in the international division of labor. From the 1990s to the mid-2000s, when German companies initially moved production to Eastern Europe and China, low-cost models or already developed models were moved overseas, while domestic production tended to maintain high-value-added production or precision technology (Krzywdzinski 2014).

However, geographical divisions of labor gradually weakened, leading to a situation in which production in Germany and production in low-wage countries became a direct competitive relationship. Amid new competition for overseas local consumers, German companies felt increasing pressure to cut costs in all product areas, while facing local consumers' demand for high-quality products tailored to their tastes. German companies were no longer free from price competition. For example, German companies had to produce locally in emerging markets such as China, rather than avoid price competition in high-end niche markets, and were required to innovate, reduce costs, and adjust their local parts procurement system to meet intensified competition in these emerging markets (Herrigel 2015: 140). German companies had to strengthen their engineering and R&D capabilities in overseas local production sites to adapt to this competition in emerging markets, establish new parts procurement systems overseas, and coordinate R&D capabilities, engineers, and production capabilities.

To ensure a competitive advantage, German corporations created "sophisticated production clusters" for parts procurement overseas. These overseas clusters were designed to imitate or supplement domestic production clusters for automobile or machine production (Herrigel et al. 2017: 80–141). German companies' strategy to build "sophisticated production clusters" overseas in local production sites such as China is distinct from the U.S. strategy of establishing cost-effective production networks based on the finance-dominant perspective. U.S. overseas production has substituted home parts makers with least-cost parts makers overseas, thus isolating home parts makers from growth opportunities (Kwon 2012).

To meet increasing demands overseas, in areas such as innovation, cost reduction in production processes, and stable delivery systems, German prime contractors tended to utilize German parts makers because local Chinese companies could not meet quality standards or delivery times. Although Germany's parts procurement system was not grouped into a one-company-affiliated organization as in Japan, German SMEs cooperated with prime contractors at local production sites based on their own high technology and innovation capabilities. German companies' coordinated networks overseas differ from Japanese companies' nationally closed circle of home subcontracting members. The German parts procurement system overseas is more open market-based, but technically coordinated. This arrangement extended beyond China. As quality and innovation increased in developing regions such as Brazil and Eastern Europe, German parts makers found new opportunities (Depner 2006: 103ff; Herrigel et al. 2017: 91–92).

Improvement of Germany's engineering and R&D and production capabilities in overseas local production did not negatively affect home production (Kwon: 2012; Herrigel 2013; 2015). Germany strengthened its domestic industry and innovation capabilities during globalization of production and finance thanks to its home country's focus in the process of reorganizing production at the global level. In this process, German companies had to redefine the role of their home country's production bases, and address how to flexibly and reliably carry out new high-quality product development, product circulation, and production process transitions at the global level.

Beyond the political logic of emotional patriotism or nationalism, German companies strengthened their domestic innovation capabilities to build high-quality global production networks. Based on their long experience of research and empirical analysis of the recent development of the German global network, German industry experts Herrigel et al. (2017) explain why German companies are centered on home country production:

> German companies … have accumulated production capacity, innovation capabilities, and experiential knowledge in their home country, that [in the home country] their prime contractors, machinery makers, and parts and materials companies are near, that they are well established in the innovative environment with other outstanding actors such as universities, and, finally, that the supportive politics exists near them. (Herrigel et al. 2017: 230)

German companies' home country development and production in the process of globalization results from the advantages of home-based production and innovation ecosystems. Germany had a wealth of research-oriented universities and polytechnic schools, high-quality engineering graduates, and well-developed clusters of closely related research and consulting companies (Herrgiel 2013: 6–9; 2015: 143). Germany has concentrated on innovation and experiential knowledge related to production as industrial commons easily accessible to German companies, and has an abundant workforce, with high levels of education and ability. Many companies have well-developed, long-lasting linkages with

R&D partners (*Entwicklungspartnern*), and political networks based on those partnerships. Lead firms, which develop consensus on product and technology trends, and transferring technologies, are easily accessed in the home country. Lead firms quickly scan and easily evaluate whether a product at the R&D stage can be made economically, identify risks, and how to reduce unnecessary costs. Experiments based on cooperative relations with skilled production labor are possible in a geographically close area (Herrigel et al. 2017: 230).

German companies further strengthened their home country's innovation capabilities as a way to adapt to intensifying competition and various needs abroad. In contrast to the case of Japan, where companies focused on transferring their domestic production method overseas with confidence in its excellence, German firms opened to new challenges from globalization, learning from overseas experiments and reflecting upon foreign demands and global standards, which in turn required further improvement of domestic innovation and production capabilities to systematically utilize the global production networks. In order to adapt to consumer preferences and local regulations overseas, the ability to develop domestic products and effective production methods expanded as various engineering capabilities and application programs for local production developed. German companies strengthened their home country's production system for innovation in applications of overseas production by redefining their home country production as a "lead plant" concept. Home country innovation centers are responsible for the transfer and applied development of production technologies to several overseas locations, and are involved in the spread and coordination of various methods tested abroad. To this end, engineers and technicians in Germany cooperate with local overseas technicians and train local personnel (Herrigel et al. 2017: 233–234).

In the global network of German companies, home country R&D and production engineering teams support and cooperate with overseas local engineering and production teams at various levels. Qualitative and quantitative expansion of central R&D and engineering in the home country proceeded as efforts to develop overseas research and product design increased. For example, German machinery and automotive companies created "continuous improvement" teams (CITs) to support local production of their products around the world and sometimes apply better solutions to other regional production based on new locally performed experiments (Herrigel 2013: 2, 6–9; 2015: 143). Germany, as the home country, serves as a control tower or coordination center (*Steuerungsstandort*) for global overseas production networks.

Actual statistics show that demand for engineers and technicians in Germany's automobile, machinery, and electronics and parts industries has increased significantly (Alphametrics and Ismeri Europa 2009: 56). For example, labor associated with direct production has remained somewhat constant since 2007, while research-related employment has increased dramatically. Automakers and parts makers now account for about a third of Germany's R&D costs. According to a 2012 report by the German Automobile Association (VDA), about 89,000 people are engaged in research and development, an increase of more than 2,000 workers compared to 2007. Increased overseas production and improved development and engineering capabilities overseas did not result in the loss of production or development capabilities at home (Herrigel 2015: 143–144). As overseas production increased, production requiring high technology became important at home. Manufacturing personnel underwent training to improve problem-solving skills to carry out new tasks. R&D increases in the home country, the need for prototyping, small batch production, and quick turnaround manufacturing capabilities increased (Herrigel 2015: 144).

Unlike the U.S., Germany's global production system was effectively reorganized through consultation with various stakeholders rather than prioritizing shareholder value set by unilateral decisions of financial capital (Berghoff 2016). Based on the export-oriented growth model and reinforced by domestic stakeholders, German stakeholders emphasized the centrality of home and improved domestic innovation and coordination capabilities to increase local adaptability and competitiveness as overseas production increased. Unlike Japan, German companies are more open to challenges and demands overseas, through reverse learning and active response to growing demands and challenges overseas. In order to support overseas production, and the new global division of labor, German companies strengthened, rather than hollowed out, their domestic innovation capabilities with globalization, creating a virtuous cycle in which strengthening domestic innovation capabilities further increased the centrality of domestic production.

Changes in Germany's Domestic Production System

Germany's focus on domestic production sites and home country centrality was not a continuation of an existing model, but a large-scale reorganization of domestic production and innovation in the process of globalization of companies. If the existing production system had remained, the relationship between overseas production bases and those of home countries would have weakened and resulted in direct competition and substitution. Here we will examine the uniqueness of the existing German production system and how it has changed in the globalization process, and then we examine how Germany improved its innovative ecosystem.

Changes in Diversified Quality Production

In much of the political-economic literature, German political economy is classified as a case model of "coordinated market economy" (Soskice 1999; Hall and Soskice 2001). Prior to 1990, social coordination by tightly intertwined institutions, including centralized bargaining, skill formation, co-determination, and bank-based corporate governance, distinguished Germany's political economic system from the Anglo-American neoliberal market model, the French and Japanese statist model, and Italian familial capitalism. The capacities for strategic coordination within German economic governance arrangements were not imposed by discretionary state power, but were largely self-organized within civil society, where large banks established a dense network with manufacturing companies, and employer and employees organized themselves and negotiated (Dyson 1986: 118–141; Windolf and Beyer 1996; Beyer and Höpner 2003).

Through social coordination, the traditional German model of political economy showed significant competitiveness and political stability. In particular, Germany's production system was regarded as the secret of its economic competitiveness. Germany's production model is often referred to as Diversified Quality Production (DQP) (Sorge and Streeck 2016; Streeck 1991, 1992; Sorge and Streeck 1987). DQP describes a production system that maintains premium prices by increasing the innovation ratio of products and production to suit consumer tastes in a saturated market. Unlike the past craft production system (Costin 2001), the DQP system does not abandon mass production. Yet unlike

Fordism, it does not ignore consumers' diverse preferences or blindly follow producers' unilateral standardization. Germany's DQP system divides total production into small batches of customized products, along with mass production, to suit consumers' tastes, thus forming a flexible production system to meet a complex market's needs (Sorge and Streeck 2016; Piore and Sabel 1984).

Germany's unique DQP production system became clearly established in the 1970s against the backdrop of global oil shocks. For example, an empirical study by Cox and Kriegbaum (1980) shows that in three major industries in Germany, companies moved to more customized and non-routine production systems, compared to British companies. Through this adjustment, they argue, Germany maintained greater profit margins and employment than the U.K.

Germany's DQP system required a unique political and social system different from the Anglo-American free-market system. Institutionalists often argue that German-style DQP is difficult to imitate and establish in countries without these specific institutional conditions. Institutionalists hold that DQP needs an ample supply of skilled workers in order to easily adapt to new forms of work based on flexible task assignment. This ample supply of skilled workers needs rich institutional conditions to organize societywide skill formation, including high levels of employment protection, preventing companies from competing on cost minimization and numerical flexibility. Rather, these conditions enable pursuit of premium markets by building the product mix upscale. All these elements need rich and clearly defined institutions to enforce reluctant employers to follow the beneficial road at the social level. In the absence of equal wage systems supported by centralized bargaining and bank-based patient finance, companies may competitively pursue low-wage-dependent production, leaving skill formation in a society as a whole at a low level, as does the U.S. free-market system (Baccaro et al. 2018: 615; Sorge and Streeck 2016: 2). Thus, institutionalists hold that DQP depends on strong unions, joint decision-making through all levels of management, and equal high wages through centralized wage negotiations (Sorge and Streeck 2016: 9).

However, Germany's unique DQP system was challenged by globalization and rapidly changing technology in the 1990s and the 2000s. First, the context of global competition changed significantly. German companies' competitors improved their innovation and production capabilities significantly. Throughout the 1980s and 1990s, Japanese lean production, regarded more efficient than German DQP, diffused globally, and the U.S. began to develop more efficient alternatives to their existing Fordist mass production. German DQP firms might excel in competition with American-style mass producers, but they lost their competitive edge in competition with new forms of post-Fordism and the U.S. new modular production which combined conception and execution (Kwon 2005, 2012; Herrigel 1997). Now, what German institutions regarded as "beneficial constraints" for DQP turned out to be rigid obstacles in the changed context of international competition.

While Japan delayed domestic reform as it transfered its existing model overseas, Germany faced new challenges overseas and was enforced to reform the existing DQP at home. In the 1990s, German export manufacturers became more price-sensitive than they once had been. Their international competitors were able to produce similar quality products at lower prices. German firms lost their competitive edge on foreign soil, such as in China, in addition to increasing domestic costs which resulted from reunification (Baccaro et al. 2018: 616).

In addition, as German firms increased overseas expansion since the 1990s, German employers easily found highly skilled workers in foreign countries, especially in Eastern Europe and China, at much lower wages than in Germany. Along with globalization of production and employer mobility, labor unions were weakened, allowing companies to experiment with simpler production systems different from those within Germany. In contrast to the case of Japan, German firms' experimenting with new practices in overseas production sites and establishing more efficient production methods put enormous pressure on unions and works councils in German domestic production (Sorge and Streeck 2016: 11).

Reflecting upon their cost problems in the changed context of global competition, German employers became offensive at reforming the existing DQP institutions. Until the early 1990s, German export-oriented manufacturing firms deliberatively agreed on the rigid institution, including centralized wage negotiations, strong employment protections, and strong rules concerning skill formation and hiring apprentices, to achieve their comparative advantages. But the Gesamtmetall (metalworking employers' association) heavily lobbied for liberalization of industrial relations during the 1990s and 2000s, not least through its pro-reform think-tank Initiative Neue Soziale Marktwirtschaft (INSM) (Diessner et al. 2022: 132).

Beyond lobbying, German employers took concrete steps that further eroded collective bargaining institutions. Initially, in the 1990s, employers in the former East Germany region began to allow employer associations to avoid the rigid, industry-level wage contract and associated wage provisions. In response, German employer associations introduced the ÖTV membership (the option of membership without having to abide by the terms of the industry-level contract). German employer associations lost much coordination capability compared to the traditional centralized system (Kwon 2002, 2005; Diessner et al. 2022: 132).

Another attempt of German employers to meet the cost competition was greater use of agency workers, domestic outsourcing, and offshoring overseas (Baccaro and Benassi 2017; Benassi 2016). Agency workers who are less securely employed typically earn 25 to 30% less than regular employees (Diessner et al. 2022: 132). Large German firms began to transfer the burdens to suppliers by increasing outsourcing of parts and squeezing the price. Further, German firms offshored the more labor-intensive parts to former communist countries. Meantime, German employers requested trade unions to agree to more concessionary bargaining, exchanging "open clauses" for the promise of job security. A representative example is the Hartz reform which lowered the wage of workers by increasing the costs of becoming unemployed (Baccaro et al. 2018: 616–617).

German manufacturing firms undermined job security for skilled workers by eroding collective bargaining, even though they rely on a skilled workforce for international competition (Benassi 2016). The industry-level collective bargaining coverage in Germany's manufacturing sector declined from 80% in 1995 to 50% in 2013, and in recent years, has declined even farther. According to the IAb Establishment Panel, only 51% of employees were covered by collective bargaining in 2020, of which 43% were covered by an industry-level agreement and 8% by a company or workplace agreement (Schulten and the WSI Collective Agreement Archive 2022: 20; Ellguth and Kohaut 2021; Baccaro et al. 2018: 616–617).

Germany also changed to a dual labor market system where stable high-wage jobs went to workers with high technical skills, while non-regular jobs increased (Artus 2013; Bosch et al. 2007; Haipeter 2013). In large firms where works councils were independent and strong, DQP-style employment systems continue, compared to SMEs. In the core sector, German firms pursued high skills and rapid innovation, while peripherally they routinized and standardized production with top-down discipline and threats of termination and outsourcing. Even in large firms, works councils were forced to negotiate significant concessions in order to avoid outsourcing to German subcontractors at lower pay (Doellgast and Berg 2018; Baccaro et al. 2018: 622).

However, Germany's adaptations in the course of globalization did not confirm the *liberalization thesis* that Germany's sweeping institutional changes resulted in a neoliberal direction or convergence toward an Anglo-Saxon-style free-market system (Streeck 2009; Baccaro and Howell 2011, 2017; Baccaro and Benassi 2017). Nor did it conform to the *dualization thesis* that the traditional model operates relatively unchanged in the core manufacturing sectors, while institutional changes occur largely in the peripheral sectors, including service sector (Thelen 2014; Palier and Thelen 2010; Hassel 2014). Contrary to the dualization thesis, Germany made far-reaching changes that have disrupted the core institutions of the traditional DQP model, as seen in the Hartz reforms of the early 2000s (Diessner et al. 2022: 119). Germany's profound changes did not spare core sectors of Germany's political economy.

However, contrary to the liberalization thesis, German reform did not result in convergence toward an Anglo-American uncoordinated free-market system. Instead, as shall be examined in the next chapter, through conflicts and social adjustments, Germany has established a new coordination system different from the U.S. free-market system. Unlike the U.S. uncoordinated free market, German stakeholders improved R&D and engineering capabilities at home in the course of globalization, based on a home country centrality, through collective negotiation by domestic stakeholders (Kwon 2012; Herrigel 2015; Diessner et al. 2022: 118). Unlike the U.S., Germany developed a new "high-end dual-training" system to connect school and workplace training within post-secondary higher education, as a layer on top of the traditional dual apprenticeship, by combining worker training with courses in a higher education setting rather than a vocational school. The number of new dual-study sites increased by 55% between 2004 and 2013 (Graf 2018). German export manufacturers now increasingly seek employees with wider skill sets in mechanical, electrical, and information technology, in order to boost innovative capacity at home (Diessner et al. 2022: 123, 126–127).

To meet the challenges of globalization and rapidly changing technology, German employers, universities, and governments collectively built a new skill formation system. German large export-oriented firms in core manufacturing industries, which traditionally supported corporatist dual apprenticeship, have become fervent supporters of deregulation of the apprenticeship system, steered clear of the American-style free-market system. Instead, German employers actively minimized the risk of future skill shortages by collectively coordinating and connecting high-quality graduate students to firms early on. In the new dual-training system, firms and universities, rather chambers of commerce and trade unions, are the key actors negotiating curricula and access to a range of dual-study programs. Considering the crucial elements for German firms to succeed in advanced ICT-intensive manufacturing, policy-makers have encouraged universities to provide the skills (STEM and engineering in particular) (Diessner et al. 2022: 129–131; Graf 2018; Thelen 2021; Busemeyer 2012; Durazzi 2019).

At the national level, Germany shifted away from traditional VoC coordination, in which employers and unions developed alliances between capital and labor for centralized coordination, to a new system in which unions became weaker and state-business relationships gained prominence (Diessner et al. 2022: 141). However, at the micro level, employers and employees, as well as local governments and research institutes, developed a new social coordination to improve the innovation and production ecosystem at home. German employers and employees redeployed their institutions to reward and retain highly skilled workers deemed vital for new production strategies in the era of knowledge-based growth.

Germany's social coordination model for high-quality production has survived challenges from the pressure of globalization and financialization since the 2000s. Germany's innovation capabilities strengthened its role in coordinating professional functions for the global network. Innovation replaced traditional forms of production (Herrigel et al. 2017: 229). According to DQP advocate Wolfgang Streeck, Germany had to reconceptualize DQP, leading to a more heterogeneous production system which emphasized quality over consumer customization, combining commercialization and non-routinized operations. The new system emphasized the overlap between new and old industries through piecemeal innovation of existing companies, rather than fundamental industrial ruptures (Sorge and Streeck 2016: 9). Germany maintained its export competitiveness in major industries such as consumer-sensitive goods and premium cars. Despite the strength of Japanese automobiles, Germany has held the premium automobile market (The Economist,

June 7, 2014: 59–60), and has held leadership in high-technology, high-quality production (Herrigel 2015). According to Venohr and Meyer, Germany maintained the world product quality leadership position in more than 1,000 products, from high-quality screws to high-quality washing machines. Lufthansa Technik is also the maintenance services leader in the global aviation industry and maintenance services (Venohr and Meyer 2007; Sorge and Streeck 2016: 14). Despite overseas production, Germany succeeded in upgrading its domestic industry (Sorge and Streeck 2016: 15).

Building and Innovation Ecosystem and the Role of the State

Various support measures of the German state enabled expansion of the industrial commons and the upgrading of its domestic industries. However, the role of the state in European social-coordinated corporatist countries such as Germany is different from those of developmental states such as Korea and Japan that adopted state-led development. The federal government of Germany, unlike East Asian developmentalist countries, supports development of the industrial ecosystem through indirect, horizontal industrial policies rather than directly intervening in fostering industries through strategic-selective industrial policies. Compared to them, the German state is much more liberal and neutral. However, the German state, unlike the U.S., supports industry rather than takes a non-interventionist attitude toward private actors. For example, the U.S. innovation system focuses on pure basic research, often defense-related, neutral to market actors, while the German state indirectly supports industry-related application research and industry-related environments. In this section, we briefly examine how Germany has built an innovation ecosystem at home with its government's assistance.

The German government's industrial policy to promote domestic production and innovation capabilities differs from that of the East Asian developmental state. The role of government in the East Asian developmental state model is to first set specific goals for industrial development and provide various selective support systems and incentives accordingly. In contrast, Germany, while giving financial and institutional support, does not take the initiative in controlling or coordinating various actors (Belzer and Hilbert 1996; Hirsch-Kreinsen 1994; Rose 1995). Germany's role in social coordination corporatism is to indirectly support private economic actors to establish an autonomous coordination system within which actors can negotiate and cooperate with each other. In other words, corporatist government focuses on creating an industrial ecosystem so that companies and research institutes can autonomously establish cooperative networks, assisted by various institutional arrangements.

In Germany not only the federal government but also state (*Land*) and local governments support R&D at various levels of policy. In particular, since 1992, the German government has actively supported technology and applied science universities to participate in consortia that strengthen R&D capabilities in cooperation with SMEs, providing a venue for cooperation and encouragement.

The German government uses policies to foster an innovative ecosystem where companies can enhance their innovation capabilities rather than rely on direct industrial policies as in Japan and East Asian countries. Notably, German innovation policy first focuses on SMEs (*Mittelstand*). While large and multinational corporations drive German innovation, the government focuses on strengthening SMEs to commercialize innovation and conduct cutting-edge R&D (Frietch and Kroll 2008: 5). The federal and state governments support SMEs through university–industrial collaboration for innovative ecosystems.

Recently, the German federal government has initiated the High-Tech Strategy (HTS) to set the overall direction and enhance innovation capabilities by coordinating public research and innovation policies. With HTS, Germany aims to enhance international competitiveness by reviewing conditions for an innovation system. HTS seeks to enhance research capabilities by expanding existing research policy measures, and by strengthening linkage and cooperation between universities and industry, while focusing on the application and commercialization of research. The German government is committed to supporting innovative SMEs while developing cutting-edge technology (Frietsch and Kroll 2008: 5–7). SMEs and startups operating in cutting-edge fields (biotech, nanotech, ITC, production and energy-efficient technologies, optical technology) all benefit from HTS.

Furthermore, German governments have played an active interventionist role in promoting innovation capabilities. After the Second World War, Germany had firmly committed itself to open markets and was resolutely opposed to state intervention, in contrast to the East Asian developmental states (Katzenstein 1977: 900; Abelshauser 2016: 12–14). More recently German governments have actively promoted the improvement of domestic industrial and innovative capabilities. For example, in

February 2019, the Ministry of Economy startled many people when it announced its ambitious National Industrial Strategy 2030 (NIS 2030). To improve the German economy in a world transformed by new technologies, a rapidly rising China, and a protectionist U.S., NIS 2030 proposed that the state invest in strategic growth sectors, foster national champions big enough to withstand global competition, protect flagship companies from unwanted foreign takeover, and defend its technological sovereignty (Bundesminiserium für Wirtwschaft und Energie [BMWi] 2019a, 2019b; Germann 2023: 1749–1750). NIS 2030 shows a paradigm shift toward a far more proactive, interventionist state.

However, the most important feature of Germany's innovation research system is its close cooperation between private companies, social organizations, universities, and government research institutes, which serves as a model for the U.S. and Britain. The Fraunhofer model emerging from the Fraunhofer research institutes strengthens innovation ecosystems through cooperative networks with private research companies in applied science. The Fraunhofer Society conducts application-oriented research used directly by public and private companies, thus bridging the gap between universities and industries (Jewell 2017: 1; Hoffmann 2018).

The Fraunhofer Society consists of over 70 institutes and research units across Germany. In 2017 the institutes employed a total of 25,327 researchers and staff, a marked increase over the 23,236 employed in 2013. Scientists increased from 8,837 in 2013 to 9,792 in 2017. Approximately 30% of funds come from German federal and state governments, and 70% come from corporate and public research institute contracts. As of 2017, Fraunhofer's research budget was about 2.1 billion euros (Hoffmann 2018; Jewell 2017: 2).

To boost the industrial innovation ecosystem, Fraunhofer works directly with SMEs, such as a cooperative project with Bavarian Butcher to develop fat-free sausages, in cooperation with SMEs. While the Society works with automobile and consumer electronics companies, most of its partners (approximately 60%) are SMEs (Jewell 2017: 2).

Fraunhofer transfers new technologies from development and research to industries, thus developing innovation ecosystems. With about 10,000 projects currently in progress, the Society conducts specific industry-related projects and provides research results directly to corporations, along with patenting and technology licensing. Fraunhofer also brings up next generations of research scientists, with about 900 scientists leaving Fraunhofer every year for corporations (Jewell 2017: 5).

Meanwhile, the Fraunhofer Society's strong connection with universities cross-fertilizes to reinforce both industry and universities. Composed mainly of university professors and researchers, it provides companies with easy access to basic research universities. The Fraunhofer Society easily attracts young scientists, students, and interns. The Society integrates the interests and needs of industry with education by providing interns and students with access to real-world problems. Companies are able to recruit excellent talent with access to advanced research. The Fraunhofer Society trains Ph.D. students to pursue startup companies. These SMEs are an important part of the Fraunhofer incubation system to ensure that their findings are applied to or commercialized in the industry (Jewell 2017: 2–3; Hoffmann 2018). The Society conducts technical research on areas that have not yet emerged as main market interests, based on autonomous long-term prospects.

In summary, German companies have improved their home country's innovation capabilities in order to strengthen their innovation competitiveness at the global level, through cooperative networks based on industry–university links, between federal and state governments, and the work of the Fraunhofer Society. Germany's global strategy was built through the active involvement and coordination of many stakeholders, including the state and trade associations. In the next chapter, we will examine the politics of transformation in the course of globalization.

CHAPTER 8

Politics of Transformation in Germany

Despite the globalization of production and finance, Germany's domestic production has not been hollowed out; rather, its innovation and production capacities have improved. In order to effectively adapt to global competition and challenges in the process of expanding overseas production, German companies felt the need to further develop their innovation capabilities and cooperative corporate relationships built over time in their home country. High technology, local application capability, and intensifying competition required German companies to actively utilize domestic production and innovation ecosystems.

Germany's adaptation method was not based on any centralized pre-planning or single group of actors, but on mutual coordination and adaptation among stakeholders such as national and local governments, industry associations, unions, works councils, and investment experts. In particular, its adaptation through social consultations marks a notable difference between Germany and other countries. Despite the trend in neoliberal financialization and globalization, Germany engaged in a different development method. Germany was in a situation of financialization and globalization similar to the U.S., but while the U.S. drove changes according to maximum shareholder value based on unilateral decisions by financial capital, Germany sidestepped the unilateral claim of shareholder priority through collective consultations, upgraded

H. Kwon, *Openness and Coordination*,
https://doi.org/10.1007/978-981-97-3352-1_8

its domestic industrial innovation ecosystem, and coordinated overseas-domestic production based on social consultation among stakeholders.

In this chapter, we explore the political process among German stakeholders in the globalization of production and finance. First, we examine how Germany reinforces its export-driven growth strategy in the course of overseas expansion, focusing on changes in the social alliances for export growth at national level politics. And then, we explore the politics at a micro level, discussing coordination of interfirm conflicts, labor–management conflicts, and the politics of R&D employees and works councils, in the course of reorganization of corporate governance and production.

Export-Oriented Growth Strategy and Social Alliances

Since the end of the Second World War, Germany achieved its economic development by continuously using an export-driven growth strategy. Export expansion was not only the secret of success for the German economy's high growth until the 1970s, but also the way of recovering economic crises, including oil shocks and the 2008 global financial crisis (Kreile 1977: 775–776; Baccaro and Pontusson 2016; Höpner 2019; Hünnekes et al. 2019). Germany's basic economic policy has been to increase export competitiveness, including a policy mix of aggressive deflation and restrained domestic consumption, as well as low-wage employment and rationalization of supply chains while protecting the most productive and highly coordinated manufacturing sector (Hopkin and Voss 2022: 388).

However, reinforcement of export-driven growth strategy in Germany does not exclude changes in social alliances to support that strategy. As seen in Chapter 7, in order to increase export-led growth in globalization, Germany underwent significant changes, including deregulation of its labor market, limiting unemployment insurance, decentralization of collective bargaining, liberalization of capital markets, and offshoring. These domestic adjustments in the course of overseas expansion and adapting to rapidly changing technology involved serious conflicts and changes in social alliances to support an increasingly export-led growth strategy. In this section, we explore how Germany continues its export-led growth strategy, and how Germany's export-led growth coalition has changed in the course of adapting to globalization.

Germany's export growth regime relies on a number of institutions and political strategies that are directed at maintaining a current account surplus, often by suppressing domestic demand, unlike the U.S. consumption-led growth. Traditionally, the German export regime built upon safeguarding and relative undervaluation of the national currency (e.g., through restrictive central bank policies) as well as securing market access for German products and services and integrating global supply chains (e.g., through development aid and economic diplomacy) (Kreile 1977; Höpner 2019; Nölke 2020; Germann 2021a).

Traditionally, the axis of the policy network for export growth strategy in Germany included a close network linking the ministerial bureaucracy to export manufacturers, trade associations, and banking. Germany's policy networks, based on the principle of liberalism, differed from French and Japanese statist networks where state bureaucrats have initiative and guidance over industrialists. Germany's policy networks also differed from Italian policy networks, in which bureaucrats were captured and colonized by interest groups (Kreile 1977: 778–779). In German policy-making, the main interest groups are entitled to be heard and consulted during the drafting stage of legislation. Through quiet politics, these interest groups participate in the legislative process at a stage when draft projects are still kept secret from the Bundestag. Parliament is more or less eclipsed by cooperation between bureaucrats and interest groups. For example, between 1952 and 1964, only eight out of 286 petitions filed by the BDI (the umbrella organization of German industry) on subjects related to foreign economic policy were addressed to the Bundestag (Kreile 1977: 784).

Furthermore, unlike the American-style lobby system, German trade associations have developed a self-governing system, organizing their members and dealing with their internal issues and rules. German industry is highly concentrated and remarkably well organized. German trade associations assume functions which go far beyond traditional interest group activities. For example, the Iron and Steel Association has features of an industry-wide planning institution, as it collects and distributes information on planned sales, production capacities, and investment plans (Arndt 1966: 73).

The continuity and reinforcement of Germany's export growth strategy relies on the dominant growth coalition which reflects upon the social interests of cross-class alliance of employers and labor in the export manufacturing sector. Powerful groups, as a social bloc for a growth strategy, can shape models to their needs in ways which bypass formal and visible policy processes altogether (Hopkin and Voss 2022: 377). Particularly in the general consensus that the German economy depends on global markets—imports and exports relative to overall GDP in 2020 stand at 82%, far higher than the U.S. (26%) and Japan (37%) (World Bank 2021 database)—the structural economic influence of the export sector has effectively translated into political power (Wadbrook 1972: 80; Kasper 1972: 283). Reflecting upon its outstanding dependence on global markets, economic exchange with the rest of the world is a critical issue in political debate due to its vulnerability and sense of urgency (Kundnani 2011: 36–37).

Thus, large German corporations in export manufacturing industries carry much political clout and also dominate crucial industry associations central to Germany's political economy (Koddenbrock and Mertens 2022: 146). Reflecting upon their share of German export goods, the dominant manufacturing sectors include automobile (€187.1 billion in 2020), machinery and equipment (€174.54 billion), chemicals and chemical products (€111.28 billion), and computer, electronics and optical products (€109.51 billion) (Federal Statistical Office 2021).

Labor in the German export industries is also part of a grand coalition for Germany's export growth regime as a beneficiary of export growth. German workers and unions have restrained wages with inflation-consciousness for concern for export performance. In particular, *IG Metall*, the powerful metal union, has its center of strength in export-intensive industries, and has led wage negotiations in Germany. As much Comparative Political Economy (CPE) literature points out, wage growth suppression, which German unions such as the IG Metall exercised, contributed to the growth of German exports (Baccaro and Benassi 2017; Di Carlo 2018; Hall 2017; Hassel 2014). German unions, although not docile, suspended class conflicts for the benefit of export growth (Kreile 1977: 777, 786).

With this postwar export growth regime, industrialists, union leaders (particularly in export industries), and politicians alike adhered to the principle that German competitiveness in world markets had to be maintained and strengthened. Acknowledging that Germany is a trading nation, they put highest priority on Germany's export competitiveness. Price stability and export competitiveness became the overriding objectives of economic policy throughout the postwar decades (Koddenbrock and Mertens 2022: 144; Kundnani 2011: 36–37; Kreile 1977: 777).

However, Germany's continuity of export growth and export profile does not mean the simple persistence of an export growth regime. German export manufacturers faced new challenges in the world market throughout the 1990s and 2000s, such as diffusion of Japanese lean production, new global production networks, and a rapidly changing technology and knowledge economy. Losing its premium competitive edge, German export manufacturers became more price-sensitive. Where German competitors were able to produce similar quality products at lower prices due to their changed production methods, the existing German Diversified Quality Production turned out rigid and costly (Herrigel 1997; Kwon 2005, 2012; Baccaro et al. 2018).

German export corporations and policy-makers went on the offensive to improve their international competitiveness. In particular, contrary to the expectation of the VoC literature, German employers began to readjust rather than reinforce their existing DQP institutions. German employers decentralized and liberalized central wage negotiations, while employers in the former East Germany region left employer associations, to reduce the production costs. They also increased expanding overseas production, to change domestic power relations with labor and to reduce costs, while at the same time, German export firms struggled to improve their export competitiveness through strengthening technology-based innovation capabilities (Baccaro et al. 2018: 616–617; Storm and Naastepad 2015).

These processes of adjustments to improve German export competitiveness include significant conflicts and realignment of social alliances for Germany's export regime. For example, the Hartz reform fractured the existing German growth coalition between employers and core workers, because the reinforced neoliberal trend from the Hartz reform encroached upon not only the interests of peripheral workers but also the benefits of core workers, which brought about the crisis of the existing growth coalition (Nachtwey 2018; Diessner et al. 2021). Contrary to the *dualization thesis* (Thelen 2014), as mentioned earlier, even Germany's core export manufacturing sectors underwent significant deregulation and liberalization, which dissolved the existing DQP institutions and encroached upon the benefits of core workers. In party politics since 2008, the electoral support base of the dominant growth coalition shrank, causing anti-system politics in Germany. The alternative to reduction of the electorate base to support the existing export-led growth was grand coalitions between SPD and CDU (Hopkin and Voss 2022: 393).

However, unlike the *liberalization thesis* (Streeck 2009), the social alliances of German export growth coordination did not dissolve and converge toward an American-style free-market system. Rather, Germany successfully built a new social alliance to continue its export growth regime, rather than shifting toward American-style domestic consumption-led growth. German export employers emphasize a new alliance with skilled graduates, rather than traditional core blue collar workers, in order to adopt IT technology and improve technology-based innovation capabilities. German employers shifted to giving preference to college graduates with a STEM (Science, Technology, Engineering, and Mathematics) background through linkage with universities, rather than traditional apprenticeships (Diessner et al. 2022; Graf 2018).

Even on the side of capital, the dominant factions for German export growth regime also changed. Export manufacturers gained more voice, while banks lost relative power (Braun and Deeg 2019). Traditionally, banks held hegemonic power in Germany's political economy, unlike the U.S. Until the 1990s, Germany's DQP-based export regime had been sustained by banks' patient capital investment, as the VoC literature argues. German banks, which lent extensively and simultaneously held shares and controlled large blocks of voters in large enterprises, enabled export manufacturing firms to make long-term investment in workforce skills and incremental product innovation, a foundation of German export success (Hall and Soskice 2001; Deeg 1999; Zysman 1983).

However, Germany has continuously reinforced its economic system toward an overwhelmingly full-fledged export-led growth model, from a traditionally relatively balanced model of export and domestic consumption, where the export ratio relative to GDP increased from approximately 20% in the early 1990s, to 40% of GDP in 2007, and further to 50.9% in 2022 (Baccaro and Pontusson 2016: 14; Braun and Deeg 2019: 1–4; OECD 2024 Database), German manufacturing employers became more independent of banks, due to their accumulated profits resulting from the growth of exports, and self-financing rather than relying on bank loans. For example, German non-finance corporations (NFCs)' profit share of GDP increased from 38% in 1995 to 47% in 2007, which contrasts with the decline of U.K. non-finance corporations' share from 40 to 35%. German NFCs' debt declined from 60% in 2003 to 52% in 2017 in contrast to the growth of corporate debt in Italy, France, and the U.K. (Braun and Deeg 2019: 7). Based on a high profit share and low debt levels of German NFCs, these NFCs relied on self-financing by 76% since

1995, rather than bank loans and stock markets. This trend of internal financing occurs not only in Germany's large corporations but also in SMEs (Braun and Deeg 2019: 7–12).

As bank lending declines, the relative power of banks in Germany's political economy also reduces. In particular, commercial banks in Germany significantly lost power over industry, as manufacturing firms increased profitability and access to capital markets. The share of bank lending in total NFC debt declined from 75% in 1991 to 50% in 2017 (Braun and Deeg 2019: 12).

While the relative power of banks in Germany's political economy declines, German state bureaucracy as a new partner gains ascendancy to reinforce export growth strategy. For example, as commercial banks' lending to manufacturing industries from a combined 36% in 1993 to 26% in 2017 (Braun and Deeg 2019: 13), public banks increased their power, including the Landesbanken and the KfW (Kreditanstalt für Wiederaufbau). The KfW, which has long focused on export finance and lending in strategic sector, increased its NFC financing along with the intensification of the German export model (Naqvi et al. 2018). The success of Airbus and the renewable energy industry in Germany, which has become an important export sector, is practically unimaginable without large-scale funding from the KfW (Ergen 2015: 232–233).

Traditionally, since the Second World War, Germany had been firmly committed to liberalism and resolutely opposed to state intervention (Abelshauser 2016: 12–14; Katzenstein 1977: 900). More recently the German state has turned toward more active intervention, considering the rise of China, U.S.–China rivalry, and geopolitics. For example, in February 2019, the economics ministry announced an ambitious and deeply controversial National Industrial Strategy 2030 (NIS 2030). Reflecting upon an international competition transformed by new technologies, a rapidly rising China, and a protectionist U.S., the NIS 2030 proposed that the state invest in strategic growth sectors, foster national champions big enough to withstand global competition, and protect flagship companies from unwanted foreign takeovers, in order for Germany to gain the lead on game-changing technologies in a global race (BMWi 2019a, 2019b; Germann 2023: 1749–1750, 1757).

Recently, despite organized opposition from German industry (BDI 2019a: 13; Lohr 2019), the German government has continued to pursue far more proactive developmental policy, such as the NIS 2030 that has continued under the Scholz government (Bofinger 2019; Zettelmeyer

2019). The reason for this paradigm shift toward developmentalism is mainly due to sectoral differences within the export regime, which need authoritative coordination from the perspective of an entire national economy, rather than individual corporate interests.

Even German export manufacturing firms have different preferences regarding foreign economic policy due to sectoral differences. For example, German export sectors including electrical industries and chemical industry, which depend less on Chinese markets, support the state's mercantilist developmental policy. By contrast, German export sectors including automobile industry, which depend far more on Chinese markets, oppose the defensive mercantilist policy outlined in the NIS 2030. Large corporations and SMEs in Germany also have different ideas on economic policy. For example, BDI (the German industry federation) actively supports market-driven formation of European champions through EU regulations to foster M&A, while the *Mittelstand* (SMEs) actively oppose it (BDI 2019b: 9; Kohler-Koch 2016: 67; Germann 2023: 1756–1759).

Germany increased its coordinating role for its export growth regime, considering the seriously changing contexts of national rivalry and domestic divisions of key export actors. In particular, as traditional social alliances including the bank-centered finance-industry nexus, core workers, and SMEs, weakened and dissolved, new social alliances to move toward a knowledge economy and improve innovation capabilities needed new partners including skilled graduates, research institutes, universities, and the bureaucracy. Germany's export-led growth model has been reinforced not by traditional social alliances of export manufacturers, banks, and trade unions, but by export manufacturers and public bureaucracy, through improving technology-based innovation capabilities.

The next section examines the politics of transformation at micro levels, including interfirm relations, and employer–employee relations.

Conflicts and Cooperation Between Companies

We look now at how German companies have reorganized interfirm relationships since the 1990s in the process of globalizing production and finance, to understand the challenges caused by outsourcing and offshoring. Germany's development method is the product of the political process of conflict and coordination among companies. We will explore the politics of interfirm relations in Germany's core automotive and machinery industries in two dimensions: first, the vertical, representing the relationship between prime contractors (OEMs) and SMEs, and the horizontal, representing the relationship among SMEs.

What distinguished German companies from American companies since the 1990s in the process of outsourcing and offshoring is that German companies actively developed cooperative relationships through social coordination, while U.S. OEMs and SMEs traded mainly on the basis of free-market relations (Kwon 2004a: Chapter 2). Domestic parts makers in the U.S. went bankrupt or independently moved overseas to escape the breakdown of traditional domestic parts procurement systems and adapted to the emergence of new global production systems. Despite Germany's expansion of overseas projection by OEMs, domestic SMEs developed a newly defined cooperative relationship and further strengthened the domestic innovation ecosystem (Kwon 2012).

The way of Germany's overseas expansion also differs from that of Japan. In the case of Japan, as seen in Chapter 5, Japanese lead firms and subcontractors went abroad together, based on their closed circles of subcontracting. This nationally closed circle delayed domestic reform and isolated Japan from rapidly changing technology and world markets. By contrast, Germany's interfirm relations had more open relations, compared to those of Japan. Germany's interfirm cooperation resulted from severe conflicts and resistance between lead firms and parts makers, unlike Japan, as well as through social coordination, which involved collective resolution and coordination by governments, trade associations, lead firms, and parts makers, unlike U.S. individual choice in the free market.

By establishing cooperative networks in the course of overseas expansion, Germany's core industries further enhanced their domestic innovation capabilities. For example, since the 1990s, the German automobile industry has shown a high degree of innovation in expanding overseas production of automotive products, automobile models, and overall expansion of R&D, achieving unrivaled performance (Blöcker 2001: 22ff; Jürgens and Meissner 2005: 19ff; Wymann 2012: 22ff). In the early 1990s, Audi, BMW, and Mercedes had only seven or eight models. After that, the numbers rapidly expanded, and even tripled (Wymann 2012: 18f). German automakers had to adapt to new challenges—not just new demands from consumers, but also regulations and demands for environment-friendly production and improved energy efficiency. German companies made massive R&D investments in innovation rather than focus on cost reduction, and nearly doubled their R&D expenditures (99%) from the mid-1990s to 2000. Between 2000 and 2013, R&D expenditures in the German automobile industry increased by about 35% (VDA-Jaresberichte 2001, 2013; Kalkowski and Mickler 2015: 93–94).

In addition to increased support for R&D, German automakers made the best use of SMEs' capabilities and technologies through outsourcing, moving production bases overseas to utilize global production networks. The intention was to establish a global production network to combine optimal inputs such as low wages, good technology, and parts at both the global and domestic levels. In fact, this globalization process caused serious conflicts between prime contractors and parts makers, but German companies succeeded in globalization because they navigated the conflicts with SMEs and established a new governance system.

Changes occurred in interfirm relationships in the 1990s, conflicts resulting in the process of reorganizing production, when German automakers shifted from an in-house production system to one that reduced internal development and production and relied instead on outsourcing (Blöcker 2001: 77ff). In the 1960s and 1970s, when German companies' vertical system was at its peak, Volkswagen kept about 80% of its automobile production value inside the company, while in the 1990s it dismantled the system and outsourced much of its parts production and R&D. This move reduced in-house production to about 30% of total value by the end of the 1990s. The same occurred in R&D. In automotive R&D prime contractors accounted for 70–75% before the 1990s; by Fraunhofer's estimate, the share would decrease to 32%–36% in 2015 (Kwon 2004a: 30–31; Roth 2013: 7; Kalkowski and Mikler 2015).

However, this disintegration and outsourcing to external companies caused many conflicts between companies. Division of roles became ambiguous, allowing powerful prime contractors to easily abuse it. Traditionally, German and American automobile prime contractors delivered detailed blueprints to parts makers (*Pfichtenheft* or *Lastenheften*). However, during the 1990s, interfirm relationships of OEMs and SMEs were reestablished so that SMEs participated in the development of parts. Conflicts arose where OEMs cooperated with SMEs based on rough, black-box style guidelines (Kalkowski and Mickler 2015: 98–99; Roth 2013: 22, 41).

Amid the ambiguous governance in these new interfirm relations, German and American OEMs often acted unfairly, causing many conflicts, unlike Japanese trustful interfirm relationships based on the closed circles of *Keiretsu* subcontracting. Both German and U.S. OEMs initially shifted their burden to SMEs to reduce costs, causing serious conflicts and confrontations among them.[1] German OEMs entrusted parts makers with more work and R&D tasks while pressuring them to reduce costs and lower parts prices. Like U.S. companies, German OEMs pressured parts makers through "unfair behavior" in long-term contractual relationships (Kwon 2004a: 58–62). For example, they pressured SMEs to reduce prices while making long-term contracts of three to five years, threatening to switch contracts to other SMEs if they refused to accept these unfair demands. Sometimes OEMs even deceived parts makers into parts development projects by promising long-term contracts, and once the projects were over, they threatened to abandon the relationship, exposing SMEs to free-market competition with producers who proposed much cheaper supply of parts.

However, unlike the U.S., Germany eventually established more stable and mutually recognized "fair and collaborative relations" through arbitration and coordination by industrial associations and social organizations to resolve serious conflict between OEMs and SMEs.[2] In the U.S., lacking social coordination, OEMs and SMEs relied on one-on-one market relations, maintaining a remote rather than cooperative relationship due to OEMs' free exercise of power. As global outsourcing developed, U.S. prime contractors sought cost savings based on new market relationships abroad. In contrast, Germany was able to mediate unfair practices and build more stable cooperative relations based on fair trade, by collectively asking "what is fair trade" and "who is the problem" in long-term transactions, through intervention by industrial associations and various social organizations.

For example, trade groups including OEMs and SMEs within the German automobile industry were unified into one organization, the German Automobile Association (VDA). However, in 1993, when German automobile companies engaged in unfair practices, German

[1] See Kwon (2004a) for conflicts and confrontations between prime contractors and parts makers in the German automobile industry in the 1990s, and for the process of establishing new cooperative relationships different from those in the U.S. Further explanation on confrontation and conflict over Germany's new long-term contractual relationship and the social coordination process through the association is based on Kwon (2004a).

[2] See Chapter 4 of Kwon (2004a) for the politics of conflict and coordination in Germany, in particular.

parts makers created the *Arbeitsgemeinschaft Zulieferindustrie* (ArGeZ) as an independent organization and as a collective protest. In order for German SMEs to address huge automakers in protesting unfair practices, six trade associations related to major parts companies organized, including the Metal Industry Association (WVM), the Steel Forging Association (WSU), German Casting Association (DGV), the Steel Plate Metal Industry Association (EBM), Synthetic Industry Association (GKV), and the Rubber Industry Association (W.d.K.). ArGeZ has since contributed greatly to continuing protests against unfair transactions by OEMs as well as seeking globalization strategies for SMEs themselves.

Germany was able to establish fair and stable cooperation in the vertical relationship between prime contractors and parts makers both through consolidated power, as in the case of ArGeZ, and by valid and fair social norms achieved through social consultation. Due to long-term transactions and new divisions of labor in the 1990s, responsibilities and gains in the perfunctory cooperative labor process became unclear, along with criteria for fairness. In this situation, organizations such as the German Industrial Federation (BDI), the German Automobile Association (VDA), and the ArGeZ publicly and privately held serious discussions to set fairness criteria. For example, as German parts makers collectively protested, organizations such as VDA reconciled conflicts between OEMs and SMEs through "conversations for peace" or "supplier days" to establish standards for fair norms. Trade associations crafted and published standards of fair norms such as the German Industrial Federation Guidelines (*BDI-Leitsetze*) and German Automobile Association Guidelines (*VDA-Leitfaden*).

Through the process of collective discussion of social norms for fairness, German parts makers achieved horizontal solidarity and established alternative development strategies. In Korea and the U.S., SMEs and parts makers were separated and isolated in the absence of collective resistance and discussion, resulting in the absence of horizontal solidarity. Even if tier 1 component companies accepted the demands of prime contractors and established cooperative relationships in Korea and the U.S., the relationship between tier 1 parts makers and subcontractors below them worsened, since tier 1 companies could withstand the pressure of price reduction from the prime contractor by transferring it to tier 2 and tier 3 companies. As a result, the relationship among parts makers became noncooperative and conflictual, thus weakening overall innovative capabilities. This phenomenon remains common in Korea and the U.S.[3]

In Germany, however, as SMEs protested against OEMs, the democratic process of discussing the social norms of fair transactions led to social policing against unfair trade and to effective implementation of fairness norms across society. Above all, in transactions with lower tier parts makers, German parts makers were unable to break their own social norms that had been set based on voluntary and democratic participation. Recalling the experience of participating in the discussion and censure in numerous unfair transactions, the CEO of a German parts maker company stated in an interview with the author:

> If one declares that they disagree with a proposal on certain kinds of fairness and act differently according to the declaration, that's fine. Everyone will accept those actions. However, an action that can never be accepted is the case of "unfair" behavior, when one's actions differ from what was said during discussions or meetings. If one does not abide by the norms they agreed to in the formal meeting, they will not be able to get respect from others in this society. (quoted in Kwon 2004a: 181)

The development of fair governance and horizontal solidarity through the process of social and political coordination has enabled Germany to enhance its domestic production network and innovation capabilities during the process of production globalization. This social horizontal solidarity distinguishes Germany from both the liberal U.S. method and the statist methods of Korea and Japan. In the U.S., market relations are dominant, while in Korea and Japan, governance through closed membership centering on affiliates of prime contractors is dominant. In the U.S., it was difficult to establish societywide norms and accumulate

[3] According to analyses by industry experts in Ulsan, Korea, "The unfair trade practices between prime contractors and the tier-1 vendor have improved a lot compared to the past, but the unfair trade at the lower level, between the tier-1 vendor and the tier-2 and -3 vendors has relatively not yet improved." See Ulsan Metropolitan City Government (2012) "The Labor-Management Conflict Prevention Team Report on the First Session Meeting in 2012 for the Development of Labor-Management Relations" (Buk-gu, Ulsan Metropolitan City). See also *JoongAng Ilbo* (June 18, 2020) "Declaration of abandonment of business by Hyundai Motor's partner companies: Inefficient supply chain, only a matter of time" for recent cases.

industrial commons due to free-riders in the free market during globalization. In Japan, due to the closed structure centered on *Keiretsu* affiliates, conflicting and estranged relationships dominated outside the affiliates, and the governance of nonstate actors has remained weak and hierarchical. The closed circles of *Keiretsu* affiliates in Japan had problems in flexibly adopting new ideas and technology, which in turn made the industrial commons outdated. In recent years, in Korea and the U.S., the relationships between tier 1 subcontractors and lower tier subcontractors have caused more problems than between prime contractors and tier 1 subcontractors, due to the absence of societywide norms. By contrast, for reasons explained above, Germany was able to develop a horizontal cooperative system throughout the society, unlike the U.S. free-market system and the Japanese and Korean closed affiliates-centered systems (Kwon 2004: 139–185).

In 2010, a coalition of German parts makers developed small-sized electric vehicles (EVs), serving as a representative example of horizontal cooperation among the companies.[4] This partnership was initially formed by a small number of parts makers and academic-based *Hochschule* researchers to develop practical and inexpensive small EVs. Soon, about 11 automobile parts companies joined the partnership, and through joint investment formed an independent joint venture, *Fahrzeug GmbH*. The venture was operated through a democratic joint decision-making system of participating companies, all of which produced different parts, enabling them to divide their labor within the alliance.

Hochschule institutes and the Fraunhofer Society for applied science worked closely with the venture's research center with the support of public research funds, although they did not invest in the venture directly. These technical institutes formed a cooperative network with about 50 parts companies, mobilizing their own research capabilities and the use of public research funds. Although these 50 parts companies did not invest in the venture, they actively participated in the cooperative development network as strategic partners.

Parts makers had diverse motives to participate in the horizontal alliance network for EV development, but the predominant reason was to acquire new EV technology capabilities. According to one participating

[4] See Kalkowski and Mickler (2015) for a detailed explanation of the development of cooperative organizations among parts markers for the development of small electric vehicles in 2010.

CEO, "They eventually wanted to experience it together and thus acquire knowledge for themselves that they had never had before" (CEO "B" who participated in the project, quoted in Kalkowski and Mickler 2015: 142). Most participants emphasized the advantages of a horizontal cooperation system over the hierarchical relationship between existing OEMs and parts makers. Such open and democratic cooperation allowed quick adaptation to markets based on trust, while teams gained technical possibilities and innovations from each other. The informal negotiation process enabled participants to mutually improve technical and coordinating skills without unilateral guidelines or regulations from OEMs. Participating companies experienced mutual learning, project success, competitiveness, and economic improvement.

Germany's machinery industry is also notable for its innovative ecosystem through cooperation between various industries and companies. The machinery industry provides important industrial commons for almost all industries, manufacturing to meet the unique needs of consumer companies. In this process, the machinery industry not only enhances the innovation capabilities of consumer companies, but acts as a mediator and driver of innovation to upgrade applied science and technology in the process of solving consumer companies' problems.

Germany's machinery industry remains strong despite globalization, unlike the U.S. According to the 2014 *Verband Deutscher Maschinen-und Anlagenbau* (VDMA), of Germany's 6000 machinery enterprises, most maintain production facilities in Germany, although more than 30% have overseas production bases. The German machinery industry has required continuous innovation due to the development of electronic technology in the 1980s and IT technology in the 1990s, and has strengthened its innovation strategy by increasing R&D investment to gain expertise in its domestic innovation capabilities. The majority of machinery workers have traditionally received technical education or graduated from technical colleges, bur recently, recruitment of research personnel with a college degree or higher is increasing (Hirsch-Kreinsen 1994; Kowol and Kronhn 1995; Rose 1995).

Despite the globalization of production, Germany's machinery industry enhanced its domestic innovation capabilities while remaining competitive due to a rich innovation ecosystem based on a close connection with research institutes, such as *Fachhochschule,* the University of

Applied Sciences, trade association research centers such as *Arbeitsgemeinschaft Industrieller Forschungsvereinigungen* (AIF), and government-funded research institutes like the Fraunhofer Society. In addition, the German machinery industry utilized various subsidies and funds, including support from each regional chamber of commerce and the federal government.

German companies have kept their home production robust despite the globalization of production and finance, by strengthening their home production and innovation capabilities in parts procurement in order to reorganize production at the global level, even while increasing overseas production. This German adaptation method is the result of collectively coordinating OEMs and SMEs based on collective vertical and horizontal coordination. Despite the globalization of production, German companies strengthened their home country's ability to innovate through conflict mediation and cooperative network development between various stakeholders, especially private companies and trade associations, unlike the U.S. model. Collective social coordination, indirect government support, and close support and connection with public research institutes and universities served as the framework for stability and growth, along with sponsorship of research institutes such as the German federal government or Fraunhofer, and the provision of industrial commons.

Politics of Labor and Management

In this section, we examine the labor–management relationship in light of the politics of social coordination in Germany. In Germany's globalization process, organized labor and managers, along with local research institutes and related organizations, jointly discussed where to invest and how to expand overseas production. In particular, organized labor in Germany actively intervened in the collective coordination process of seeking new alternatives in globalization through legally and institutionally guaranteed works councils as well as nationwide unions. This social coordination in Germany weakened the influence of financialization and offered an alternative model of stakeholder capitalism, which prioritizes coordination between various stakeholders over shareholder value. By way of contrast, in the globalization process in the U.S., organized labor had little influence while managers made unilateral decisions. In particular, in the process of financialization, U.S. employers focused on short-term profits which prioritized shareholder value, with little consideration of domestic production and innovation capabilities, nor of innovation ecosystems in the decision process.

We will look first at the politics between organized labor and employers at the national level, particularly regarding co-determination in the course of financialization; then, we explore the politics of employment relations at the micro level. At the micro level, we examine first the relationship between employers and labor in the workplaces, and the relationship between general workers and R&D workers in works councils in the process of creating alternatives to enhance innovation capabilities of wage labor.

Politics of Capital and Labor at National Level

In Germany, neoliberal criticism toward the rigidity and inefficiency of existing coordinated capitalism and organized labor prevailed against the backdrop of globalization and financialization. Some party politicians and associations on the capital side criticized the German-style corporatist negotiation model, its *Mitbestimmung* (co-determination system), and works councils. In fact, centralized wage negotiations in the 1990s and 2000s were considerably decentralized and weakened. Institutionalists such as Wolfgang Streeck (2009) call this phenomenon "deconstruction of the German model and convergence to neoliberalism," but through the lens of German labor–management politics we see a switch to a more flexible coordination system rather than "convergence to an Anglo-American free market model." The *Mitbestimmung*, criticized by neoliberals in discussions over corporate governance, survives and operates as a more flexible coordination system in the globalization process. Before examining how the micro politics of coordination surrounding the works councils actually works based on co-determination in the next section, we look at the politics of capital and labor at the national level, focusing on reform of corporate governance institutions.

With globalization and financialization as the backdrop, neoliberal voices have prevailed in Germany since the 1990s. Neoliberal forces, led by some employer associations, politicians, and neoclassical economists, criticized Germany's corporatist coordination system and the rigidity and inefficiency of organized labor. In the *Standortdebatte* (debate on where to locate production in globalization), neoliberals argued that German companies had no choice but to move abroad, given the protective powers of strong labor unions. To maintain domestic production and attract foreign companies, they argued that German companies should switch to the Anglo-American free-market model (Sinn 2005; Thurow 1999; Henkel 1995).

In fact, in the process of adapting to globalization since the mid-1990s, Germany's centralized collective bargaining system has been greatly weakened. Previously, negotiations on wages and working conditions were conducted at the national level in each industrial unit. Once central organizations of the trade union (IG Metall) and the employers' organization (Gesamtmetall) in Germany's strongest industry, metals, finished negotiation and set guidelines, other industries followed suit, allowing for corporatist coordination between labor and management. The proportion of laborers included in the negotiations was very high, as nonunion workers were also included in each industry's centralized negotiations.

However, since the mid-1990s, the number of workers and workplaces covered by centralized industry-wide collective bargaining has decreased significantly. Contrary to the expectation of the VoC literature (Hall and Soskice 2001), instead of reinforcing the existing coordination method, German employers sought to deviate from the agreement set out in centralized industry-specific negotiations for more flexible adaptation in the process of globalization of production. The number of employees included in negotiations decreased from 72% in 1995 to 57% in 2006. The number of workplaces included in industry negotiations decreased from 53% in 1995 to 37% in 2006 (Streeck 2009: 38–39). Deviation from industry-wide agreement (*Flächentarifbindung*) was particularly severe in the former East German region, where the proportion of employees included in industry-specific agreements decreased from 56% in 1996 to 37% in 2010. Between 1991 and 2010, companies in the former West German region included in the industry-specific agreement in Germany's metal industry decreased from 8,168 to 3,495, while companies in the former East German region decreased from 1,365 to 218 during the same period (Bispinck and Dribbusch 2011: 19; Ellguth and Kohaut 2011: 242–247). Germany's labor–management negotiation system decentralized from the industry to the company level. In Germany's core metal and electronics industries, the number of company-level agreements increased from only 70 in 2004 to about 730 in 2009 (Haipeter 2011a: 11; 2011b: 117). According to IG Metall's research data, although many company-level agreements expired in 2010, about 1,060 agreements remain valid (Bispinck and Dribbusch 2011: 40–41).

Regarding these changes in Germany's existing corporatist coordination system, not only neoliberals but also many institutionalists who argued for capitalist diversity now argue that Germany's coordinated capitalism has been dismantled and converged into the Anglo-American free-market model (Streeck 2009; Lane 2005; Meardi and Toth 2006). Still, it is difficult to say that Germany's coordinated capitalist system was completely dismantled and converged into the Anglo-American free-market system. Decentralized negotiations now conducted at the company level, and the preference for works councils over centralized unions, is by no means a waiver of social coordination. Rather, it demonstrates a transition to a more flexible coordination system for more effective adaptation against the backdrop of new production globalization and financialization (Diessner et al. 2022; Kwon 2012; Reisenbichler and Morgan 2012).

Therefore, some scholars of historical and discourse institutionalism emphasize pragmatic adaptation. Germany shifts to company-level negotiations along with financialization, but with a method of adjustment based on Germany's co-determination (Mitbestimmung) system. In this system employees negotiate and coordinate with employers, unlike in the U.S., despite financialization and globalization, a method referred to as "hybridity between heterogeneous factors" (Crouch 2005), "negotiated shareholder value" (Vitols 2004), or "contextual interpretation of ideas" (Goutas and Lane 2009). The Anglo-American shareholder-value-priority principle following financialization was interpreted and accepted differently in Germany by several stakeholder coalitions under this decentralized coordination system (Jackson 2003; Goutas and Lane 2009). The national politics surrounding co-determination (*Mitbestimmung*) as a minimum system ensured this.

Neoliberals argued that Germany's *Mitbestimmung*, a unique characteristic of German corporate governance that legally allows equal participation of labor in major corporate decisions, should be abolished. German companies' "codetermination system" weakens German companies' competitiveness, they argued, because it threatens international investors and weakens Germany's financial status, and further increases capital costs due to investment avoidance (Schmidt and Seger 1998: 454, 468; Gorton and Schmid 2004). They asserted that the shareholder-value-priority principle gave exclusive rights to shareholders, and thus joint decision-making should be dismantled (Wagner 1997). Studies by neoliberals argue that abolishing equal employee representation would increase companies' shareholder value by more than 20%, and would better position Germany in the competition for European corporate governance (Schmidt and Seger 1998: 46; Zuckerman 1999).

Neoliberals' arguments were not only ideological, but applied in the political process. At the national level of politics, representatives of major industrial associations, such as the German Industry Federation (BDI) and the German Employers Association (BDA), violently attacked the system. However, member companies took a different approach. German companies rarely withdrew from the co-determination system despite international managers' encouragement to do so (Höpner 2003: 157–158). Nevertheless, the arguments of representatives of major industrial associations resonated greatly in German political society. Members of the Liberal Democratic Party and Christian Democratic Party began to openly attack the co-determination system (Faust 2012: 159).

Political discussions were concentrated in the activities of the Commission on the Co-determination System (*Mitbestimmungskommission*), consisting of industry representatives, scholars, and experts under the Schröder administration in 2005. Representatives of BDI and BDA argued that labor representation "should be reduced to one-third of current share in the corporate supervisory committee, abandoning the joint labor-management representative system." As labor and employer representatives independently submitted their arguments, scholars and experts agreed only to the common recommendation which was limited to partial modification of the current co-determination system (Mitbestimmungskommission 2006; Streeck and Höpner 2006).

Subsequently, scholars' reports gained support from lawmakers from the coalition government of the Christian and Social Democratic Parties. Eventually, the 2005 federal general election failed to lead to a neoliberal reform of the co-determination system, and reaffirmed the system's basic rules. The popularity of neoliberal reform began to fade in Germany and reform of the co-determination system became almost impossible. Although German institution reforms in the late 1990s and early 2000s favored the shareholder value principle, formal legal stability for the co-determination system was reaffirmed (Jackson 2005: 236; Höpner 2003: 157–158).

Meanwhile, German unions did not unconditionally oppose the shareholder value priority of employer organizations. Workers' representatives in German unions and the Company Supervisory Commissions showed a shareholder-friendly attitude to maintain "communication systems" through the existing consensus model (Höpner 2003). Labor unions and works councils' representatives emphasized transparency in corporate management as the "prerequisites and means of the co-determination system" as a viable reform alternative, and justifying the voices of workers' representatives during reform discussions (Höpner 2007: 413; Jürgens et al. 2008: 74).

In the end, discussions on corporate governance reform in Germany since the late 1990s have moved toward enhancing corporate transparency, strengthening the role and authority of the supervisory board toward employers and corporate managers, and emphasizing closer cooperation between management and supervisory boards. Due to this reform, the supervisory board, in which workers' representatives participate, has transformed from a retroactive controlling body into a forward-looking advisory body that actively presents alternatives to the company's development direction in the process of production globalization. By playing an active role in agenda setting or regulating major transactions and matters within the company that require board approval, such as overseas investment, the supervisory board enables active participation and social coordination of stakeholders, including labor. According to an empirical survey, more than 60% of workers' representatives participating in the supervisory boards of major German joint stock companies (AG) considered them as future-oriented advisory committees. The majority of respondents (70.6%) reported that these supervisory boards and the co-determination system had influenced the company's strategic decisions (52.9%), improving the quality of decisions as well as contributing to "social integration" (64.7%) (Jürgens et al. 2008: 52–54, 96–105; Gerum 2007).

Eventually, Germany developed a new social coordination system by coordinating roles between German co-determination and supervisory boards, resulting in the strengthened authority of both, and greater transparency and authority of the supervisory board over managers. These reforms were actively welcomed by employees' works councils and unions (Höpner 2007: 413). Germany's corporate governance reform following financialization eventually renewed and strengthened its consensus model (Faust 2012: 160–161).

Politics of Labor and Management at Micro Level[5]

Maintaining the legal co-determination system at national level politics is not the only reason that Germany could successfully establish a new social coordination system. Apart from the formal co-determination system, social coordination of labor and stakeholders would not have been possible without valid strategies and responses. The active, constructive intervention of German organized labor in the process of globalization greatly contributed to the creation of a new adaptation model in Germany. Labor did not simply resist corporate relocation to overseas nor obsess over preserving the existing centralized model. Rather, German organized labor created a new adaptation model while gaining organizational justification for more constructive alternatives for corporate competitiveness.

Unlike the globalization of American companies, Germany did not experience an industrial hollowing-out or employment reduction in its home country's main industries. Rather, German companies promoted German exports, and maintained or improved domestic employment by strengthening domestic competitiveness along with expansion of overseas production. In the process of globalization of production, German companies continuously adjusted their home country's role in the newly created global production network and established an improved international division of labor. Domestic industry upgrades were made by continuous collective consultations and political compromises between various stakeholders, especially between labor and management.

The case of Volkswagen, which produces mass cars rather than luxury cars (*Klassenwagen*), illustrates how Germany's globalization strengthened its domestic competitiveness through upgrading domestic production. BMW and Mercedes-Benz, which produce luxury cars, already had a considerable degree of vertical division of labor. However, in the case of Volkswagen in the late 1990s, direct competition between home country

[5] This section is basically written as a revision and supplement of the author's previous articles, especially based on a portion from an article in *Korean Journal of International Relations* Vol. 52, No. 1, 2012, and a portion explaining the politics of German labor during the globalization process from an article in *Politics & Society*, the December 2012 issue. See Kwon Hyeong-ki (2012) "Globalization of Production and Possibilities of Labor Politics" *International Political Discussion*, Vol. 52, No. 1, pp. 233–238; and Kwon Hyeong-ki (2012) "Politics of Globalization and National Economy: The German Experience Compared with the United States," *Politics & Society*, vol. 40, no. 4, pp. 589–592 for further explanation.

and overseas production sites grew sharply. Labor was facing loss of home production due to direct competition between overseas production sites in Eastern Europe and domestic production in Germany. Until the early 1990s, domestic production showed high technical superiority compared to production sites in Eastern Europe, so the possibility of a transfer of production to Eastern Europe was not a major threat to domestic production. However, as Volkswagen built an increasingly international labor division through standardized production and parts in the mid- to late 1990s, production in Germany and in Eastern Europe began to directly compete.

Yet despite direct competition between home and abroad, labor organizations such as the IG Metall and the Volkswagen Works Council (VW Works Council) sought better alternatives through active negotiations with management. In particular, works councils (*Betriebsrat*), which had access to major corporate decisions based on co-determination (*Mitbestimmung*), contributed to upgrading domestic production by accepting management's global strategy and suggesting better globalization alternatives.

After the corporation faced a crisis in 1993, the VW Works Council abandoned its previous defensive stance on management's global strategy and sought more efficient production alternatives through active negotiations with management. Volkswagen's worker organizations (metal workers' unions and the works council) did not unconditionally oppose or resist management's globalization strategy, as U.S. labor unions did, but actively supported a strategy, based on the same platform as globalization, devised by management. Volkswagen was under pressure to withstand international competition due to bureaucratic ills. However, the VW Works Council accepted management's new strategies, including globalization, platform strategy, and benchmarking, and actively intervened and negotiated major company decisions through the *Mitbestimmung*.

Expansion of investment for commercial vehicles production in Pozan, Poland, was not threatening to German labor in the mid-1990s. It was an international division of labor that allowed for differences in technology levels. Volkswagen collaborated with Tarpan, a Polish commercial vehicle producer in Pozan, in 1993, to produce commercial cars (*Nutzfahrzeuge*) previously produced in Hanover, and in 1996 VW acquired the Polish production facility and converted it to an independent integrated production facility in the early 2000s. While Hanover produced the

T5 variant, Poland focused on producing Caddy and relatively inexpensive vans, allowing room for production bases in Germany.

However, parallel divisions of labor and direct competition between the two production sites began in earnest around 1999 when competition between the German home country and Eastern European production sites arose over the production of expensive SUVs. A sharp confrontation between Volkswagen and organized labor continued for months over the production site of the Touareg SUV (Jürgens and Krzywdzinski 2010: 53–54; Kloves 2005: 177). Prior to that, an implicit agreement existed between labor and management that high-value-added vehicles should be produced in Germany, while low-cost vehicles should be produced in Eastern Europe. Labor expected that the high-value Touareg would be produced in Germany. However, the Hanover plant was unable to meet management's production cost requirements. Management believed that for the company to survive, even SUVs had to be competitive in cost. In response, organized labor believed that missing production of high-value SUVs would close out future high-value opportunities. IG Metall and the VW Works Council tried to attract Touareg production, but failed. The company's management did not budge on cost competitiveness, which meant life or death to the company. Labor was forced to yield Touareg production to the Bratislava plant in Slovakia. Yet in the process of negotiations, labor yielded Touareg production to overseas bases, but achieved a contract for a new automobile production project instead, the Benchmark Production 5000 × 5000 project. Benchmark 5000 created a strategy for upgrading German production sites through specific negotiations.

Based on Benchmark 5000, Volkswagen organized an independent company called Auto 5000 GmbH, which attracted more academic and public attention throughout Germany than any other company, including the successful merger with Volkswagen's headquarters in 2009. Auto 5000 was an important test case for whether Germany could maintain production under rigid negotiations with strong unions, amid debate over Germany's expansion of overseas production. The success of Volkswagen's Auto 5000 offered a successful alternative to neoliberalism in the process of globalization.

The Auto 5000 company was established as an independent organization, through negotiations with management along with active proposals from VW Works Council and IG Metall, to show that competitive production is possible in Germany amid growing overseas production sites. The Touran vehicle, scheduled to be produced by Auto 5000, was originally planned to be produced in Eastern Europe. However, the Works Council, IG Metall, and VW management agreed on production in Germany by finding ways to secure competitiveness not only in wages but also in production methods. Accepting the demands of the Niedersachsen state government, a major shareholder of Volkswagen, Auto 5000 hired about 3500 unemployed workers with little experience in automobile production to produce Touran. After six months of training, production began in November 2002. Auto 5000 has since been economically successful despite domestic production. According to an interim evaluation conducted in 2004 by the Sociological Research Institute (SOFI) of the University of Göttingen, famous for industrial sociology, Auto 5000 has already succeeded in generating profits, as well as showing tremendous results in production efficiency and automobile quality.

Auto 5000's economic success was not due to its lower wages (about 20% lower compared to VW's general workers). Their wages were similar to the average wage of skilled workers in Germany's metal industry. VW's workers' wages were relatively high, as stipulated by Volkswagen's house arrangement (*Haustarifvertrag*) apart from metal industry wage negotiations. While wages for Auto 5000 workers were somewhat lower than for other VW workers at the beginning, the gap diminished with annual increases in bonuses and wages based on the success of Auto 5000's Touran sales, and in January 2009, as Auto 5000 was fully integrated into VW, wage negotiations were unified as well. In addition to lower wages, Auto 5000 was economically successful due to its continuous innovation, resulting in a profits increase of 25% every year (Schuman et al. 2006a: 304–306; Schumann 2008: 379–386).

Auto 5000 continuously improved productivity through collective consultations involving management, the Works Council, and the expertise of institutes such as SOFI. Through this collective deliberation process, Auto 5000 allowed workers to fully demonstrate their innovative potential. Through all stages of production, company management, the Works Council, IG Metall, and newly reorganized labor participated through discussions facilitated by SOFI.

Auto 5000's production method is distinct from both the American Taylorist mass production system and Japanese Toyotaism (Schumann et al. 2006b). The key difference is continuous innovation through collective discussion. Auto 5000 simplifies the hierarchy of the company's organization and develops collective horizontal consultations to include all functions, inducing autonomous innovation, mutual consultation, and compromise in the process of direct and indirect value creation. In this organizational structure, all workers participate and make decisions together in the process of finding optimum points for production innovation and processes.

Auto 5000 production emphasizes "learning plants" (*Lernfabriken*). Beyond the initial six months of vocational training, Auto 5000 developed continuous worker training. Labor and management agreed on workers' participation in three hours of vocational training per week, far greater than that of other automakers, and which systematically combined work and learning. A large conference room next to the production line allowed managers, engineers, various functional experts, and production workers to gather to discuss ways to improve production. These collective deliberations boosted workers' abilities and opened possibilities for more efficient methods in production.

According to a study (Schumann et al. 2006a), Auto 5000 reduced production costs by about a third through effective organization of production. With notable improvements in quality and productivity, VW management entrusted production of its new Tiguan SUV to Auto 5000, and production began in August 2007. Contrary to neoliberal arguments, the success of Auto 5000 signals that in the process of globalizing production, high-wage advanced countries such as Germany still hold potential to maintain production and be competitive.

Another example of direct competition between production in Germany and overseas production sites was between Eastern Europe and Germany over Audi's engine production. Volkswagen's engine production is based on the most parallel division of production of any sector, and provides a good example of direct competition for production. By the early 1990s, Volkswagen had produced engines for VW and Audi vehicles at Salzgitter and Ingolstadt in Germany, respectively. However, when VW faced a crisis in the first half of the 1990s, it began to produce engines in Chemnitz in the former East Germany and by the late 1990s introduced a new international division of labor by building engine factories in Eastern Europe. In 1994, Audi began operating an engine factory in Györ, Hungary, and gradually expanded production for a while, finally transferring engine production from Ingolstadt, Germany, to Hungary in the late 1990s. Starting with the transfer to Hungary, Ingolstadt's engine production gradually declined, and in 2000, production eventually stopped. Volkswagen management initially promised that only Audi engines would be produced in Györ, but soon the gasoline engines for

Golf platform vehicles previously produced in Salzgitter gradually moved to Hungary. The Salzgitter Works Council hoped that its plant would produce diesel engines and the Hungarian plant would produce gasoline engines through the international division of labor. However, in 1997, competition between Salzgitter and Györ for diesel engine production began, and part of the production was transferred to Hungary. In short, engine production was stopped in Ingolstadt, and production was reduced in Salzgitter.

This outcome did not mean reduced production at German domestic production sites. Rather, in Ingolstadt, production staffing was expanded and relocated to other parts. As a result, Ingolstadt's employment in 1994 was 22,391, but in 2003, two years after the end of engine production, it increased by 40%, to 31,013. A similar change happened in Salzgitter as well. This development of German domestic production sites was the result of consultation with the Works Council, similar to the case of Auto 5000 discussed earlier.

A new vertical complementary relationship can still be observed between Germany's Salzgitter and Eastern European production bases. Salzgitter, with higher production capacities, produces all the main components including engine body, pipes, pumps, and pillars. Therefore, as engine production in Eastern Europe increased, German parts exports also increased. In other words, as Eastern Europe turned into an engine production base and Germany turned into a core parts production base for engines, engine production in Eastern Europe developed into a form that relied on German core parts. For example, in 2005, 36% of engine value produced in Hungary was imported from Germany. This form of vertical complementary division of labor, through a "vertical specialization of production stages" as seen between East and West Europe, results in high-technology high-value-added sectors and low-cost labor-intense sectors, but not as a "vertical complementary production specialization," or a division between high-price and low-price products.

In short, in contrast to Japanese companies' closed circles, Volkswagen introduced market principles such as comparative benchmarking and competition among production bases, and global outsourcing in the process of globalization of production as in the U.S. But unlike the Americans, VW presented a competitive alternative by realizing the politicization of market control which forms market control measures based on social coordination among stakeholders. The new social coordination for production of Auto 5000 and Audi engines meant that strong unions and collective negotiations offered a substantially valid alternative that refutes the neoliberal claims that Germany is no longer a valid location for production.

Thanks to VW's Auto 5000 model, the German metal union (IG Metall) allowed workers to actively participate in company-level negotiations to counter employers' threat of production relocation. As the crisis of Germany's multinational companies emerged in the wake of the 2008 global financial crisis, the move to establish VW's production model gained strength through active efforts by IG Metall. For example, when Opel in Germany was in crisis, discussions were held to upgrade domestic production through a new innovative production method by making Opel's ownership independent from GM, and further developing strategic partnerships with management through participation of the Works Council and labor unions. When family managed SMEs such as Schoeffler faced crisis, IG Metall actively intervened to establish a works council, introduced a joint decision system to develop new partnerships, and devoted joint effort to improve domestic competitiveness.

In addition, strategic labor–management partnerships based on co-determination played an important role in many of the Employment Security Pacts (*Beschäftigungspakte*) signed between works councils and managers in Germany.[6] With the globalization of production in the 2000s, employment pacts (*Beschäftigungspakte*) became widespread at the company level, and about a third of all German companies with works councils adopted the pacts in the mid-2000s. According to a study by Gesamtmetall, the number of *Beschäftigungspakte* in metalworking and electronics increased from 70 in 2004 to 730 in 2009 (Kwon 2012: 592–593; Haipeter 2011a: 11; Bispinck and Dribbusch 2011).

The *Beschäftigungspakte* is based on the basic principle of political reciprocal exchange between labor and management, where management offers job security, expansion of investment, and production commitments, while labor agrees to wage freezing or concessions, extension

[6] Traditional labor–management relations in Germany are characterized by a dual system divided into industry-level unions and company-level works councils. While unions negotiate basic issues encompassing individual companies at the industrial level, works councils supervise whether the industry-level agreement is properly implemented at the company level, and encourage their members to join the unions and mobilize organizations. Negotiations by works councils were almost meaningless when centralized corporatism was at its peak in the 1980s. However, since the 1990s, the role of works councils has been strengthened by globalization and a flexible production system (Haipeter 2011a, 7–12).

of working hours, enhanced flexibility, and cooperative production. This collective and political exchange balances employment stability and competitiveness. Unlike employment agreements during the German economic crisis of 1993 to 1996, the post-2000s *Beschäftigungspakte* pacts, referred to as Coalition for Competitiveness Enhancement (*Wettbewerbskoalitionen*), focus on improving the competitiveness of domestic production sites along with globalization of production. Allowing revisions of the collective agreement by industry at the company level shows that management holds an advantage in globalization of production. Nonetheless, German labor organizations gained strength and legitimacy by actively intervening in specific negotiation processes.

German law requires companies to justify any changes to the pact when making company-level changes to the agreement between labor and management at the industrial level. According to Haipeter (2011c)'s empirical study, companies in Germany's metal and chemical industries must first submit reports on the company's economic situation to the industry-level union to change the agreement at the company level. The union then reviews the validity of the reports and proposes how to deal with the company's demand based on them. In the course of these negotiations, the works council strengthens its bargaining power through collaboration with the union in negotiations with the company's management, or proposes an alternate constructive compromise.

Germany's labor–management structure has shifted from the industry level to the corporate, and plays a crucial role in social coordination during the globalization process. In the end, while adopting financialization and opening to global competition unlike Japan, Germany also, unlike the U.S., was able to establish a new high-value-added innovative production system through collective negotiations and social coordination of stakeholders that distinguished itself from the traditional professional production system.

R&D Employees and Ordinary Workers at Works Council

Unlike the U.S., Germany was able to strengthen its home country's production and innovation capabilities through social coordination even during the globalization process. As discussed earlier, this social coordination was possible because Germany's unique system of co-determination not only systematically provided space for unions and works councils to participate in major corporate decisions, but also created effective alternatives by stakeholders such as organized labor, state governments, social associations, and research institutes. In particular, solidarity with ordinary workers and researchers in the R&D sector was critical to creating innovative alternatives. Traditionally, Germany had no close cooperative relationship between R&D employees and ordinary workers, but the new social solidarity between the two was created in the process of struggling with the shareholder-value-priority principle which is based on financialization. As a result, this principle was weakened in Germany, even while a similar trend of financialization advanced in the U.S. In this section, we will examine how social solidarity between R&D employees and general workers was created.

Traditionally, tense conflictual relationships existed between R&D employees and works councils. Representatives of works councils in codetermination systems were predominantly production or office workers, and R&D employees tended to be underrepresented by the councils. R&D employees were reluctant to politically participate in the works councils and were dissatisfied with their underrepresentation in the codetermination process. Ordinary workers had a critical view of R&D employees, viewing them as weakening their bargaining power because their wages and working conditions deviated from the work and wage system set by collective bargaining (Kädtler et al. 2013: 132, 214).

Despite traditional tensions, works councils and R&D employees have sought a new relationship in light of the possibility of overseas relocation of companies with globalization. In addition, companies' rationale due to financialization acted as a pressure to reduce costs in both the R&D and production sectors. Along with globalization of production, cost reduction soon became a threat of overseas relocation of production bases. These forces jointly faced by R&D employees and works councils provided an opportunity to form solidarity between them.

In Germany, labor organizations, including works councils, did not directly oppose the relocation of overseas production, as in the U.S. Rather, labor in Germany moved toward claiming that upgrading the production and innovation capabilities of domestic production bases allowed companies to compete with overseas production bases. Almost all German companies negotiated and adjusted under the framework of Germany's Production Location Assurance Agreement (*Standortsicherungsvereinbarungen*). In the process of collectively establishing a new strategy for companies in the face of globalization and intensifying competition, R&D and ordinary workers' involvement in innovation became a major concern. R&D employees actively negotiated with companies over how to materialize innovation in the research sector and how to allocate organizational staffing in R&D in the process of establishing new company strategies. In addition to innovation methods in R&D, co-determination methods for collective discussions also became the subject of readjustment (Bispinck and Dribbusch 2011; Ackermann and Vollmer 1999: 156; Berthold et al. 2003: 28; Rehder 2003: 35; Massa-Wirth 2007: 17).

In the process of collectively discussing the company's globalization strategies, a coalition was formed between R&D employees and ordinary workers of the works councils as they shared common threats. The direction and activities of works councils had changed due to threats of overseas production to reduce costs; as a result, works councils in the production sector increased their interest in the R&D sector. According to an empirical study by a German company (Kädtler et al. 2013), as the company raised the issue of outsourcing, R&D budget cuts, and overseas relocation, the works council put a brake on management's unilateral decision and told management to come up with an arbitration plan. R&D employees also responded because relocation of a company's production base overseas could eventually result in outsourcing or relocating the R&D sector overseas. Employees in R&D now actively participated in the works council or supported its coordination.

For example, when a German pharmaceutical company tried to abolish some R&D departments in 2011, the company's works council actively intervened and proposed compromises and improvements, contributing to the stabilization of domestic local production and R&D sectors (Kädtler et al. 2013: 231–232). In another case, a family-owned pharmaceutical company, under pressure from the financial sector along with a change of ownership to a foreign global corporation, converted to a stock-listed company. Since then, the company has pursued shareholder value priority. The executive power of the foreign giant has grown, and the company has lost its ability to negotiate. Pressures to reduce production costs or face overseas relocation directly affected the costly R&D sector. Company management tried to significantly reduce the R&D sector in 2011. R&D employees, traditionally in conflict with people on the works council, began to change their minds in this situation. R&D employees recognized that the works council was the only force that could counter the employers of large corporations (Kädtler et al. 2013: 232).

In this company, workers shared a proud collective memory of the works council's important role through numerous conflicts in the process of transferring ownership. The works council pursued cooperation with local managers for employment succession and stability during the transfer of company ownership. R&D employees likewise pursued employment stability in cooperation with local managers, noting that:

> The Works Council always represents the interests of local production and workers with major premises such as "employment security" (*Erhaltung von Arbeitsplätzen*) and "stabilization of local production" (*Sicherung vom Standort*). This is the main direction. It is the continuation of performance to maintain the current status. (project leader)

And in a similar vein:

> If there is any decision made by the management over the dissolution in a given area of the company, I know that the works council is always very enthusiastic to solve the problem. For example, the chemistry R&D department will be completely dismantled by 2011. There are about 400 workers. Of course, the works council will fully intervene. (group leader) (Kädtler et al. 2013: 233)

As this pharmaceutical company shows, R&D employees recognized that their interests were similar to those of local production workers in Germany amid new challenges brought about by globalization and financialization, and began to recognize the existing works council and unions as representing their interests.

The pharmaceutical company is not the only case of joint response to the threat to local production caused by the financialization and globalization. The case of a German company in the machinery industry is similar. This company began listing its shares about 10 years ago, strengthening the financial sector within the company. Pressure increased on product innovation to reduce R&D costs. In 2012, this pressure challenged existing social partnerships. In the past, the company's *Standortvereinbarungen* (Agreements for local production site) did not set the budget for R&D. Since then, as the financial sector's demand for cost reduction increased, pressure also increased to revise existing R&D agreements downward. To this end, management proposed an objective investigation and evaluation through an external service company on the efficiency of R&D and research expenditure. To management's surprise, it was possible to successfully stabilize local production by clearly fixing the necessary budget for R&D through joint efforts of the works council and R&D employees (Kädtler et al. 2013: 233–234).

Cooperation between R&D employees and works councils to jointly address threats caused by production globalization and financialization takes various forms, depending on the company. In some companies, the works council actively supports the R&D sector through official agreements; in others, cooperation is strengthened through personnel who informally mediate between the two sides. Official agreements have the advantage of institutional stability, but inefficiency may increase due to excessive administrative demands in R&D performance evaluation. Informal cooperation's weakness is that the continuity of cooperation may rely too much on the mediator (Kädtler et al. 2013: 236).

Despite these various types of advantages and disadvantages, cooperation between R&D employees and general production workers of works councils in German companies could serve as a security agreement of local production (*Standortsicherungsvereinbarung*) as an alternative to globalization and financialization, in contrast to uncoordinated overseas transfers following unilateral management decisions that represent the interests of the U.S. financial sector. Social solidarity between production workers and R&D employees through works councils provided an organizational basis for seeking alternative strategies against unilateral claims from financial capital. Such solidarity also encouraged local managers to actively participate in actions against the institutional investors' priority of shareholder value.

The attitudes of British and American institutional investors have changed considerably since the 1990s, when institutional investors at Anglo-American investment banks believed that co-determination was an obstacle to the rights of shareholders. However, since the late 2000s in Germany, Anglo-American fund managers have never viewed Germany's co-determination or social coordination model as a brake against economic growth or competitive improvement (Faust, Bahnmüller, and Fisecker 2011: 150–155). According to an empirical study by Faust, Bahnmüller, and Fisecker (2011) targeting fund managers and investment analysts,[7] none of the Anglo-Saxon fund managers, contrary to neoliberal claims, mentioned Germany's co-determination system as "a disability to investment." Instead, according to the opinions of the survey subjects, some opined that "German co-determination is not bad," while others were satisfied, saying "the co-determination system has a rather positive effect on company development" (Faust, Bahnmüller, and Fisecker 2011: 154–155; Faust 2012: 167–168). In addition, an empirical study by Jirjahn (2010) shows that a company's co-determination system has a positive effect not only on productivity, but also on a company's profit rate and market value.

Why has shareholder value priority changed in corporate internal decisions in Germany? British and American investors' changed perception of Germany's co-determination system reveals that institutional investors recognize how German companies actually work with their investor relations managers. Anglo-American investors recognize that a co-determination system can contribute to stable labor–management relations. This change in perception took place in the microscopic political process surrounding German companies.

Changes in Germany's shareholder value priority mainly appear through negotiations at the supervisory board. After witnessing that companies' long-term development capacities were weakened by short-term investment early on, German companies negotiated to block this harmful effect. Even if a company's returns fell short of investors' expectations, German employers and management were not preoccupied with arbitrary decisions based solely on realizing shareholder value. Collectively they discussed and negotiated practical solutions to increase profits through co-determination.

Questions arose: How much time should be given to subunit organizations with poor performance to meet their profit goals? What measures should be taken to produce better results? Are there alternatives to simple cost reduction, especially labor cost reduction? If not, can dismissal of workers be avoided? German employees and management jointly discussed and decided together on such questions. According to a union

[7] Their empirical study was mainly conducted through in-depth qualitative interviews with large listed companies in Germany between 2005 and 2006. In addition to in-depth interviews with finance managers and other related department managers inside the company, they also conducted interviews with fund managers and bank analysts (Faust 2012: 151, 155–157).

leader, the issue of turning existing outsourcing back into the company was discussed to avoid labor cuts. The company supervisory board jointly decides whether to sell, merge, or outsource some of the company's organizations (Faust 2012: 174–176; Faust et al. 2011: 107–138).

German companies' investment managers do not accept the positions of foreign investors who are unfamiliar with the German co-determination system, but actively try to persuade them that their concerns lack evidence, and that co-determination is well suited to investors' interests. The co-determination system never prevents necessary workforce reduction programs. Conversely, without co-determination, managers face greater resistance and waste more time to reduce the workforce. During an in-depth interview, an investor relations manager explains well what he does when he meets institutional investors:

> More than anything else, I explain how this [co-determination system] has developed historically in our industry. I explain that our major competitors have the same structure, and that they have mimicked us. ... Then I mention day-to-day business. And I say: "I'm sorry, but as you can see from our cost-saving and staffing cuts programs, we're developing constructive cooperation with the works council." Without the support of the council, rapid changes in our company would not be so swift. Of course, we also mention the problems of the co-determination system. Not everything that glitters is gold. In this way, you gain more trust. I'm not saying that the relationship with the works council is always good. What I say is that it's generally OK. (IR Manager, quoted in Faust 2012: 169)

Empirical studies show that the mediating and persuading roles of investment-related managers in German companies have increased the institutional investors' and bank analysts' understanding of the co-determination system, and that this also offers them a balanced view that the works council is a major partner in communication (Faust 2012: 169). Institutional investors have become aware that even if they want to move production bases overseas to reduce costs, they may proceed without serious labor disputes by consulting through the co-determination system.

As can be seen above, since the 1990s Germany has experienced the financialization trend of companies similar to the U.S. In Germany, with financialization, institutional investors and bank analysts began to make more demands on the direction of operations of companies. In Germany, however, financial capital's unilateral demands were not accepted. Rather, the unilateral demands of shareholder value priority or neoliberal free-market models were eased or transformed in the process of coordinating with the company's stakeholders of various positions. Unlike the U.S., managers of German companies play a role in easing or transforming unilateral financial logic by focusing on social consultation and coordination.

Despite a similar globalization and financialization process, Germany was able to continuously upgrade its domestic production and innovation capabilities because of the process of social coordination involving various stakeholders, including organized labor, industrial associations, social organizations, research institutes, and state governments. Constructively organizing collective consultation based on unions and works councils, strengthening linkages to research institutes and social organizations for innovation, and promoting consensus on an alternative development strategy through consultation with company managers based on solidarity, are the pillars that enable Germany to maximize the strength of social coordination, unlike the U.S.

CHAPTER 9

Conclusion

Since the 1990s, in most advanced capitalist countries, major corporations have dismantled existing vertically integrated production systems and reorganized elements of production across borders. Nationally recognized corporations such as Apple (U.S.), Volkswagen (Germany), Toyota (Japan), Samsung, and Hyundai (Korea) have globally organized elements of production including labor, technology, and parts in order to survive intensified competition. Major companies have strengthened their competitiveness by segmenting entire value chains, from product development and design to production of detailed parts, assembly, and sales, deploying each factor at the global level.

In an era of intensifying international competition against the rapidly changing world of technology and markets, the globalization of national corporations seemed inevitable, even following the COVID-19 pandemic and U.S.–China hegemonic rivalry, because without openness to globalization and connectedness to global integration, even the most competitive firm cannot sustain a competitive edge against the rapidly changing technology and competition games (Nguyen-Quoc 2023; Ito et al. 2023; Bathelt and Li 2020; Bloom et al. 2016; Buera and Oberfield 2020). Global production networks, led by U.S. companies, forced companies in other developed countries to follow suit, including Germany, Japan, Korea, and now China and other emerging industrial countries, reflecting a massive paradigm shift from the past one-nation-based production

H. Kwon, *Openness and Coordination*,
https://doi.org/10.1007/978-981-97-3352-1_9

system toward global production networks. However, this trend comes at a price.

The unanticipated problem is that the overseas production of national corporations causes serious gaps and tensions between the interests of individual companies and the interests of national economies as a whole. For example, Apple, a leading U.S. company and producer of the iPhone 14 Plus, gathers worldwide resources, parts, skills, and innovative ideas, including hardware chip design in Cupertino, excellent chips in Taiwan, and semiconductor production machines in the Netherlands, assembles them in China and exports them to U.S. markets (DeLong 2023; Nanto 2010: 5–8). In this production structure, private U.S. companies make huge operating profits, but the U.S. economy suffers from an account deficit and a decline in domestic production and employment. Automakers, a leading U.S. industry, have increased overseas production, including in China, to contain costs, since the 1990s. As a result, employment in the U.S. domestic automobile industry decreased to 66.7% in 2008 compared to 1998 (US Bureau of Labor Statistics). Expansion of overseas production in industries beyond electronics and automobiles brought a risk of hollowing-out domestic production. However, traditional nationalist protectionism does not solve the problem. If the U.S. wants to resolve domestic unemployment and account deficits, then regulating Chinese imports will cause decisive damage to the global network of U.S. companies producing in and exporting from China.

Despite the globalization of production, how can national economies and corporate globalization be compatible? How can national economies reconstitute themselves in an era of corporate globalization? Political economists and policymakers have argued seriously about the direction, method, and effect of production globalization, and about changes in the national economy following the globalization of production. Neoliberals expressed optimism based on the free market principle, while those in the position of traditional nationalism were concerned about the collapse of the national economy and the hollowing-out of industries due to globalization of production. However, despite neoliberal optimism and nationalist pessimism, globalization does not necessarily result in an upgrade toward high-value-added industries or industrial hollowing-out. As seen from our cases of the U.S., Japan, Korea, and Germany, globalization may lead to deindustrialization of the home country, or to an improvement in the quality of the domestic industry, depending on the politics among the major actors of each nation-state.

In particular, this study emphasized the importance of "the politics of coordination" concerning how to develop industrial commons and innovation ecosystems consisting of production factors and parts with increased transferability in order to strengthen the production and innovation capabilities of the national economy in the process of globalization. Now I wish to summarize the main argument of this study, comparing it to the existing theories.

This study argues that the globalization of major national corporations does not necessarily lead to denationalization in which differences between national economies disappear. Our argument is distinct from the view of neoliberal globalism and GVC literature that globalization means the decline of the nation-state or the disappearance of differences and competition among national economies. The denationalization argument has dominated the globalization debate since the 1990s, predicting that the economies of each country will converge into the free market following a global standard, and that various existing nationalist development methods will disappear. The denationalization view has been widely spread not only among neoliberals and GVC proponents, but also among sociologists such as Sassen (2006), Marxist political economists (Cerny 2010; Harvey 2007; Joseph 1999), and nationalists concerned about the domestic industrial hollowing-out of their own countries. Despite their varied positions in the normative evaluation of globalization, they share the view that the globalization of major national corporations will not only remain inconsistent with the interests of national economies as a whole but will also converge into the global free market method.

The denationalization view is basically the argument of neoliberal globalists and GVC proponents, based on neoclassical economics (Singh 2023; World Bank 2020; Aichele and Heiland 2018; Yeung 2017; Bhagwati 2010a, 2010b; Gibbon et al. 2008; Friedman 2005; Edwards 2004; Ohmae 1990, 1995). They hold that the free movement of capital, labor, and goods resulting from globalization guarantees the best efficiency; thus, almost all countries will competitively lift regulations and move toward the free market to attract capital and direct investment that moves freely across borders. They hold that the freer or more open to a globalized world a national economy becomes, the more prosperous it will be. Therefore, they argue that nation-states will abolish their patterns of economic development or nationalist elements and converge into the free market. Thus, neoliberals and GVC proponents hold that the decline of state interference, along with free markets across borders, will benefit not only home countries but also developing countries.

The view that globalization means denationalization is also shared by left-wing intellectuals who criticize neoliberalism. John Gray (2005) has pointed out that the globalization of neoclassical liberals following Adam Smith's tradition is in line with that of Marx and Engels. For example, Thomas Friedman, a global neoliberalist, acknowledged that his perspective was fundamentally the same as that of Marx and Engels, saying "Globalization will eventually result in the single economic system" (Friedman, 2005; 2013). Left-wing intellectuals criticize globalization in that neoliberalism unilaterally strengthens the power of capital, reduces welfare, and expands social inequality, but they share the neoliberal view that globalization will eventually dissolve the national economy into one globalized economy, diminish the nation-state's decision-making role, and eliminate differences in national economic governance patterns (Cerny 2010; Harvey 2007; Robinson 2004; Jessop 1999; Giddens 1999).

For example, the global capitalism school, led by Robinson, a global networks analyst who builds on the Marxist tradition, argues that the emergence of a transnational production system will dismantle the existing national economy and accelerate convergence into a single global standard. Philip Cerny, a leading left-wing political economist, also stresses that, with globalization, countries can no longer play the traditional "strategic" or "developmental" role, and that economies are increasingly converging into marketization and "commodification" (Cerny 2010: 38). Sociologists such as Sassen (2006) also argue that as globalization progresses, the nation-state undergoes a fundamental "epochal transformation" called "de-nationalization" in terms of territory, authority, and rights. Sassen believes that globalization dismantles the traditional logic based on national economy through denationalization, and that "global assemblies" will emerge that reorganize authority and rights with new organizational logic at the global level.

However, whether from a neoliberal GVC view or a left-wing position, arguments that globalization is denationalization may overlook that in reality, patterns and impacts of globalization can vary from country to country. Empirical studies (in addition to this one) on multinational corporations reveal that companies show differences in governance and organizational logic by their nationality in the process of internationalization (Harzing and Noorderhaven 2008; Lane and Probert 2009; Lane 2001).

This study emphasizes that despite globalization, competition and tension among nation-states still exist, and that competition continues as a major structural force that defines society, if not as nationalism as in the past. This point represents a position that is distinct from modern liberalism handed down since Adam Smith or Marxist thinking, a representative trend that criticizes liberalism. In Adam Smith's classical liberalism or Karl Marx's class struggle, by emphasizing the universal Cosmopolitan position beyond the boundaries of nation-states, competition and tension among nation-states, and pressure to reorganize them—whether furiously or peacefully—are largely ignored.

As demonstrated in the previous chapters, this study makes clear that the way of globalization does not necessarily result in denationalization. The globalization of production by leading national corporations does not result in a single outcome such as industrial hollowing-out in the home country, nor converge into a single governance structure based on the free market. National corporations cause tensions within the existing national economy as they increase overseas production, but this does not necessarily result in denationalization, such as the hollowing-out of domestic production. As can be seen in Korea and Germany, not all national economies experience industrial hollowing-out and denationalization as the U.S. has experienced. Rather, some countries strengthen their competitiveness by reorganizing their innovation capabilities in the globalization process. Rather than eliminating diversity among nation-states and leading to a single process, the globalization of production itself shows various patterns.

For example, the U.S., Japan, Korea, and Germany show a wide variety of patterns in ways to establish global networks covering overseas production sites, linkages between domestic and overseas production, and modes of production and innovation ecosystems in their home countries. In the U.S., domestic parts makers and prime contractors (OEMs) had relationships based on free market relations, and in the process of globalization they naturally separated from each other and signed free contracts with local companies or global parts makers. In contrast, Japan tended to establish close cooperative relationships overseas with parts companies based on affiliates in the home country.

Significant differences emerge in the way companies enhance their home country's production and innovation capabilities in the globalization process. According to the principle of free market and financial capital advantage, the U.S. experienced a hollowing-out phenomenon in which the home country's production and innovation capabilities were weakened through uncoordinated migration. In the case of Japan and Germany, through statist and social coordination respectively, a pattern emerged of linking home and overseas production and strengthening production and innovation capabilities through coordinated methods in the globalization process, although coordination based on too much closed structure, as seen in Japan, causes negative effects on improvement of industrial commons at home.

Openness and Coordination, which shows the diverse reconstruction patterns of national economies in the process of production globalization, may look similar to those of the neoinstitutionalists, as in Varieties of Capitalism (VoC) literature. However, the diversity of national economies that continues despite globalization is different from neo-institutionalism. Contrary to institutionalists' static, path-dependent, or self-reinforcing diversity based on each country's inherited cultures and institutions, we emphasize the "politics of recomposition" to account for dynamic changes, as seen in the radical shifts, including the recent U.S. changes from neoliberalism to statist coordination in the late 2010s and Japan's shift toward U.S.-style open innovation system. Through the politics of recomposition, major actors struggle for solutions to new challenges and construct new alternatives to respond to challenges raised by evolving nation-states competing in national rivalry.

The politics of dynamic recomposition emphasizes tension and pressure from competition among nation-states, contrary to the arguments of the "global capitalist school" or "global assembly" of neoliberal or left-wing intellectuals. Also, contrary to institutionalists' static understanding of diversity, we argue that diverse patterns of development and governance of national economies are due to rivalry among nation-states and the continuous changes in types of diversity. This position is quite different from seeing institutions and cultures as heritage, or a unidirectional, path-dependent consequence of traditional institutions and cultures, as institutionalists or their simple static classification argues.

For example, as seen in the main body of this book, when the U.S., based on mass production lost to Japan's and Germany's more flexible specialization systems, the U.S. was initially inspired by the Japanese Lean Production system, and in the course of emulating that flexible system, the U.S. developed a modular flexible production system and global network. These changes and upgrades put a competitive strain on Japan's flexible production system based on closed structures like *Keiretsu*. Japan, the world's most competitive nation until the 1980s, lost its edge in the face of the U.S.'s and Germany's open flexible production systems (Kwon 2005). Japanese companies could no longer insist on their own way of development based on traditional institutions. In order to compete with the U.S. again, Japan tried to enhance national competitiveness through adopting more open innovation, inspired by the U.S., and building a new sophisticated and complex production system in the global production network.

The neoinstitutionalists' diversity of capitalist states argument (Iversen and Soskice 2019; Hall and Soskice 2001; Whitley 2007) expressed in terms of unidirectional, path-dependent, or self-reinforcing consequences by existing institutions could not explain the dynamics of competitors' changes and new challenges arising from competition among national economies. New production and innovation patterns emerging in the process of globalization were not unilaterally defined results by the unique culture or historically inherited domestic system in certain domestic institutional environments, as Whitley (2007) and other institutionalists argue. Major actors in each country utilized and actively reconstructed the existing system, rather than passively defining it, through new experiences and choices acquired in overseas production processes, especially through introspective reflections on competitors' production methods and their own. Therefore, new diversity is created through dynamic changes in the national economy, which reflects changes in the domestic system through local experiences abroad.

The reorganization of national economies and the creation of new diversities in the process of production globalization manifest differently, especially depending on the politics of the main actors and how they coordinate with each other. How nation-states reconstruct their domestic production and innovation system in the process of production globalization, and how they construct industrial and innovative commons to enhance industrial innovation capabilities are crucial. This form of politics reflects how actors coordinate with various interests to create industrial commons.

Industrial commons and innovative ecosystems are key sources of national competitiveness that reconstruct the national economy in the process of globalization. Industrial commons refer to various complementary capabilities that exist beyond individual companies—embedded in a network of major economic actors, including customers, subcontractors, public and private research institutes, and technical personnel—and to the public goods including abundant labor, science and technology, vocational training, research institutes, various components, and a supportive social network. Industrial commons lie beyond the scope and capacities of individual companies, must be produced socially, and represent more than financial, quantitative value.

Contrary to nationalists' pessimism about globalization, the national economy can be upgraded to the next level when the industrial commons are well created in the globalization process. And, contrary to neoliberalist optimism, the national economy can be dismantled when the industrial commons are lost. Industrial commons are not automatically created or inevitably extinguished by globalization. Contrary to neoliberal optimism, surplus profits generated by overseas outsourcing are not automatically reinvested in strengthening domestic industrial capabilities and require intentional adjustment. As with all common goods, "free-riders" motivated by personal interests and profit-seeking lead to a collective loss of innovative capabilities and common goods for the national economy as a whole.

In the political process of problem-solving, collective action, and coordination in the process of globalization, each country's national economy creates a variety of production and innovation systems. There exists no sole, ultimate method to create an industrial commons and innovation ecosystem for production and innovation capabilities. As shown in this study, there exists the American neoliberal free market method, as well as the statist coordination method found in Japan and Korea, and the social coordination method found in Germany.

Openness and Coordination reveals, through these diverse coordination methods, that the proposition that free market is the most effective model in the globalization process, and that all countries should imitate it, may not be true. Contrary to the neoliberal argument, industrial commons or innovative ecosystems are not naturally and automatically created by the free market, although openness to a rapidly changing world is crucial for the improvement of innovation capabilities at home. Openness without coordination can result in suboptimal outcomes. For example, U.S. companies may invest surplus profits from globalization in other parts of the world for financial gain rather than reinvesting domestically. Decisions based on the finance-dominant free market logic without a coordination process can cause many losses to domestic industrial links and industrial commons, a challenge to neoliberal optimism, and weakening the capacity for innovation.

In addition to the problem of simple openness without coordination, as seen in the case of Japan, coordination without openness to a rapidly changing world can cause suboptimal outcomes because a closed structure or insularity deters the free flow of inputs, including new technology, better parts, and innovative ideas, and renders the industrial commons outdated. Openness to a rapidly changing world not only engenders stimulus for innovation and learning from foreign competitors but also facilitates the enrichment of innovative ideas and skills (Ito et al. 2023; Bathelt and Li 2020; Bloom et al. 2016). Thus, *Openness and Coordination* emphasizes an appropriate coordination given openness to a rapidly changing world in order to improve innovation capabilities and competitiveness.

Openness and Coordination argues that the active role of the nation-state is decisive for coordination in openness to a rapidly changing world. Contrary to neoliberalist and left-wing intellectual claims, the state's active role does not naturally decline with globalization. Rather, the role of the state can be newly emphasized, as the need increases to enrich the industrial commons and create a competitive industrial ecosystem in the process of globalization. The cases of Korea, and recently Japan, clearly show that the role of the state is necessary to strengthen domestic industrial commons. Of course, the effectiveness of state coordination in Japan and Korea works by switching to a new model and method. In the past, both were limited in creating an innovation ecosystem among companies with various innovation capabilities, as Japan's past developmentalism had created "closed reciprocity," and Korea's past developmentalism excluded SMEs, concentrating capital instead in large companies. Although reform was delayed, Japan moved to an open innovation system by fostering innovative start-up companies and strengthening industry-academic cooperation through university reform, following the state's initiatives. Korea succeeded in strengthening domestic innovation capabilities and international competitiveness based on the new developmentalist state that focused on joint learning and enhanced innovation capabilities through a comprehensive cooperative network. Thus, *Openness and Coordination* emphasizes that the role of the state, not the free market, is vital for coordination to qualitatively strengthen the domestic industrial ecosystem in the process of globalization, as demonstrated in Japan and Korea, and as the U.S. discovered in the late 2010s.

However, statist coordination is not the only option to strengthen industrial commons and innovation capabilities. In Germany, the social coordination system is a viable alternative. Even with similar globalization and openness to a changing world, as in the U.S., Germany advanced, rather than reduced, domestic production and innovation capabilities. Unlike in the U.S., German companies collectively adjusted their production globalization by major actors inside and outside the company. In social coordination systems like Germany's, actors such as labor, parts makers, and industrial associations actively participated and negotiated in the decision-making process of major companies, allowing them to upgrade their domestic production and innovation ecosystems to the next level, as well as expand overseas production. Despite globalization, the national economy's success depends on the politics surrounding how major actors such as the state, SMEs, labor, and industrial associations build industrial commons at home in the course of openness to a globalized world.

Openness and Coordination holds that in order to build successfully competitive national economies in response to a rapidly changing world of markets and technology, openness is needed first; as seen in the case of Japan, the closed structure for coordination deters flexible adaptation in the rapidly changing world and makes the industrial commons outdated. However, simple openness itself does not secure improved industrial commons in a national economy. As seen in the U.S., simple openness without coordination easily results in the loss of industrial commons. Openness has its own costs. Thus, *Openness and Coordination* concludes that the more open and the more decentralized a national economy becomes, the more coordination it needs. An appropriate balance of openness and coordination in a nation-state is not predetermined or fixed. Reflecting upon each nation's current problems and resources which the nation has, each nation must build its own methods of openness and coordination.

References

Abelshauser, W. (2016). "Einleitung: Der deutsche Weg der Wirtschaftspolitik." In W. Abelshauser (ed.), *Das Bundeswirtschaftsministerium in der Ära der Sozialen Marktwirtschaft: Der deutsche Weg der Wirtschaftspolitik*. Berlin: De Gruyter.

Acharya, Viral, Matthew Richardson, Stijn van Nieuwerburgh, and Lawrence White. (2011). *Guaranteed to Fail: Fannie Mae, Freddie Mac, and the Debacle of Mortgage Finance*. Princeton: Princeton University Press.

Ackermann, K.-F., and S. Vollmer. (1999). "Firmenspezifische Bündnisse für Arbeit und Wettbewerbsfähigkeit in der Unternehmenspraxis." In K. F. Ackermann and M. Kammüller (eds.), *Firmenspezifische Bündnisse für Arbeit. Ziele, Strategien, Unternehmensbeispiele*. Stuttgart: Schäffer-Poeschel Verlag.

Ahmadjian, Christina L., and James Lincoln. (2001). "Keiretsu, Governance and Learning: Case Studies in Change from the Japanese Automotive Industry." *Organization Science* 12, no. 6, pp. 683–701.

Aichele, R., and I. Heiland (2018). "Where Is the Value Added? Trade Liberalization and Production Networks." *Journal of International Economics* 115, pp. 130–144.

Ali, Anuwar. (1994). "Japanese Industrial Investments and Technology Transfer in Malaysia." In K. S. Jomo (ed.), *Japan and Malaysian Development: In the Shadow of the Rising Sun*. London: Routledge.

Alphametrics, and Ismeri Europa. (2009). *Comprehensive Sectoral Analysis of Emerging Competences and Economic Activities in the European Union*. European Commission, DG Employment, Social Affairs and Equal Opportunities.

Amable, Bruno. (2003). *The Diversity of Modern Capitalism*. Oxford, UK: Oxford University Press.

H. Kwon, *Openness and Coordination*,
https://doi.org/10.1007/978-981-97-3352-1

———. (2017). *Structural Crisis and Institutional Change in Modern Capitalism: French Capitalism in Transition*. Oxford: Oxford University Press.

Amsden, Alice H. (2013). "Securing the Home Market: An New Approach to Korean Development." Research Paper 2013-1, United Nations Research Institute for Social Development (UNRISD), April 2013.

Amyx, J. (2002). "Okurasho Nettowaku: Kenryoku No Kakudai To Seiyaku No Kiketsu [The MoF Network: The Expansion of Authority and the Outcome of Restrictions]." In M. Muramatsu and M. Okuno (eds.), *Heisei Baburu No Kenkyu. Houkaigo No Fukyo To Furyosaiken Shori Mondai* [The Study of the Heisei Bubble (Vol. II). The Recession After the Collapse and Non-Performing Loan Problem]. Tokyo: Toyo Keizai Shinposha.

———. (2004). *Japan's Financial Crisis: Institutional Rigidity and Reluctant Change. Princeton*, NJ: Princeton University Press.

Ando. (2019). "Japan Inc. Sitting on ¥506.4 Trillion Mountain of Cash." *Japan Times*, September 3, 2019.

Anuroj, Bonggot. (1995). "Japanese Investment in Thailand: The Nature and Extent of Backward Linkages." Ph.D. dissertation, University of New South Wales.

Aoki, M. (1987). "The Japanese Firm in Transition." In K. Yamamura and Y. Yasuba (eds.), *The Political Economy of Japan*, vol. 1. Stanford, CA: Stanford University Press.

———. (1988). *Information Incentives and Bargaining in the Japanese Economy*. Cambridge: Cambridge University Press.

———. (1998). "Unintended Fit: Organizational Evolution and Government Design of Institutions in Japan." In M. Aoki, H. Kim, and M. Okuno-Fujiwara (eds.), *The Role of Government in East Asian Economic Development: Comparative Institutional Analysis*. Oxford: Clarendon.

Aoki, M., G. Jackson, and H. Miyajima (eds.). (2007). *Corporate Governance in Japan: Institutional Change and Organizational Diversity*. Oxford: Oxford University Press.

Arndt, Hans-Joachim. (1966). *West Germany. Politics of Non-planning*. Michigan: Syracuse University Press.

Artus, I. (2013). "Precarious Delegates: Irregular Forms of Employee Interest Representation in Germany." *Industrial Relations Journal* 44, no. 4, pp. 409–424.

Asahi Shimbun. (2009). *Ushinawareta* 20 Nen [The Lost Two Decades]. Tokyo: Iwanami Shoten.

Atkinson, Robert D. (2009). *Effective Corporate Tax Reform in the Global Innovation Economy*. Washington, DC: ITIF. http://www.itif.org/files/090723_CorpTax.pdf.

———. (November 24, 2010). "Don't Believe Amity Shales (or Most Neoclassical Economists): Obama's Accelerated Depreciation Proposal will Boost Economic Growth and Is a Good Idea," The Innovation Files.

———. (2018). *Big Is Beautiful: Debunking the Myth of Small Businesses*. Cambridge: MIT Press.

———. (2022). "The Abandonment of Growth and the Decline of the West." *The Independent Review* 27, no. 2, pp. 201–226.

———. (2023). "What Kind of Industrial Policy: Progressives or Hamilton?" Hamilton Center on Industrial Strategy, Information Technology & Innovation Foundation.

Atkinson, Robert D., and Stephen Ezell. (2012). *Innovation Economics: The Race for Global Advantage*. New Haven: Yale University Press.

Baccaro, L., and C. Benassi (2017). "Throwing Out the Ballast: Growth Models and the Liberalization of German Industrial Relations." *Socio-Economic Review* 15, no. 1, pp. 85–115.

Baccaro, Lucio, and Chris Howell. (2011). "A Common Neoliberal Trajectory: The Transformation of Industrial Relations in Advanced Capitalism," *Politics & Society* 39, no. 4 (2011): 521–563.

Baccaro, L., and C. Howell. (2017). *Trajectories of Neoliberal Transformation: European Industrial Relations after the 1970s*. Cambridge: Cambridge University Press.

Baccaro, Lucio, and Jonas Pontusson. (2016). "Rethinking Comparative Political Economy: the Growth Model Perspective." *Politics & Society* 44, no. 2, pp. 175–207.

Baccaro, Lucio, Mark Blyth, and Jonas Pontusson. (2022). "Introduction: Rethinking Comparative Capitalism." In Baccaro, Blyth, and Pontusson (eds.), *Diminishing Returns: The New Politics of Growth and Stagnation*. Oxford University Press, pp. 1–50.

Baccaro, Lucio, Mark Blyth, and Jonas Pontusson (eds.). (2022). *Diminishing Returns: The New Politics of Growth and Stagnation*. Oxford: Oxford University Press.

Baccaro, Lucio, Virginia Doellgast, Tony Edwards, and Josh Whitford. (2018). "Diversified Quality Production 2.0." *Socio-Economic Review* 16, no. 3, pp. 613–635.

Bailey, D., M. Bellandi, A. Caloffi, and L. De Propris. (2010). "Place-Renewing Leadership: Trajectories of Change for Mature Manufacturing Regions in Europe." *Policy Studies* 31, no. 4, pp. 457–474.

Baily, David, and Lisa De Propis. (2014). "Manufacturing Reshoring and Its Limits: The UK Automotive Case." *Cambridge Journal of Regional Economy and Society* 7, pp. 379–395.

Bair, J. (2009). "Global Commodity Chains: Genealogy and Review." In J. Bair (ed.), *Frontiers of Commodity Chain Research*. Stanford: Stanford University Press.

Baker, Deam. (2022, December 21). "Industrial Policy Is Not a Remedy for Income Inequality." Center for Economic and Policy Research, from https://cepr.net/industrial-policy-is-not-a-remedy-for-income-inequality/.

Baldwin, C., and K. Clark. (2000). *Design Rules*. Cambridge: MIT Press.

Banerji, K., and R. Sambharya. (1996). "Vertical Keiretsu and International Market Entry: The Case of the Japanese Automobile Ancillary Industry." *Journal of International Business Studies* 27, pp. 89–113.

Barzotto, Mariachiara, Giancarlo Coro, and Mario Volpe. (2018). "Global Value Chains and the Role of MNEs in Local Production Systems." In V. de Marchi, E. D. Maria, and G. Gereffi (eds.), *Local Clusters in Global Value Chains: Linking Actors and Territories Through Manufacturing and Innovation*. London: Routledge.

Bathelt, H., and P. Li. (2020). "Processes of Building Cross-Border Knowledge Pipelines." *Research Policy* 49, p. 103928. https://doi.org/10.1016/j.respol.2020.103928.

Bawn, Kathleen, Martin Cohen, David Karol, Seth Masket, Hans Noel, and John Zaller. (2012). "A Theory of Political Parties: Groups, Policy Demands and Nominations in American Politics." *Perspectives on Politics* 10, pp. 571–597.

BDI. (2019a, May 6). "Deutsche Industriepolitik: Zum Entwurf der Nationalen Industriestrategie 2030 [German Industrial Policy: On the Draft National Industrial Strategy]." https://issuu.com/bdi-berlin/docs/20190506_position_bdi_industriepoli.

———. (2019b, January). "Partner and Systemic Competitor: How Do We Deal with China's State-Controlled Economy?" https://english.bdi.eu/publication/news/china-partner-and-systemiccompetitor/.

Beason, Richard, and David Weinstein. (1996). "Growth, Economies of Scale, and Targeting in Japan (1995–1990)." *The Review of Economics and Statistics* 78, no. 2, pp. 286–295.

Belzer, V., and J. Hilbert. (1996). "Virtuelle Unternehmen: schlank, aber innovative." In P. Brödner, U. Perkruhl, and D. Rehfeld (eds.), *Arbeitsteilung ohne Ende? Von den Schwierigkeiten inner- und überbetrieblicher Zusammenarbeit*. Müchen: R Hampp.

Benassi, Chiara (2016). "Liberalization Only at the Margins? Analysing the Growth of Temporary Work in German Core Manufacturing Sectors." *British Journal of Industrial Relations* 54, no. 3, pp. 597–622.

Berger, Suzanne. (2005). *How We Compete: What Companies around the World Are Doing to Make It in Today's Global Economy*. New York: Currency/Doubleday.

———. (2013) *Making in America: From Innovation to Market*. Cambridge, MA: The MIT Press.

Berghoff, Hartmut. (2016). "Varieties of Financialization? Evidence from German Industry in the 1990s." *The Business History Review* 90, no. 1, pp. 81–108.

Bergholt, Drago, Francesco Furlanetto, and Nicolo Maffei-Faccioli. (2022). "The Decline of the Labor Share: New Empirical Evidence." *American Economic Journal: Macroeconomics* 14, no. 3, pp. 163–198.

Bernaciak, Magdalena. (2010). "Cross-Border Competition and Trade Union Responses in the Enlarged EU: Evidence from the Automotive Industry in Germany and Poland." *European Journal of Industrial Relations* 16, no. 2, pp. 119–135.

Berthold, N., M. Brischke, and O. Stettes. (2003). *Betriebliche Bündnisse für Arbeit. Eine empirische Untersuchung für den deutschen Maschinen- und Anlagenbau*. Wirtschaftswissenschaftliche Beiträge des Lehrstuhls für Volkswirtschaftslehre, Wirtschaftsordnung und Sozialpolitik, no. 68.

Beyer, Jürgen, and Martin Höpner. (2003). "Corporate Governance and the Disintegration of Organized Capitalism." *West European Politics* 26, no. 4, pp. 179–198.

Bhagwati, Jagdish. (2010a). "The Computer Chip vs. Potato Chip Debate." *The Moscow Times*, September 1, 2010.

———. (2010b). "The Manufacturing Fallacy." *Project Syndicate*, August 27, 2010.

Bispinck, Reinhard, and Heiner Dribbusch. (2011). "Collective Bargaining, Decentralization and Crisis Management in the German Metalworking Industries since 1990." WSI Discussion Paper, no. 177.

Blöcker, Antje. (2001). *Reorganisationsmuster von Forschung und Entwicklung in der Automobilindustrie am Beispiel von BMW, Mercedes-Benz und Volkswagen*. Aachen: Shaker Verlag.

Bloom, N., M. Draca, and J. van Reenen. (2016). "Trade Induced Technical Change? The Impact of Chinese Imports and Innovation, IT and Productivity." *Review of Economic Studies* 83, pp. 87–117. https://doi.org/10.1093/restud/rdv039.

Blyth, Mark. (2002). *Great Transformations: Economic Ideas and Institutional Change in the Twentieth Century*. Cambridge: Cambridge University Press.

BMWi. (2019a, February 5). National Industrial Strategy 2030: Strategic Guidelines for a German and European Industrial Policy. https://www.bmwi.de/Redaktion/EN/Publikationen/Industry/national-industry-strategy-2030.html.

———. (2019b, November 29). Industrial Strategy 2030: Guidelines for a German and European Industrial Policy. https://www.bmwi.de/Redaktion/EN/Publikationen/Industry/industrial-strategy-2030.html.

Bofinger, P. (2019). “Paradigmenwechsel in der deutschen Wirtschaftspolitik.” *Wirtschaftsdienst: Zeitschrift fur Wirtschaftspolitik* 99, no. 2, pp. 95–98.

Bohle, Dorothee, and Aidan Regan. (2021). “The Comparative Political Economy of Growth Models: Explaining the Continuity of FDI-Led Growth in Ireland and Hungary.” *Politics & Society* 49, no. 1, pp. 75–106.

Bonvillian, William B. (2022). *Industrial Innovation Policy in the United States*. Norwell, MA: Now Publishers.

Bonvillian, William B., and Peter L. Singer. (2017). *Advanced Manufacturing: The New American Innovation Policies*. Cambridge, MA: The MIT Press.

Bosch, G., T. Haipeter, E. Latniak, and S. Lehndorff. (2007). “Demontage oder Revitalisierung? Das Deutsche Beschäftungsmodell im Umbruch.” *Zeitschrift für Soziologie* 64, pp. 839–853.

Boston Consulting Group (BGC) and Semiconductor Industry Association (SIA). (April 2021). “Strengthening the Global Semiconductor Supply Chain in an Uncertain Era” Policy Report, SIA. https://www.semiconductors.org/wp-content/uploads/2021/05/BCG-x-SIA-Strengthening-the-Global-Semiconductor-Value-Chain-April-2021_1.pdf.

Bown Chad, P. (2020). “How the United States Marched the Semiconductor Industry into Its Trade War with China.” Working Paper 20-16, Peterson Institute for International Economics.

Boyd, J. P., and R. Samuels. (2008). “Prosperity’s Children: Generational Change and Japan’s Future Leadership.” *Asia Policy* 6 (July), pp. 15–51.

Braun, Benjamin, and Richard Deeg. (2019). “Strong Firms, Weak Banks: The Financial Consequences of Germany’s Export-led Growth Model.” MPIfG Discussion Paper 19/5, Max Planck Institute for the Study of Societies.

Broz, J. L., J. Frieden, S. Weymouth. (2021). “Populism in Place: The Economic Geography of the Globalization Backlash.” *International Organization* 75, no. 2, pp. 464–494.

Browning, L. D., and J. C. Shetler. (2000). “SEMATECH History.” In *Saving the U.S. Semiconductor Industry*. College Station: Texas A&M University Press from http://www.sematech.org/corporate/history.htm.

Buchanan, John, Dominic H. Chai, and Simon Deakin. (2012). *Hedge Fund Activism in Japan: The Limits of Shareholder Primacy*. New York: Cambridge University Press.

Buciuni, G., and G. P. Pisano. (2015). “Can Marshall’s Clusters Survive Globalization?” Harvard Business School Working Paper 15-088.

Buera, F. J., and E. Oberfield. (2020). “The Global Diffusion of Ideas.” *Econometrica* 88, no. 1, pp. 83–114. https://doi.org/10.3982/ECTA14044.

Busemeyer, Marius R. (2012). “Business as a Pivotal Actor in the Politics of Training Reform: Insights from the Case of Germany.” *British Journal of Industrial Relations* 50, no. 4, pp. 690–713

Calder, Kent E. (1988). *Crisis and Compensation: Public Policy and Political Stability in Japan, 1949–1986*. Princeton: Princeton University Press.

———. (1989). "Elites in an Equalizing Role: Ex-Bureaucrats as Coordinators and Intermediaries in the Japanese Government-Business Relationship." *Comparative Politics* 21, no. 4, pp. 379–403.

———. (2017). *Circles of Compensation: Economic Growth and the Globalization of Japan*. Stanford: Stanford University Press.

Calomiris, Charles W., and Charles P. Himmelberg. (1995). "Government Credit Policy and Industrial Performance." Policy Research Working Paper, No. 1434. Washington, DC: World Bank.

Capello, R., and C. Lenzi. (2015). "The Knowledge—Innovation Nexus: Its Spatially Differentiated Returns to Innovation." *Growth and Change* 46, no. 3, pp. 379–399.

Carlin, Wendy, and David Soskice. (2008) "German Economic Performance: Disentangling the Role of Supply-Side Reforms, Macroeconomic Policy and Coordinated Economy Institutions." *Socio-Economic Review* 7, no. 1, pp. 67–99.

———. (2015). *Macroeconomics: Imperfections, Institutions, and Policies*. New York: Oxford University Press.

Castellani, D., and F. Pieri. (2015). "Outward Investments and Productivity: Evidence from European Regions." *Regional Studies* 50, no. 12, pp. 1945–1964.

Cerny, Philip G. (2010). *Rethinking World Politics: A Theory of Transnational Neopluralism*. Oxford: Oxford University Press.

Cha, Seok-rok. (2020). "Japan—Revisioning Open Innovation Promotion Tax System." *Nanum Economy News*, August 2, 2020. http://nanumy.co.kr/View.aspx?No=929074.

Chen, Edward K. Y., and Teresa Y. C. Wong. (1997). "Hong Kong: Foreign Direct Investment and Trade Linkages in Manufacturing." In Wendy Dobson and Chia Siow Yue (eds.), *Multinationals and East Asian Integration*. Ottawa: International Development Research Centre.

Chesbrough, H. W. (2006). *Open Innovation: The New Imperative for Creating and Profiting from Technology*. Cambridge: Harvard Business Press.

Chokki, Shun, Hiroshi Odawara, André Rocha, Christoph Sandler, and Takuya Tsuda. (2020). *A New Era for Industrial R&D in Japan*. McKinsey & Company. https://www.mckinsey.com/capabilities/operations/our-insights/a-new-era-for-industrial-rnd-in-japan#/Springer.

Clark, Colin. (1940). *The Conditions of Economic Progress*. London: Macmillan.

Clark, K. B., and T. Fujimoto. (1991). *Product Development Performance: Strategy, Organization, and Management in the World Auto Industry*. Boston MA: Harvard Business Review Press.

CNBC. (March 11, 2021). “Biden Signs $1.9 Trillion COVID Relief Bill, Clearing Way for Stimulus Checks, Vaccine Aid.”
Cole, Robert E., and D. Hugh Whittaker. (2006). “Introduction.” In Whittaker and Cole (eds.), *Recovering from Success*. Oxford: Oxford University Press.
Costin, Cathy Lynne. (2001). “Craft Production Systems.” In G. M. Feinman and T. D. Price (eds.), *Archaeology at the Millennium*. Boston: Springer.
Cox, Joan C., and Herbert Kriegbaum. (1980). *Growth, Innovation and Employment: An Anglo-German Comparison*. London: Anglo-German Foundation for the Study of Industrial Society.
Crouch, Colin. (2005). “Three Means of Complementarity,” *Socio-Economic Review* 3, no. 2, pp. 359–363.
Culpepper, Pepper D. (2010). *Quiet Politics and Business Power: Corporate Control in Europe and Japan*. Cambridge: Cambridge University Press.
Curtis, Gerald L. (1988). *The Japanese Way of Politics*. New York: Columbia University Press.
Davis, Gerald F. (2011). “The Twilight of the Berle and Means Corporation.” *Seattle University Law Review* 34, no. 4, pp. 1121–1138.
Deeg, Richard. (1999). *Finance Capitalism Unveiled: Banks and the German Political Economy*. Ann Arbor: University of Michigan Press.
De Graaff, Nana, and Bastiaan van Apeldoorn. (2019). “The Transnationalist US Foreign-Policy Elite in Exile? A Comparative Network Analysis of the Trump Administration.” *Global Networks* 21, no. 2, pp. 238–264.
De Marchi, V., and R. Grandinetti. (2014). “Industrial Districts and the Collapse of the Marshallian Model: Looking at the Italian Experience.” *Competition and Change* 18, no. 1, pp. 70–87.
Delgado, Mercedes, Michael E. Porter, and Scott Stern. (2012). *Clusters, Convergence, and Economic Performance*. National Bureau of Economic Research. http://www.nber.org/papers/w18250.
Deloitte-MI (Deloitte and Manufacturing Institute). (2011). *Unwavering Commitment. The Public's View of the Manufacturing Industry Today*. From http://www.deloitte.com/assets/Dcom-UnitedStates/Local%20Assets/Documents/us%20cip%202011PublicViewonManufacturingReport%20090811.pdf.
Delong, Brad. (2023). “Theses on China, be U.S., Political-Economic Systems, Global Value Chains, & be Relationship.” 2023 Brad DeLong in Internet.
Denning, Steve. (2011). “Clayton Christensen: How Pursuit of Profits Kills Innovation and the U.S. Economy,” *Forbes*, November 18, 2011.
Depner, Heiner. (2006). *Transnationale Direktinvestitionen und kulturelle Unterschiede: Lieferanten und Joint Ventures deutscher Automobilzulieferer in China*. Bielefeld: Transcript.
Di Carlo, Donato. (2018). “Does Pattern Bargaining Explain Wage Restraint in the German Public Sector?” MPIfG Diiscussion Paper 18/3.

Di Tommaso, Marco R., and Stuart O. Schweitzer. (2013). *Industrial Policy in America: Breaking Taboo.* Cheltenham, UK: Edward Elgar.

Dicken, Peter. (2011). *Global Shift: Mapping the Changing Contours of the World Economy*, 6th edition. New York: The Guilford Press.

Diessner, Sebastian, Niccolo Durazzi, and David Hope (2021) "Skill-Biased Liberalization: Germany's Transition to the Knowledge Economy." *Politics & Society* 50, no. 1, pp. 117–155.

Doellgast, V., and P. Berg. (2018). "Negotiating Flexibility: External Contracting and Working Time Control in German and Danish Telecommunications Firms," *ILR Review* 71, pp. 117–142.

Dore, Ronald. (2005). "Deviant or Different: Corporate Governance in Japan and Germany." *Corporate Governance: An International Review* 43, no. 3, pp. 437–446.

Doremus, Keller, Louis Pauly, and Simon Reich. (1998). *The Myth of the Global Corporation.* Princeton: Princeton University Press.

Dujarric, Robert, and Ayumi Takenaka. (2019). "Parochialism: Japan's Failure to internationalize." In Jeff Kingston (eds.), *Critical Issues in Contemporary Japan.* New York: Taylor & Francis.

Durazzi, Niccolo. (2019). "The Political Economy of High Skills: Higher Education in Knowledge Based Labour Markets." *Journal of European Public Policy* 26, no. 12. pp. 1799–817.

Dyer, J. H., and K. Nobeoka. (2000). "Creating and Managing a High-Performance Knowledge-sharing Network: The Toyota Case." *Strategic Management Journal* 21, no. 3, pp. 345–367.

Dyson, Kenneth. (1986). "The State, Banks and Industry: The West German Case." In Andrew Cox State (ed.), *Finance and Industry: A Comparative Analysis of Post-war Trends in Six Advanced Industrial Economies.* Brighton, UK: Wheatsheaf.

Edwards, Ben. (2004). "A World of Work." *The Economist*, November 11, 2004.

Eisner, Marc Allen. (2014). *The American Political Economy: Institutional Evolution of Market and State.* New York: Routledge.

Elia, S., I. Mariotti, and L. Piscitello. (2009). "The Impact of Outward FDI on the Home Country's Labour Demand and Skill Composition." *International Business Review* 18, no. 4, pp. 357–372.

Eliasson, Gunnar. (2007). "Divergence among Mature and Rich Industrial Economies: The Case of Sweden Entering a New and Immediate Economy." In Timo J. Hämäläinen and Risto Heiskala (eds.), *Social Innovations, Institutional Change and Economic Performance*, pp. 214–279. Cheltenham: Edward Elgar.

Ergen, Timur. (2015). *Große Hoffnungen und brüchige Koalitionen: Industrie, Politik und die schwierige Durchsetzung der Photovoltaik.* Frankfurt: Campus Verlag.

Ernst & Young. (2006). *Deutschlands Zukunft als Automobilstandort*. Stuttgart: Ernst & Young.

Evans, Peter B. (1995). *Embedded Autonomy: States & Industrial Transformation*. Princeton, NJ: Princeton University Press.

———. (2010). "Constructing the 21st Century Developmental State: Potentialities and Pitfalls." In O. Edigheji (Ed.), *Constructing a Democratic Developmental State in South Africa: Potentials and Challenges* (pp. 37–58). Cape Town: HSRC Press.

———. (2014) "The Korean Experience and the Twenty First-Century Transition to a Capability-Enhancing Developmental State." In Ilcheong Yi and Thandika Mkandawire (eds.), *Learning from the South Korean Developmental Success: Effective Developmental Cooperation and Synergistic Institutions and Policies* (pp. 31–53). New York: Palgrave Macmillan.

Evans, Peter B., and Patrick Heller. (2015). "Human Development, State Transformation, and the Politics of the Development State." In Stephan Leibfried et al. (eds.), *The Oxford Handbook of Transformations of the State*, pp. 691–713. Oxford: Oxford University Press.

Farnham, Wallace. (1963). "The Weakened Spring of Government: A Study in Nineteenth Century American History." *American Historical Review*, LXVIII, pp. 662–680.

Farrell, Diana et al. (2003). *Offshoring: Is It a Win-Win Game?* San Francisco: McKinsey Global Institute.

Faust, Michael. (2012). "The Shareholder Value Concept of the Corporation and co-Determination in Germany: Unresolved Contradictions or Reconciliation of Institutional Logics?" In Christel Lane and Geoffrey T. Wood (eds.), *Capitalist Diversity and Diversity within Capitalism*. London: Routledge.

Faust, Michael, Reinhard Bahnmüller, and Christiane Fisecker. (2011). *Das Kapitalmarkt-orientierte Unternehman: Externe Erwartungen, Unternehmenspolitik, Personalwesen, und Mitbestimmung*. Edition Sigma.

Felbermayr, Gabriel. (2023). "Deglobalization: Reasons and Effects." *Economist Voice* 20, no. 2, pp. 249–253.

Ferner, Anthony, Jacques Bélanger, Olga Tregaskis, Michael Morley, and Javier Quintanilla (2013). "US Multinationals and the Control of Subsidiary Employment Policies." *Industrial & Labor Relations Review* 66, pp. 645–669.

Ferner, Anthony, Phil Almond, Ian Clark, Trevor Colling, Tony Edwards, Len Holden, and Michael Muller-Camen (2004). "Dynamics of Central Control and Subsidiary Autonomy in the Management of Human Resources: Case-Study Evidence from US MNCs in the UK." *Organization Studies* 25, pp. 363–391.

Fligstein, Neil. (2021). *The Banks Did It: An Anatomy of the Financial Crisis*. Cambridge: Harvard University Press.

Friedman, Thomas. (2005). *The World Is Flat: A Brief History of the Twenty-First Century*. New York: Farrar, Straus and Giroux.
Frietsch, Rainer, and Henning Kroll. (2008). "Recent Trends in Innovation Policy in Germany." In *New Challenges for Germany in the Innovation Competition*, Final Report at Fraunhofer Institute Systems and Innovation Research, Karlsruhe, Germany.
Froud, J., S. Johal, J. Law, A. Leaver, and K. Williams. (2011). "Rebalancing the Economy (or Buyer's Remorse)." CRESC Working Paper No. 87. Manchester: CRESC.
Fujimoto, T. (2002). "Architecture, Capability, and Competitiveness of Firms and Industries," Working Paper, University of Tokyo.
———. (2004) *Nihon no monozukuri tetsugaku* [The Philosophy of Japanese Production]. Tokyo: Nihon Keizai shinbunsha.
Fujimoto, T., A. Takeishi, and Y. Aoshima. (2001). *Bijinesu akitekuchia, seihin, soshiki, purosesu no senryakuteki sekkei nijumon* [A Primer on Business Architecture, Strategic Design of Products, Organizations, and Processes]. Tokyo: Nihon Keizai shinbunsha.
Fukuda, Kayano. (2020). "Science, Technology and Innovation Ecosystem Transformation toward Society 5.0." *International Journal of Production Economics* 220, p. 107460.
Fukuda, S. (2015). "Abenomics: Why Was It so Successful in Changing Market Expectations?" *Journal of the Japanese and International Economies* 37, pp. 1–20.
Fukuyama, Myumi. (2018). "Society 5.0: Aiming for a New Human-Centered Society." *Japan Spotlight*, July/August: 47–50.
Gabrisch, Hubert, and Karsten Staehr (2014). "The Euro Plus Pact: Cost Competitiveness and External Capital Flows in the EU Countries." Working Paper Series No. 1650. European Central Bank, Frankfurt.
Gaulier, G., and V. Vicard (2012). "The Signature of Euro Area Imbalances." *Quarterly Selection of Articles—Bulletin de la Banque de France*, issue 27, pp. 5–26.
Gereffi, Gary, and Timothy Sturgeon. (2004). "Globalization, Employment, and Economic Development: A Briefing Paper." Sloan Workshop Series in Industry Studies Rockport, Massachusetts, June 14–16, 2004.
Germann, Julian. (2021a). "Global Rivalries, Corporate Interests and Germany's 'National Industrial Strategy 2030." Unpublished Manuscript.
———. (2021b). *Unwitting Architect: German Primacy and the Origins of Neoliberalism*. Stanford: Stanford University Press.
———. (2023). "Global Rivalries, Corporate Interests and Germany's 'National Industrial Strategy 2030.'" *Review of International Political Economy* 30, no. 5, pp. 1749–1775.

Gertner, Jon. (2012). *The Idea Factory: Bell Labs and the Great Age of American Innovation*. New York: Penguin Press.

Gerum, E. (2007). *Das deutsche Corporate Governance-System: eine empirische Untersuchung*. Stuttgart: Schäffer-Poeschel.

Gibbon, P., J. Bair, and S. Ponte. (2008). "Governing Global Value Chains: An Introduction." *Economy and Society* 37, no. 3, pp. 315–338.

Giddens, A. (1999). *Runaway World: How Globalization Is Reshaping Our Lives*. London: Profile Books.

Gilpin, Robert. (1975). *U.S. Power and the Multinational Corporation: The Political Economy of Foreign Direct Investment*. New York: Basic Books.

Global Tech Security. (2023). "History of the CHIPS and Science Act." *Global Tech Security* 2023, from https://globaltechsecurity.com/history-of-the-chipsand-science-act/.

Gorton, G., and F. A. Schmid. (2004). "Capital, Labor, and the Codetermi-nated Firm: A Study of German Codetermination." *Journal of the European Economic Association* 2, pp. 863–905.

Gotoh, Fumihito. (2020). "Industrial Associations as Ideational Platforms: Why Japan Resisted American-Style Shareholder Capitalism." *The Pacific Review* 33, no. 1, pp. 125–152.

Götz, Marta. (2019). "Unpacking the Provision of the Industrial Commons in Industry 4.0 Cluster." *Economic and Business Review* 5, no. 4, pp. 23–48.

Gourevitch, Peter A., and James J. Shinn. (2005). *Political Power and Corporate Control: The New Global Politics of Corporate Governance*. Princeton: Princeton University Press.

Goutas, L., and C. Lane. (2009). "The Translation of Shareholder Value in the German Business System: A Comparative Study of DaimlerChrysler and Volkswagen AG." *Competition and Change* 13, no. 4: pp. 327–346.

Grabow, Colin. (2024). "Technology and Innovation, Not Just Policy, Help Drive Globalization." *Globalization: Then and Now* 12 Parts Series paper, CATO Institute from https://www.cato.org/publications/technology-globalization-ie-box-ict.

Graf, Lukas. (2018). "Combined Modes of Gradual Change: The Case of Academic Upgrading and Declining Collectivism in German Skill Formation." *Socio-Economic Review* 16, no. 1, pp. 185–205.

Grant, Wyn. (2001). "Pressure Politics: From 'Insider' Politics to Direct Action?" *Parliamentary Affairs* 54, no. 2, pp. 337–348.

Graw, A. (2019. May 9). Stimmt in unserem Land etwas nicht? Der Bundestag debattiert uber € die 'Wirtschaftsverfassung Deutschlands' [Is There Something Wrong in Our Country? The Bundestag debates 'Germany's Economic Constitution']. Die Welt. https://www.welt.de/print/welt_kompakt/print_politik/article193198869/Stimmt-in-unserem-Land-etwas-nicht.html.

Gray, John. (2005). "The World Is Round." *The New York Review of Books*, vol. 52, no. 13.

Green, Kenneth. (2010). "Why the U.S. Shouldn't Panic." *New York Times*, November 9, 2010.

Haipeter, Thomas. (2013). "Perspektiven der Sozialpartnerschaft." In Stefan Schmalz and Kluas Dörre (eds.), *Comeback der Gewerkschaften?* Frankfurt a. M.: Campus.

———. (2000). *Mitbestimmung bei VW*. Münster: Westfälisches Dampfboot.

———. (2011a). "Einleitung: Intressenvertretungen, Krise und Mondernisierung -über alte und neue Leitbilder." In T. Haipeter and K. Dörre (eds.), *Gewerkschaftliche Modernisierung*. Wiesbaden, Germany: VS Verlag für Sozialwissenschaften.

———. (2011b). "The Global Reorganisation of the Value Chain and Industrial Relations in the Automobile Industry." In O. Struck, ed., *Industrial Relations and Social Standards in an Internationalized Economy*. München, Germany: Rainer Hampp Verlag.

———. (2011c). "Works Councils as Actors in Collective Bargaining: Derogations and the Development of Codetermination in the German Chemical and Metalworking Industries." *Economic and Industrial Democracy* 32, no. 4, pp. 679–695.

Hall, Peter A. (2015). "The Changing Role of the State in Liberal Market Economies." In Leibfried, Stephan, Evelyne Huber, Matthew Lange, Jonah D. Levy, Frank Nullmeier, and John D. Stephens (eds.), *The Oxford Handbook of Transformations of the State*, pp. 426–444. Oxford: Oxford University Press.

———. (2018). "Varieties of Capitalism in the Light of the Euro Crisis." *Journal of European Public Policy* 25, no. 1, pp. 7–30.

Hall, Peter A., and David Soskice. (2001). "An Introduction to Varieties of Capitalism." In P. Hall and D. Soskice (eds.), *Varieties of Capitalism: The Institutional Foundations of Comparative Advantage*. Oxford: Oxford University Press.

Hancke, Bob, Martin Rhodes, and Mark Thatcher. (2007). "Introduction: Beyond Varieties of Capitalism." In B. Hancke, M. Rhodes, and M. Thatcher (eds.), *Beyond Varieties of Capitalism*. Oxford: Oxford University Press.

Harvey, David. (2007). *A Brief History of Neoliberalism*. Oxford: Oxford University Press.

Harzing, Anne-Wil, and N. G. Noorderhaven. (2008). "Headquarters-Subsidiary Relationships and the Country-of-Origin Effect." In M. P. Feldman and G. D. Santangelo (eds.), *New Perspectives in IB Research—Progress in International Business Research*, vol. 3, pp. 13–40. Emerald Group Publishing Limited.

Hassel, Anke. (2014). "The Paradox of Liberalization: Understanding Duralism and the Recovery of the German Political Economy." *British Journal of Industrial Relations* 52, no. 1, pp. 57–81.

Hatch, Walter F. (2010). *Asia's Flying Geese: How Regionalization Shapes Japan*. Ithaca: Cornell University Press.

Hatch, W., and Yamamura, K. (1996). *Asia in Japan's Embrace: Building a Regional Production Alliance*. Cambridge: Cambridge University Press.

Helper, S. (1991). "How Much Has Really Changed between U.S. Automakers and their Suppliers?" *Sloan Management Review* 32, pp. 15–28.

Helper, Susan, Timothy Krueger, and Howard Wial. (2012). *Locating American Manufacturing: Trends in the Geography of Production*. Washington, DC: Brookings Institution.

Henkel, H.-O. (1995). "Interview." *Neuen Osnabrücker Zeitung*, 21 October 1995.

Henning, C. Randall. (1994). *Currencies and Politics in the United States, Germany, and Japan*. Washington, DC: Institute for International Economics.

Herrigel, Gary. (1997) "The Limits of German Manufacturing Flexibility." In Lowell Turner (ed.), *Negotiating the New Germany*. Ithaca: Cornell University Press.

———. (2010). *Manufacturing Possibilities: Creative Action and Industrial Recomposition in the United States, Germany, and Japan*. Oxford: Oxford University Press.

———. (2013) "Recent Trends in Manufacturing Globalization and Their Effects on the Distribution of R&D, Design, and Production within US, German and Japanese Automobile, Electro-Mechanical, Machinery, and related Component MNCs," Report to European Commission, Directorate General for Research and Innovation.

———. (2015). "Globalization and the German Industrial Production Model." *Journal for Labour Market Research* 48, pp. 133–149.

Herrigel, Gary, Ulrich Voskamp, and Volker Wittke (2017). *Globale Qualitätsproduktion: Transnationale Produktionssysteme in der Automobilzulieferindustrie und im Maschinenbau*. Campus.

Hirsch-Kreisen, H. (1994). "Innovationspotentiale und Innovationsprobleme des Werkzeugmachinenbaus: Zum Verhältnis von Verwissenschaftlichung und industrieller Praxis." *WSI-Mitteilungen* 2, pp. 94–102.

Hirsh, M. (2010). *Capital Offense: How Washington's Wise Men Turned America's Future Over to Wall Street*. Hoboken: Wiley.

Hiwatari, Nobuhiro, and Mari Miura (eds.). (2002). *Ryudoki no Nihon seiji: 'Ushinawareta 10 nen'no Seijigaku teki Kensho* [Japanese Politics in a Period of Fluidity: A Political Science Analysis of the 'Lost Decade']. Tokyo: University of Tokyo Press.

Hoffmann, Marianne. (2018). "The Fraunhofer Model: Technology Transfer from Universities to Industry." Commentary 2018 Japanese-German Symposium, Tokyo, Fraunhofer Headquarters.

Holroyd, Carin. (2022). "Technological Innovation and Building a 'Super Smart' Society: Japan's Vision of Society 5.0." *Journal of Asian Public Policy* 15, no. 1, pp. 18–31.

Holstein, William J. (2009). *Why GM Matters: Inside the Race to Transform an American Icon*. New York: Walker & Company.

Honma, Masayaoshi, and Aurelia George Mulgan. (2018). "Political Economy of Agricultural Reform in Japan under Abe's Administration." *Asian Economic Policy Review* 13, no. 1, pp. 128–144.

Hopkin, Jonathan, and Dustin Voss. (2022). "Political Parties and Growth Models." In Lucio Baccaro, Mark Blyth, and Jonas Pontusson (eds.), *Diminishing Returns: The New Politics of Growth and Stagnation*. Oxford: Oxford University Press.

Hopkin, Jonathan, and Kate Alexander Shaw. (2016). "Organized Combat or Structural Advantage? The Politics of Inequality and the Winner-Take All Economy in the United Kingdom." *Politics & Society* 44, no. 3, pp. 345–371.

Hopkin, Jonathan, and Mark Blyth. (2019). "The Global Economics of European Populism: Growth Regimes and Party Change in Europe." *Government and Opposition* 54, no. 2, pp. 193–225.

Höpner, Martin. (2003). *Wer beherrscht die Unternehmen? Shareholder Value, Managerherrschaft und Mitbetstimmung in Deutschland*. Frankfurt am Main: Campus.

———. (2007). "Corporate Governance Reform and the German Party Paradox." *Comparative Politics* 39, no. 4, pp. 401–420.

———. (2019). "The German Undervaluation Regime under Bretton Woods: How Germany Became the Nightmare of the World Economy." MPIfG Discussion Paper 19/1, Max-Planck Institute for the Study of Societies.

Hoshi, Takeo. (2017). "Two Decades of Stalled Reforms: Why the Government's Growth Strategies All Look the Same." Working Paper, Tokyo Foundation for Policy Research from https://www.tokyofoundation.org/research/detail.php?id=460.

Houseman, Susan, Christopher Kurz, Paul Lengermann, and Benjamin Mandel. (2011). "Offshoring Bias in U.S. Manufacturing." *Journal of Economic Perspectives* 25, no. 2, pp. 111–132.

Hughes, Kent. (2005). *Building the Next American Century: The Past and Future of American Economic Competitiveness*. Washington, DC: Woodrow Wilson Center Press.

Hünnekes, F., M. Schularick, and C. Trebesch. (2019). "Exportweltmeister: The Low Returns on Germany's Capital Exports." Working Paper, Kiel Institute for the World Economy.

Huo, Jingjing, and John D. Stephens. (2015). "From Industrial Corporatism to the Social Investment State." In Stephan Leibfried et al. (eds.), *The Oxford Handbook of Transformations of the State*, pp. 410–425. Oxford: Oxford University Press.

Hynes, Casey. (2017). "Beijing—Not Silicon Valley—Is the World's Top Tech Hub, Report Says." *Forbes*, November 2, 2017 from https://www.forbes.com/sites/chynes/2017/11/02.

Imai, K., ed. (1998). *Benchaazu infura* [The Infrastructure of Venture Companies]. Tokyo: NTT Shuppan.

Imai, K., I. Nonaka, and H. Takeuchi (1985). "Managing the New Product Development Process: How Japanese Companies Learn and Unlearn." In K. Clark, R. Hayes, and C. Lorenz (eds.), *The Uneasy Alliance: Managing the Productivity-Technology Dilemma*. Boston: Harvard Business School Press.

Inagami, T., and D. H. Whittaker. (2005). *The New Community Firm: Employment, Governance and Management Reform in Japan*. Cambridge: Cambridge University Press.

Incerti, Trevor, and Phillip Y. Lipsey. (2018). "The Politics of Energy and Climate Change in Japan under Abe: Abenergynomics." *Asian Survey* 58, no. 4, 607–634.

Inomatsu, Satoshi. (1998). "Japanese Direct Investment and Changes in East Asian Industrial Structure." In Sano Takao and Osada Hiroshi (eds.), *Deepening Industrial Linkages among East Asian Countries*. Tokyo: Institute of Developing Economies.

Isogai, A., A. Ebizuka, and H. Uemura. (2000). "The Hierarchical Market-Firm Nexus as the Japanese Mode of Regulation." In R. Boyer and T. Yamada (eds.), *Japanese Capitalism in Crisis*. London: Routledge, 32–53.

Itami, Hiroyuki. (1998). "The Structural Upgrading of East Asian Economies and Networks." In Institute of Developing Economics (IDE) and JETRO (eds.), *Can Asia Recover Its Vitality? Globalization and the Roles of Japanese and U.S. Corporations*. Tokyo: IDE.

Ito, Keiko, Kenta Ikeuchi, Chiara Criscuolo, Jonathan Timmis, and Antonin Bergeaud (2023). "Global Value Chains and Domestic Innovation." *Research Policy* 52, pp. 1–22.

Iversen, Torben, and David Soskice. (2019). *Democracy and Prosperity: Reinventing Capitalism through a Turbulent Century*. Princeton, NJ: Princeton University Press.

Jackson, Gregory. (2003). "Corporate Governance in Germany and Japan: Liberalization Pressures and Responses during the 1990s." In K. Yamamura and W. Streeck (eds.), *The End of Diversity*. Ithaca: Cornell University Press.

———. (2005). "Contested Boundaries: Ambiguities and Creativity in the Evolution of German Codetermination." In W. Streeck and K. Thelen (eds.),

Beyond Continuity: Institutional Change in Advanced Political Economies. Oxford: Oxford University Press.

Jacoby, Wade. (2020). "Surplus Germany." *German Politics* 29, no. 3, pp. 498–521.

Jamrisko, Michelle, and Wei Lu. (2020). "Germany Breaks Korea's Six-Year Streak as Most Innovative Nation." https://www.bloomberg.com/news/articles/2020-01-18/germany-breaks-korea-s-six-year-streak-as-most-innovative-nation.

Janco Associates. (2003, September). *The Coming Commodization of Compensation*, from http://comon.ziffdavisinternet.com/download/o/02216/Baseline0901-p28-29.pdf.

Janssen, M. J., and K. Frenken. (2019) "Cross-specialisation policy: Rationales and Options for Linking Unrelated Industries." *Cambridge Journal of Regions, Economy and Society* 12, no. 2, pp. 195–212.

Jessop, Bob. (1999). "Narrating the Future of the National Economy and the National State: Remarks on Remapping Regulation and Reinventing Governance." In G. Steinmetz (ed.), *State/Culture: State-Formation after the Cultural Turn*. Ithaca: Cornell University Press.

JETRO. (1997). *Jetro Hakusho, Toshi Hen* [1997 White Paper on Foreign Direct Investment].

Jewell, Catherin. (2017). "Forging the Future the Fraunhofer Way." *WIPO Magazine*, April 2017.

Jirjahn, U. (2010). "Ökonomische Wirkungen der Mitbestimmung in Deutschland: Ein Update." Arbeitspapier 186 der Hans-Böckler-Stiftung, Düsseldorf: Hans-Böckler Stiftung.

Johnson, Chalmers. (1982). *MITI and the Japanese Miracle: The Growth of Industrial Policy, 1925–1975*. Stanford: Stanford University Press.

Johnston, Alison, Gregory Fuller, and Aidan Regan. (2020). "It Takes Two to Tango: Mortgage Markets, Labor Markets, and Rising Household Debt in Europe." *Review of International Political Economy* 28, no. 4, pp. 843–873.

Johnstone, B. (1999). *We Were Burning: Japanese Entrepreneurs and the Forging of the Electronic Age*. Boulder, CO: Basic Books.

Jung, Hyun-joo, Kyung-sun Choi, and Young-joo Ko. (2014). "Bioplastic Saneop-eoseo Hankookkwa Ilbonui Gaebanghyeong Hyeoksin Bigyo Yeongu" (Korean) [Open Innovation in Bioplastic Industiry: Comparison between Korea and Japan]." *Korea Technology Innovation Society 2014nyeondo Choogyehaksooldaehuoi Nonmoonjip*. [KOTIS Collection from Autumn Research Conference, 2014], October 31, 2014. pp. 493–507.

Jung, Sung-Chun. (2020a). "Open Innovation in Japan." *KIEP Opinions*, February 12, 2020.

———. (2020b). *Ilbonui Gaebanghyung Hyuksinjunryak: Sanhak Hyupryukul Joongsimuro* (Korean) [*Open Innovation in Japan: Focusing on Cooperation between Business and National Universities*], Policy References 20-02. Sejong: Korea Institute for International Economic Policy.

Jürgens, U., and H. Meißner. (2005). *Arbeiten am Auto der Zukunft – Produktinnovationen und Perspektiven der Beschäftigten*. Berlin: Edition Sigma.

Jürgens, U., I. Lippert, and F. Gaeth. (2008). *Information, Kommunikation und Wissen im Mitbestimmungssystem: Eine Umfrage under Arbeitnehmervertretern im Aufsichtsrat*. Baden-Baden: Nomos.

Jürgens, Ulrich, and Martin Krzywdzinski. (2010). *Die neue Ost-West-Arbeitsteilung: Arbeitsmodelle und inustrielle Beziehungen in der europäischen Automobilindustrie*. Frankfurt: Campus Verlag.

Kabashima, Ikuo, and Gill Steel. (2007). "The Koizumi Revolution." *PS: Political Science and Politics* 40, no. 1, pp. 79–84.

Kädtler, Jürgen, H. J. Sperling, Volker Wittke, and Harald Wolf. (2013). *Mitbestimmte Innovationsarbeit: Konstellationen, Spielregeln und Partizipationspraktiken*. Düsseldorf: Edtion Sigma.

Kalinowski, Thomas. (2015). "Crisis Management and the Diversity of Capitalism: Fiscal Stimulus Packages and the East Asian (Neo-)developmental State." *Economy and Society* 44, no. 2, pp. 244–270.

Kalkowski, Peter, and Otfried Mickler. (2015). *Kooperative Produktentwicklung: Fallstudien aus der Automobilindustrie, dem Maschinenbau under der IT-Industrie*. Baden-Baden: Nomos.

Kamikawa, R. (2010). *Koizumi Kaikaku no Seijiagaku: Koizumi Junichiro ha Hontouni Tsuyoi Shusho dattanoka* [The Politics of the Koizumi Reform: Was Junichiro Koizumi Really a Strong Prime Minister?]. Tokyo: Toyo Kezai.

Kano, Yoshikazu. (1996) "Ajia no sangyoka ga Noho shijo o Nerau" [The Industrialization of Asia, Which Is Aimed at the Japanese Market]. *Shukan Toyo Keizai* (September 14), pp. 78–82.

Kasper, Wolfgang (1972) "Stabilization Policies in a Dependent Economy: Some Lessons from the West German Experience of the 1960s." In E. Claassen and P. Stalin, eds. *Stabilization Policies in Interdependent Economies*. Amsterdam and London: North-Holland Publishing Co.

Katz, Richard. (2003). *Japanese Phoenix: The Long Road to Economic Revival*. Routledge.

Katzenstein, P. (1977). "Conclusion: Domestic structures and Strategies of Foreign Economic Policy." *International Organization* 31, no. 4, pp. 879–920.

Kawai, Masahiro, and Shujiro Urata. (1996). "Trade Imbalances and Japanese Foreign Direct Investment: Bilateral and Triangular Issues." Discussion Paper no. F-52, APEC Study Center, Waseda University and Institute of Developing Economies, Tokyo.

Kawakita, T. (1985) *Tsusan Yusei Senso* [The War between MITI and MPS]. Tokyo: Kyoikusha.

———. (2011). *Zaikai no Shotai* [The Truth of the Industrial Associations]. Tokyo: Kodansha.

Kazuhiko, Toyama. (2015). "The Curse of "Japan, Inc." and Japan's Microeconomic Competitiveness." In Yoichi Funabashi and Barak Kushner (eds.), *Examining Japan's Lost Decades*. London: Routledge.

Keidanren. (2006). "A Suitable Corporate Governance System for Japan." Press release dated 20 June from https://www.keidanren.or.jp/japanese/policy/2006/040.html.

Kikai Shinko Kyokai. (1995). "Ajia Chiiki e no Seisan Shifuto to Sono Eikyo: Ryosan-gata kikai buhin sangyo no kudoka no shiten kara" [The Shift of Manufacturing to Asia and Its Effects on Large-scale Machinery Parts Industries: From the Perspective of Hollowing-out]. Working Paper H6-4. May.

Kim, Bo-min, Min-soo Han, Jong-hyuk Kim, Hee-chae Ko, and Sung-hee Lee (2014). "Strengthening U.S. Manufacturing Competitiveness and Its Implications" *KIEP Policy Analysis 14–12*. Sejong: Korea Institute for International Economic Policy.

Kim, Kyung Mi, and Hyeong-ki Kwon. (2017). "The State's Role in Globalization: Korea's Experience from a Comparative Perspective." *Politics & Society* 45, no. 4, pp. 505–531.

Kim, Si-yoon. (2012). "The Usefulness of Selective Industrial Policy: Focused on the Bioindustrial Policy in Japan." *Korea Public Administration Quarterly* 24, no. 3, pp. 693–710.

Kimura, Fukinari. (1996). "Nihon no Taigai Chokusetsu Toshi no Tokucho" [The Characteristics of Japanese Foreign Direct Investment]. *NIRA Seisaku Kenkyu* 9, no. 10, pp. 8–13.

Kishii, Daitaro. (1999). "Historical Features of Japan's Public Utility Laws and the Limits of Deregulation." *Social Science Japan Journal* 2, no. 1, pp. 45–63.

Klobes, Frank. (2005). *Produktions-strategien und Organisationsmode: Internationale Arbeitsteilung am Beispiel von Zwei Standorten der Volkswagen AG*. Hamburg: VSA-Verlag.

Kochan, Thomas A. (2012). "A Jobs Compact for America's Future." *Harvard Business Review* 90, no. 3, March 2012 Special Report.

Koddenbrock, Kai, and Daniel Mertens. (2022). "Geoeconomics and National Production Regimes: On German Exportism and the Integration of Economic and Security Policy." In Milan Babic, Adam D. Dixon, Inogen T. Liu (eds.), *The Political Economy of Geoeconomics: Europe in a Changing World*. Cham: Palgrave Macmillan.

Kohler-Koch, Beate. (2016). "Deutsche Industrieverbände: Studie zur Heterogenität der Verbandswirklichkeit." *Zeitschrift für Politikwissenschaft* 26, pp. 53–74.

Kornprobst, Markus, and T. V. Paul (2021). "Globalization, Deglobalization and the Liberal International Order." *International Affairs* 97, no. 5, pp. 1305–1316.

Kowol, U., and W. Kronhn. (1995). "Innovationsnetzwerke: Ein Modell dere Technikgenese." In J. Halfmann, G. Bechmann, and W. Rammert (eds.), *Technik und Gesellschaft. Jahrbuch 8. Theoriebausteine der Techniksoziologie*. Frankfurt am Mein.

Krauss, E. S., and Benjamin Nyblade. (2005). "'Presidentialization' in Japan? The Prime Minister, Media and Elections in Japan." *British Journal of Political Science* 35, no. 2, pp. 357–368.

Krehmeyer, Dean, Matthew Orsagh, and Kurt Schacht. (2006). *Breaking the Short-Term Cycle: Discussion and Recommendations on How Corporate Leaders, Asset Managers, Investors, and Analysts Can Refocus on Long-Term Value*. Charleottesville, VA: CFA Institute, from http://www.darden.virginia.edu/corporate-ethics/pdf.

Kreile, Michael. (1977). "West Germany: The Dynamics of Expansion." *International Organization* 31, no. 4, pp. 775–808.

Krein, J. (2022). "Where the Chips Fell, American Affairs." *American Affairs* 5, no. 2.

Kruse, Kevin M., and Julian E. Zelizer. (2019). *Fault Lines: A History of the United States since 1974*. New York: W. W. Norton.

Krzywdzinski, Martin. (2014). "How the EU's Eastern Enlargement Changed the German Productive Model: The Case of the Automotive Industry." *Revue de la regulation, Capitalisme institutions, pouvoirs* 15.

Kundnani, H. (2011). "Germany as a Geo-economic Power." *The Washington Quarterly*, 34, no. 3, pp. 31–45.

Kushida, Kenji E. (2006). "Japan's Telecommunications Regime Shift: Understanding Japan's Potential Resurgence." In John Zysman and Abraham Newman (eds.), *How Revolutionary Was the Digital Revolution? National Responses, Market Transitions, and Global Technology*. Stanford: Stanford Business Books.

———. (2011). "Leading without Followers: How Politics and Market Dynamics Trapped Innovations in Japan's Domestic 'Galapagos' Telecommunications Sector." *Journal of Industry, Competition, and Trade* 11, no. 3, pp. 279–307.

———. (2017). "Innovation and Entrepreneurship in Japan: Why Japan (Still) Matters for Global Competition." SVNJ Working Paper 2017-2, Japan Program at Stanford University.

———. (2018a) "Abenomics and Japan's Entrepreneurship and Innovation Is the Third Arrow Pointed in the Right Direction for Global Competition in the Digital Era of Silicon Valley?" SVNJ Working Paper 2018–1, Japan Program at Stanford University.

———. (2018b) "Departing from Silicon Valley: Japan's New Startup Ecosystem." In M. Fackler and Y. Funabashi (eds.), *Reinventing Japan: New Directions in Global Leadership*. Santa Barbara, CA: Praeger.

———. (2021). "Abenomics and Japan's Entrepreneurship and Innovation: Is the Third Arrow Pointed in the Right Direction for Global Competition in the Silicon Valley Era?" In Takeo Hoshi and Philip Y. Lipsey (eds.), *The Political Economy of the Abe Government and Abenomics Reforms*. Cambridge: Cambridge University Press.

Kwon, Hyeong-ki. (2002). "The German Model Reconsidered." *German Politics & Society*, 20, no. 4, pp. 48–72.

———. (2004a). *Fairness and Division of Labor in Market Societies: A Comparison of U.S. and German Automotive Parts Markets*. New York: Berghahn Books.

———. (2004b). "Japanese Employment Relations in Transition." *Economic and Industrial Democracy* 25, no. 3, pp. 325–345.

———. (2005). "National Model under Globalization: The Japanese Model and Its Internationalization," *Politics and Society* 33, no. 2, pp. 234–252.

———. (2012). "Politics of Globalization and National Economy: The German Experience Compared with the United States." *Politics & Society* 40, no. 4, pp. 581–607.

———. (2021). *Changes by Competition: The Evolution of the South Korean Developmental State*. Oxford: Oxford University Press.

Kwon, Hyeong-ki, and Kyung Mi Kim. (2020). "Varieties of Globalisation and National Economy: Korea's Experience from a Comparative Perspective." *Journal of International Relations and Development* 23, no. 3, pp. 728–754.

Lane, Christel. (2001). "The Emergence of German Transnational Companies: A Theoretical Analysis and Empirical Study of the Globalization Process." In G. Morgan, P. H. Kristensen and R. Whitley (eds.), *The Multinational Firm*, pp. 69–96. Oxford: Oxford University Press.

———. (2005). "Institutional Transformation and System Change: Changes in the Corporate Governance of German Corporations." In G. Morgan, R. Whitley, and E. Moen (eds.), *Changing Capitalism? Internationalization, Institutional Change, and Systems of Economic Organization*. Oxford: Oxford University Press.

Lane, Christel, and Jocelyn Probert. (2009). *National Capitalisms, Global Production Networks: Fashioning the Value Chain in the UK, USA, and Germany*. Oxford: Oxford University Press.

Lang, A., and Schneider, V. (2007). "Wirtschaftsverbande. Verbandspolitik im Spannungsfeld von divergierenden Interessen und hierarchischer Integration [Business associations. Association politics between divergent interests and hierarchical integration]." In T. von Winter & U. Willems (Eds.), *Interessenverb€ande in Deutschland* [Interest groups in Germany], pp. 221–243. VS Verlag fur Sozialwissenschaften.

Lapavitsas, C., A. Kaltenbrunner, D. Lindo, J. Meadway, J. Michell, J. P. Painceira, E. Pires, J. Powell, A. Stenfors, N. Teles, and L. Vatikiotis. (November 2011). *Breaking Up? A Route Out of the Eurozone Crisis.* RMF Occasional Report 3. Research on Money and Finance.

Larrue, Philippe. (2021). "Challenges and Opportunities of Mission-Oriented Innovation Policy in Japan." Policy Paper no. 106, OECD Science, Technology, and Industry, OECD.

Lauridsen, L. (2010). "Strategic Industrial Policy and Latecomer Development: The What, the Why and the How." *Forum for Development Studies* 37, no. 1, pp. 7–32.

Lechevalier, Sebastien. (2016). "Is Japanese Capitalism Still Coordinated?" In Sebastien Lechevalier (ed.), *The Great Transformation of Japanese Capitalism.* London: Routledge.

Lee, Jung-Hwan. (2018). "Ilbon Nongup Yiikyodojungchiui Shoete: Abe Jungkwon, Jamindang Nongrimjok, Nongupgaehyuk" (Korean) [The Decline of Pork-Barrel Politics in Japan's Agricultural Sector: The Abe Cabinet, The LDP Norin Zoku, and Agricultural Reform]. *Journal of Contemporary Politics* 11, no. 2, pp. 43–72.

Lee, Seung-Joo. (2018a). "Abe Jungboowa Jungryakjuk Dajajoouiui Boosang: TPP/CPTPP Junryakul Joongsimero" (Korean) [The Emergence of Strategic Multilateralism in Japan: The Abe Administration's TPP and CPTPP Strategy]. *National Strategy* 26, no. 2, pp. 97–121.

———. (2018b). "Abenomicsui Jungchikyungjae: Jungchakjuk Chabyulsungui Jungchijuk Kiwon" (Korean) [The Political Economy of Abenomics: The Political Origins of Policy Differentiation]. *Kookmin Social Science Review* 25, no. 4, pp. 95–118.

———. (2022). "Ilbon Jungchikyungjae Yonsoksungkwa Byunhwa: Baljunjoouiwa Hookyunjoouiui Dongtaejuk Sanghojakyong" (Korean) [Continuity and Change in Japan's Development Model: Dynamic Interaction Between Developmentalism and Clientelism]. *Asia Review* 12, no. 2, pp. 73–105.

———. (2023). "Ilbonkwa Saeroun Sanupjungchaekui Daedoo: Yiik Jungchaekeyum Jaedo Gan Sanghojakyong" (Korean) [The Emergence of a New Industrial Policy in Japan]. *Korean Political Science Review* 57, no. 1, pp. 143–168.

Legewie, Jochen. (1999). "Economic Crisis and Transformation in Southeast Asia: Strategic Responses by Japanese Firms in the Area of Production." DIJ Working Paper 99/3, Deutshes Institut für Japanstudien.

Lehrer, M., and K. Asakawa. (2004). "Rethinking the Public Sector." *Research Policy* 33, pp. 921–938.

Levinson, Marc. (2020). *Outside the Box: How Globalization Changed from Moving Stuff to Spreading Ideas*. Princeton: Princeton University Press.

Levy, Jonah D. (2015). "The Transformations of the Statist Model." In S. Leibfried et al. (eds.), *The Oxford Handbook of Transformations of the State*. Oxford: Oxford University Press.

Lincoln, Edward J. (2001). *Arthritic Japan: The Slow Pace of Economic Reform*. Washington, DC: Brookings Institution Press.

Lincoln, James R. (2006). "Interfirm Networks and the Management of Technology and Innovation in Japan." In D. H. Whittaker and R. E. Cole (eds.), *Recovering from Success*. Oxford: Oxford University Press.

Lincoln, J., and M. Gerlach. (2004). *Japan's Network Economy: Structure, Persistence, and Change*. New York: Cambridge University Press.

Lincoln, James R., and Masahiro Shimotani (2009). "Whither the Keiretsu, Japan's Business Networks? How Were They Structured? What Did They Do? Why Are They Gone?" Working Paper 188' 09 Institute for Research on Labor and Employment, University of California, Berkeley.

List, Friedrich. (2016 [1910]). *Das National System der Politischen Oekonomie*. 2nd Version Translated by Lee Sung Moo (in Korean). Jena: Verlag von Gustav Fischer.

Locke, Richard M., and Rachel L. Wellhausen (eds.). (2014) *Production in the Innovation Economy*. Cambridge, MA: The MIT Press.

Lohr, J. (2019, May 6). "Showdown im Ministerium [Showdown in the ministry]." *Frankfurter Allgemeine Zeitung*. https://www.faz.net/aktuell/wirtschaft/altmaiers-umstrittene-industriestrategie-showdown-im-ministerium-16173210.html.

Lynn, Barry C. (2005). *End of the Line: The Rise and Coming Fall of the Global Corporation*. New York: Currency Doubleday.

Macher, J., D. Mowery, and D. Hodges (1998). "Reversal of Fortune? The Recovery of the U.S. Industry." *California Management Review* 41, no. 1, pp. 107–136.

Marukawa, Tomo. (2006). "Chûgoku jiôsha sangyô no Buhin kyôkyû to Kigyô ricchi" (Japanese) [Parts Supply and Enterprises' Location in Chinese Automobile Industry], University of Tokyo, Institute of Social Science Studies, Working Paper no. 2006-21.

Massa-Wirth, H. (2007). *Zugeständnisse für Arbeitsplätze? Konzessionäre Beschäftigungsvereinbarunggen im Vergleich Deutschland-USA*. Berlin: Edition Sigma.

Matsutani, A. (2009). *'Jinko Gensho Keizai' no Atarashi Koshiki: 'Chizimu Sekai' no Hasso to Shisutemu* [Shrinking Population Economics: Lessons from Japan]. Tokyo: Nikkei Publishing.

Mazzucato, M. (2020). *Mission Economy: A Moonshot Guide to Changing Capitalism*. New York: Harper Business.

Mazzucato, M., R. Kattel, and J. Ryan-Collins. (2020). "Challenge Driven Innovation Policy: Towards a New Toolkit." *Journal of Industry, Competition and Trade* 20, no. 2, pp. 421–437.

McCarthy, Nolan M., Keith T. Poole, and Howard Rosenthal. (2013). *Political Bubbles: Financial Crises and the Failure of American Democracy*. Princeton: Princeton University Press.

Meardi, G., and A. Toth. (2006). "Who Is Hybridizing What?" Insights on MNCs' Employment Practices in Central Europe." In A. Ferner, J. Quintanilla and C. Sanchez-Runde (eds.), *Multinationals and the Construction of Transnational Practices: Convergence and Diversity in the Global Economy*. Basingstoke: Palgrave.

METI (Ministry of Economy, Trade and Industry). (2019). *Heisei 30nen Sangyo Kizutsu Chousazigyo (Daigakubatsu Venture Zittaichousa)* [Industrial Technology Survey Project Heisei Year 30. (Survey for the Current Situation of University Ventures)] [Japanese]. https://www.meti.go.jp/policy/innovation_corp/start-ups/h30venturereport.pdf.

MEXT (Ministry of Education, Culture, Sports, Science and Technology). (2018). *Daigaku nadoniokeru Sangakurenkeidou Zitsizyokyonitsuite* [Report on the Current Situation of the Industry-University Cooperation Programs in Universities]. [Japanese] https://www.mext.go.jp/a_menu/shinkou/sangaku/sangakub.htm.

MEXT (Ministry of Education, Culture, Sports, Science and Technology). (2008). *Kagoku Gijutsu Hakusho* [White paper on science and technology]. Tokyo: MEXT.

Mikuriya, Takashi. (2015). *Abe Seikenwa Hontoni Tsuyoinoka?* [Is the Abe Administration Strong?]. PHPGenkyuzyo.

Mingsarn, Santikarn Kaosaard. (1993). "Comparative Analysis of Direct Foreign Investment in Thailand." Paper for a conference "Japan and the Regionalization of Asia" sponsored by the Hoover Institution, Stanford University.

Mingsarn, Santikarn Kaosaard. (1994). "Regional Investment and Technology Transfer in Asia: A Thai Case Study." In Asian Productivity Organization (ed.), *Intra-Regional Investment and Technology Transfer in Asia*. Tokyo: APO.

Ministry of Science, ICT and Future Planning. (2014). *Survey of Research and Development in Korea, 2014*. Seoul: Korea Institute of S&T Evaluation and Planning.

Ministry of Trade, Industry and Energy. (2019). "Mi Jaejo-eop Hyeonhwang Mit Jooyo hyeosin Jeongchaek: Migook Jaejo Hwankyeong-eo Ddareun Jeonryak Mit Hyeoksin Jeongchaek" (Korean) [Current Status and Major Policies of American Manufacturing Industry: Policy Strategy and Innovation depending on the Manufacturing Environment in the USA]. *Global Tech Korea Simcheungbunseok Bogoseo* [Global Tech Korea In-depth Analysis Report]. November 2019, Korea Institute for Advanced Technology.

Mitbestimmungskommission (Kommission zur Modernisierung der deutschen Unternehmensmitbestimmung). (2006). *Bericht der wissenschaftlichen Mitglieder der Kommission mit Stellungnahmen der Vertreter der Unternehmen und der Vertreter der Arbeitnehmen*. Berlin.

MITI. (1996). *Wagakumi Kigyo no Kaigai Jigyo Katsudo, Dai 25 kai* [Overseas Business Activities of Japanese Firms, no. 25]. Tokyo: MOF Printing Bureau.

———. (1998a). *Wagakumi Kigyo no Kaigai Jigyo Katsudo, Dai 26-Kai* [The Overseas Business Activities of Japanese Firms, Number 26]. Tokyo: MOF Printing Bureau.

———. (1998b) *Tsusho Hakusho, Heisei 10-nenban* [White Paper on Trade and Industry for 1998]. Tokyo: MOF Printing Bureau.

Mizruchi, Mark. (2013). *The Fracturing of the American Corporate Elite*. Cambridge: Harvard University Press.

Mizuho Research Institute. (2017). "Five Years of Abenomics and Policy Issues Going Forward: Japan's Economic Revival Remains the Abe Administration's Focus as It Takes a Step Forward a Long-Term Administration." *Mizuho Economic Outlook & Analysis*, December 21.

Mogaki, Masahiro. (2019). *Understanding Governance in Contemporary Japan*. Manchester: Manchester University Press.

Moretti, Enrico. (2012). *The New Geography of Jobs*. New York: Houghton Mifflin Harcourt Publishing.

Morgan Stanley. (2018). "Japan's Journey from Laggard to Leader." Morgan Stanley Research from https://www.morganstanley.com/ideas/japan-equities-turnaround.

Morgan, Glenn, and Christian Lyhne Ibsen. (2021). "Quiet Politics and the Power of Business: New Perspectives in an Era of Noisy Politics." *Politics & Society* 49, no. 1, pp. 3–16.

Mukoyama, Hidehiko. (1996). "Development of Asian Small and Medium Companies and Japanese Small Business Investment in Asia." *Rim: Pacific Business and Industries* 1, no. 31.

Mulgan, Aurelia George. (2002). *Japan's Failed Revolution: Koizumi and the Politics of Economic Reform*. Canberra: Asia Pacific Press.

———. (2019). *The Abe Administration and the Rise of Prime Ministerial Executive*. New York: Routledge.

Nachtwey, Oliver. (2018). *Germany's Hidden Crisis: Social Decline in the Heart of Europe*. London: Verso Books.

Nagata, Kyosuke. (2018). "University Reform in Japan." Paper presented at Japan-France Symposium in Higher Education, December 7, 2018, The Japan

Association of National Universities from https://www.janu.jp/eng/globalization/files/20181207-jp-fr3.pdf.

Nakano, Y. (2011). "A Positive Observation of Long-term Knowledge Industries Change in France and Japan," from http://www.iioa.org/files/conference-2/379_20110430091_19th_iioa_alox_NAKANO_Yukinori.pdf.

Nakashima, Takamasa. (1998). "Industrial Relations and Ethnicity: The Case of MSC, a Japanese-Owned Automobile Manufacturer in Thailand." Paper for the Asian Regional Conference on Industrial Relations, Tokyo.

Nanto, Dick K. (2010). "CRS Report for Congress: Globalized Supply Chains and U.S. Policy," Congressional Research Service 7-5700.

Naqvi, Natalya, Anne Henow, and Ha-Joon Chang (2018) "Kicking Away the Financial Ladder? German Development Banking under Economic Globalisation." *Review of International Political Economy* 25, no. 5, pp. 672–698.

Nguyen-Quoc, Thang. (2024, January 19). "The Deglobalization Myth: How Asia's Supply Chains are Changing." Oxford Economics and Hinrich Foundation report. https://www.oxfordeconomics.com/wp-content/uploads/2024/01/How-Asia-supply-chains-are-changing-Hinrich-Foundation-January-2024.pdf.

Nicholas, John. (2024). "The Progressives Who Give Us Hope for 2024." *The Nation*, January 2024 from https://www.thenation.com/article/society/shawn-fain-rashid-khalidi-progressive/.

Nishiuchi, Toshihiro. (1994). *Strategic Industrial Sourcing: The Japanese Advantage*. Oxford: Oxford University Press.

Nishiguchi, Toshiro, and Alexandre Beaudet. (1999). "Kaosu ni okeru Jiko Soshiki-ka: Toyota Grupu to Aishin Seiki Kasai" [Self Organization in Chaos: The Toyota Group and the Aishin Fire]. *Soshiki Kagaku* 32, no. 4, pp. 58–72.

Nitta, K. (2009). *On the Resurgence of Cross-Shareholding—Data from the Fiscal 2008 Survey of Corporate Ownership Structure*. Tokyo: NLI Research Institute.

Noble, Gregory W. (2010) "The Decline of Particularism in Japanese Politics." *Journal of East Asian Studies* 10, pp. 239–273.

Nölke, A. (2020). "Exportism as an Ideology in World Politics." In K. G. Giesen (Ed.), *Ideologies in World Politics*. Wiesbaden: Springer VS.

Nunnenkamp, P. (2004). "The German Automobile Industry and Central Europe's Integration into the International Division of Labour: Foreign Production, Intra-industry Trade, and Labour Market Repercussions," Papeles del Este 9, Universidad Complutense, Madrid.

O'Donnell, G. (2022). "The Chips Act Puts the Semiconductor Industry Back on the Right Path." *Barron's*, pp. 1–3.

OECD. (2012). *Economic Survey of Germany 2012*. Paris: OECD.

———. (2020). *STAN: OECD Structural Analysis Statistics*. Paris: OECD.

———. (2021). "Mission-Oriented Innovation Policy in Japan: Challenges, Opportunities, and Future Options." OECD Science, Technology and Industry Policy Papers. April 2021. No. 106.

———. (2023). *Measuring Progress towards Inclusive and Sustainable Growth in Japan*. Paris: OECD.

Oh, Moon-suk, and Hyung-joo Kim. (1996). *Hae-euo Jikjeop Toojaga Woorigyeongjae-eo Michineun Yeonghyang* (Korean) [Effects of Foreign Direct Investment on Korean Economy]. Research Report 96-12. LG Business Research.

Ohmae, Kenichi. (1990). *The Borderless World: Power and Strategy in the Interlinked Economy*. New York: Harper Business.

———. (1995). *The End of the Nation State*. New York: Free Press.

Okamoto, Y. (2007). "Paradox of Japanese Biotechnology" from http://www.waseda.jp/assoc-jsie-2007/okamoto-thesis.pdf.

Okazaki, Tetsuji. (2001). "The Government-Firm Relationship in Postwar Japan: The Success and Failure of Bureau Pluralism." In J. Stiglitz and S. Yusuf (eds.), *Rethinking of the East Asian Miracle*. New York: Oxford University Press.

Okazaki, Tetsuji, et al. (1996). *Sengo Nippon Keizai to Keizai Doyukai* [Postwar Japanese Economy and Keizai Doyukai]. Tokyo: Iwanami Shoten.

Okimoto, Daniel I. (1989). *Between MITI and the Market: Japanese Industrial Policy for High Technology*. California: Stanford University Press.

Okimoto, Daniel, and Yoshio Nishi. (1996). "R&D Organization in Japanese and American Semiconductor Firms." In Masahiko Aoki and Ronald Dore (eds.), *The Japanese Firm: The Sources of Competitive Strength*. Oxford: Oxford University Press.

Okuno-Fujiwara, M. (1991). "Industrial Policy in Japan." In P. Krugman (ed.), *Trade with Japan: Has the Door Opened Wider?* Chicago: University of Chicago Press.

Oliver Koppel, Thomas Puls, and Enno Röben (2018). "Die Patentleistung der deutschen KFZ-Unternehmen: Eine Analyse der Patentanmeldungen beim deutschen Patentund Markenamt unter Berücksichtigung von branchen- und technologiespezifischen Schwerpunkten," IW-Reports 34/2018.

Onaran, Ö., E. Stockhammer, and L. Grafl (2011). "Financialization, Income Distribution and Aggregate Demand in the USA." *Cambridge Journal of Economics* 35, no. 4, pp. 637–661.

Orhangazi, Özgür. (2008). *Financialization and the US Economy*. Cheltenhamm UK: Edward Elgar.

Pack, Howard, and Kamal Saggi. (2006). "Is There a Case for Industrial Policy? A Critical Survey." *World Bank Research Observer* 21(2): 267–297.

Panglaykim, J. (1983). *Japanese Direct Investment in ASEAN: The Indonesian Experience*. Singapore: Maruzen.

Panitch, L (2012). "Situating Obama's response to the crisis: Finance, regulation and the American state." In Lawrence R. Jacobs, and Desmond King (eds.), *Obama at the crossroads: Politics, Markets, and the Battle for America's Future*, pp. 117–152. Oxford: Oxford University Press.

Park, Yoo-mi. (2019). "Migook Jaejo-eop Renaissance-ui Ui-miwa Gyohoon" (Korean) [The Meaning of American Manufacturing Renaissance and What Can Be Learned]. *KIET Industrial Economic Review*, July 2019.

Pauly, Louis W., and Simon Reich. (1997). "National Structures and Multinational Corporate Behavior: Enduring Differences in the Age of Globalization." *International Organization* 51, no. 1, pp. 1–30.

Pempel, T. J. (1998). *Regime Shift: Comparative Dynamics of the Japanese Political Economy*. Ithaca: Cornell University Press.

———. (2004) "Review: Japan's Failed Revolution: Koizumi and the Politics of Economic Reform by Aurelia George Mulgan." *The Journal of Japanese Studies* 30, no. 1, pp. 240–245.

Peng, M. W., S. H. Lee, and J. J. Tan. (2001). "The Keiretsu in Asia: Implications for Multilevel Theories of Competitive Advantage." *Journal of International Management* 7, pp. 253–276.

Peng, M. W., and A. Delios. (2006). "What Determines the Scope of the Firm over Time and Around the World?" An Asia Pacific Perspective." *Asia Pacific Journal of Management* 23, pp. 385–405.

Pereira, L., and G. A. Plonski. (2009). "Shedding Light on Technological Development in Brazil." *Technovation* 29, no. 6–7, pp. 451–464.

Pfeffer, Jeffrey, and James N. Baron. (1988). "Taking the Workers Back Out: Recent Trends in the Structuring of Employment." *Research in Organizational Behavior* 19, pp. 257–303.

Pierson, Paul. (2004). *Politics in Time: History, Institutions, and Social Analysis*. Princeton: Princeton University Press.

Piore, Michael J., and Charles F. Sabel. (1984). *The Second Industrial Divide*. New York: Basic Books.

Pisano, G. P, and W. C. Shih. (2009). "Restoring American Competitiveness." *Harvard Business Review* 87, no. 7–8, pp. 114–125.

———. (2012a). "Does America Really Need Manufacturing." *Harvard Business Review* 90, no. 3, pp. 94–102.

———. (2012b). *Producing Prosperity: Why America Needs a Manufacturing Renaissance*. Boston: Harvard Business Review Press.

Ponte, Stefano. (2019). *Business Power and Sustainability: In a World of Global Value Chains*. London: ZED.

Porter, Michael. (1990). *The Competitive Advantage of Nations*. New York: Free Press.

Porter, Michael E., and Jan W. Rivkin. (2012). "The Looming Challenge to U.S. Competitiveness." *Harvard Business Review* 90, no. 3, March 2012 Special Report.

Prasad, Monica. (2006). *The Politics of Free Markets: The Rise of Neoliberal Economic Policies in Britain, France, Germany, and the United States.* Chicago: University of Chicago Press.

President's Council of Advisors on Science and Technology (PCAST). (July 2012). *Report to the President on Capturing Domestic Competitive Advantage in Advanced Manufacturing.* Executive Office of the President.

Prestowitz, Clyde. (1992). "Beyond Laissez Faire," *Foreign Policy* no. 87, pp. 67–87.

———. (2010). *The Betrayal of American Prosperity.* New York: Free Press.

Primabase Team. (2018). "Top Tech Hubs around the World." *Primabase*, August 10, 2018, from https://medium.com/primalbase/top-tech-hubs-around-the-world-8c2941d67651.

Quinn, M. (2022). "What's in the Inflation Reduction Act, Democrats' Health Care, Climate and Tax Bill?" *CBS News.*

Ramaswamy, Ramana, and Robert Rowthorn. (2000). "Does Manufacturing Matter?" *Harvard Business Review* (November–December).

Rattner, Steven. (2011). "The Secrets of Germany's Success: What Europe's Manufacturing Powerhouse Can Teach America," *Foreign Affairs* 90, no. 4, pp. 7–11.

Rehder, B. (2003). *Betrieebliche Bündnisse für Arbeit in Deutschland. Mitbetstimmung und Flächentarif im Wandel.* Franfurt am Main: Campus.

Reich, Robert B. (1991). *The Work of Nations: Preparing Ourselves for 21st-Century Capitalism.* New York: Vintage Books, a Division of Random House.

Reisel, Mary. (2017). "From 'Galapagos Syndrome' to Globalization: Japanese Business between Tradition and Virtual Reality." *International Journal of Business Anthropology* 7, no. 2.

Reisenbichler, Alexander. (2022). "Entrenchment or Retrenchment: The Political Economy of Mortgage Debt Subsidies in the United States and Germany." *Comparative Politics* 54, no. 4, pp. 717–740.

Reisenbichler, Alexander, and Andreas Wiedemann. (2022). "Credit-Driven and Consumption-Led Growth Models in the United States and United Kingdom." In Lucio, Blyth, and Pontusson (eds.), *Diminishing Returns: The New Politics of Growth and Stagnation*, pp. 213–237. Oxford University Press.

Reisenbichler, Alexander, and Kimberly J. Morgan. (2012). "From 'Sick Man' to 'Miracle': Explaining the Robustness of the German Market During and After the Financial Crisis 2008–2009." *Politics & Society* 40, no. 4, pp. 549–579.

Reynolds, Elisabeth B., Hiram M. Samel, and Joyce Lawrence. (2014). "Learning by Building: Complementary Assets and Migration of Capabilities in U.S.

Innovative Firms." In R. M. Locke and R. L. Wellhausen (eds.). *Production in the Innovation Economy*. Cambridge, MA: The MIT Press.

Robinson, W. I. (2004). *A Theory of Global Capitalism: Production, Class, and State in a Transnational World*. Baltimore: The Johns Hopkins University Press.

Rodergas, Esther. (2018). "Opportunities for Cooperation between EU and Japan on Biotechnology in Healthcare: Japan Bioventures Landscape." Report at the EU-Japan Centre for Industrial Cooperation, Tokyo (April 2018) from https://www.eu-japan.eu/sites/default/files/publications/docs/min17_2_rodergas_biotechnology_in_healthcare_bioventures.pdf.

Rodrik, Dani. (1996). "Coordination Failures and Government Policy: A Model with Applications to East Asia and Eastern Europe." *Journal of International Economics* 40, no. 1–2, pp. 1–22.

Romer, Christina D. (2012). "Do Manufacturers Need Special Treatment?" *New York Times*, February 4, 2012.

Rose, H. (1995). "Herstellerübergreifende Kooperation und nutzerorientierte Produktentwicklung als Innovationsstrategie." In H. Rose (ed.), *Nutzerorientierung im Innovationsmanagement: Neue Ergebnisse der Sozialforschung über Technikbedarf und Technikentwicklung*. Frankfurt a. M.

Rosenbluth, Francis McCall, and Michael F. Thies. (2010). *Japan Transformed: Political Change and Economic Restructuring*. Princeton: Princeton University Press.

Roth, Siegfried. (2013). *Vertrag und Vertrauen: Die Regelung von Entwicklungskooperationen in der Automobilindustrie*. Aachen: Shaker Verlag.

Rtischev, Dimitry, and Robert E. Cole. (2003). "The Role of Organizational Discontinuity in High Technology: Insights from a U.S.-Japan Comparison." In J. Bachnik (ed.), *Roadblocks on the Information Highway*. Lanham, MD: Rowman Littlefield Publishers.

Ruttan, Vernon. (2006). *Is War Necessary for Economic Growth? Military Procurement and Technology Development*. New York: Oxford University Press.

Sasada, Hinonori. (2015). "The "Third Arrow" or Friendly Fire? The LDP Government's Reform Plan for the Japan Agricultural Cooperatives." *The Japanese Political Economy* 41, no. 1–2, pp. 14–35.

Sassen, Saskia. (2006). *Territory, Authority, Rights: From Medieval to Global Assemblages*. Princeton: Princeton University Press.

Saxenian, A. (1994). *Regional Networks: Industrial Adaptation in Silicon Valley and Route 128*. Cambridge: Harvard University Press.

Schaede, Ulrike. (1995) "The Old Boy Network and Government-Business Relationships in Japan." *Journal of Japanese Studies* 21, no. 2, pp. 293–317.

———. (2000). *Cooperative Capitalism: Self-regulation, Trade Associations, and the Antimonopoly Law in Japan*. Oxford University Press.

———. (2006). "The Strategic Logic of Japanese Keiretsu, Main Banks and Cross Shareholdings, Revisited," CJEB Working Papers, No. 247.

———. (2012). "From Developmental State to the 'New Japan': The Strategic Reflection Point in Japanese Business." *Asia Pacific Business Review* 18, no. 2, pp. 167–185.

———. (2020). *The Business Reinvention of Japan: How to Make Sense of the New Japan and Why It Matters*. Stanford: Stanford University Press.

Schimada, Go. (2017). "Inside the Black Box of Japan's Institution for Industrial Policy: An Institutional Analysis of the Development Bank, Private Sector, and Labor." In Akbar Noman and J. E. Stiglitz (eds.), *Efficiency, Finance, and Varieties of Industrial Policy: Guiding Resources, Learning, and Technology for Sustained Growth*. New York: Columbia University Press.

Schmidt, E., and Y. Bajraktari (2022). "How America Could Lose the Tech War Contest with China: How Washington Can Craft a New Strategy." *Foreign Affairs*. September.

Schmidt, F. A., and F. Seger. (1998). "Arbeitnehmermitbestimung, Allokation von Entscheidungsrechten und Shareholder Value." *Zeitschrift für Betriebswirtschaft* 68, no. 5, pp. 453–473.

Schmitz, H., and P. Knorringa. (2000). "Learning from Global Buyers." *Journal of Development Studies* 37, pp. 177–205.

Schoppa, L. J. (1997). *Bargaining with Japan: What American Pressure Can and Cannot Do*. New York: Columbia University Press.

———. (2001). "Japan, the Reluctant Reformer." *Foreign Affairs* 80, no. 5, pp. 76–90.

———. (2006). *Race for Exits: The Unravelling of Japan's System of Social Protection*. Ithaca: Cornell University Press.

Schröder, E. (2011). "Trade Balances in Germany and the United States: Demand Dominates Price." Term Paper for Advanced Macroeconomics. Department of Economics, New School for Social Research, New York.

Schulten, Thorsten, and the WSI Collective Agreement Archive. (2022). "Collective Bargaining in Germany 2021." Annual Report, WSI Collective Agreement Archive, WSI.

Schumann, M., M. Kuhlmann, F. Sanders, and H. J. Sperling. (2006a). "Vom Risko-zum Vorzeigeprojekt. Auto 5000 bei Volkswagen," *WSI-Mitteilungen* 59, no. 6, 299–306.

Schumann, M., M. Kuhlmann, F. Sanders, and H. J. Sperling (eds.). (2006b). *VW Auto 5000: ein neues Produktionskonzept: Die deutsche Antwort auf den Toyota-Weg?* Hamburg: VSA-Verlag.

Schumann, Michael. (2008). "Kampf um Rationalisierung – Suche nach neuer Übersichtlichkeit," *WSI Mitteilungen* 7, pp. 379–386.

Sedgwick, Mitchell W. (1996). "Does Japanese Management Travel in Asia? Managerial Technology Transfer at Japanese Multinationals in Thailand." Working Paper MTTJP 96-04, MIT Japan Program.

SIA (Semiconductor Industry Association). (June 15, 2018). "SIA Statement on Trump Administration Tariff Announcement," from Semiconductor Industry Association Latest News, from https://www.semiconductors.org/sia-statement-on-trump-administration-tariff-announcement/.

———. (May 2021). "The Positive Impact of the Semiconductor Industry on the American Workforce and How Federal Industry Incentives Will Increase Domestic Jobs," from https://www.semiconductors.org/wp-content/uploads/2021/05/SIA-Webinar-May-2021-hg-fy.pdf.

Semiconductor Industry Association and Nathan Association. (2016). *Beyond Borders—The Global Semiconductor Value Chain: How an Interconnected Industry Promotes Innovation and Growth*. The Washington, DC: Semiconductor Industry Association. https://www.semiconductors.org/wp-content/uploads/2018/06/SIA-Beyond-Borders-Report-FINAL-May-6-1.pdf.

Semiconductor Manufacturing Industry Association. (2020). "SEMI Statement on New U.S. Export Control Regulations," *SEMI Press Release*, August 24. https://www.semi.org/en/news-media-press/semi-press-releases/semi-export-control.

Singh, Kulwant, Joseph Putti, and George Yip. (1998). "Singapore: Regional Hub." In George Yip (ed.), *Asian Advantage: Key Strategies for Winning in the Asian-Pacific Region*. Reading, MA: Addison-Wesley.

Singh, Surendar. (2023). "Global Value Chains, Neoliberalism and Development Practice: Reflections on Kenya's Experience." *Journal of International Development*. 10.1002./jid.3786.

Sinn, H.-W. (2005). *Die Basar-Ökonomie: Deutschland, Exportweltmeister oder Schusslicht?* Berlin: Ullstein Buchverlag.

Sirkin, Harold L., Michael Zinser, and Douglas Hohner. (2011). "Made in America, Again: Why Manufacturing Will Return to the United States." Boston Consulting Group. http://www.bcg.com/documents/file84471.pdf.

Sorge, A., and W. Streeck. (1987). *Industrial Relations and Technical Change: The Case for an Extended Perspective*. Berlin: Wissenschaftszentrum Berlin für Sozialforschung.

———. (2016). "Diversified Quality Production Revisited: The Transformation of Production Systems and Regulatory Regimes in Germany." MPIfG Discussion Paper 16/13, Max Planck Institute for the Study of Societies.

Soskice, D. (1999). "Divergent Production Regimes: Coordinated and Uncoordinated Market Economies in the 1980s and 1990s." In H. Kitschelt, P. Lange, G. Marks, and J. D. Stephens (eds.), *Continuity and Change in Contemporary Capitalism*. Cambridge: Cambridge University Press.

Steffensen, Sam K. (1998). "Informational Network Industrialization and Japanese Business Management." *Journal of Organizational Change Management* 11, no. 6, pp. 515–529.

Stewart, Charles, T., Jr. (1985). "Comparing Japanese and U.S. Technology Transfer to Less Developed Countries." *Journal of Northeast Asian Studies* 4, pp. 3–19.

Stiglitz, Joseph E., Justin Yifu Lin, and Celestin Monga. (2013). "Introduction: The Rejuvenation of Industrial Policy." In Joseph E. Stiglitz and Justin Yifu Lin (eds.), *The Industrial Policy Revolution I: The Role of Government beyond Ideology*. London: Palgrave Macmillan.

Stockhammer, E. (2011). "Peripheral Europe's Debt and German Wages. The Role of Wage Policy in the Euro Area." Research on Money and Finance Discussion Paper No. 29.

Storm, Servaas, and C. W. M. Naastepad. (2015). "Crisis and Recovery in the German Economy: The Real Lessons." *Structural Change and Economic Dynamics* 32, pp. 11–24.

Story, Louise. (2012). "As Companies Seek Tax Deals, Governments Pay High Price." *New York Times*, December 1.

Straits Times. (March 17, 2016). "Manufacturing to Get Boost from 3D Printing."

Streeck, W., and M. Höpner. (2006). "Reform der Unternehmensmitbestimmung," *MPIfG* 07-08 06.

Streeck, Wolfgang. (1991). "On the Institutional Preconditions of Diversified Quality Production." In E. Matzner and W. Streeck (eds.), *Beyond Keynesianism: The Socio-Economics of Production and Full Employment*. Aldershot: Elgar.

———. (1996). "Lean Production in the German Automobile Industry: A Test Case for Convergence Theory." In Suzanne Berger and Ronal Dore (eds.), *National Diversity and Global Capitalism*. Ithaca: Cornell University Press.

———. (2009). *Re-Forming Capitalism: Institutional Change in the German Political Economy*. Oxford: Oxford University Press.

Sturgeon, T. J. (2002). "Modular Production Networks: A New American Model of Industrial Organization." *Industrial and Corporate Change* 11, no. 3, pp. 451–496.

Suehiro, Akira. (1998). "Social Capabilities for Industrialization in Asia: Government Polices, Technology Formation, and Small Business." Paper for the Institute of Small Business Research and Business Administration, Osaka University of Economics (March).

Suehiro, Akira, and Natenapha Wailerdsak. (2004). "Top Executive Origins: Comparative Study of Japan and Thailand." *Asian Business and Management* 3, pp. 84–104.

Susskind, R. (2011). *Confidence Men: Wall Street, Washington and the Education of a President*. New York: HarperCollins.

Takahashi, Hiroaki. (1996). "Activities of Japanese Machinery Makers in Southeast Asia." *NRI Quarterly* (Winter).

Tamura, Ei. (1996). "Wagakuni Seizo Kigyo no Kaigai Toshi no Genjo to Kongo no Hoko nit suite" [The Current State and Future Direction of Foreign Investment by Japanese Manufacturing Firms]. *Chusho Koko Geppo* (November), pp. 16–22.

Tassey, Gregory. (2010). "Rationales and Mechanisms for Revitalizing US Manufacturing R&D Strategies." *Journal of Technology Transfer* 35, pp. 283–333.

———. (2014). "Competing in Advanced Manufacturing: The Need for Improved Growth Models and Policies." *The Journal of Economic Perspectives* 28, no. 1, pp. 27–48.

———. (2023). "A Four-Asset Technology-Based Growth Policy." *Science and Public Policy*, pp. 1–13 from https://doi.org/10.1093/scipol/scad039.

Teece, David. (1998). "Capturing Value from Technology Assets: The New Economy, Markets for Know How and Intangible Assets." In R. Cole (ed.), *California Management Review* 40, pp. 55–79.

Teixeira, Ruy. (2009). "New Progressive America: Twenty Years of Demographic, Geographic, and Attitudinal Changes across the Country Herald a New Progressive Majority." Center for American Progress from www.americanprogress.org.

The Economist. (November 20, 2010). "Leaving Home: Japanese Manufacturers," 73–74.

Teranishi, J. (2003). *Nippon no Keizai Shisutemu* [The Japanese Economic System]. Tokyo: Iwanami Shoten.

Thelen, Kathleen. (2014) *Varieties of Liberalization and the New Politics of Social Solidarity*. New York: Cambridge University Press.

———. (2019). "Transitions to the Knowledge Economy in Germany, Sweden, and the Netherlands." *Comparative Politics* 51, no. 2, pp. 295–315.

———. (2021). "Transitions to the Knowledge Economy in Germany, Sweden, and the Netherlands." In Anke Hassel and Bruno Palier (eds.), *Growth and Welfare in Advanced Capitalist Economies: How Have Growth Regimes Evolved?* Oxford: Oxford University Press.

Thelen, K., and B. Palier. (2010). "Institutionalizing Dualism: Complementarities and Change in France and Germany." *Politics and Society* 38, no. 1, pp. 119–148.

Thurow, L. C. (1999). *Building Wealth: The New Rules for Individuals, Companies, and Nations in a Knowledge Based-Economy*. New York: HarperCollins.

Tiberghien, Yves. (2007). *Entrepreneurial States: Reforming Corporate Governance in France, Japan and Korea*. Ithaca: Cornell University Press.

———. (2016). "Thirty Years of Neo-liberal Reforms in Japan." In Sebastien Lechevalier (ed.), *The Great Transformation of Japanese Capitalism*. London: Routledge.

Tilton, Mark. (1994). "Informal Market Governance in Japan's Basic Materials Industries." *International Organization* 48, no. 4, pp. 663–685.

Tooze, Adam. (2018). *Crashed: How a Decade of Financial Crisis Changed the World*. New York: Viking.

Toya, T. (2006). *The Political Economy of the Japanese Financial Big Bang*. Oxford: Oxford University Press.

Toya, T. M. Aoki, and R. Toya. (2003). *Kin'yubiggubanno Seiji Keizaigaku. Kin'yu to Kokyoseisakusakutei ni okeruseidohenka* [The Political Economy of the Japanese Financial Big Bang: Institutional Change in Finance and Public Policy Making]. Tokyo: Toyo Keizai Shinposha.

Tu, Jenn-haw (1997). "Taiwan: A Solid Manufacturing Base and Emerging Regional Source of Investment." In Wendy Dobson and Chia Siow Yue (eds.), *Multinationals and East Asian Integration*. Ottawa: International Development Research Centre.

Tucker, Todd (2019). "Industrial Policy and Planning: What It Is and How to Do It Better." Working paper at Roosevelt Institute, https://rooseveltinstitute.org/wp-content/uploads/2020/07/RI_Industrial-Policy-and-Planning-201707.pdf.

Van Apeldoorn, Bastiaan, and Nana de Graaff. (2017). "Obama's Economic Recovery Strategy Open Markets and Elite Power: Business as Usual." *International Politics* 54, pp. 356–372.

Vassiliouk, Svetlana. (2019). "Globalization in Japan: Tackling the Galapagos Syndrome.'" Paper presented at Twelfth Global Studies Conference, Jagiellonian University, 27–28 June 2019.

VDA-Jahresberichte, from http://212.108.163.130/de/publikationen/jahresberichte.

Venohr, Bernd, and Klaus E. Meyer. (2007). "The German Miracle Keeps Running: How Germany's Hidden Champions Stay Ahead in the Global Economy." Working Paper 30, Berlin: Institute of Management Berlin at the Berlin School of Economics.

Vitols, S. (2004). "Negotiated Shareholder Value: The German Variant of an Anglo-American Practice." *Competition and Change* 8, no. 4, pp. 357–374.

Vittas, Dimitri, and Yoon Je Cho. (1996). "Credit Policies: Lessons from Japan and Korea." *The World Bank Research Observer* 11, no. 2, pp. 277–298.

Vogel, David. (1978). "Why Businessmen Distrust Their State: The Political Consciousness of American Corporate Executives." *British Journal of Political Science* 8, no. 1, pp. 45–78.

Vogel, Steven K. (2006). *Japan Remodeled: How Government and Industry Are Reforming Japanese Capitalism?* Ithaca: Cornell University Press.

———. (2019) "Japan's Ambivalent Pursuit of Shareholder Capitalism." *Politics & Society* 47, no. 1, pp. 117–144.

von Staden, P. (2012). "Fettered by the Past in the March Forward: Ideology as an Explanation for the Malaise in Today's Japan." *Asia Pacific Business Review* 18, no. 2, 185–200.

Wadbrook, William P. (1972) *West German Balance-of-Payments Policy: The Prelude to European Monetary Policy.* New York: Praeger.

Wagner, F. (1997). "Shareholder Value: Eine neue Runde im Konflikt zwischen Kapitalmarkt und Unternehmensinteresse." *BfuP* 5, pp. 473–498.

Watanabe, Hiroaki Richard. (2020). *The Japanese Economy.* Agenda Publishing.

Weber, Max. (1949). "Objectivity in Social Science and Social Policy." In *The Methodology of the Social Sciences.* New York: The Free Press.

Werner, Marion. (2016). "Global Production Networks and Uneven Development: Exploring Geographies of Devaluation, Disinvestment, and Exclusion." *Geography Compass* 10, no. 11, pp. 457–469.

Whitley, Richard. (1999). *Divergent Capitalisms: the Social Structuring and Change of Business Systems.* Oxford: Oxford University Press.

———. (2001). "How and Why are International Firms Different? The Consequences of Cross-Border Managerial Coordination for Firm Characteristics and Behaviour." In G. Morgan, P. H. Kristensen, and R. Whitley (eds.), *The Multinational Firm: Organizing Across Institutional and National Divides.* Oxford: Oxford University Press.

———. (2007). *Business Systems and Organizational Capabilities: The Institutional Structuring of Competitive Competences.* Oxford: Oxford University Press.

Williams, Michelle. (2014). "Introduction" and "Rethinking the Developmental State in the Twenty-First Century." In Michelle Williams (ed.), *The End of the Developmental State?* London: Routledge.

Williamson, O. (1996). *The Mechanisms of Governance.* New York: Oxford University Press.

Windham, P., C. Hill, and D. Cheney (2020). "Improving the Endless Frontier Act." *Issues in Science and Technology.*

Windolf, Paul, and Jürgen Beyer. (1996). "Co-operative Capitalism: Corporate Networks in Germany and Britain." *British Journal of Sociology* 47, pp. 205–231.

Winter, Markus. (2016). "Abe and the Bureaucracy: Tightening the Reins." *The Diplomat*, June 16, from https://thediplomat.com/2016/06/abe-and-the-bureacracy-tightening-the-reins/.

Womack, James P., Daniel T. Jones, and Daniel Roos. (1990). *The Machine that Changed the World: The Story of Lean Production.* New York: Harper Perennial.

Wong, Joseph. (2011). *Betting on Biotech: Innovation and the Limits of Asia's Developmental State*. Cornell University Press.
World Bank. (2020). *World Development Report 2020: Trading for Development in the Age of Global Value Chains*. World Bank.
Wymann, O. (2012). *FAST 2025- Future Automotive Industry Structure*. VDA-Materialien.
Yamakawa, Y., M. Peng, and D. Deeds. (2008). "What Drives New Ventures to Internationalize from Emerging to Developed Economies?" *Entrepreneurship Theory and Practice* 32, no. 1, pp. 1–14.
Yamamura, Kozo. (2003). "Germany and Japan in a New Phase of Capitalism: Confronting the Past and the Future." In Kozo Yamamura and Wolfgang Streeck (eds.), *The End of Diversity? Prospects for German and Japanese Capitalism*. Ithaca: Cornell University.
Yamashita, Nobuaki. (2021). "Economic Crisis and Innovation Capacity of Japan: Evidence from Cross-Country Patent Citations." *Technovation* 101, pp. 1–14.
Yang, Xiaohua, Yi Jiang, Rongping Kang, and Yinbin Ke. (2009). "A Comparative Analysis of the Internationalization of Chinese and Japanese Firms." *Asia Pacific Journal of Management* 26, pp. 141–162.
Yeung, Henry Wai-Chung. (2017). "State-led Development Reconsidered: The Political Economy of State Transformation in East Asia since the 1990s." *Cambridge Journal of Regions, Economy, and Society* 10, no 1, pp. 83–98.
———. (2022). *Interconnected Worlds: Global Electronics and Production Networks in East Asia*. Stanford: Stanford Business Books.
Yoffe, David. (2009). "Why the U.S. Tech Sector Doesn't Need Domestic Manufacturing," *Harvard Business Review Blog Network*, October 5, 2009.
Yun, J. (2016). "The Setback in Political Entrepreneurship and Employment Dubaization in Japan, 1998–2012." *British Journal of Industrial Relations* 54, no. 3, pp. 473–495.
Zanker, Chrisoph, and Djerdj Hovat. (2015). "Globale FuE-Aktivitäten deutschedr Unternehmen." Mitteilungen aus der ISI-Erhebung. März, Ausgabe 68.
Zettelmeyer, J. (2019, March 29). "The Return of Economic Nationalism in Germany (Policy Brief 19-4)." Peterson Institute for National Economics. https://www.piie.com/publications/policy-briefs/return-economic-nationalism-germany.
Zuckerman, E. W. (1999). "The Categorical Imperative: Securities Analysts and the Illegitimacy Discount." *American Journal of Sociology* 104, no. 5, pp. 1398–1438.
Zysman, John. (1983). *Governments, Markets, and Growth: Financial Systems and the Politics of Industrial Change*. Ithaca: Cornell University Press.

Index

H. Kwon, *Openness and Coordination*,
https://doi.org/10.1007/978-981-97-3352-1

K

L

M

N

O

P

The manufacturer's authorised representative in the EU is Springer Nature Customer Service Centre GmbH, Europaplatz 3, 69115 Heidelberg, Germany. If you have any concerns regarding our products, please contact ProductSafety@springernature.com

Printed and bound by CPI Group (UK) Ltd, Croydon, CR0 4YY

01/10/2026

02225852-0005